Strategic Marketing

Kent Series in Marketing

Strategic Marketing

Planning, Implementation, and Control

Barton A. Weitz
The Wharton School of Finance and Commerce,
The University of Pennsylvania

Robin Wensley
London School of Business

Kent Publishing Company

A Division of Wadsworth, Inc.
Boston, Massachusetts

Senior Editor: David S. McEttrick
Production Editor: Marianne L'Abbate
Designer: Carol Rose
Cover Designer: Nancy Lindgren
Production Coordinator: Linda Siegrist

KENT PUBLISHING COMPANY
A Division of Wadsworth, Inc.

Printed in the United States of America

1 2 3 4 5 6 7 8 9 — 88 87 86 85 84

LIBRARY OF CONGRESS CATALOGING IN PUBLICATION DATA
Main entry under title:

Strategic marketing.

   Includes bibliographical references and index.
   1. Marketing.   I. Weitz, Barton A.   II. Wensley,
Robin, 1944–
HF5415.S8689   1983   658.8'02   83–4324
ISBN 0–534–00971–9

Credits

Article 1: "Customer Oriented Approaches to Identifying Product Markets," by George S.
Day, Alan D. Shocker, and Rajendra K. Srivastava. Reprinted from the *Journal of Marketing*,
published by the American Marketing Association, Fall 1979, pp. 8–19. *Article 2:* Copyright ©
1979 by the President and Fellows of Harvard College; all rights reserved. Reprinted by
permission of the *Harvard Business Review*. "How Competitive Forces Shape Strategy" by
Michael E. Porter, March–April 1979, pp. 137–145. *Article 3:* "Competitor Analysis: The Missing Link in Strategy" by William E. Rothschild. Reprinted, by permission of the publisher,
from *Management Review*, July 1979 © 1979 by AMACOM, a division of American Management
Associations. All rights reserved. *Article 4:* "Defining Corporate Strengths and Weaknesses"
by Howard H. Stevenson. Reprinted from *Sloan Management Review*, Vol. 17, No. 3, pp. 51–68,
by permission of the publisher. Copyright © 1976 by the Sloan Management Review Association. All rights reserved. *Article 5:* "Market Cost Analysis: A Modularized Contribution Approach" by Patrick M. Dunne and Harry I. Wolk. Reprinted from the *Journal of Marketing*,
published by the American Marketing Association, July 1977, pp. 83–94. *Article 6:* "The
Marketing Audit Comes of Age" by Philip Kotler, William Gregor, and William Rogers.
Reprinted from *Sloan Management Review*, Vol. 18, No. 2, pp. 25–44, by permission of the
publisher. Copyright © 1977 by the Sloan Management Review Association. All rights re-
(continued on page 495)

Preface

The area of marketing strategy has experienced rapid growth in recent years. Few undergraduate and MBA programs are without a course on marketing strategy or planning, and similar concepts are to be found in many business policy or strategy courses. This rapid growth has brought with it two concerns: the nature of what is taught and how it is taught has often caused some confusion, and rapid developments have made it difficult to design courses which are relevant to students' needs while still reflecting the state of knowledge in both marketing and allied disciplines.

For these reasons, it does not seem appropriate at this time to develop an overall synthesis in the form of a traditional textbook. This book, therefore, represents a halfway point, with key articles grouped into related areas rather than chapter-by-chapter discussions.

This book follows what might be described as a traditional structure: identification of opportunities, evaluation of alternatives, models for allocating resources, planning and development, and finally implementation and control. It is organized on the assumption that the sections will be treated in the order that we present them. Each section is accompanied by an introduction, which is an important part of the book. The section introductions suggest various contexts in which the readings themselves should be evaluated. This is not to imply that some of the readings are "better" than others: they have been carefully selected so that each is representative of an important and legitimate perspective on the particular problem.

One particular theme runs throughout the book, as well as, indeed, throughout much current discussion in the area of marketing strategy. This theme was appropriately encapsulated by the title of Walter Kiechel's recent article in *Fortune:* "The Real World Strikes Back." The dilemma can be expressed in various terms: analysis versus implementation, top-down versus bottom-up, marketing versus finance, generalities versus detail, and so on. Each perspective not only brings us back to a central dilemma, but also sheds a different light on the overall problem.

Our hope would be that the use of this book in a marketing strategy course, alongside a number of appropriate case studies, will mean that students can assess both the strengths and limitations of the various approaches. The central dilemma will not go away, but we can become much better informed about it.

For writing this book, we owe a great deal to colleagues *and* students.

Our former MBA students, particularly at UCLA but also at both the London Business School and Wharton, have often acted as the testing ground for the ideas and teaching material presented here: they have not only willingly accepted this role but also provided additional insights. It is always misleading to list just a few colleagues, but we do feel particularly indebted to Dick Rumelt at UCLA, Tom Evans and Jules Goddard at the London Business School, and George Day at the University of Toronto. We also extend special thanks to our reviewers, Gert Assmus, Arun Jain, James Nelson, and William Staples, who read our work at various stages. Their insightful comments assisted us greatly in selecting, ordering, and developing the material. Thanks must also go to Dave McEttrick, our editor, and finally to our families, for their patience.

Barton A. Weitz
Robin Wensley

Contents

Introduction to Strategic Marketing

THE ORIENTATION OF MARKETING MANAGEMENT and management in general is going through a dramatic change. Marketing executives have traditionally been concerned with operating or tactical decisions. During the last five years, this emphasis on tactical decisions has been supplanted by a growing involvement in strategic planning decisions. Philip Kotler suggests that "strategic planning has been moving into today's companies with the same rapidity and appeal as marketing ideas moved into firms of the 1960s. It is happening so fast that many marketers still haven't noticed it."[1]

This growing interest in strategic considerations

> . . . has been attributed to the increased uncertainty that businessmen feel these days when they can contemplate the future — what will government intrusion, roaring inflation, or the sudden appearance of competition from abroad do to them next?[2]

In addition to the enormous changes in the rate of political, economic, social, and technological events, the increased complexity of business organizations has also created a need for a strategic orientation. Between 1949 and 1970, the majority of the Fortune 500 companies shifted from single-product-line firms to multiple industries, and even multinational organizations.[3] This change in complexity means that a business can no longer be guided by a single key idea in the head of an entrepreneur. Modern businesses need analytical tools to assist corporate managers in directing complex organizations as they encounter rapidly changing environments.

In response to this need for help with strategic decisions, there has been a rapid growth in industry-strategic consulting. In 1979, companies paid over $100 million for work labeled "corporate strategy." The Boston Consulting Group (BCG) has been a leading force in this area. The most well-known analytical tools — the experience curve and the growth share

1

matrix — were developed by Bruce Henderson, the founder of BCG. Growing opportunities in strategic consulting have led to the formation of thirteen spin-offs established by former BCG consultants. In addition, the large general-practice consulting firms such as McKinsey; Arthur D. Little; and Booz, Allen & Hamilton are making substantial efforts to satisfy this growing need.

The interest in strategy is also reflected in business publications. Annual reports of companies such as General Electric, Shell Oil, American Hospital Supply, Texas Instruments, Mead, Becton-Dickinson, Borg-Warner, and FMC place major emphasis on strategic analyses. *Business Week* has inaugurated a weekly section of "Corporate Strategies," in which strategic problems and solutions of firms are discussed in terms of the new strategic concepts, such as *cash cow, dog, problem child,* and *SBUs.*

The objective of this volume of readings is to familiarize both marketing students and marketing executives with these concepts and the principles of marketing strategy and planning. In this introductory section, we define strategic marketing decisions and compare them with operational or tactical marketing decisions.

Strategic Versus Tactical Decisions

The word *strategy* has been used in a variety of ways by marketing people. In an early paper, Alfred Oxenfeldt applied the concept of marketing strategy to the selection and evaluation of market targets.[4] Nowadays, however, *strategy* is a term commonly associated with various elements of the marketing mix. For example, marketers frequently talk about product, pricing, distribution, advertising, and copy strategies. Clearly, there is a wide spectrum of marketing decisions that have been labeled "strategic." These decisions range from broad market directions at one extreme to detailed choices at the other.

It is often useful to distinguish between strategic and tactical decisions because they differ in terms of the way in which they are formulated and implemented. George Steiner and John Miner have suggested the following set of dimensions with which to distinguish strategic from tactical decisions:[5]

1. *Importance.* Strategic decisions are significantly more important to the organization than tactical decisions. As Peter Drucker says, doing the right thing is more important than doing things right. If an organization directs its efforts toward the appropriate product markets, it will be successful even if it makes mistakes in implementation. However, exceptionally good marketing tactics (advertising campaigns, sales contests, etc.), according to Drucker, will not overcome the selection of poor product-market targets.

2. *Level at Which Conducted.* Due to their importance, strategic decisions are made by top-level marketing managers while tactical decisions are made at the level of product and functional managers.

3. *Time Horizons.* Strategies last for long periods of time, while tactics have short durations. Strategic plans might have a ten-year horizon, in contrast to annual marketing plans that deal primarily with tactical issues.

4. *Regularity.* The formulation of strategy is continuous and irregular. The ongoing process of monitoring the environment might trigger an intense strategic planning activity when new opportunities or threats appear. Tactics are determined on a periodic basis with a fixed time schedule, typically designed to correspond to the annual budgeting cycle.

5. *Nature of Problems.* Strategic problems are typically unstructured and unique. Hence, there is great uncertainty and risk associated with the formulation of strategies. Tactical problems, such as setting an advertising level or selecting salespeople, are more structured and repetitive in nature, so the risks associated with tactical decisions are easier to assess. In addition, strategy formulation involves the consideration of a wider range of alternatives than the formulation of tactics.

6. *Information Needed.* Since strategies represent an organization's response to its environment, the formulation of strategies requires large amounts of information external to the organization. Much of the information is related to an assessment of the future and thus is quite subjective. Tactical decisions rely much more on internally generated accounting or market research information.

7. *Detail.* Strategic plans are typically broad statements based on subjective judgments, while tactical plans are quite specific, supported by much more detailed information.

8. *Ease of Evaluation.* Strategic decisions are much more difficult to evaluate than tactical decisions. The results of strategies might become evident only after many years. In addition, it is difficult to disentangle the quality of the decision from changes that might have occurred in the forecasted environment. In contrast, the results of tactical decisions are quickly evident and much more easily associated with the decision.

While the preceding list provides some characteristics that differentiate strategic and tactical decisions, there is no generally accepted definition of strategy.[6] Even though controversy exists concerning the exact nature of organizational strategy, we will adopt the Hofer/Schendel definition in this book:

> An organization's strategy is the fundamental pattern of present and planned resource deployments and environmental interactions that indicates how the organization will achieve its objectives.[7]

This definition recognizes that strategic decisions are concerned with resource allocation that is based on an analysis of the interaction between
environmental factors and organizational capabilities. Thus, strategic decisions determine where a company places its efforts, which markets and
market segments it chooses to participate in, and what products it attempts
to sell to those markets. These strategic decisions provide direction for the
company's effort, while tactical or operating decisions are needed to implement strategic decisions.

Corporate Strategy Versus Marketing Strategy

Strategic decisions are made at all levels of the corporation from the chief
executive officer (CEO) to the individual salesperson. The CEO's strategic
decisions determine how the corporation allocates capital to various divisions, while the salesperson's strategic decisions determine how the salesperson allocates his or her scarce resource, time, to various customers. In
reading the articles in this book it is important to recognize that there is a
hierarchy of strategic decisions for a corporation. Two of its major levels
are corporate strategy, and business-level and marketing strategy.

As discussed previously, modern firms are quite complex. They are
often composed of numerous divisions and even separate legal entities.
Corporate-level strategy deals primarily with determining what portfolio of
businesses the corporation should hold. Strategic decisions at the corporate level are concerned with acquisition, divestments, and diversification.
Thus, corporate strategists manage a portfolio of businesses just as a
mutual fund manager manages a portfolio of stocks. The businesses in a
corporate portfolio are frequently referred to as strategic business units
(SBUs).

Lower in the hierarchy, at the business or SBU level, strategic decisions
focus on how to compete in an industry or a product-market. Business-
level strategy deals with achieving and maintaining a competitive advantage. Strategic decisions at the business level are concerned with selecting
target market segments and determining the range of products to offer.
Bruce Henderson emphasizes the relevance of understanding competition
and competitive strengths in making these decisions:

> A market can be viewed in many different ways, and a product can be used in
> many different ways. Each time the product–market pairing is varied, the
> relative competitive strength is varied too. Many businessmen do not recog-
> nize that a key element in strategy is choosing the competitor whom you wish
> to challenge, as well as choosing the market segment and product characteris-
> tics with which you will compete.[8]

Analyzing competitors, segmenting markets, and exploiting competitive advantages to penetrate markets are primarily marketing activities.

Even though marketing is just one functional area in a business, marketing strategy plays a principal role in business-level strategy. Thus, in this book, marketing strategy is closely identified with business-level strategy; we adopt the following definition of marketing strategy: the allocation of resources to achieve a sustainable competitive advantage in selected product-markets.

To realize and exploit this competitive advantage, the business must engage in numerous functional-level decisions, such as developing new products, establishing and managing a distribution network and a sales force, and creating and implementing advertising and promotion programs. These decisions, while critical to the success of a marketing strategy, are of a more tactical than strategic nature. They are associated with the efficient implementation of a program based on the direction outlined in the marketing strategy. In the next section, we clarify the distinction between strategic and tactical decisions by showing the steps in the strategic marketing planning process.

Developing a Marketing Strategy

A prescriptive planning model for developing a marketing strategy is illustrated in Figure I.1. The shaded portions of this figure are typically associated with strategic decisions, while the unshaded portions are associated with more tactical implementation decisions. Thus our chief concern in this book is with the shaded boxes in the planning model. After we look at the elements of the model, we shall relate the stages it shows to the organization of this book.

Define Business Mission

The first decision in the prescriptive planning process shown in Figure I.1 is the definition and purpose of the business unit. At this stage, managers address the following questions: Who are our customers and what value are we providing to them? What business are we in? What should our business be? The answers to these simple-sounding questions can determine the future success of the organization. Levitt suggested that railroad companies would not be in their present deplorable condition if they had defined their mission as transporting people and products rather than simply as "being in the railroad business."[9] By adopting a broader definition, railroad companies could have taken advantage of transportation opportunities involving airplanes, trucks, and pipelines.

Another example of the breadth of definition of the business mission concerns Gillette. During the fluorocarbon propellent controversy, a number of Gillette's customers were switching to competitive roll-on and stick deodorants. In analyzing this situation, one executive commented:

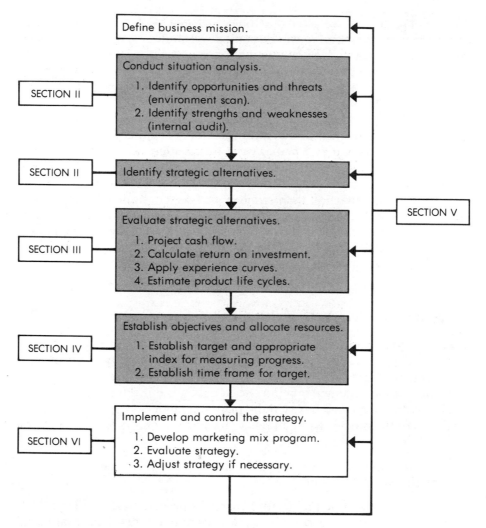

FIGURE I.1   The Strategic Marketing Planning Process

We were like the railroad (that) didn't realize they were in the transportation business. We thought we were in the aerosol business because 80 percent of all users preferred aerosols and we were the leader in that segment. But when the ozone controversy broke, we found we were really in the underarm business.[10]

Once Gillette redefined its mission as being in the underarm business, it allocated significant resources to develop alternate deodorant delivery systems.

The two preceding examples are compelling, but, as several writers have recognized, the "correct" answers to the question of business mission are far from clear in most specific situations.[11] The question "What business are we in?" is often really a question about the nature of the firm's capabilities and customer franchise. It could be argued, particularly in the railroad example, that it would be more valuable to ask: "In what businesses are we capable of maintaining a competitive advantage?" and "What business do our customers think we are in?"

We have seen that there can be problems with narrowly defined missions, but problems can also arise when the mission statement is too broad. For example, it would be dangerous for a manufacturer of felt-tip pens to say that its mission was manufacturing communication equipment. Such a broad statement could lead the company to attempt to develop products for which it had no experience or expertise and thus no competitive advantage. A too-broad mission statement can result in a business failing to exploit its differential advantage, while a too-narrow mission definition can result in a failure to capitalize on new opportunities.

Conduct Situation Analysis

Since a marketing strategy indicates the direction that a business takes to realize a sustainable competitive advantage in the marketplace, an analysis of the position of a business relative to its environment is an important input throughout the planning process. Figure I.1 indicates that this analysis is typically composed of two elements: (1) the identification of opportunities and threats that might arise from changes in economic, political, social, legal, technological, and competitive factors and (2) the identification of the strengths and weaknesses of the business relative to competition. These strengths and weaknesses indicate the degree to which the business can exploit the environmental opportunities and blunt the threats. It is important to note that competitive analysis plays a key role in both aspects of the situation analysis.

Identify Strategic Alternatives

The next decision in the planning process is to identify strategic alternatives. Typically, alternatives are defined in terms of products provided to a market. For example, an SBU in the climate control business might consider products such as central, room, and automobile air conditioners for OEM (original equipment manufacturers), industrial, replacement, new construction and consumer markets. The product-market alternatives facing a pet food business might be dry, canned, and semimoist products to be sold to dog owners and cat owners.

These alternatives may include product-markets that the business is presently serving as well as new opportunities identified by a scan of the environment. Of course, the business mission restricts the nature of the alternatives that are considered: a firm in the climate control business would not consider the growing market for home video tape recorders because this opportunity would be inconsistent with its business mission.

Factors related to conducting a situation audit and identifying strategic alternatives are presented in Section II.

Evaluate Strategic Alternatives

After a number of alternatives have been identified, the next decision is to evaluate each of these alternatives. This evaluation is accomplished by an assessment of the degree to which the business can develop a sustainable competitive advantage and realize long-term profits in a product-market. The assessment weighs the characteristics of the product-market opportunity against the characteristics of the business that enable it to exploit this potential. Thus, the business considers the match between its strengths and weaknesses and its opportunities.

On the basis of this evaluation, managers decide that some product-markets will receive major investments, in terms of financial resources and human effort; other alternatives will receive little or no investment; and still other alternatives receive negative investments. This final group of alternatives is expected to generate funds rather than receive them. Thus strategic decisions are reflected in the level of investment made in a product-market; the pattern of investments across product-markets reflects the strategy of the business.

The traditional methods for evaluating strategic investment opportunities rely on financial analysis — the projection of cash flows and the calculation of return on investment. But currently there is more emphasis on the use of the concepts of the experience curve and the product life cycle. All these approaches are taken up in Section III.

Establish Objectives and Allocate Resources

The next set of decisions in the planning process establishes objectives for each of the product-markets in which the business will be participating. Each objective should have the following two components: (1) the target sought, with an appropriate index for measuring progress, and (2) a time frame within which the goal is to be achieved. In conjunction with each objective, an appropriate investment level is established so that the business will have sufficient resources to achieve the objectives.

Traditionally, businesses have adopted financial performance targets — such as profits as a percent of sales, earnings per share, dividends, and return on assets employed. Some of the new strategic planning models discussed in Section IV suggest that these financial objectives should be supplanted by market share and cash flow targets.

Implement and Control the Strategy

The next set of decisions in the planning process is to develop a marketing mix program for each product-market. This program is designed to achieve the objective with the resources that have been allocated. It requires decisions about product characteristics, price, promotional activities, and distribution functions.

Finally, managers need to evaluate the results of the strategic marketing plans. If the business is achieving the strategic objectives, changes are unnecessary. However, when the business is failing to meet its strategic objectives, a reanalysis is required. Such a reanalysis would start with the implementation program; but it could possibly indicate that the entire strategy should be reconsidered, even including the situation analysis and the business mission. Issues related to the implementation and control of marketing strategies are discussed in Section VI.

Illustrations of the Strategic Planning Process

Since its inception, the mission of Walt Disney Productions has been to provide entertainment for children.[12] The specific product-markets emphasized were theme parks, television programs, and motion pictures directed toward U.S. families with children between 6 and 13 years old. The phenomenal success of Walt Disney Productions is, in part, due to the fact that the 6-to-13-year-old segment grew from 14.7 percent of the U.S. population in 1950 to 18.2 percent of the population in 1960. But this market segment is beginning to decline. In 1980, it accounted for only 15 percent of the U.S. population, and by 1990 it is expected to fall to 12 percent.

This change in the business environment has led Walt Disney Productions to recognize the disadvantages of continuing to aim at a declining product-market, and to place more emphasis instead on the growing segment of 21-to-24-year-old adults. To implement this new strategy, Disney has made changes in its marketing mix. "PG" rated movies are replacing the traditional "G" rated movies, thrill rides are being added to the amusement parks, and new entertainment products (ski resorts) and international markets (Japan) are being pursued.

Decisions made at Texas Instruments in the early 1970s offers another illustration of strategy development and reformation. Prior to 1971, TI's efforts had been directed primarily toward supplying semiconductor products to industrial customers. When surveying the environment, TI recognized that recent technological advances would result in a large, rapidly growing market for consumer electronics. TI felt that it was in a good position to exploit this opportunity because of their experience in manufacturing the critical components in consumer electronic products. Thus, TI decided to

" . . . put most of its development money for the next few years into the consumer business rather than into computer memories and microprocessors, as its competitors did. 'We penalized semiconductors — that was the price for allocating our resources,' Bucy [CEO of TI] said."[13]

While this strategic decision resulted in TI playing a major role in the consumer hand-held calculator and digital watch product-market, the limited resources directed toward semiconductors was a major factor in Intel's domination of semiconductor memories.

Most of the examples presented in this book concern profit-oriented corporations. However, nonprofit institutions also develop and reformulate strategies. For example, the University of California has a mission to provide graduate and undergraduate education to the residents of California. The departments (management, law, history, physics, etc.) at the seven campuses can be considered the product-market alternatives toward which resources can be directed. In light of declining enrollments, the total resources allocated to the university system have been reduced. Thus the university is forced to re-evaluate its strategy — its pattern of resource allocations. One option would be to reduce the funding to each department by the same percentage as the entire university funding is reduced. Another option would be to direct resources toward strong departments on campuses with high student demand and reduce funding or even eliminate funding to weak departments. Whatever strategy is selected, operational changes will have to be made. The price charged to students (tuition) might be increased and the quality of the service might be altered by increasing class sizes.

Comparisons of Prescriptive and Actual Planning Processes

The prescriptive planning process shown in Figure I.1 implies that strategic decisions are made in a hierarchical process. After the business mission is defined, the situation analysis is performed, the product-market alternatives are identified, objectives are established, and finally resources are allocated. However, one must recognize that there are substantial interactions between the decisions made at each step of the process. For example, when strategic alternatives are identified, they may lead to a reformulation of the business mission; or an analysis of implementation decisions might lead to a re-evaluation of the resource allocation decisions previously made, and perhaps ultimately to a re-evaluation of the entire strategic decision.

Even though we acknowledge these interactions in the prescriptive planning model, the model still seems to imply that the process is dominated by a top-down rather than a bottom-up direction. In addition, the model may suggest that a clear distinction exists between the strategic marketing decisions made by top management and tactical decisions made at operating levels.

Much of this book is devoted to the hierarchical perspective for making strategic marketing decisions; however, some alternative views will be examined in Sections V and VI. Specifically, we will examine the contention that, in practice, strategy formulation and evaluation cannot be so readily differentiated from implementation. This problem concerns strategists continually: the tradeoff between the top-down approaches that incorporate the grand view but lack practicality and the bottom-up views, which are clearly practical but may be unnecessarily limited in perspective. The top-management perspective is "strategic," but its high-level generalities may mask the richness of options that a different approach could suggest. For example, product positioning and distribution are operating-level decisions which may be critical in creating a strategic advantage over competition.

Organization of Book

This book is organized around the prescriptive planning model shown in Figure I.1. Following is Section II, which contains articles that address the identification of strategic marketing opportunities. The environmental and internal analyses are also treated in this section.

Section III examines concepts used to evaluate the identified alternatives, or opportunities. This section contains articles that illustrate how financial, product life cycle, and experience curve analyses are used to determine the attractiveness of a strategic market opportunity.

Section IV focuses on normative models used to determine objectives and investment levels for strategic opportunities. The three models presented in this section are the market-share/market-growth matrix associated with the Boston Consulting Group; the market attractiveness/competitive position matrix associated with GE, McKinsey, and UK Shell; and the PIMS model associated with the Strategic Planning Institute. In addition to articles describing each model, there are also some articles examining the strengths and weaknesses of these models.

The first four sections of the book are primarily concerned with the nature of strategic decisions and factors that need to be considered in making these decisions. Section V contains articles that examine how marketing strategies are and should be developed. Thus the first four sections focus on the strategic plan while the fifth section discusses the planning process.

Section VI is devoted to considerations in implementing marketing strategies. Some topics discussed in the articles in this section are examples of how marketing strategies are implemented, how the annual marketing plan is integrated with the marketing strategy, the importance of timing in implementing strategies, and methods for monitoring the effectiveness of marketing strategies. The two concluding articles in this final section examine the degree to which broad strategic approaches can effectively adapt to environmental change.

Notes

1. *Marketing News,* "Corporate Strategy: New Role for Marketers: Kotler," 30 June 1978, p. 4.
2. Walter Kiechel, II, "Playing by the Rules of the Corporate Strategy Game," *Fortune,* 24 September 1979, pp. 110–115.
3. Richard P. Rumelt, *Strategy, Structure and Economic Performance* (Boston: Graduate School of Business Administration, Harvard University, 1974).
4. Alfred R. Oxenfeldt, "The Formulation of a Marketing Strategy," in *Managerial Marketing: Perspectives and Viewpoints,* ed. E. J. Kelly and W. Lazer (Homewood, Ill.: Richard D. Irwin, 1978), pp. 34–44.
5. George A. Steiner and John B. Miner, *Management Policy and Strategy: Text, Readings, and Cases* (New York: Macmillan, 1977), pp. 22–24.
6. For a review of various definitions of strategy that have been proposed, see C. W. Hofer and D. E. Schendel, *Strategy Formulation: Analytical Concepts* (St. Paul: West Publishing, 1981), Chap. 2.
7. Charles W. Hofer and Dan Schendel, *Strategy Formulation: Analytical Concepts,* (St. Paul: West Publishing, 1978), p. 25.
8. Bruce D. Henderson, *Henderson on Corporate Strategy,* Cambridge, Mass.: Abt Books, 1981, p. 8.
9. Theodore Levitt, "Marketing Myopia," *Harvard Business Review* 38, no. 4 (July/August 1960), pp. 26–34.
10. *Business Week,* "Gillette: After Diversification that Failed," 28 February 1977, p. 59.
11. Ken Simmonds, "Removing the Chains from Product Strategy," *Journal of Management Studies* 5, no. 1 (1968), pp. 29–40.
12. *Business Week,* "Can Disney Still Grow on Its Founder's Dream?" 31 July 1978, pp. 58–63.
13. *Business Week,* "Texas Instruments Shows U.S. Business How to Survive in the 1980's," 10 September 1978, pp. 66–92.

Additional Readings

Abell, Derek F. *Defining the Business.* Englewood Cliffs, N.J.: Prentice-Hall, 1980. Focuses on identifying strategic opportunities. Proposes a three-dimensional scheme for defining opportunities, based on customer segments, customer uses, and substitute technology. Particularly relevant to the material in Section II of this book.

Abell, Derek F., and Hammond, John S. *Strategic Marketing Planning: Problems and Analytical Approaches.* Englewood Cliffs, N.J.: Prentice-Hall, 1979. A textbook on strategic marketing, containing sections on methods for assessing the strategic position of a company, analytical tools for making strategic decisions, and creative aspects of the planning process. About 50 percent of the book is devoted to cases that illustrate the use of strategic planning tools.

Ansoff, H. Igor. *Corporate Strategy: An Analytic Approach to Business Policy for Growth and Expansion.* New York: McGraw-Hill, 1965. A classic book on the steps involved in strategy formulation. Extensive and highly readable discussion of the concept of synergy and the use of this concept to generate and evaluate strategic alternatives.

Britt, Stewart H., and Boyd, Harper W., Jr., eds. *Marketing Management and Administrative Action,* 4th ed. Englewood Cliffs, N.J.: Prentice-Hall, 1978. A collection of forty-one articles in a paperback volume with a principal focus on tactical marketing decisions concerning new product development, pricing, advertising, personal selling, and distribution.

Cravens, David W. *Strategic Marketing.* Homewood, Ill.: Richard D. Irwin, 1982. A textbook of strategic marketing that discusses the relationship between corporate and marketing strategies, the identification and selection of target markets, the link between marketing strategy and the marketing mix variables, and strategic planning process.

Glueck, William F., ed. *Readings in Business Policy for* Business Week. New York: McGraw-Hill, 1978. Eighty articles from *Business Week* that illustrate how specific companies analyze their environment, assess the advantages and disadvantages of strategic alternatives, choose strategies, and implement strategic decisions.

Henderson, Bruce D. *Henderson on Corporate Strategy,* Cambridge, Mass.: Abt Books, 1979. A collection of short essays written by the founder of the Boston Consulting Group. Essays are directed toward senior-level management in large businesses.

Hofer, Charles W., and Schendel, Dan E. *Strategy Formulation: Analytical Concepts.* St. Paul: West Publishing, 1978. A paperback book that defines the concept of strategy; explains why strategic decisions play a central role in organizational performance; and describes the analytical concepts, models, and techniques that are useful for the formulation of strategy. Distinctions are made between strategy formulation at the corporate, business, and functional level. More oriented toward academics and students than toward a business audience.

Jain, Subhash C., *Marketing Planning and Strategy.* Cincinnati: South-Western Publishing, 1981. A textbook on marketing strategy that is quite similar to the textbook by Cravens mentioned previously.

Kerin, Roger A., and Peterson, Robert A., eds. *Perspectives on Strategic Marketing Management.* Boston: Allyn & Bacon, 1980. A collection of 31 articles on strategic marketing. The articles are divided between the formulation of corporate and marketing strategies and marketing management decisions concerning the implementation of the marketing strategy. There are a mix of theoretical articles and practical articles from trade magazines. Some attempt has been made to develop a framework to link the articles together.

Levitt, Theodore. *Marketing for Business Growth.* New York: McGraw-Hill, 1974. A very readable book for executives on how to get more out of people, products, and resources. Discusses the importance and role of marketing in the strategic planning process.

Lorange, Peter. *Corporate Planning Systems: An Executive Viewpoint.* Englewood Cliffs, N.J.: Prentice-Hall, 1980. A thorough discussion of practical problems in implementing a corporate planning system. Particularly relevant to the material in Sections V and VI of this book.

Porter, Michael E. *Competitive Strategy: Techniques for Analyzing Business, Industry and Competitors.* New York: Free Press, 1980. Excellent book describing how to analyze the degree of competition and profit potential in an industry. Also, it includes techniques for examining vertical integration and new business entry decisions.

Rothschild, William E. *Putting It All Together: A Guide to Strategic Thinking.* New York: ATACON, 1976. An excellent "how-to" book written by a strategic planning specialist of General Electric. Provides an opportunity for business people to think through their own environment, develop strategic alternatives, and evaluate those alternatives.

Schendel, Dan E., and Hofer, Charles W., eds. *Strategic Management: A New Business Policy and Planning.* Boston: Little, Brown, 1979. Collection of fourteen commissioned papers plus two commentaries per paper that were presented at a conference in 1977. The papers are written by leading scholars with the objectives of defining the field of strategic management, presenting major research findings, and suggesting the direction for future research in strategic management. This is a comprehensive book covering goal formulation, strategy formulation, evaluation and implementation of strategies, and company organizational forms; it was written primarily for an academic audience.

Steiner, George A., and Miner, John B. *Management Policy and Strategy: Text, Readings, and Cases.* New York: Macmillan, 1977. A comprehensive text, supplemented with readings and case studies, for use in a capstone business policy course. While this text is primarily oriented for students, the material would be quite useful to business people.

The Identification of Strategic Opportunities

WE CAN LEARN to define strategic opportunities by thinking carefully about this simple principle: overall success in a competitive marketplace depends on marketing one's products to customers in a more cost-effective manner than the competitors do. Using this principle, we can consider the following three dimensions or aspects of strategic opportunities: customers, competitors, and company capabilities. These three dimensions are related, but there are also clear distinctions among them. Traditional economic analysis would readily recognize the distinction between the first and the third dimensions: it is the difference between demand and supply. The dimension of competitive analysis is added because an observation of actual business practice indicates that, contrary to the classic economic assumption, competitors are not homogeneous. Most competitor companies are as much different from each other as they are similar. Hence we need to recognize explicitly that the ways in which competitors compete in the marketplace is critical.

To a considerable extent the degree to which businesses compete against each other is determined by customers. Customers define the nature of competition by the alternatives they consider when making purchase decisions. Some definitions of competitive products are obvious; for example, Coca-Cola against Pepsi-Cola in the cola drink market. However, Coca-Cola also competes against Seven-Up in the broader soft drink market, and against coffee in the still broader beverage market. Some of the competitive products are, however, much less obvious (until we think about them). For example, convenience foods prepared at home compete with fast food outlets. "Home" computers with word-processing capabilities compete with secretarial services.

It is often easiest, from a company point of view, to define the nature of competition in terms of products that look similar and perform similar functions. In some markets, this may be an appropriate way to characterize the nature of customer perceptions as well. After all, customers are also likely to think that one brand of detergent competes against another brand because they look alike and are both used to launder clothes. When this product-based approach is justified in terms of consumer behavior and perceptions, it is certainly a convenient approach because it is easy to relate market-based product dimensions to internal measures of production and distribution.

Unfortunately there is a growing number of markets where product-related distinctions are less and less justified. There is ample evidence, both at broad level of industry sectors and in many specific markets as well, that physical characteristics of the product are becoming less important relative to services associated with the overall offering. As this situation evolves, we have to consider two crucial issues in our analysis of the customers. First, we cannot relate the competitive offerings purely in terms of the characteristics of their physical products; second, we must be careful to base our analysis of the customers on their perceptions of crucial offerings, hence, of competitors.

This emphasis on customer perception of services extends much wider than it used to; we once thought of "service" in connection only with banking and hotels. For instance, the advent of both store brands and now of generic brands have led businesses to recognize the substantial service elements, not only in the convenience and choice of products the retailer should provide but also in the implicit quality certification proffered by the retailer rather than just the traditional certification manufacturers offered with their brand names.

The rising emphasis on service means that we can expect to encounter many situations in which the nature of the market as customers see it is significantly different from the nature of the market defined in terms of the companies' physical products.

A number of businesses successfully compete against manufacturers of branded products by adopting new approaches. Rather than competing for customers by offering similar branded products, they specialize in low-cost manufacturing and supply store brand products instead. For example, Design and Manufacturers, one of the largest world-wide manufacturers of appliances during the 1960s and early 1970s, had no branded products.[1] Thus, powerful competition can exist between businesses that have chosen very different strategic directions.

Finally, the efforts of a business to exploit its strength can result in the business embracing opportunities that are not related to its existing customer franchise and not related to activities of existing competitors. Hence, Texas Instruments and IBM have both decided to enter into a retailing activity so as to have direct access to new customers; in so doing, they find themselves competing with retail outlets as well as with electronics manufacturers.

The preceding discussion illustrates that we must not expect our analysis of the customer, competitor, and capabilities dimensions of competition to yield the same set of opportunities. In addition, there is one other problem. So far we have been considering the analysis of the past and the present, but what we really want to know is what might happen in the future, or at least we want to make sure we are reasonably aware of any large changes around the corner. We must consider how far the overall process of information gathering and analysis can be pushed. It is the essence of strategy that decisions have to be made in an ambiguous and confusing world, so we cannot expect to arrive at neat, unambiguous answers. If such situations arise, people are either deceiving themselves or doctoring the data.

In the whole process of strategic analysis, companies should be looking for something different. They need to look for various partial facts derived from empirical data, information that will either cast doubt on or support one or more of the critical assumptions in the proposed strategy.[2] The fact that such a process is only partial does not mean it is of limited value. It is critical that as much information as possible is gathered and analyzed so that reasoned judgments can be made about the appropriate opportunities.

Customers

Customers have never really been forgotten in strategy; nonetheless, there is a danger that analysts can talk rather glibly about market niches in which the premium price will hold, but, in fact, no such niche exists. Understanding customers is a way of avoiding such pitfalls and of identifying more meaningful ways in which the market might be split up. The only critical proviso is that analysts must remember that customers are not a very reliable source of information on the nature of market evolution. After all, a business cannot expect its customers to forecast how the market will develop, since customers typically have not been exposed to the developing products and choices.

On the other hand, market research can provide a lot of information on current behaviors and attitudes toward existing offerings. There are essentially two different ways of obtaining the information about customer behavior and attitudes — from an analysis of purchase and usage behavior, or from customer judgments. Indeed, balance between these two sources is a critical concern: ever since Mason Haire's classic article demonstrating the usefulness of projective market research techniques, we have had to recognize the need to relate empirical evidence to attitude data.[3] The first article in this section, "Customer-Oriented Approaches to Identifying Product-Markets," provides a detailed critique of these approaches.

Competitors

One of the more recent and obvious developments in marketing strategy has been a renewed focus on the impact of competitors on strategies. This focus first developed within the context of cost competition (the experience curve described in Section III), in which emphasis was placed on getting down the experience curve faster than the competition. More recently, however, firms have recognized the more complex nature of the experience curve, with its many shared components, and also the heterogeneity of most competition. Heterogeneous competition means that firms have to expect to find themselves competing not only with businesses that are very similar but also with some that are very different.

Competition can therefore be considered from a number of different points of view. There are companies that

- provide the same product or service to the market,
- provide a substitute product or service, or
- use a similar production technology.

In addition, each competitor must be considered from a number of different perspectives:

- their relative performance in terms of costs,
- the relationship between the specific products and other related ones that they produce or sell, and
- the relationship of this product group to the competitors' overall portfolio.

Any analysis of competition must therefore consider two rather distinct elements. First, the overall nature of competition in terms of the institutional structure of the market (including both alternative intermediate suppliers and alternative distribution channels). Second, a more detailed analysis of how individual competitors are changing in response to their objectives, priorities, and overall portfolio.

The second article, "How Competitive Forces Shape Strategy," considers in detail the issues raised by the competitive structure of the market, while Article 3, "Competitor Analysis: The Missing Link in Strategy," focuses more on the detailed analysis of individual competitors.

The Company Itself

The final input into the process of identification of opportunities is obviously the detailed analysis of the company itself. One traditional component in such a corporate appraisal has been a strengths and weaknesses analysis. This analysis is often combined with the competitive and market analysis previously discussed; the combination is described by the acronym SWOT, to cover Strengths, Weaknesses, Opportunities and Threats. A number of critics have claimed that the output from a strengths and weaknesses analysis is often either trivial or so broad as to be relatively meaningless in the face of actual strategic choices. Article 4, "Defining Corporate Strengths and Weaknesses," reports on a detailed piece of research designed to investigate this problem further. Overall it suggests that most descriptions are highly subjective and, in the classic psychoanalytical framework, they "tell us more about the person performing the analysis than the firm." Such research, supported by more recent work,[4] clearly suggests that one should be wary of the results of a traditional SWOT analysis. Such an analysis might, however, be useful as feedback to the relevant managers as they formulate and recommend strategy.

An understanding of both current and future performance also requires a clear idea of the firm's actual costs associated with servicing a particular market segment. Unfortunately, many accounting systems tend to reflect a rather restricted set of different elements in the costing system. To make more effective marketing strategy decisions, we need a refined costing structure capable of analyzing contribution margins at various different levels of aggregation — including products, distribution channels, and customers. Such information can be generated at a cost in response to each particular inquiry. However, the development of a cost accounting system having such built-in flexibility would have a very significant impact on strategy development even though the set-up costs are likely to be quite high. Article 5 in this section, "Marketing Cost Analysis: A Modularized Contribution Approach," describes such a system in detail.

Finally, in marketing analysis there has been a traditional method to identify the current corporate position: the marketing audit. A well-executed marketing audit results in the recognition of a number of important questions and new options to consider. On the other hand, it often works most effectively as feedback into the relevant organization to be assessed and acted upon. In the last article in this section, "The Marketing Audit Comes of Age," the process and type of questions are described in some detail; the final emphasis is on the fact that the audit report will help in placing priorities on ideas and directions already within the company rather than propose startling new opportunities.

Notes

1. The original research work in this area was in domestic appliances; see M. S. Hunt, "Competition in the Major Home Appliance Industry" (Ph.D. diss., Harvard University, 1972).

2. Such a process is discussed in more detail in Robin Wensley, "The Effective Strategic Analyst," *Journal of Management Studies* 16, no. 3 (1979) and also relates to the concept of strategic assumptions analysis developed by James R. Emshoff and Ian I. Mitroff, "Improving the Effectiveness of Corporate Planning," *Business Horizons,* October 1976, pp. 49–60.

3. Mason Haire, "Projective Techniques in Marketing Research," *Journal of Marketing,* April 1950, pp. 646–656.

4. Lynn W. Phillips, "Assessing Measurement Error in Key Informant Reports: A Methodological Note on Organizational Analysis in Marketing," *Journal of Marketing Research* 18 (November 1981): 395–415.

1. Customer-Oriented Approaches to Identifying Product-Markets

George S. Day
Allan D. Shocker
Rajendra K. Srivastava

The problems of identifying competitive product-markets pervade all levels of marketing decisions. Such strategic issues as the basic definition of the business, the assessment of opportunities presented by gaps in the market or threats posed by competitive actions, and major resource allocation decisions are strongly influenced by the breadth or narrowness of the competitive arena. Share of market is a crucial tactical tool for evaluating performance and guiding territorial advertising, sales force, and other budget allocations. The quickening pace of antitrust prosecution is a further source of demands for better definitions of relevant market boundaries that will yield a clearer understanding of the competitive consequences of acquisitions.

This paper is primarily concerned with the needs of marketing planners for strategic analyses of competitive product-markets.[1] Their needs presently are served by approaches to defining product-markets which emphasize similarity of production processes, function, or raw materials used. Seldom do these approaches give a satisfactory picture of either the threats or the opportunities facing a business. In response, there has been considerable activity directed toward defining product-markets from the customers' perspective. Our objectives are first, to examine the merits of a customer perspective in the context of a defensible definition of a product-market, and second, to evaluate progress toward providing this perspective. The paper's structure corresponds to these objectives. The first two

This article first appeared in the *Journal of Marketing*, Fall 1979, pp 8–19.

When this article was published, the authors were Professor of Marketing at the University of Toronto, Associate Professor of Business Administration at the University of Pittsburgh, and Associate Professor of Business Administration at the University of Texas at Austin, respectively.

sections are concerned with the nature of the strategic problem, and the development of a customer-oriented definition of a product-market. This definition is used in the third section to help evaluate a variety of methods for identifying product-market boundaries. In this discussion, a sharp distinction is drawn between methods which rely on purchase or usage behavior and those which use customer judgments.

Sources of Demand for Better Insights

Ultimately all product-market boundaries are arbitrary. They exist because of recurring needs to comprehend market structures and impose some order on complex market environments. But this situation could not be otherwise. One reason is the wide variety of decision contexts which dictate different definitions of boundaries.

Market and product class definitions appropriate for tactical decisions tend to be narrow, reflecting the short-run concerns of sales and product managers who regard a market as "a chunk of demand to be filled with the resources at my command." These resources are usually constrained by products in the present product line. A longer-run view, reflecting strategic planning concerns, invariably will reveal a larger product-market to account for (1) presently unserved but potential markets; (2) changes in technology, price relationships, and supply which broaden the array of potential substitute products; and (3) the time required by present and prospective buyers to react to these changes.

Of necessity, a single market definition is a compromise between the long-run and the short-run views. All too often, the resulting compromise is not consistent with customer's views of the competitive alternatives to be considered for a particular usage situation or application. One consequence of these problems is the development of different definitions for different purposes. Thus, for some strategic planning purposes, General Electric treats hair dryers, hair setters, and electric brushes as parts of distinct markets while for other purposes they are part of a "personal appliance" business since they tend to compete with one another in a "gift market." General Foods has taken an even broader approach in a reorganization of its process-oriented divisional structure into strategic business units. Each SBU now concentrates on marketing families of products made by different processing technologies but consumed by the same market segments (Hanon 1974). Thus, all desserts are in the same division whether they are frozen, powdered, or ready-to-eat.

A further reason for the inevitable arbitrariness of product-market boundaries is the frequent absence of natural discontinuities which can be readily identified — and accepted — without argument. Moran (1973) states the problem bluntly:

> In our complex service society, there are no more product classes — not in any meaningful sense, only as a figment of file clerk imagination. . . . To some degree, in some circumstances, almost anything can be a partial substitute for almost anything else. A (fifteen-cent) stamp substitutes to some extent for an airline ticket.

When a high degree of ambiguity or compromise is present in the identification of the product-market, a number of problems are created. Some will stem from inadequate and delayed understanding of emerging threats in the competitive environment. These threats may come from foreign competition, product substitution trends, shifts in price sensitivity, or changed technological possibility. Thus fiberglass and aluminum parts have displaced steel in many automotive applications due in some measure to increasing willingness to pay higher prices to obtain lower weight and consequent gas economy. Conversely, opportunities may be overlooked when the definition is drawn too narrowly for tactical purposes and the nature and size of the potential market are understated. Finally, whenever market share is used to evaluate the performance of managers or to determine resource allocations (Day 1977), there is a tendency for managers to manipulate the market boundaries to show an increasing or at least static share.

A Customer-Oriented Concept of a Competitive Product-Market

Market definitions have, in the past, focused on either the *product* (as with the following definition, ". . . products may be closely related in the sense that they are regarded as substitutes by consumers." Needham 1969, which assumes homogeneity of consumer behavior), or on the *buyers* (". . . individuals who in the past have purchased a given class of products," Sissors 1966). Neither approach is very helpful for clarifying the concept, or evaluating alternative approaches for identifying product-market boundaries.

A more productive approach can be derived from the following premises:

> People seek the benefits that products provide rather than the products per se. Specific products or brands represent the available combinations of benefits and costs.

> Consumers consider the available alternatives from the vantage point of the usage contexts with which they have experience or the specific applications they are considering (Belk 1975; Lutz and Kakkar 1976; Stout et al. 1977). It is the usage requirement which dictates the benefits being sought.[2]

From these two premises, we can define a product-market as the *set of products* judged to be substitutes, within those usage situations in which similar patterns of benefits are sought, and the *customers* for whom such usages are relevant.

This definition is *demand* or customer-oriented in that customer needs and requirements have primacy. The alternative is to take a *supply* perspective and define products by such operational criteria as similarity of manufacturing processes, raw materials, physical appearance, or function. These criteria are the basis of the Standard Industrial Classification (SIC) system — and have generally wide acceptance because they appear easy to implement. They lead to seemingly stable and clear-cut definitions, and importantly, involve factors largely controllable by the firm; implying that the definition is somehow controllable as well. They are also helpful in identifying potential competitors, because of similarities in manufacturing and distribution systems. Demand-oriented criteria, on the other hand, are less familiar and consequently appear more difficult to implement (as a consequence of the variety of methods available and the inevitable problems of empirical measurement, sampling errors, and aggregation over individual customer differences). Moreover, such definitions may be less stable over time because of changing needs and tastes. Finally, the organization must initiate a research program to collect and analyze relevant data and monitor change rather than relying on government or other external sources to make the information available. The consequence is most often a decision to use supply-oriented measures despite their questionable applicability in many circumstances (Needham 1969).

Hierarchies of Products

The notion of a unique product category is an oversimplification in the face of the arbitrary nature of the boundaries. Substitutability is a measure of degree. Thus it is better to think in terms of the levels in a hierarchy of products within a generic product class representing all possible ways of satisfying a fundamental consumer need or want. Lunn (1972) makes the following useful distinctions between:

> Totally different *product types* or subclasses which exist to satisfy significantly different patterns of needs beyond the fundamental or generic. For example, both hot and cold cereals serve the same need for breakfast nutrition, but otherwise are different. Over the long run, product types may behave like substitutes.

> Different *product variants* are available within the same overall type, e.g., natural, nutritional, presweetened, and regular cereals. There is a high probability that some short-run substitution takes place among subsets of these variants (between natural and nutritional, for ex-

ample). If there is too much substitution, then alternatives within the subset do not deserve to be distinguished.

Different *brands* are produced within the same specific product variant. Although these brands may be subtly differentiated on many bases (color, package type, shape, texture, etc.), they are nonetheless usually direct and immediate substitutes.

There may be many or few levels in such a hierarchy, depending on the breadth and complexity of the genuine need and the variety of alternatives available to satisfy it. Thus, this typology is simply a starting point for thinking about the analytical issues.

Submarkets and Strategic Segments

The product-market definition proposed above implies submarkets composed of customers with common uses or applications of the product. These are segments according to the traditional definition of groups that have similar purchase or usage behavior or reactions to marketing efforts (Frank, Massy, and Wind 1973). For our purposes, it is more useful to consider these as submarkets within *strategic market segments*. While each of these submarkets may serve as the focus of a positioning decision, the differences between them may not present significant strategic barriers for competitors to overcome. Such barriers may be based on factors such as differences in geography, order quantities, requirements for technical assistance and service support, price sensitivity, or perceived importance of quality and reliability. The test of strategic relevance is whether the segments defined by these or other characteristics must be served by substantially different marketing mixes. The boundaries could then be manifested by discontinuities in price structures, growth rates, share patterns, and distribution channels when going from one segment to another.

Analytical Methods for Customer-Oriented Product-Market Definitions

Customer-oriented methods for identifying product-markets can be classified by whether they rely upon behavioral or judgmental data. Purchase behavior provides the best indication of what people actually do, or have done, but not necessarily what they might do under changed circumstances. As such, its value is greater as a guide to tactical planning. Judgmental data, in the form of perceptions or preferences, may give better insights into future patterns of competition and the reasons for present patterns. Consequently, it may better serve as the basis for strategic planning. In this section we will evaluate seven different analytical approaches within the two basic classes as follows:

Purchase or Usage Behavior	*Customer Judgments*
A1. Cross-elasticity of demand	**B1.** Decision sequence analysis
A2. Similarities in behavior	**B2.** Perceptual mapping
A3. Brand switching	**B3.** Technology substitution analysis
	B4. Customer judgments of substitutability

Within the broad category of customer judgments of substitutability (B4), five related approaches, using free associations, the "dollar metric," direct grouping of products, products-by-uses analysis and substitution-in-use analysis will be examined.

Analysis of Purchase or Usage Behavior

A1. *Cross-elasticity of demand* is considered by most economists to be the standard against which other approaches should be compared (Scherer 1970). Despite the impressive logic of the cross-elasticity measure, it is widely criticized and infrequently used:

> The conceptual definition of this measure presumes that there is no response by one firm to the price change of another (Needham 1969). This condition is seldom satisfied in practice.

> It is a static measure, and "breaks down in the face of a market characterized by changing product composition" (Cocks and Virts 1975). This is so because a priori it is not known what all the potential substitutes or complements may be. Over time new entrants or departures from a market may affect the cross-elasticity between any two alternatives.

> Finally, "in markets where price changes have been infrequent, or all prices change together, or where factors other than prices have also changed, there is simply not enough information contained in the data to permit valid statistical estimation of the elasticities" (Vernon 1972).

These problems may be overcome with either an experimental study, which can introduce problems of measure validity, or extensive monitoring of the factors affecting demand and use of econometric methods to control, where possible, for the effects of such factors. Not surprisingly, such studies are expensive and rather infrequently undertaken. Generally, empirical cross-elasticity studies have focused on only two goods (typically product-types as opposed to variants or brands). It is also worth noting that if simultaneous estimation of all cross-elasticities were to be attempted, some a priori determination of the limits to a product-market would be needed in order to include price change and other market data for all potential competitive brands. The estimation of any specific cross-elasticity should be sensitive to such product-market definition.

A2. *Similarities in customer usage behavior.* This approach was successfully used in a study of the ethical pharmaceutical market (Cocks and Virts 1975). The basic question was the extent to which products made up of different chemicals, but with similar therapeutic effects, could be significant substitutes. The key to answering this question was the availability of a unique set of data on physician behavior. Each of the 3,000 physicians in a panel recorded: (1) patient characteristics, (2) the diagnosis, (3) the therapeutic measures — drugs — used to treat the patient, (4) the desired action of the drugs being used, and (5) characteristics of the reporting physician.

The first step in the analysis was to estimate the percentage usage of each drug in the treatment of patients diagnosed as having the same ailment. When a drug was found to be the only one used for a certain disease, and seldom or never used in the treatment of any other diagnosis, it was assumed to represent a distinct class. Generally, it was found that several drugs were used in several diagnosis categories. The next step was to see if drugs which were used together had similar desired actions. Some drugs, such as analgesics, are frequently used along with other drugs, without being substitutes (strictly speaking, they also are not complements). Finally, drugs were classed as substitutes — and hence in the same product class — if 10 percent or more of the total usage of each drug was in the treatment of a specific diagnosis.

While it was not claimed that every drug in the resulting product-market competed for all uses of every other drug in that market, the data revealed a substantial amount of substitutability. The key to understanding the patterns of competition in this market was knowledge of the usage situation. As yet, few consumer panels have incorporated similar data with the usual measures of purchase behavior. The potential to conduct similar analyses suggests that usage data could be valuable when available for categories which are purchased for multiple uses.

A3. *Brand switching* measures are usually interpreted as conditional probabilities, i.e., the probability of purchasing brand A, given that brand B was purchased on the last occasion. Such measures are typically estimated from panel data where the purchases of any given respondent are represented by a sequence of indefinite length. The probabilities are computed from counts of the frequency with which each condition arises in the data (e.g., purchases of brand A are preceded by different brands in the sequence). The premise is that respondents are more likely to switch be-

tween close substitutes than distant ones and that brand switching propor-
tions provide a measure of the probability of substitution.

As with cross-elasticity, the brand-switching measure is usable only
after a set of competitive products has first been established. Since estimation of brand-switching rates is based upon a sequence of purchases, there
must be some logical basis to determine which brands to include in such a
sequence. Similarity of usage patterns, as discussed above, is one promising basis.

Brand switching rates as measures of degree of substitutability are
flawed in several respects. (1) Applicability is typically limited to product
categories having high repeat purchase rates to ensure that a sufficiently
long sequence of purchases is available over a short time period for reliable
estimates of switching probabilities. (2) The customer choice process,
which determines switching, must be presumed stable throughout the
sequence of purchases. If a long time series is used to provide reliable
estimates, this assumption may be questionable. (3) Panel data, upon
which switching probabilities are based, often obscure individual switching behavior since data are typically reported by only one member of a
family who completes a diary of purchases. Apparent switching can result
from different members of the family making consistent but different
brand choices at differing points in time. A similar distortion is created by
an individual who regularly purchases different brands for different usage
occasions. (4) Analyses of panel data are further complicated by multiple
brand purchases at the same time (does purchase of A precede B or vice
versa in determining the sequence?), by lack of uniformity in package sizes
across brands (since package size affects frequency of purchase), and by
different sized packages of the same brand (is purchase of a large size
equivalent to some sequence of purchases of smaller sizes?).

The Hendry model (Butler and Butler 1970, 1971) uses brand switching
data directly to determine the market structure. Although details have
been slow to appear in the literature (Kalwani and Morrison 1977; Rubison
and Bass 1978) there has been a good deal of utilization of the empirical
regularities uncovered by the model for marketing planning purposes.

This model does not rely solely on behavioral data, as it can also incorporate retrospective reports of switching or purchase intentions data from
surveys. In essence, the model seeks an underlying structure of brand-
switching maximally "consistent" with the input data. It posits a hierarchical ordering in consumer decision making: consumers are presumed to
form categories within the product class (e.g., cold or hot, presweetened or
regular, Kellogg's, General Mills, or Post cereals), select those classes in
which they are interested, and then consider for purchase only the alternatives within the chosen class (e.g., brands within a particular type of product *or* product types within a brand name). Analysis is carried out at each
submarket level. Customers may purchase brands within more than one
submarket, but within any submarket all customers are considered poten-

tial purchasers of all brands. Each customer is assumed, at equilibrium, to have stable purchase probabilities.

To determine which ordering or structuring of the market best characterizes customer views, a heuristic procedure is employed. Initially, judgment is used to hypothesize a limited number of plausible partitionings of a market, i.e., *alternative* submarket definitions. For each hypothesized definition, the Hendry framework is used to predict various switching probabilities among the products/brands within each submarket and between submarkets (switching *between* submarkets should be much less than *within* any one submarket). The predictions can then be compared with the actual data. That hypothesized partitioning (market structure) yielding switching patterns in closest correspondence with actual data is selected as the appropriate definition for the structure of the market.

A procedure elaborating hierarchical partitioning concepts similar to those of Hendry, but with the ability to incorporate usage occasion has recently been discussed by Urban and Hauser (1979). As in the Hendry model, a hierarchical tree structure is specified. More switching should occur within than between branches. Individual probability estimates are derived by measuring preferences among products with a consumer interview and statistically matching these preferences to observed or reported purchase behavior using the conditional logit model (McFadden 1970). The derived trees are tested by comparing predicted with actual choices in a simulated buying situation which occurs at the end of the consumer interview.

The Hendry procedure has a substantial subjective component, depending upon the criterion used to generate the hypothetical market structure definitions to be evaluated. (The alternative to a good criterion is the testing of potentially large numbers of definitions.) It is also quite arbitrary, possessing elements of the chicken–egg controversy: the prior specification of "the market" is quite critical to the empirical determination of "market shares" for each brand but these in turn are necessary to calibrate the Hendry model (i.e., estimate its parameters). Thus the "correct" definition of the market will depend upon how well predictions of the model correspond to the actual data. The model ought to always do reasonably well in predicting switching patterns in the same market environment from which share data were taken. In other words, to use the model for purposes of selecting the superior market definition, one must presume the model valid. But to test its validity, one must already possess a valid definition of the market. Thus the Hendry model may provide a reasonable approach to market definition only if either the model itself can be independently validated or if independent criteria exist for validating the market definition it suggests.

The Hendry model presumes all customers have stable probabilities of purchasing every brand within a partition (submarket). This assumes preferences, market shares, attitudes, and all other factors of significance are stable and that learning is negligible. Such assumptions may suggest applicability of the Hendry framework only in mature product categories, where such conditions may reasonably hold. Moreover, confirmation of any a priori partitioning of a market rests solely upon analysis of the aggregate switching probabilities as these become the measures of substitutability. Since analysis is carried out on an aggregate level, individual or segment differences are largely ignored. The premise that any given brand may have a varying set of competitors depending upon intended usage and brand familiarity is assumed away by such aggregation.

Summary. Behavioral measures suffer from an endemic weakness because they are influenced by what "is" or "was" rather than what "might be." Actual switching is affected by current market factors such as the set of existing brands, their availability, current pricing structures, promotional message and expenditures, existing legislation and social mores, etc. An imported beer could be substitutable for a local brand insofar as usage is concerned, but price differences may discourage actual substitution. Similarly, a private label brand may be substitutable for a nationally distributed one, but unless the customer shops the stores in which the private label is sold, they cannot make the substitution. If data are developed over long periods of time or from a diverse set of people in differing circumstances, sufficient variability may have taken place in the determinants of demand to reveal such potential substitutability. Otherwise, if some kind of behavioral measure is desired, laboratory manipulation may be necessary.

Analyses Based upon Customer Judgments

Customers often have considerable knowledge of existing brands through personal or friends' experiences and exposure to promotion. Their perceptions may not always correspond to what manufacturers may believe about their own or competitive products. They may have purchase and consumption objectives which influence their consideration of alternatives and choices among them. They may create new uses for existing products. If such perceptual and decision making processes prove relatively stable, they may be useful for predicting which products and brands will be regarded as potential or actual substitutes and why.

B.1. *Decision Sequence Analysis* utilizes protocols of consumer decision making, which indicate the sequence in which various criteria are employed to reach a final choice (Bettman 1971; Haines 1974). The usual procedure asks individuals to verbalize what is going through their mind as they make purchase decisions in the course of a shopping trip. This verbal record is called a protocol as distinguished from retrospective questioning of subjects about their decisions. With such data, a model of the way the subject makes decisions can be developed. These models specify the *attributes* of the choice objects or situations that are considered and the *sequence* and *method* of combination of these attributes or cues. Generally, the attributes or cues are arrayed in a hierarchical structure called a decision tree. The order in which they are examined is modeled by the path structure of the tree. The branches are based merely on whether or not the level of the attribute is satisfactory or a certain condition is present ("Is the price too high?" "Is the store out of my favorite brand?").

Analysis of protocols is at the individual level. This has the advantage of enabling individual differences in knowledge and beliefs about alternative products and choice criteria to be recognized. Individuals may, in principle, be grouped into segments on the basis of similar decision procedures. Measures of the extent of competition between brands can be obtained from protocols of different segments by noting which alternatives are even considered and when they are eliminated from further consideration by criteria used at each stage of the decision process (alternatives eliminated at later stages should be more competitive than those eliminated earlier).

Applications of decision sequence analysis have focused on choices at the brand level. Yet the real benefits of this approach would seem to be better insights into the hierarchy of product types and variants within a generic product class. Thus in understanding patterns of competition in the vegetable market, it is important to know whether buyers first decide on the type of vegetable (corn, beans, peas, etc.) or the form (fresh, frozen, or canned). Proposals for a similar kind of study have been made by economists in connection with the concept of a "utility tree" (Strotz 1957) and are similar in intent to the Hendry procedure.

There are numerous empirical problems to be considered in any effort to collect protocols of choice hierarchies. The typical representations of decision sequences appear quite complex and pose serious difficulties for aggregation of the individual models into any small number of segments. Aggregation requires some definition of "similarity" in order to group different decision structures. Further, since it is generally expensive to develop protocols, a representative sample of customers may be unrealizable. Customers are not used to reporting their decision processes so explicitly. A trained interviewer is needed to coax information which is specific enough to be meaningful (e.g., what is too high a price or a satisfactory level of preference?) and yet not unduly bias the process. Since customer decision making for some product categories may take place over prolonged periods of time it may be necessary for the length of the interviewing to be similarly extended or to rely on respondent's recall of certain events. Finally, since protocol data are collected in the context of the purchase situation, factors associated with that situation may assume greater importance than factors of intended usage. This could place misleading emphasis on in-store factors as determinants of competition.

B.2. *Perceptual mapping* includes a large family of techniques used to create a geometric representation of customers' perceptions of the qualities possessed by products/brands comprising a previously defined product-market (Green 1975). Brands are represented by locations (points or, possibly, regions) in the space. The dimensions of this space distinguish the competitive alternatives and represent benefits or costs perceived important to the purchase. Thus any product/brand might be located in such a space according to a set of coordinates which represent the extent to which the product is believed to possess each benefit or cost attribute. Relative "distances" between product alternatives may be loosely interpreted as measures of perceived substitutability of each alternative for any other.

There are several different techniques which can be used to create perceptual configurations of product-markets (e.g., direct scaling, factor analysis, multiple discriminant analysis, multidimensional scaling). Analysis may be based upon measures of perceived overall similarity/dissimilarity, perceived appropriateness to common usage situations, and correlations between attribute levels for pairs of products. Unfortunately such diversity of criteria and method can lead to somewhat different perceptual maps and possibly different product-market definitions. Much empirical research is still needed to compare the alternatives and assess which produce definitions that are more valid for particular purposes (Shocker and Srinivasan 1979).

When perceptual maps can be represented in two or three dimensions without destroying the data, there is a great improvement in the understanding of the competitive structure. Further, to the extent that substitutability in such a representation corresponds in some straightforward way to interproduct distance, analytic techniques such as cluster analysis (or simply looking for "open spaces" in the map) could prove useful in identifying product-market boundaries. The eventual decision must necessarily be judgmental, with the geometric representation simply facilitating that judgment. Customers or segments may also be represented in such a space by the location of their "most preferred" combination of attribute levels — termed their ideal point.

The major advantage offered by perceptual mapping methods is versatility. Maps can be created for each major usage situation. When care is taken to control for customer knowledge of available product/brand alternatives, perceptual homogeneity may be sufficient to permit the modeling of preference and choice for different user segments within a common perceptual representation (Pessemier 1977). Moreover, perceptual maps can be created for different levels of product competition to explore competitive relations at the level of product types, variants, or brands. For example, Jain and Etgar (1975) have used multidimensional scaling to provide a geometric representation of the beverage market which incorporates all these different levels in the same configuration. These analyses become cumbersome when it is not possible to assume perceptual homogeneity

(Day, Deutscher, and Ryans 1976). Then it is necessary to cluster the respondents into homogeneous "points-of-view" groups, based on the commonality in their perceptions, and conduct a separate analysis for each group. Alternatively, one can assume that respondents use the same perceptual dimensions, but differ with respect to the weights they attach to the various dimensions.

In principle, new product concepts can be positioned in the space, or existing brands repositioned or deleted, and the effects on the individual or segment choice behavior predicted. Unfortunately, the relation between interproduct distances in the perceptual space and substitutability is not rigorously established. Stefflre (1972) has argued that a perceptual space contains only labeled regions and hence that gaps may simply represent discontinuities. The question is not whether such discontinuities in fact exist, but rather whether a preference model based upon distances from ideal-points to products remains a reasonable predictor of individual or segment behavior. If so, the decision framework of a common perceptual space coupled with models of individual/segment decision making can be used to assess the relative substitutability of different brands for each segment. These measures can then be aggregated over segments to estimate patterns of competition for the broader market.

B.3. *Technology substitution analysis* adapts the idea of preference related to distance in a multiattribute space to the problem of forecasting the substitution of one material, process, or product for another — aluminum for copper in electrical applications and polyvinyl for glass in liquor bottles, for example. Each successful substitution tends to follow an S-shaped or "logistic" curve representing a slow start as initial problems and resistance to change have to be overcome, followed by more rapid progress as acceptance is gained and applications can be publicized, and finally a slowing in the pace of substitution as saturation is reached.

A simple approach to forecasting the course and speed of the substitution process is to project a function having the appropriate logistics curve, using historical data to determine its parameters (Lenz and Lanford 1972). This curve-fitting method overlooks many potential influences on the process, such as: the age, condition, and rate of obsolescence of the capital equipment used in the old technology; the price elasticity of demand; and the "utility-in-use" or relative performance advantage. Recent efforts to model substitution rates have focused on relative "utility" as the basis for improvements in forecasting ability (Stern, Ayres, and Shapanko 1975). The procedure for assessing "utility-in-use" involves: first, identifying the relevant attributes and performance characteristics of each of the competing products or technologies, followed by ratings by experts of the extent to which each alternative possesses each attribute and the perceived importance of each attribute in each end-use market. Finally, an overall utility for each product in each usage situation is obtained by multiplying the

attribute possession score by the importance ratings, summing the resulting products, and adjusting for differences in unit price. While criticism
can be made of the model structure and the seeming reliance on measurable physical properties to specify the attributes, the value of the basic
approach should not be discounted. The outcome is a highly useful quantitative measure of utility which can be used to estimate substitutability
among competing products or technologies in specific usage situations.

B.4. *Customer judgments of substitutability* may be obtained in a variety of
ways. The simplest is to ask a sample of customers to indicate the degree of
substitutability between possible pairs of brands on a rating scale such as:
none, low, some, or substantial substitutability. Beyond this familiar approach, several methods of utilizing customer judgments have recently
been developed which provide far greater diagnostic insights into patterns
of competition.

1. *The free response approach* (Green, Wind, and Jain 1973). Respondents
are presented with various brands and asked to free-associate the names of
similar or substitute brands. Two kinds of data are obtained. One is the
frequency of mention of one brand as a substitute for another, which could
be used as a measure of similarity of the two brands in order to establish a
perceptual space. Secondly, the *order of mention* of substitute brands can be
treated as rank-order data (Wind 1977). These data represent an aggregate
judgment across situations, and leave it to the respondent to decide how
similar two brands must be before they become substitutes.

A useful variant of the free-response question asks respondents what
they would do if they were unable to buy their preferred brand. One
advantage of this question is that it can realistically be tailored to specific
situations. For example, one study asked scotch drinkers what they would
do if scotch were not available in a variety of situations, such as a large
cocktail party in the early evening. Evidently, there were some situations
where white wine was the preferred alternative.

2. *The dollar metric approach* (Pessemier et al. 1970/71). Respondents first
are presented with all possible pairs of brands, each of the brands being
marked with their regular prices. In each case, the respondent selects the
brand he/she would buy in a forced-choice purchase. They are then asked
the price to which the preferred brand must rise before they would switch
their original preference. Strength of preference is measured in terms of
this price increment. Such data must be further "processed" to compute
aggregated preference measures.

This procedure is somewhat analogous to a laboratory measurement of
cross-elasticity of demand. The set of potentially competitive brands must
be again identified in advance. The procedure is reasonably easy to ad-
minister and analyze; although the simplicity may be eroded if considera-

tions of intended usage, brand familiarity, and market segmentation are incorporated. It appears that respondents are able to reveal their preferences for different alternatives in the forced-choice situation. Whether they can relate validly how they arrived at the preference — by estimating the minimum price change that would cause a switch — remains an open question (Huber and James 1977).

3. *Direct grouping into product categories.* Bourgeois, Haines, and Sommers (1979) have taken broadly related sets of brands and asked samples of customers to: (1) divide the set into as many groups as they consider meaningful, (2) explain the criteria used for each grouping, and (3) judge the similarity of the brands within each group. A measure of the similarity of brands is created by summing across customers to find the frequency with which pairs of brands are assigned to the same group. These data are analyzed by nonmetric, multidimensional scaling programs to obtain interval-scaled measures of brand similarity (according to their proximity in a reduced space). These are input to a cluster analysis routine to obtain groupings of brands regarded as "customer product types." Products are assigned to one type only. An application of this procedure to the generic "personal care" market yielded intuitively appealing groups of brands. However the data were reported to be quite "noisy," which is not surprising in view of the wide latitude given the respondents. Potentially, respondents could differ both in the frame of reference for the task (the intended application or usage) and the criterion for grouping. Some, for example, might emphasize physical similarity while others might elect appropriateness-in-use or similarity of price as the criterion.

4. *Products-by-uses analysis.* In the procedure developed by Stefflre (1979; Myers and Tauber 1977), a sample of customers is given a list of target products or brands and asked to conjecture as many uses for them as possible. They are then asked to suggest additional products or brands appropriate to these same uses and additional uses appropriate to these new products. This sequence of free-response questions generates large lists of products/brands and potential uses. An independent sample is then asked to judge the appropriateness of each product for each use. In one study of proprietary medicines, for example, respondents were asked to judge the acceptability of each of 52 medicines for 52 conditions of use ranging from "when you have a stuffy nose" to "when the children have a fever."

Two assumptions underlie analyses of the products-by-uses matrix: (1) the set of products constitutes a representative sample of the benefits sought by customers and (2) two usage situations are similar if similar benefits are desired in both situations. If these assumptions are valid, then grouping usage situations according to similarity of products judged appropriate should be equivalent to grouping them explicitly by the benefits desired. The net result is a somewhat circular procedure:

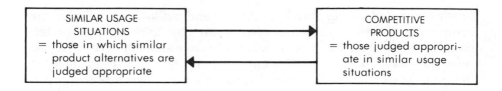

The merits of the Stefflre (1972, 1979) procedure are first, that the introduction of specific situations gives respondents frames of reference for their judgments of substitutability or appropriateness and second, that the criteria can be modified to reflect greater concern with *potential* competition (respondents are asked which existing products or descriptions of concepts would be appropriate to specified uses) or with *actual* competition (which products they would consider for purchase in the situation). This ability to use descriptions of concepts greatly extends the flexibility of the approach to provide data relevant to actual or proposed changes in the product-market. A further advantage, shared with the direct grouping approach, is an ability to cope with large numbers of alternatives if necessary, without a requirement for large numbers of respondents because of a high degree of homogeneity in perceptual judgments.

These advantages are seemingly offset by the evident impracticability of the demands on respondents to complete a matrix with as many as 2,500 cells. For many purposes, however, it is not necessary that each respondent complete the entire matrix. A related problem is the lack of a sound basis for deciding how many situations, and at what level of specificity, to include in the matrix.

5. *Substitution-in-use analysis.* This extends the Stefflre procedure in two directions (Srivastava, Shocker, and Day 1978). First, a separate analysis step is introduced to ensure that the set of usage situations is parsimonious and representative. If the latter condition is not met, it is likely there will be too many of one "type" of situation, with consequent distortion in the grouping of products. Secondly, the measure of appropriateness-in-use is modified to measure the degree of suitability. This is feasible as the number of situations the respondents are given is significantly smaller than in the Stefflre procedure. The result is a three-stage procedure:

1. The *exploratory* stage uses free response plus repertory grid and focused group methods to elicit usage situations associated with a generic need.
2. A *typology* of usage situations is then developed from a principal components analysis of the products-by-uses matrix (after a check for perceptual homogeneity). Both uses and products can be plotted in the reduced space described by the first two or three principal components. A typology of uses may be derived from factorial combinations of different levels of the independent dimensions of this space.

3. A new sample is employed to obtain a measure of the suitability or appropriateness of each brand or product for each of the usage situations in the typology. Each alternative can be rated separately, or all alternatives can be ranked, within each situation.

There are several ways to analyze the resulting matrix. Insights into a firm's competitive position within distinct situational submarkets can be obtained from a principal components analysis similar to stage 2 of the procedure described above. Experience with breath fresheners and banking services (Srivastava and Shocker 1979) indicates that ideas for new products or product positions can come from the identification of inadequately served usage situations. A useful test of the effectiveness of a company's positioning efforts is the extent of variability of customer perceptions of the appropriateness of a specific brand for a distinct usage submarket. The analysis can also help assess the possibility of cannibalization. If two or more products or brands of a single manufacturer are seen as appropriate for the same usage submarket, then efforts to promote one may be at the expense of a loss in sales of the other.

The data can also be analyzed with categorical conjoint or similar procedures, as long as the factorial combinations of usage situations are properly balanced. Here the focus would be on both the patterns of competition within a usage situation and the elements of the situation which have the greatest influence on these patterns. Wind (1977) used this approach to study the relative positions of finance companies. Automobile dealers were given 16 different financing situations and asked to assign each to one of five possible financing alternatives. The situations represented combinations of six different factors including customer's credit rating, familiarity with customer, amount to finance, and length of term. The estimated utility functions suggested the degree of appropriateness of each source of financing for each level of the six factors. It was found, for example, that the client (a finance company associated with an automobile dealer) faced quite different competition depending on the amount to be financed.

Many of the advantages of the substitution-in-use approach derive from the consistency of the approach with the conceptual definition of a product-market. Despite these potential advantages, the procedure produces only a relative measure of substitutability. Managerial judgment must still decide the level of judged appropriateness that permits each product/brand to be considered as part of a situational submarket.

Summary and Conclusions

The questions of how to identify product-market boundaries cannot be separated from the ways results are to be used. Strategic or long-run definitions of market structure inevitably hold more significance even though they are mainly obtainable from customer judgments rather than behavior. Very narrowly defined boundaries appear adequate for short-run, tactical decisions in most product categories. The value of a valid and strategically relevant product-market definition lies in "stretching" the company's perceptions appropriately far enough so that significant threats and opportunities are not missed, but not so far as to dissipate information gathering and analysis efforts on "long shots." This is a difficult balance to achieve given the myriad of present and potential competitors faced by most companies.

The principal conclusions from the analysis of the nature of boundaries and the various empirical methods for identifying competitive product-markets are:

Boundaries are seldom clear-cut — ultimately, all boundaries are arbitrary.

The suitability of different empirical methods is strongly influenced by the character of the market environment.

On balance, those empirical methods which explicitly recognize the variety of usage situations have widest applicability and yield maximum insights. The concept of usage situation appears to be the most prevalent common denominator of market environments which can be used as the basis for empirical methods.

Most methods, particularly those based upon behavioral measures, are static and have difficulty coping with changes in preferences or additions and deletions of choice alternatives in the market.

Regardless of method, the most persistent problem is the lack of defensible criteria for recognizing boundaries.

These conclusions add up to a situation where the state of knowledge has not kept abreast of either the present need to understand, or the changing technological, social, and economic factors which are constantly reshaping market environments. To redress this situation, there is a clear need for a strategically oriented program of research in a variety of market situations. Research in each market should be characterized by the use of multiple techniques to seek confirmation through cross validation and longitudinal approaches in which judgmental methods are followed by behavioral methods which can validate inferences. As we have noted, different methods have different strengths and weaknesses, and more needs to be learned about the sensitivity of results to the shortcomings of each method. Also there will inevitably be points of contradiction and consistency in the insights gained from boundaries established by different methods. The process of resolution should be most revealing, both in terms of understanding a firm's competitive position and suggesting strategy alternatives.

Notes

1. Many of the same issues are encountered during efforts to define the relevant product-market for antitrust purposes. Here the question is whether a company so dominates a market that effective competition is precluded, or that a past or prospective merger has lessened competition. The conceptual approach to this question is very similar to the one developed in this paper (Day, Massay, and Shocker 1978). However, because of the adversarial nature of the proceedings and the existence of prior hypotheses of separation to be tested, the treatment of "relevant market" issues is otherwise quite different.

2. This premise was directly tested, and supported, in a study of the variation of judged importance of various fast food restaurant attributes across eating occasions (Miller and Ginter 1979). This study and others also have found that some needs, and benefits sought, are reasonably stable across situations. Thus it is usually productive to segment a market on the basis of both people and occasions (Goldman and McDonald 1979).

References

Belk, Russell (1975), "Situational Variables and Consumer Behavior," *Journal of Consumer Research*, 2 (December), 157–164.

Bettman, James R. (1971), "The Structure of Consumer Choice Processes," *Journal of Marketing Research*, 8 (November), 465–471.

Bourgeois, Jacques D., George H. Haines, and Montrose S. Sommers (1979), "Defining an Industry," paper presented to the TIMS/ORSA Special Interest Conference on Market Measurement and Analysis, Stanford, CA, March 26.

Butler, Ben, Jr., and David H. Butler (1970 and 1971), "Hendrodynamics: Fundamental Laws of Consumer Dynamics," Hendry Corp., Croton-on-Hudson, NY, Chapter 1 (1970) and Chapter 2 (1971).

Cocks, Douglas L., and John R. Virts (1975), "Market Definition and Concentration in the Ethical Pharmaceutical Industry," Internal publication of Eli Lilly and Co., Indianapolis.

Day, George S. (1977), "Diagnosing The Product Portfolio," *Journal of Marketing*, 41 (April), 29–38.

———, Terry Deutscher, and Adrian Ryans (1976), "Data Quality, Level of Aggregation and Nonmetric Multidimensional Scaling Solutions," *Journal of Marketing Research*, 13 (February), 92–97.

———, William F. Massy, and Allan D. Shocker (1978), "The Public Policy Context of The Relevant Market Question," in *Public Policy Issues in Marketing*, John F. Cady, ed., Cambridge, MA: Marketing Science Institute, 51–67.

Frank, Ronald, William F. Massy, and Yoram Wind (1973), *Market Segmentation*, Englewood Cliffs, NJ: Prentice-Hall, Inc.

Goldman, Alfred, and Susan S. McDonald (1979), "Occasion Segmentation," paper presented to American Marketing Association Attitude Research Conference, Hilton Head, S.C., Feb. 25–28.

Green, Paul E. (1975), "Marketing Applications of MDS: Assessment and Outlook," *Journal of Marketing*, 39 (January), 24–31.

———, Yoram Wind, and Arun K. Jain (1973), "Analyzing Free Response Data in Marketing Research," *Journal of Marketing Research*, 10 (February), 45–52.

Haines, George H. (1974), "Process Models of Consumer Decision-Making," in *Buyer/Consumer Information Processing*, G. D. Hughes and M. L. Ray, eds., Chapel Hill, NC: University of North Carolina Press.

Hanon, Mack (1974), "Reorganize Your Company Around Its Markets," *Harvard Business Review*, 79 (November–December), 63–74.

Huber, Joel, and Bill James (1977), "The Monetary Worth of Physical Attributes: A Dollarmetric Approach," in *Moving A Head with Attitude Research*, Yoram Wind and Marshall Greenberg, eds., Chicago: American Marketing Association.

Jain, Arun K., and Michael Etgar (1975), "How to Improve Antitrust Policies with Marketing Research Tools," in *1975 Combined Proceedings of the American Marketing Association*, Edward M. Mazze, ed., Chicago: American Marketing Association, 72–75.

Kalwani, Manohar U., and Donald G. Morrison (1977), "A Parsimonious Description of the Hendry System," *Management Science*, 23 (January), 476–477.

Lenz, Ralph C., Jr., and H. W. Lanford (1972), "The Substitution Phenomena," *Business Horizons*, 15 (February), 63–68.

Lunn, Tony (1972), "Segmenting and Constructing Markets," in *Consumer Market Research Handbook*, R. M. Worcester, ed. Maidenhead, Berkshire: McGraw-Hill.

Lutz, Richard J., and Pradeep Kakkar (1976), "Situational Influence in Interpersonal Persuasion," in *Advances in Consumer Research*, Vol. III, Beverlee B. Anderson, ed., Atlanta: Association for Consumer Research, 370–378.

McFadden, Daniel (1970), "Conditional Logit Analysis of Qualitative Choice Behavior" in *Frontiers in Econometrics*, P. Zarembka, ed., New York: Academic Press, 105–142.

Miller, Kenneth E., and James L. Ginter (1979), "An Investigation of Situational Variation in Brand Choice Behavior and Attitude," *Journal of Marketing Research*, 16 (February), 111–123.

Moran, William R. (1973), "Why New Products Fail," *Journal of Advertising Research*, 13 (April), 5–13.

Myers, James H., and Edward Tauber (1977), *Market Structure Analysis*, Chicago: American Marketing Association.

Needham, Douglas (1969), *Economic Analysis and Industrial Structure*, New York: Holt, Rinehart, and Winston, Chapter 2.

Pessemier, Edgar A. (1977), *Product Management: Strategy and Organization*, Santa Barbara, CA: Wiley/Hamilton, 203–254.

———, Philip Burger, Richard Teach, and Douglas Tigert (1970/71), "Using Laboratory Brand Preference Scales to Predict Consumer Brand Purchases," *Management Science*, 17 (February), 371–385.

Rubison, Joel R., and Frank M. Bass (1978), "A Note on 'A Parsimonious Description of the Hendry System,' " paper 658, West Lafayette, IN: Krannert School, Purdue, March.

Scherer, Frederic (1970), *Industrial Market Structure and Economic Performance*, Chicago: Rand McNally.

Shocker, Allan D., and V. Srinivasan (1979), "MultiAttribute Applications for Product Concept Evaluation and Generation: A Critical Review," *Journal of Marketing Research*, 16 (May), 159–180.

Sissors, Jack Z. (1966), "What is a Market?" *Journal of Marketing*, 30 (July), 17–21.

Srivastava, Rajendra, and Allan D. Shocker (1979), "The Validity/Reliability of a Method for Developing Product-Specific Usage Situational Taxonomies" working paper, Pittsburgh: University of Pittsburgh, Graduate School of Business (September).

———, ———, and George S. Day (1978), "An Exploratory Study of Situational Effects on Product Market Definition," in *Advances in Consumer Research*, Vol. V, H. Keith Hunt, ed., Ann Arbor: Association for Consumer Research, 32–38.

Stefflre, Volney (1972), "Some Applications of Multidimensional Scaling to Social Science Problems," in *Multidimensional Scaling: Theory and Applications in the Behavioral Sciences*, Vol. III, A. K. Romney, R. N. Shepard, and S. B. Nerlove, eds., New York: Seminar Press.

——— (1979), "New Products: Organizational and Technical Problems and Opportunities," in *Analytic Approaches to Product and Marketing Planning*, A. D. Shocker, ed., Cambridge, MA: Marketing Science Institute, April Report 79–104, 415–480.

Stern, M. O., R. V. Ayres, and A. Shapanko (1975), "A Model for Forecasting the Substitution of One Technology for Another," *Technological Forecasting and Social Change*, 7 (February), 57–79.

Stout, Roy G., Raymond H. S. Suh, Marshall G. Greenberg, and Joel S. Dubow (1977), "Usage Incidents as a Basis for Segmentation," in *Moving A Head with Attitude Research*, Yoram Wind and Marshall Greenberg, eds., Chicago: American Marketing Association.

Strotz, Robert H. (1957), "The Empirical Implications of a Utility Tree," *Econometrica*, 25 (April), 269–280.

———, and John R. Hauser (1979), "Market Definition" in *Design and Marketing of New Products and Services*. Cambridge, MA: MIT, Sloan School of Management, Ch. 5.

Urban, G. L., and J. R. Hauser (1980), *Design and Marketing of New Products*, Englewood Cliffs, NJ: Prentice-Hall.

Vernon, John (1972), *Market Structure and Industrial Performance*, Boston: Allyn and Bacon.

Wind, Yoram (1977), "The Perception of a Firm's Competitive Position," in *Behavioral Models for Market Analysis*, F. M. Nicosia and Y. Wind, eds., New York: The Dryden Press, 163–181.

2. How Competitive Forces Shape Strategy

Michael E. Porter

The essence of strategy formulation is coping with competition. Yet it is easy to view competition too narrowly and too pessimistically. While one sometimes hears executives complaining to the contrary, intense competition in an industry is neither coincidence nor bad luck.

Moreover, in the fight for market share, competition is not manifested only in the other players. Rather, competition in an industry is rooted in its underlying economics, and competitive forces exist that go well beyond the established combatants in a particular industry. Customers, suppliers, potential entrants, and substitute products are all competitors that may be more or less prominent or active depending on the industry.

The state of competition in an industry depends on five basic forces, which are diagrammed in Figure 2-1. The collective strength of these forces determines the ultimate profit potential of an industry. It ranges from *intense* in industries like tires, metal cans, and steel, where no company earns spectacular returns on investment, to *mild* in industries like oil field services and equipment, soft drinks, and toiletries, where there is room for quite high returns.

In the economists' "perfectly competitive" industry, jockeying for position is unbridled and entry to the industry very easy. This kind of industry structure, of course, offers the worst prospect for long-run profitability. The weaker the forces collectively, however, the greater the opportunity for superior performance.

Whatever their collective strength, the corporate strategist's goal is to find a position in the industry where his or her company can best defend itself against these forces or can influence them in its favor. The collective

Reprinted by permission of the *Harvard Business Review*, March–April 1979, pp. 137–145. Copyright © 1979 by the President and Fellows of Harvard College; all rights reserved.

When this article was published, Mr. Porter was an associate professor of business administration at the Harvard Business School.

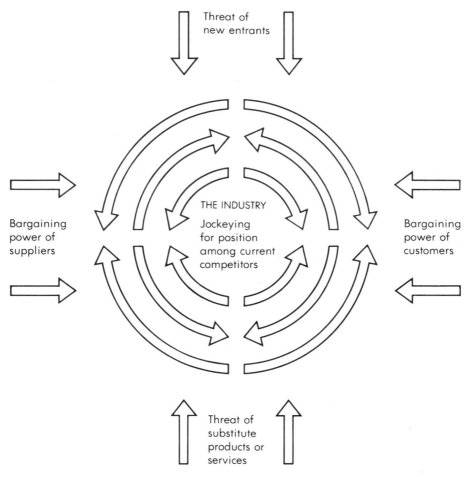

FIGURE 2.1   Forces Governing Competition in an Industry

strength of the forces may be painfully apparent to all the antagonists; but to cope with them, the strategist must delve below the surface and analyze the sources of each. For example, what makes the industry vulnerable to entry? What determines the bargaining power of suppliers?

Knowledge of these underlying sources of competitive pressure provides the groundwork for a strategic agenda of action. They highlight the critical strengths and weaknesses of the company, animate the positioning of the company in its industry, clarify the areas where strategic changes may yield the greatest payoff, and highlight the places where industry trends promise to hold the greatest significance as either opportunities or threats. Understanding these sources also proves to be of help in considering areas for diversification.

Contending Forces

The strongest competitive force or forces determine the profitability of an industry and so are of greatest importance in strategy formulation. For example, even a company with a strong position in an industry un- threatened by potential entrants will earn low returns if it faces a superior or a lower-cost substitute product — as the leading manufacturers of vacuum tubes and coffee percolators have learned to their sorrow. In such a situation, coping with the substitute product becomes the number one strategic priority.

Different forces take on prominence, of course, in shaping competition in each industry. In the ocean-going tanker industry the key force is proba- bly the buyers (the major oil companies), while in tires it is powerful OEM buyers coupled with tough competitors. In the steel industry the key forces are foreign competitors and substitute materials.

Every industry has an underlying structure, or a set of fundamental economic and technical characteristics, that gives rise to these competitive forces. The strategist, wanting to position his company to cope best with its industry environment or to influence that environment in the company's favor, must learn what makes the environment tick.

This view of competition pertains equally to industries dealing in ser- vices and to those selling products. To avoid monotony in this article, I refer to both products and services as "products." The same general princi- ples apply to all types of business.

A few characteristics are critical to the strength of each competitive force. I shall discuss them in this section.

Threat of Entry

New entrants to an industry bring new capacity, the desire to gain market share, and often substantial resources. Companies diversifying through acquisition into the industry from other markets often leverage their re- sources to cause a shake-up, as Philip Morris did with Miller beer.

The seriousness of the threat of entry depends on the barriers present and on the reaction from existing competitors that the entrant can expect. If barriers to entry are high and a newcomer can expect sharp retaliation from the entrenched competitors, obviously he will not pose a serious threat of entering.

There are six major sources of barriers to entry:

1. *Economies of scale* — These economies deter entry by forcing the aspir- ant either to come in on a large scale or to accept a cost disadvantage. Scale economies in production, research, marketing, and service are probably the key barriers to entry in the mainframe computer industry, as Xerox and GE sadly discovered. Economies of scale can also act as

hurdles in distribution, utilization of the sales force, financing, and nearly any other part of a business.

2. *Product differentiation* — Brand identification creates a barrier by forcing entrants to spend heavily to overcome customer loyalty. Advertising, customer service, being first in the industry, and product differences are among the factors fostering brand identification. It is perhaps the most important entry barrier in soft drinks, over-the-counter drugs, cosmetics, investment banking, and public accounting. To create high fences around their businesses, brewers couple brand identification with economies of scale in production, distribution, and marketing.

3. *Capital requirements* — The need to invest large financial resources in order to compete creates a barrier to entry, particularly if the capital is required for unrecoverable expenditures in up-front advertising or R&D. Capital is necessary not only for fixed facilities but also for customer credit, inventories, and absorbing start-up losses. While major corporations have the financial resources to invade almost any industry, the huge capital requirements in certain fields, such as computer manufacturing and mineral extraction, limit the pool of likely entrants.

4. *Cost disadvantages independent of size* — Entrenched companies may have cost advantages not available to potential rivals, no matter what their size and attainable economies of scale. These advantages can stem from the effects of the learning curve (and of its first cousin, the experience curve), proprietary technology, access to the best raw materials sources, assets purchased at preinflation prices, government subsidies, or favorable locations. Sometimes cost advantages are legally enforceable, as they are through patents. (For an analysis of the much-discussed experience curve as a barrier to entry, see the appendix to this article.)

5. *Access to distribution channels* — The new boy on the block must, of course, secure distribution of his product or service. A new food product, for example, must displace others from the supermarket shelf via price breaks, promotions, intense selling efforts, or some other means. The more limited the wholesale or retail channels are and the more that existing competitors have these tied up, obviously the tougher that entry into the industry will be. Sometimes this barrier is so high that, to surmount it, a new contestant must create its own distribution channels, as Timex did in the watch industry in the 1950s.

6. *Government policy* — The government can limit or even foreclose entry to industries with such controls as license requirements and limits on access to raw materials. Regulated industries like trucking, liquor retailing, and freight forwarding are noticeable examples; more subtle government restrictions operate in fields like ski-area development and coal mining. The government also can play a major indirect role by affecting entry barriers through controls such as air and water pollution standards and safety regulations.

The potential rival's expectations about the reaction of existing competitors also will influence its decision on whether to enter. The company is likely to have second thoughts if incumbents have previously lashed out at new entrants or if:

- the incumbents possess substantial resources to fight back, including excess cash and unused borrowing power, productive capacity, or clout with distribution channels and customers;
- the incumbents seem likely to cut prices because of a desire to keep market shares or because of industrywide excess capacity;
- industry growth is slow, affecting its ability to absorb the new arrival and probably causing the financial performance of all the parties involved to decline.

Changing Conditions.   From a strategic standpoint there are two important additional points to note about the threat of entry.

First, it changes, of course, as these conditions change. The expiration of Polaroid's basic patents on instant photography, for instance, greatly reduced its absolute cost entry barrier built by proprietary technology. It is not surprising that Kodak plunged into the market. Product differentiation in printing has all but disappeared. Conversely, in the auto industry economies of scale increased enormously with post–World War II automation and vertical integration — virtually stopping successful new entry.

Second, strategic decisions involving a large segment of an industry can have a major impact on the conditions determining the threat of entry. For example, the actions of many U.S. wine producers in the 1960s to step up product introductions, raise advertising levels, and expand distribution nationally surely strengthened the entry roadblocks by raising economies of scale and making access to distribution channels more difficult. Similarly, decisions by members of the recreational vehicle industry to vertically integrate in order to lower costs have greatly increased the economies of scale and raised the capital cost barriers.

Powerful Suppliers and Buyers

Suppliers can exert bargaining power on participants in an industry by raising prices or reducing the quality of purchased goods and services. Powerful suppliers can thereby squeeze profitability out of an industry unable to recover cost increases in its own prices. By raising their prices, soft drink concentrate producers have contributed to the erosion of profitability of bottling companies because the bottlers, facing intense competition from powdered mixes, fruit drinks, and other beverages, have limited freedom to raise *their* prices accordingly. Customers likewise can force down prices, demand higher quality or more service, and play competitors against each other — all at the expense of industry profits.

The power of each important supplier or buyer group depends on a number of characteristics of its market situation and on the relative importance of its sales or purchases to the industry compared with its overall business.

A *supplier* group is powerful if:

It is dominated by a few companies and is more concentrated than the industry it sells to.

Its product is unique or at least differentiated, or if it has built up switching costs. Switching costs are fixed costs buyers face in changing suppliers. These arise because, among other things, a buyer's product specifications tie it to particular suppliers, it has invested heavily in specialized ancillary equipment or in learning how to operate a supplier's equipment (as in computer software), or its production lines are connected to the supplier's manufacturing facilities (as in some manufacture of beverage containers).

It is not obliged to contend with other products for sale to the industry. For instance, the competition between the steel companies and the aluminum companies to sell to the can industry checks the power of each supplier.

It poses a credible threat of integrating forward into the industry's business. This provides a check against the industry's ability to improve the terms on which it purchases.

The industry is not an important customer of the supplier group. If the industry *is* an important customer, suppliers' fortunes will be closely tied to the industry, and they will want to protect the industry through reasonable pricing and assistance in activities like R&D and lobbying.

A *buyer* group is powerful if:

It is concentrated or purchases in large volumes. Large-volume buyers are particularly potent forces if heavy fixed costs characterize the industry — as they do in metal containers, corn refining, and bulk chemicals, for example — which raise the stakes to keep capacity filled.

The products it purchases from the industry are standard or undifferentiated. The buyers, sure that they can always find alternative suppliers, may play one company against another, as they do in aluminum extrusion.

The products it purchases from the industry form a component of its product and represent a significant fraction of its cost. The buyers are likely to shop for a favorable price and purchase selectively. Where the product sold by the industry in question is a small fraction of buyers' costs, buyers are usually much less price sensitive.

It earns low profits, which create great incentive to lower its purchasing costs. Highly profitable buyers, however, are generally less price sensitive (that is, of course, if the item does not represent a large fraction of their costs).

The industry's product is unimportant to the quality of the buyers' products or services. Where the quality of the buyers' products is very much affected by the industry's product, buyers are generally less price sensitive. Industries which this situation pertains to include oil field equipment, where a malfunction can lead to large losses, and enclosures for electronic medical and test instruments, where the quality of the enclosure can influence the user's impression about the quality of the equipment inside.

The industry's product does not save the buyer money. Where the industry's product or service can pay for itself many times over, the buyer is rarely price sensitive; rather, he is interested in quality. This is true in services like investment banking and public accounting, where errors in judgment can be costly and embarrassing, and in businesses like the logging of oil wells, where an accurate survey can save thousands of dollars in drilling costs.

The buyers pose a credible threat of integrating backward to make the industry's product. The Big Three auto producers and major buyers of cars have often used the threat of self-manufacture as a bargaining lever. But sometimes an industry engenders a threat to buyers that its members may integrate forward.

Most of these sources of buyer power can be attributed to consumers as a group as well as to industrial and commercial buyers; only a modification of the frame of reference is necessary. Consumers tend to be more price sensitive if they are purchasing products that are undifferentiated, expensive relative to their incomes, and of a sort where quality is not particularly important.

The buying power of retailers is determined by the same rules, with one important addition. Retailers can gain significant bargaining power over manufacturers when they can influence consumers' purchasing decisions, as they do in audio components, jewelry, appliances, sporting goods, and other goods.

Strategic Action.   A company's choice of suppliers to buy from or buyer groups to sell to should be viewed as a crucial strategic decision. A company can improve its strategic posture by finding suppliers or buyers who possess the least power to influence it adversely.

Most common is the situation of a company being able to choose whom it will sell to — in other words, buyer selection. Rarely do all the buyer groups a company sells to enjoy equal power. Even if a company sells to a single industry, segments usually exist within that industry that exercise less power (and that are therefore less price sensitive) than others. For example, the replacement market for most products is less price sensitive than the overall market.

As a rule, a company can sell to powerful buyers and still come away with above-average profitability only if it is a low-cost producer in its industry or if its product enjoys some unusual, if not unique, features. In supplying large customers with electric motors, Emerson Electric earns high returns because its low-cost position permits the company to meet or undercut competitors' prices.

If the company lacks a low cost position or a unique product, selling to everyone is self-defeating because the more sales it achieves, the more vulnerable it becomes. The company may have to muster the courage to turn away business and sell only to less potent customers.

Buyer selection has been a key to the success of National Can and Crown Cork & Seal. They focus on the segments of the can industry where they can create product differentiation, minimize the threat of backward integration, and otherwise mitigate the awesome power of their customers. Of course, some industries do not enjoy the luxury of selecting "good" buyers.

As the factors creating supplier and buyer power change with time or as a result of a company's strategic decisions, naturally the power of these groups rises or declines. In the ready-to-wear clothing industry, as the buyers (department stores and clothing stores) have become more concentrated and control has passed to large chains, the industry has come under increasing pressure and suffered falling margins. The industry has been unable to differentiate its product or engender switching costs that lock in its buyers enough to neutralize these trends.

Substitute Products

By placing a ceiling on prices it can charge, substitute products or services limit the potential of an industry. Unless it can upgrade the quality of the product or differentiate it somehow (as via marketing), the industry will suffer in earnings and possibly in growth.

Manifestly, the more attractive the price-performance trade-off offered by substitute products, the firmer the lid placed on the industry's profit potential. Sugar producers confronted with the large-scale commercialization of high-fructose corn syrup, a sugar substitute, are learning this lesson today.

Substitutes not only limit profits in normal times; they also reduce the bonanza an industry can reap in boom times. In 1978 the producers of fiberglass insulation enjoyed unprecedented demand as a result of high energy costs and severe winter weather. But the industry's ability to raise prices was tempered by the plethora of insulation substitutes, including cellulose, rock wool, and styrofoam. These substitutes are bound to become an even stronger force once the current round of plant additions by fiberglass insulation producers has boosted capacity enough to meet demand (and then some).

Substitute products that deserve the most attention strategically are those that (a) are subject to trends improving their price-performance trade-off with the industry's product, or (b) are produced by industries earning high profits. Substitutes often come rapidly into play if some development increases competition in their industries and causes price reduction or performance improvement.

Jockeying for Position

Rivalry among existing competitors takes the familiar form of jockeying for position — using tactics like price competition, product introduction, and advertising slugfests. Intense rivalry is related to the presence of a number of factors:

> Competitors are numerous or are roughly equal in size and power. In many U.S. industries in recent years foreign contenders, of course, have become part of the competitive picture.

> Industry growth is slow, precipitating fights for market share that involve expansion-minded members.

> The product or service lacks differentiation or switching costs, which lock in buyers and protect one combatant from raids on its customers by another.

> Fixed costs are high or the product is perishable, creating strong temptation to cut prices. Many basic materials businesses, like paper and aluminum, suffer from this problem when demand slackens.

> Capacity is normally augmented in large increments. Such additions, as in the chlorine and vinyl chloride businesses, disrupt the industry's supply-demand balance and often lead to periods of over-capacity and price cutting.

> Exit barriers are high. Exit barriers, like very specialized assets or management's loyalty to a particular business, keep companies competing even though they may be earning low or even negative returns on investment. Excess capacity remains functioning, and the profitability of the healthy competitors suffers as the sick ones hang on.[1] If the entire industry suffers from overcapacity, it may seek government help — particularly if foreign competition is present.

> The rivals are diverse in strategies, origins, and "personalities." They have different ideas about how to compete and continually run head-on into each other in the process.

As an industry matures, its growth rate changes, resulting in declining profits and (often) a shakeout. In the booming recreational vehicle industry of the early 1970s, nearly every producer did well; but slow growth since then has eliminated the high returns, except for the strongest members, not to mention many of the weaker companies. The same profit story has been played out in industry after industry — snowmobiles, aerosol packaging, and sports equipment are just a few examples.

An acquisition can introduce a very different personality to an industry, as has been the case with Black & Decker's takeover of McCullough, the producer of chain saws. Technological innovation can boost the level of fixed costs in the production process, as it did in the shift from batch to continuous-line photo finishing in the 1960s.

While a company must live with many of these factors — because they are built into industry economics — it may have some latitude for improving matters through strategic shifts. For example, it may try to raise buyers' switching costs or increase product differentiation. A focus on selling efforts in the fastest-growing segments of the industry or on market areas with the lowest fixed costs can reduce the impact of industry rivalry. If it is feasible, a company can try to avoid confrontation with competitors having high exit barriers and can thus side-step involvement in bitter price cutting.

Formulation of Strategy

Once the corporate strategist has assessed the forces affecting competition in his industry and their underlying causes, he can identify his company's strengths and weaknesses. The crucial strengths and weaknesses from a strategic standpoint are the company's posture vis-à-vis the underlying causes of each force. Where does it stand against substitutes? Against the sources of entry barriers?

Then the strategist can devise a plan of action that may include (1) positioning the company so that its capabilities provide the best defense against the competitive force; and/or (2) influencing the balance of the forces through strategic moves, thereby improving the company's position; and/or (3) anticipating shifts in the factors underlying the forces and responding to them, with the hope of exploiting change by choosing a strategy appropriate for the new competitive balance before opponents recognize it. I shall consider each strategic approach in turn.

Positioning the Company

The first approach takes the structure of the industry as given and matches the company's strengths and weaknesses to it. Strategy can be viewed as building defenses against the competitive forces or as finding positions in the industry where the forces are weakest.

Knowledge of the company's capabilities and of the causes of the competitive forces will highlight the areas where the company should confront competition and where avoid it. If the company is a low-cost producer, it may choose to confront powerful buyers while it takes care to sell them only products not vulnerable to competition from substitutes.

The success of Dr Pepper in the soft drink industry illustrates the coupling of realistic knowledge of corporate strengths with sound industry analysis to yield a superior strategy. Coca-Cola and Pepsi-Cola dominate Dr Pepper's industry, where many small concentrate producers compete for a piece of the action. Dr Pepper chose a strategy of avoiding the largest-selling drink segment, maintaining a narrow flavor line, forgoing the development of a captive bottler network, and marketing heavily. The company positioned itself so as to be least vulnerable to its competitive forces while it exploited its small size.

In the $11.5 billion soft drink industry, barriers to entry in the form of brand identification, large-scale marketing, and access to a bottler network are enormous. Rather than accept the formidable costs and scale economies in having its own bottler network — that is, following the lead of the Big Two and of Seven-Up — Dr Pepper took advantage of the different flavor of its drink to "piggyback" on Coke and Pepsi bottlers who wanted a full line to sell to customers. Dr Pepper coped with the power of these buyers through extraordinary service and other efforts to distinguish its treatment of them from that of Coke and Pepsi.

Many small companies in the soft drink business offer cola drinks that thrust them into head-to-head competition against the majors. Dr Pepper, however, maximized product differentiation by maintaining a narrow line of beverages built around an unusual flavor.

Finally, Dr Pepper met Coke and Pepsi with an advertising onslaught emphasizing the alleged uniqueness of its single flavor. This campaign built strong brand identification and great customer loyalty. Helping its efforts was the fact that Dr Pepper's formula involved lower raw materials cost, which gave the company an absolute cost advantage over its major competitors.

There are no economies of scale in soft drink concentrate production, so Dr Pepper could prosper despite its small share of the business (6%). Thus Dr Pepper confronted competition in marketing but avoided it in product line and in distribution. This artful positioning combined with good implementation has led to an enviable record in earnings and in the stock market.

Influencing the Balance

When dealing with the forces that drive industry competition, a company can devise a strategy that takes the offensive. This posture is designed to do more than merely cope with the forces themselves; it is meant to alter their causes.

Innovations in marketing can raise brand identification or otherwise differentiate the product. Capital investments in large-scale facilities or vertical integration affect entry barriers. The balance of forces is partly a result of external factors and partly in the company's control.

Exploiting Industry Change

Industry evolution is important strategically because evolution, of course, brings with it changes in the sources of competition I have identified. In the familiar product life-cycle pattern, for example, growth rates change, product differentiation is said to decline as the business becomes more mature, and the companies tend to integrate vertically.

These trends are not so important in themselves; what is critical is whether they affect the sources of competition. Consider vertical integration. In the maturing minicomputer industry, extensive vertical integration, both in manufacturing and in software development, is taking place. This very significant trend is greatly raising economies of scale as well as the amount of capital necessary to compete in the industry. This in turn is raising barriers to entry and may drive some smaller competitors out of the industry once growth levels off.

Obviously, the trends carrying the highest priority from a strategic standpoint are those that affect the most important sources of competition in the industry and those that elevate new causes to the forefront. In contract aerosol packaging, for example, the trend toward less product differentiation is now dominant. It has increased buyers' power, lowered the barriers to entry, and intensified competition.

The framework for analyzing competition that I have described can also be used to predict the eventual profitability of an industry. In long-range planning the task is to examine each competitive force, forecast the magnitude of each underlying cause, and then construct a composite picture of the likely profit potential of the industry.

The outcome of such an exercise may differ a great deal from the existing industry structure. Today, for example, the solar heating business is populated by dozens and perhaps hundreds of companies, none with a major market position. Entry is easy, and competitors are battling to establish solar heating as a superior substitute for conventional methods.

The potential of this industry will depend largely on the shape of future barriers to entry, the improvement of the industry's position relative to substitutes, the ultimate intensity of competition, and the power captured by buyers and suppliers. These characteristics will in turn be influenced by such factors as the establishment of brand identities, significant economies of scale or experience curves in equipment manufacture wrought by technological change, the ultimate capital costs to compete, and the extent of overhead in production facilities.

The framework for analyzing industry competition has direct benefits in setting diversification strategy. It provides a road map for answering the extremely difficult question inherent in diversification decisions: "What is the potential of this business?" Combining the framework with judgment in its application, a company may be able to spot an industry with a good future before this good future is reflected in the prices of acquisition candidates.

Multifaceted Rivalry

Corporate managers have directed a great deal of attention to defining their businesses as a crucial step in strategy formulation. Theodore Levitt, in his classic 1960 article in HBR, argued strongly for avoiding the myopia of narrow, product-oriented industry definition.[2] Numerous other authorities have also stressed the need to look beyond product to function in defining a business, beyond national boundaries to potential international competition, and beyond the ranks of one's competitors today to those that may become competitors tomorrow. As a result of these urgings, the proper definition of a company's industry or industries has become an endlessly debated subject.

One motive behind this debate is the desire to exploit new markets. Another, perhaps more important motive is the fear of overlooking latent sources of competition that someday may threaten the industry. Many managers concentrate so single-mindedly on their direct antagonists in the fight for market share that they fail to realize that they are also competing with their customers and their suppliers for bargaining power. Meanwhile, they also neglect to keep a wary eye out for new entrants to the contest or fail to recognize the subtle threat of substitute products.

The key to growth — even survival — is to stake out a position that is less vulnerable to attack from head-to-head opponents, whether established or new, and less vulnerable to erosion from the direction of buyers, suppliers, and substitute goods. Establishing such a position can take many forms — solidifying relationships with favorable customers, differentiating the product either substantively or psychologically through marketing, integrating forward or backward, establishing technological leadership.

Appendix: The Experience Curve As an Entry Barrier

In recent years, the experience curve has become widely discussed as a key element of industry structure. According to this concept, unit costs in many manufacturing industries (some dogmatic adherents say in *all* manufacturing industries) as well as in some service industries decline with "experience," or a particular company's cumulative volume of production.

(The experience curve, which encompasses many factors, is a broader concept than the better-known learning curve, which refers to the efficiency achieved over a period of time by workers through much repetition.)

The causes of the decline in unit costs are a combination of elements, including economies of scale, the learning curve for labor, and capital-labor substitution. The cost decline creates a barrier to entry because new competitors with no "experience" face higher costs than established ones, particularly the producer with the largest market share, and have difficulty catching up with the entrenched competitors.

Adherents of the experience curve concept stress the importance of achieving market leadership to maximize this barrier to entry, and they recommend aggressive action to achieve it, such as price cutting in anticipation of falling costs in order to build volume. For the combatant that cannot achieve a healthy market share, the prescription is usually, "Get out."

Is the experience curve an entry barrier on which strategies should be built? The answer is: not in every industry. In fact, in some industries, building a strategy on the experience curve can be potentially disastrous. That costs decline with experience in some industries is not news to corporate executives. The significance of the experience curve for strategy depends on what factors are causing the decline.

If costs are falling because a growing company can reap economies of scale through more efficient, automated facilities and vertical integration, then the cumulative volume of production is unimportant to its relative cost position. Here the lowest-cost producer is the one with the largest, most efficient facilities.

A new entrant may well be more efficient than the more experienced competitors; if it has built the newest plant, it will face no disadvantage in having to catch up. The strategic prescription, "You must have the largest, most efficient plant," is a lot different from, "You must produce the greatest cumulative output of the item to get your costs down."

Whether a drop in costs with cumulative (not absolute) volume erects an entry barrier also depends on the sources of the decline. If costs go down because of technical advances known generally in the industry or because of the development of improved equipment that can be copied or purchased from equipment suppliers, the experience curve is no entry barrier at all — in fact, new or less experienced competitors may actually enjoy a cost *advantage* over the leaders. Free of the legacy of heavy past investments, the newcomer or less experienced competitor can purchase or copy the newest and lowest-cost equipment and technology.

If, however, experience can be kept proprietary, the leaders will maintain a cost advantage. But new entrants may require less experience to reduce their costs than the leaders needed. All this suggests that the experience curve can be a shaky entry barrier on which to build a strategy.

While space does not permit a complete treatment here, I want to mention a few other crucial elements in determining the appropriateness of a strategy built on the entry barrier provided by the experience curve:

The height of the barrier depends on how important costs are to competition compared with other areas like marketing, selling, and innovation.

The barrier can be nullified by product or process innovations leading to a substantially new technology and thereby creating an entirely new experience curve.* New entrants can leapfrog the industry leaders and alight on the new experience curve, to which those leaders may be poorly positioned to jump.

If more than one strong company is building its strategy on the experience curve, the consequences can be nearly fatal. By the time only one rival is left pursuing such a strategy, industry growth may have stopped and the prospects of reaping the spoils of victory long since evaporated.

Notes

1. For a more complete discussion of exit barriers and their implications for strategy, see Michael L. Porter, "Please Note Location of Nearest Exit," *California Management Review*, Winter 1976, p. 21.
2. Theodore Levitt, "Marketing Myopia," reprinted as a *Harvard Business Review* Classic, September–October 1975, p. 26.

*For an example drawn from the history of the automobile industry, see WIlliam J. Abernathy and Kenneth Wayne, "Limits of the Learning Curve," on page 166.

3. Competitor Analysis: The Missing Link in Strategy

William E. Rothschild

Over the past two decades, American companies have experienced dramatic changes in their domestic competitive environment. Small specialist competitors have exited or been swallowed up by larger multi-industry companies — resulting in often stronger, financially solvent, but more unpredictable competition. Foreign and multinational competitors have taken aim at the critical and more profitable US markets, which are easier to penetrate and pivotal to worldwide success, while building and maintaining in their own home markets barriers to the entry of US companies. This foreign invasion has taken many forms, including importing, acquiring US companies, and building US plants. The results have been staggering; in some industries, few or no US manufacturers have survived.

But competitive change hasn't been limited merely to new configurations of traditional competitors. It has also included a considerable number of new companies and complete substitution by new types of products. The recent digital watch invasion of the analog dial watch market is a case in point: electronics and integrated circuit manufacturers have taken share and position from the traditional watchmakers.

Neglected Task

All these facts are well known to readers of the business press. Yet competitor analysis has remained a largely neglected managerial task. Far too little emphasis has been placed on answering such basic questions as:

- who is the competition now and who will it be in the future?
- what are the key competitors' strategies, objectives, and goals?

This article was first published in *Management Review* 68, no. 7 (July 1979): 22–28, 37, 38.

When this article was published, the author was manager of strategic integration in General Electric's Corporate Planning and Development Operation.

- how important is a specific market to the competitors and are they committed enough to continue to invest?
- what unique strengths do the competitors have?
- do they have any weaknesses that make them vulnerable?
- what changes are likely in the competitors' future strategies?
- what are the implications of competitors' strategies on the market, the industry and one's own company?

On the surface these questions appear to be logical and straightforward. Yet the answers are usually lacking, for a variety of reasons.

Overconfidence. Many managers who lead profitable businesses tend to be overconfident. Because of their past success in winning the competitive battle, they begin to believe either that the competitor is inept or that they are superior.

Confusion. Some business managers are simply confused. They are confused about how to obtain competitive intelligence or what to do with it. Some companies, although they subscribe to clipping services or have elaborate systems to distribute data, never really see or understand the competitor's strategy or its implications. Other companies employ analysts or consultants to write extensive competitor reports, yet never use these analyses (which admittedly often lack insight) to determine how the competitor may affect the industry in general or themselves in particular. Competitor analysis is of strategic value only if it highlights the implications and enables management to formulate or review its own strategies.

Concern. A third cause of ineffective competitor review is fear that the company will be forced to employ illegal or unethical tactics to obtain the data it seeks. This concern is completely unwarranted: the strategic data required to make effective analyses are available from legal, ethical and relatively convenient sources. The desire to tell the world and influence investors usually leads competitors to broadcast their investment priorities and strategy in a variety of ways.

Another concern that sidetracks management from competitor review is that intelligence will be misinterpreted, resulting in wrong decisions. Of course, this is a risk in any analysis or planning — data can be misinterpreted, and misinterpretation can lead to failure. But a leader must assume some calculated risk.

Who Are They?

Now let us return to our list of basic questions. The first to consider is deceptively simple: Who is the competition now? Who will it be five years from now?

Covering all possibilities. Competition for your customers' discretionary and nondiscretionary dollars comes in many shapes and forms; there are many ways to satisfy the customers' needs and wants in the areas you serve. So we are led to the further questions: "What is the customer buying?" and "What are all the ways the customer can be satisfied in achieving this need or want?" If a consumer wants entertainment and you are in the television market, you should consider all the forms of entertainment on which a consumer might choose to spend his money: radio, stereo, home movies, hobbies, games, in-home sports, and so on. (The true scope of competition here was painfully learned by radio console manufacturers when television entered the scene.)

Industry profile. A second way to examine competition is to draw up a demographic profile of the competition in your industry. Industries dominated by small single-industry specialists or small regional producers differ significantly from those dominated or led by multi-industry companies, and these, in turn, are different from those controlled by multinational or foreign companies. It makes sense to use these classifications to profile the competitors. For instance, some companies will be dedicated to the industry and thus can be classified as "single industry." Others will have businesses in many industries and thus have the option of using one to pay for growth in others. Overlaying this classification, the competitors should be classified as domestically focused, participating abroad on a selective or opportunistic basis; foreign focused; or multinational worldwide. Combining these two assessments of company type and market focus provides a graphic display that can be used to describe the competitive position in the industry in the past and the present and to anticipate likely changes in the future.

Figure 3.1 shows the changes that have occurred over the past five years and that may take place over the next five-year period in one industry. Five years ago, this industry included a number of single-industry specialists (companies A to D) that accounted for approximately 50 percent of the market; the other major participants were divisions of larger multi-industry companies (E to H); in addition, the Japanese were beginning to make their move, with two companies (I and J) leading the way. Today, only one competitor remains in the single-industry category, and even this competitor is under attack and could be forced to merge or sell out to another company. A number of the companies have been acquired or have merged into Japanese and European companies. Thus, the competitive game in this industry has significantly changed and may continue to do so, with the possibility that two companies will exit completely in the next few years.

Change of role. A third view of competitors focuses on potential changes by reviewing the total system of interactions from supply to user. Could any of the participants in the system expand their role and become compet-

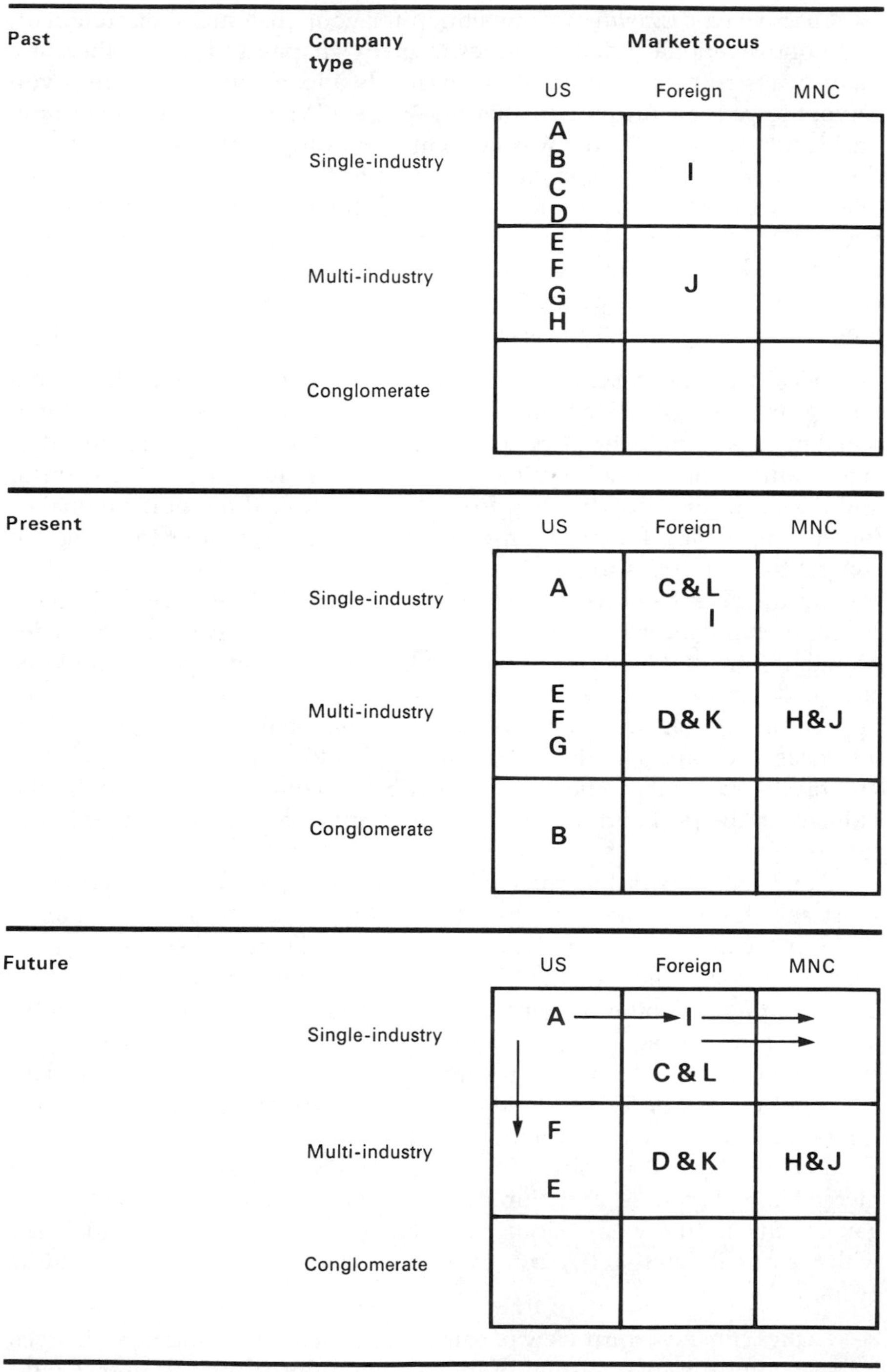

Past

Company type	Market focus		
	US	Foreign	MNC
Single-industry	A B C D	I	
Multi-industry	E F G H	J	
Conglomerate			

Present

Company type	US	Foreign	MNC
Single-industry	A	C & L I	
Multi-industry	E F G	D & K	H & J
Conglomerate	B		

Future

Company type	US	Foreign	MNC
Single-industry	A →	I →	→
		C & L	
Multi-industry	F E	D & K	H & J
Conglomerate			

FIGURE 3.1   How the Competition Changes

itors? The suppliers of components or materials, for instance, may decide to integrate forward and compete with you — or distributors may decide to integrate backward. For example, when Ford announced that it was discontinuing the manufacture of Philco appliances, Philco distributors were left empty-handed. Since the other major producers already had independent wholesalers, or sold direct, they were faced with a choice — get a new product line or quit. They decided they would band together, form a buying pool, and obtain a private label line, reintroducing the defunct Crosley brand which they will have built to their specification by other manufacturers: Rockwell/Admiral will provide the refrigerator line, Revco freezers; Hardwick, gas and electric ranges; McGraw-Edison, air conditioners. Backward integration has offered these wholesalers a chance to survive and compete effectively against the national brands; of course, only time can tell whether this strategy will be successful.

In much the same way, customers may also elect to become their own suppliers — in the manner of Ford and General Motors, who acquired component manufacturers and became competitors in the components field.

What Are They Up To?

Having established the identity of the major competitors, the next question to ask is: What are the major competitors' investment priorities and objectives? A listing or graphic display of the competition and major competitors isn't sufficient. It is important to understand their total corporate situation and intentions, a task that will vary in complexity depending on whether a competitor is a specialist, diversified, domestic, or worldwide in scope. In essence, we wish to know the competitors' total financial situation, determine whether they have profitable and balanced portfolios, and identify any serious problems they may have and the opportunities they are trying to pursue.

Single-industry specialists are the easiest to evaluate since they are dedicated to one industry. Often they are "niche"-oriented and distinguish themselves by innovation, quality, or dependability. Further, they are often led by an aggressive, strong-willed, even autocratic entrepreneur — which may be both a strength and a limitation.

Multi-industry diversified companies have a variety of business options. Each business should have its own investment and corporate purpose, and it is important to understand each one.

It is useful to ascertain how a competitor describes each of its businesses in order to determine the balance and viability of its total portfolio. Is the competitor trying to grow in too many segments simultaneously? Does it have a sufficient number of earnings and cash generators? Will the total achieve desired results? Multi-industry companies rarely have management depth sufficient to lead all their businesses effectively and, therefore, often appoint managers who are unaware of the industry's peculiarities or subtleties; this may lead to wrong decisions and reduced profitability all round.

Location or market focus can also change emphasis and objectives. Foreign competitors may be influenced, positively or negatively, by their own governments. Governments may require that competitors reduce profitability to increase employment levels or to maintain the balance of trade. They may bar a competitor from obtaining supplies in low-cost areas. On the asset side, they may subsidize profits through low-cost government loans, tax concessions, or inflated profits on government projects.

The objectives and investment priorities of multinational companies are even more difficult for an American domestic company to comprehend. Multinational companies may sacrifice profits in one country to penetrate or gain position while using profits from another country to support this aggressiveness. They have the ability to work with governments, select the least costly source of supply, and even negotiate favorable trade concessions.

Industry Commitment

Next, you should consider how important your industry is to the competitor and what its strategic purpose is. It is essential to assess a competitor's overall goals, but you should try to pinpoint your competitor's purpose in your own industry. Its commitment may be based on rational judgments or on emotions. On the rational side, it may be the anticipation of growth, strong customer needs, or some unique product or market strength — i.e., your industry may be important to the competitor's future growth, earnings performance, or cash-flow position. A rational basis is normally to be preferred, since the competitor's behavior is most likely to be consistent and logical. For example, if the competitor is depending on your industry to finance its other ventures, then it will fight hard to protect this cash-flow position.

Often, however, emotions play a significant part in decision making. The competitor's commitment may be based on such shallow reasons as: "The CEO grew up in the industry and is emotionally attached to it," "The business is the core from which the total corporation grew," or "The industry is considered glamorous and exciting." Investments are consequently made that are unjustified or even detrimental — such as adding capacity when there is already overcapacity, introducing new expensive modifications prematurely, or cutting prices to gain share in a declining market.

Key Strengths and Resources

The next area of concern is: What are the competitor's *relative* strengths and limitations? Can they support its investment strategies? These are deceptively simple questions. Many managers believe they know their own resources and have a good grasp of those of their competitors. This is rarely the case. It requires an assessment of the competitor's resources in light of the strategy it has chosen to pursue.

If the competitor wishes to gain share by innovation, does it have the proper skills to do the job? These will be different from those required to hold position, maximizing earnings via a low-cost position. Thus one must look at critical resources required by a competitor and ask if it can obtain what is required in both quantity and timing.

The major resource areas that should be assessed for each competitor are management, innovation, financing, production and marketing.

Management. Who are the key leaders and decision makers? How quickly can decisions be made? Is the management team knowledgeable or experienced in the industry? Are they risk takers? Is there depth in the management ranks?

The answers to these questions will reveal managerial skills, flexibilities, values and longevity, thus enabling you to determine the competitor's managerial fit with the strategy it is pursuing. If the strategy requires flexibility and rapid decision making, but the management team is risk-averse, slow and deliberate, the competitor will have a major problem in executing its desired strategy. If the strategy is aimed at maximizing cash flow by a slow harvest, but the management is aggressive and growth-oriented, then there is a serious mismatch that may be unresolvable.

Innovation. Assessment here must identify the driving forces behind the competitor's innovation record. It is not unusual to find a few key individuals as the driving forces behind innovation or to find the entire company's success built upon a few key patents. In such a case, the competitor's ability to continue this track record must be determined. Financing of innovation should also be studied to find out where the financing came from and how consistent it has been.

Does the competitor pride itself on its innovation ability? If so, it may have a difficult, if not impossible, job of accepting or implementing the role of follower. If a strategy requires applied research or "quick-follow" skills but the competitor has traditionally focused on basic research and is unable to follow rapidly, then this may signal a major limitation.

Financing. This review should include the traditional assessments of debt to equity, liquidity ratios, credit availability and costs, as well as an understanding of financial objectives and constraints. Here one must attempt to understand the competitor's ability to generate financing both internally and externally at the *right time* and in sufficient *quantity*. If a strategy requires large but cyclical volumes of cash and the competitor isn't able to obtain them, the strategy won't be successful. If a competitor wants to increase its worldwide sales but isn't able to provide long-term, low-cost financing, its results will be disappointing.

Production. This requires an evaluation of efficiency, cost reduction, and capacity and supply situations, along with an understanding of the competitor's total resources for production — human and material. Some useful questions to probe are:

- does the competitor manufacture in a high- or low-cost labor area?
- is its plant and equipment efficient?
- is its flexibility or response to market demands inhibited by too much integration, capital intensity, or overdependence on one technology?
- how sensitive is its break-even to capacity utilization?
- how skilled is it in maintaining equality?
- how is it affected by OSHA and EEO regulations?

Marketing. How do the competitor's marketing abilities compare to the requirements imposed by its strategy or market? Some strategies require the ability to anticipate and/or create customer needs, while others are more dependent on providing pre- and post-sale service. If the key skills aren't available, the competitor will have less than optimal results. Marketing skills, like any other resource, must be carefully nurtured and preserved and thus require consistent financing.

Figure 3.2 provides a checklist to help in assessing these critical resources.

Sources of Data

Many managers agree on the need to evaluate and anticipate changes in competitors' abilities, but seem to be at a loss on where to look for the information. It is that much of a mystery. Basically, there are three sources of "secondary" data: what the competitors say about themselves; what others say about them; and what your own people have observed in monitoring their activities.

Competitors provide data about their strategy and resources in advertising, promotional materials, speeches, personnel changes and want ads. They also provide information to the government and investors through reports, prospectuses, testimony and required documentation.

In addition, outsiders write and speak about the competitors. This includes books, articles, case histories, product evaluations, testimony in trials and special industry studies. All these sources can be evaluated and

Management	Innovation	Financing	Production	Marketing
Key people	**Technical**	**Long-term**	**Physical**	**Sales force**
●Objectives and	**resources**	●Debt/equity ratio	**resources**	●Skills
priorities	●Concepts	●Cost of debt	●Capacity	●Size
●Values	●Patents and		●Plant	●Type
●Reward	copyrights	**Short-term**	−Size	●Location
systems	●Technological	●Line of credit	−Location	
	sophistication	●Type of debt	−Age	**Distribution**
Decision	●Technical	●Cost of debt	●Equipment	**network**
making	integration		−Automation	
●Location		**Liquidity**	−Maintenance	**Research**
●Type	**Human**		−Flexibility	●Skills
●Speed	**resources**	**Cash flow**	●Processes	●Type
	●Key people and	●Days of receivables	−Uniqueness	
Planning	skills	●Inventory turnover	−Flexibility	**Service and**
●Type	●Use of external	●Accounting	●Degree of	**sales policies**
●Emphasis	technical groups	practices	integration	
●Time span				**Advertising**
	Funding	**Human**	**Human**	●Skills
Staffing	●Total	**resources**	**resources**	●Type
●Longevity and	●Percentage of	●Key people and	●Key people and	
turnover	sales	skills	skills	**Human**
●Experience	●Consistency	●Turnover	●Workforce	**resources**
●Replacement	over time		−Skills mix	●Key people and
policies	●Internally	**Systems**	−Unions	skills
	generated	●Budgeting	−Turnover	●Turnover
Organization	●Government-	●Forecasting		
●Centralization	supplied	●Controlling		**Funding**
●Functions				●Total
●Use of staff				●Consistency
				over time
				●Percentage
				of sales
				●Reward systems

FIGURE 3.2 Checklist for Competitor Resource Analysis*

*If *multi-industry*, examine portfolio of businesses (sizes, priorities, importance to company) and resources provided by parent company. If *foreign*, examine national priorities of home country, degree of government ownership, supports, incentives, home-market environment.

embellished by your own management and professionals in sales, manufacturing, finance and engineering.

The key is to develop a profile of competitors, test for validity and identify areas of agreement and disagreement. It is surprising just how much is known and what can be deduced from competitors' actions. Figure 3.3 outlines these sources of data.

Implications of Change

Another question that must be considered is: What could cause a change in competitors' priorities, strategies or resources? Any significant change in the external "macro" environment (like government, society, or the econ-

	Public	Trade professionals	Government	Investors
What competitors say about themselves	●Advertising ●Promotional materials ●Press releases ●Speeches ●Books ●Articles ●Personnel changes ●Want ads	●Manuals ●Technical papers ●Licenses ●Patents ●Courses ●Seminars	●SEC reports ●FIC ●Testimony ●Lawsuits ●Antitrust	●Annual meetings ●Annual reports ●Prospectuses ●Stock/bond issues
What others say about them	●Books ●Articles ●Case studies ●Consultants ●Newspaper reporters ●Environmental groups ●Consumer groups ●Unions ●"Who's Who" ●Recruiting firms	●Suppliers/vendors ●Trade press ●Industry study ●Customers ●Subcontractors	●Lawsuits ●Antitrust ●State/federal agencies ●National plans ●Government programs	●Security analyst reports ●Industry studies ●Credit reports

FIGURE 3.3   Sources of Competitor Information

omy) or in the internal "micro" environment can cause a change in competitive behavior. Likewise, the acquisition of a company may strengthen or weaken it (in some cases, the merger is so disruptive that it causes the competitor actually to lose strength). At other times, a competitor changes when a new chief executive officer takes over. It is always important to look at the line of succession and determine if the next in line will follow the same game plan. If an outsider obtains control, you can count on change. Another key change agent is the disruption of priorities — such as a new venture causing red ink or requiring extensive management attention.

Finally, what will be the effect of all the competitors on the industry, market, and your strategy? Most managers stop their competitors but, because they fail to interrelate their assessments, they never see the consequences of one competitor interacting with another.

The importance of this composite picture is seen in the case of one industry segment, a high break-even business requiring high capacity utilization. Four of the five competitors were aiming to grow and the leader had vowed to hold its position, so a tough battle was expected and a lot of red ink was likely to flow. Two of the companies were planning to add capacity, which could mean there would be excess capacity. Investment was likely to be heavy, ranging from $90 million to $250 million over five years. The combination of aggression, possible excess capacity and high capital investments meant the going would be expensive.

The final step is to determine how the competitors can affect your company and the worth of your strategy. If a company expects to compete in the segment just described but doesn't wish to expend heavily on capacity, then it must learn to specialize, or risk extinction.

As an aid in determining and reviewing strategy, competitor analysis is increasing in complexity and importance. If it is to have the influence it deserves, top managers must insist on a disciplined, comprehensive and strategically focused effort to assess each major competitor and the total interaction between competitors and the corporation.

4. Defining Corporate Strengths and Weaknesses

Howard H. Stevenson

Introduction

Business organizations have certain characteristics — strengths — which make them uniquely adapted to carry out their tasks. Conversely they have other features — weaknesses — which inhibit their ability to fulfill their purposes. Managers who hope to accomplish their tasks are forced to evaluate the strengths and weaknesses of the organization over which they preside. Many managers may not think in terms of "defining strengths and weaknesses." However, the evaluations which they make in determining areas for action reflect judgments of their organizations' capabilities related to either a competitive threat or a belief about what "ought to be."

Many corporate activities are aimed at helping a manager to understand what his own unit and the other units with which he comes into contact are doing well or poorly. Internally gathered information provides data for evaluating the performance of parts of the organization. Externally supplied information provides an understanding of the company's place in its competitive spectrum. It has become common for business organizations to formalize such information into a "resource evaluation program," a "capability profile," or other formally communicated assessments.

Although many organizations have undertaken such studies, the results have often been difficult to integrate into an effective planning cycle. Many of the statements which emerged were either of the "motherhood" type or else did not readily lead to operational decisions. The research for this article examined some of the characteristics which create these operational difficulties.

This article was first published in the *Sloan Management Review*, 17, no. 3 (Spring 1976): 51–68.

When this article was published, the author was a professor at the Harvard Graduate School of Business.

Research Methodology

Defining strengths and weaknesses is viewed by management theorists as an important prelude to the development of an organizational commitment to strategic purpose.[1] In the book *Business Policy: Text and Cases,* the authors identify the following four components of strategy:[2]

- market opportunity,
- corporate competences and resources,
- personal values and aspirations,
- acknowledged obligations to segments of society other than stockholders.

These components are integrated into an overall program of strategy formulation. One such process model is shown in Figure 4.1.

Other writers clearly put the objective appraisal of strengths and weaknesses high on the list of necessary activities for a company which desires to grow.[3] Almost all work available has emphasized the normative aspects of the resource evaluation process. Even those authors examining practice have to a large extent focused on the formal methods by which the evaluation process is carried out.

The study which this article presents examined the process from the viewpoint of output. Fifty managers from six companies were asked for their evaluation of the corporate strengths and weaknesses and the reasons underlying those evaluations. The sample was structured so that it provided a relatively broad representation of managers within an organization. The dimensions shown in Table 4.1 were studied. From analysis of the 191 responses examined, typologies were constructed and an evaluation was made of the consistencies of responses.

The companies selected were:

- PAPERCO — a diversified paper converter,
- AMERICAN INK — a specialty chemical producer,
- HITECH — an integrated electronic manufacturer,
- PUMPCO — a heavy machinery manufacturer,
- NATIONAL GAS — a manufacturer of gas products and transmission equipment,
- ELECTRICO — an electrical equipment manufacturer.

Despite other differences these companies had a strong commonality in their product lines. Annual sales of the selected companies ranged from $200 million to over $2 billion.

The results of the study brought into serious question the value of formal assessment approaches. It was found that an individual's cognitive perceptions of the strengths and weaknesses of his organization were strongly influenced by factors associated with the individual and not only by the organization's attributes. Position in the organization, perceived

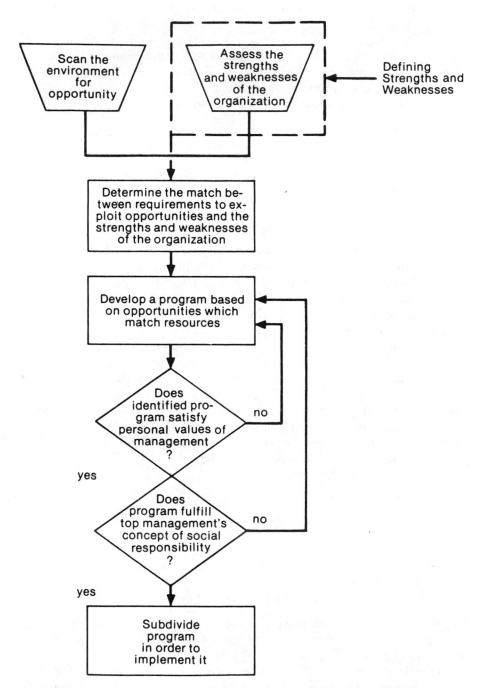

FIGURE 4.1   A Process Model of Strategy Formulation

TABLE 4.1 Steps in the Process of Assessing Strengths and Weaknesses

Which attributes can be examined?	What organizational entity is the manager concerned with?	What types of measurements can the manager make?	What criteria are applicable to judge a strength or a weakness?	How can the manager get the information to make these assessments?
Organizational structure	The corporation	Measure the existence of an attribute	Historical experience of the company	Personal observation
Major policies			Intracompany competition	Customer contacts
Top manager's skills	Groups	Measure an attribute's efficiency		Experience
Top manager's experience	Divisions		Direct competitors	Control system documents
Information system	Departments	Measure an attribute's effectiveness		Meetings
Operation procedures			Other companies	Planning system documents
Planning system	Individual employees		Consultants' opinions	Employees
Employee attitudes				Subordinate managers
Manager's attitudes				Superordinate managers
Union agreements			Normative judgments based on management's understanding of literature	Peers
Technical skills				Published documents
Research skills				Competitive intelligence
New product ideas				Board members
Production facilities			Personal opinions	Consultants
Demographic characteristics of personnel				Journals
Distribution network				Books
Sales force's skill			Specific targets of accomplishment such as budgets, etc.	Magazines
Breadth of product line				Professional meetings
Quality control procedures				Government economic indicators
Stock market reputation				
Knowledge of customer's needs				
Market domination				

role, and type of responsibility so strongly influenced the assessment that
the objective reality of the situation tended to be overwhelmed. In addition, there were wide variations among standards of measurement and
criteria for judgment employed.

Few members of management agreed precisely on the strengths and
weaknesses exhibited by their companies. To facilitate further analysis the
responses were classified within twenty-two categories. These categories
were further reduced into five major groups as follows.

General Category	Includes These Attributes
Organization	Organizational form and structure
	Top management interest and skill
	Standard operating procedures
	The control system
	The planning system
Personnel	Employee attitude
	Technical skills
	Experience
	Number of employees
Marketing	Sales force
	Knowledge of the customer's needs
	Breadth of the product line
	Product quality
	Reputation
	Customer service
Technical	Production facilities
	Production techniques
	Product development
	Basic research
Finance	Financial size
	Price-earnings ratio
	Growth pattern

The individual attributes listed are neither mutually exclusive nor collectively exhaustive in partitioning each of the general categories. They do,
however, represent the focal point of the responses from among the managers interviewed.

Analysis of Strengths and Weaknesses Reported

The list of attributes identified by the managers interviewed is notable both
for the factors which have been included and for those which were not
mentioned. Also important is the overall distribution of responses among
each of the general categories and the individual attributes. Absent from

the list were such items as: quality control procedures, channels of distribution, relationships with unions, share of market data, characteristics of the customers, growth rate of the industries in which the company is participating, purchasing and contract administration techniques, and competitive relationships.

The most obvious feature of the overall distribution of responses is the relatively equal importance attached to each of the general categories of attributes. Marketing related attributes were the subject of 26.7 percent of the responses, and technical, organizational, and personnel related attributes each accounted for over 20 percent. Since one might have predicted that the relationship to markets and customers would have been most important to the companies studied, its lack of dominance comes as a surprise. This is especially true given that over 48 percent of the responses came from managers with a marketing background. The overall distribution of the responses is shown in Table 4.2.

The study indicates that there are a variety of influences impinging upon the manager as he analyzes the strengths and weaknesses of his corporation. These influences are shown diagrammatically in Figure 4.2.

As would be expected the distribution of responses differed from company to company. The pattern of responses among the companies is shown in Table 4.3.

Some generalizations of particular interest can be drawn from this small sample. It would appear that the following statements are true.

There are some aspects of a company that are of concern in all companies.

Managers within any company examine a broad range of attributes. There is no consensus on "the corporation's strengths and weaknesses."

Attributes of Common Concern

One of the interesting phenomena observed was that there were many attributes which received roughly equal consideration from all companies.

TABLE 4.2   The Relative Importance of Attributes Identified As Strengths and Weaknesses (All Managers)

General Category	Percent of Response
Organizational	22.0%
Personnel	21.5
Marketing	26.7
Technical	22.0
Financial	7.9

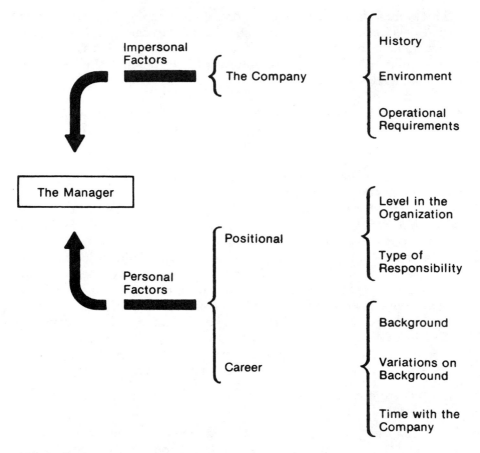

FIGURE 4.2   Factors Which Influence a Manager in Defining Strengths and Weaknesses

TABLE 4.3   The Attributes Examined in Relation to the Companies Studied

	PAPERCO	AMERICAN INK	HITECH	PUMPCO	OVERALL
Organizational	30.4%	16.5%	18.2%	20.0%	22.0%
Personnel	36.2	7.7	27.3	30.0	21.5
Marketing	15.9	36.3	45.5	10.0	26.7
Technical	14.5	29.7	—	25.0	22.0
Financial	2.9	9.9	9.1	15.0	7.9
	100.0%	100.0%	100.0%	100.0%	100.0%
Number of Responses	69	91	11	20	191

TABLE 4.4 Attributes of Common Concern to the Companies Studied
(Percentage of All Responses from the Managers Citing Attributes)

	PAPERCO	AMERICAN INK	HITECH	PUMPCO
Organizational Form	7.2%	5.5%	5.6%	5.0%
Attitudes	18.8	4.4	9.1	15.0
Technical Skills	13.0	1.1	18.2	10.0
Breadth of Line	10.1	7.7	15.5	5.0
Growth Pattern	1.4	3.3	5.0	10.0
Percentage of Total Response for Company	37.7%	22.2%	36.9%	45.0%

There was not a statistically significant difference among the attributes
examined by the companies. Evidence of the interest of the company in a
particular type of problem was shown by a tendency to examine additional
attributes of the same category.

The clearest examples of this phenomenon were the "organization"
and "marketing" categories. Within these categories, there were similar
responses for some individual attributes, for example, organizational form.
This attribute was mentioned in the following percentages of responses:
7.2 percent for PAPERCO, 5.5 percent for AMERICAN INK, 5.6 percent for
HITECH, and 5.0 percent for PUMPCO. The wide variation between companies in examining the "organizational" category arose as people in PA-
PERCO examined the other organizational attributes, such as top management, standard procedures, the control system, and the planning system.

Managers in all companies were concerned with the attributes listed in
Table 4.4. Variations arose as the managers examined other attributes
which affected their companies' strengths and weaknesses in the organizational, personnel, marketing, technical and financial categories.

The Range of Concern

The broad range of attributes examined in each company should at once be
a comfort and a warning signal to those interested in the process of
defining strengths and weaknesses. PAPERCO managers evaluated seventeen of the twenty-two categories. AMERICAN INK managers had at least
one response in each category. Even in the companies where only three or
four executives were questioned, more than half of the list of twenty-two
attributes were cited as being either a strength or a weakness.

This broad dispersal of responses indicated the situation that one staff
manager stated: "My job is to worry about certain aspects of the company's
business. To cover others with real meaning, you can talk to some other

people." There was apparently an effective, if informal, division of the effort of "scanning the internal environment." The managers assumed certain territories upon which they felt qualified and responsible for judgment. These territories did not overlap; therefore, a majority of the important aspects of the company's existence was surveyed for relative strengths or weaknesses.

Most attributes were found to be both strengths and weaknesses. The results of the definition process were therefore ambiguous. The dynamic reasons underlying this difficulty were perhaps best expressed by the planning director at NATIONAL GAS who said:

> We have a formal system to develop a list of corporate strengths and weaknesses. We held a two-day planning session with our top corporate officers in which we were to review the results of the formal planning process including the list of strengths and weaknesses. Unfortunately, or perhaps fortunately, we found the list to offer only a very marginally useful guide to action. The "yes, but" phenomenon took hold. We found that by the time we got through discussing the strengths on the list, we weren't so certain that they were that strong. Conversely, the weaknesses were, upon examination, not so weak.

The resolution of the process of defining strengths and weaknesses into a list often did not produce the expected results. Further management judgment needed to be applied in order to develop a meaningful guide to action.

Although the strengths which a manager identifies depend in part upon his company affiliation, it is also apparent that certain characteristics of the manager's position influence his evaluations. Level in the organization, type of responsibility, functional background, time with the company and variations in background were all studied as possible explanatory variables. The results indicated that only level in the organization and type of responsibility were significantly related to the attributes which a manager cited as being strengths or weaknesses.

Importance of the Manager's Level in the Organization

The traditional theory of organization rests on the differentiation of responsibility within a hierarchical structure. With this as a framework, the hypothesis is that the attributes which are cited as strengths and weaknesses will vary by organizational level within a company. The results of the study show variations which are consistent from company to company. Table 4.5 shows variations among the overall sample in the attributes examined as they were related to the organizational level of the respondent. The organizational levels are defined as follows: level one is presidents and board chairmen; level two reports to either the company president or board chairman; level three is two steps removed; and level four is three or more steps removed from the company's executive officers.

Table 4.5 suggests several tentative conclusions. The level of responsi-

TABLE 4.5   The Relationship Between the Category of Attribute Examined and the Manager's Organizational Level

	One	Two	Three	Four	Overall
Organizational	25.0%	17.3%	24.2%	26.9%	22.0%
Personnel	32.1	22.7	17.7	15.4	21.5
Marketing	10.7	28.0	33.9	23.1	26.7
Technical	7.1	24.0	21.0	34.6	22.0
Financial	25.0	8.0	3.2		7.9
Percentage of Total Response by Level	14.7%	39.3%	32.5%	13.6%	100.0%

bility is connected with the type of attribute cited. Personnel attributes, for example, are of increasing concern as the level of responsibility goes up. This finding is consistent with the frequently made statement that the problems of managers at higher levels of responsibility increasingly become questions of the management of people. Comments have often been heard that judgments have to be made on the basis of whether the person is right for the job rather than on other more measurable dimensions. An interesting aspect of the citation of personnel attributes is that an individual's technical skills and experience tended to be examined equally at all levels. The consideration of attitudes of the individual, on the other hand, was definitely an increasing function of the organizational level of the examiner. The incidence of citation by levels of personnel attitudes as strengths or weaknesses is shown in Table 4.6.

Technical attributes exhibited the opposite pattern from that observed in the personnel attributes. Managers at higher levels were less concerned with the technical aspects of running the business. This finding is consistent with the traditional theory. Among the four attributes which comprise the technical category, only facilities and basic research were cited at all by the top management personnel (level one). Techniques and product development were of roughly equal concern to each of the other three levels. Facilities were of increasing concern to the lower levels of management. These detailed trends appear in Table 4.7.

TABLE 4.6   Concern for Personnel Attitudes by Organizational Level (Percentage of Responses Dealing with All Attributes)

	Organizational Level				
	One	Two	Three	Four	Overall
Attitudes	21.4%	12.0%	6.5%	7.7%	11.0%

TABLE 4.7   Concern for Technical Attributes by Level (Percentage of All Responses at Each Level)

		Organizational Level			
	One	Two	Three	Four	Overall
Facilities	3.6%	4.0%	8.1%	11.5%	6.3%
Techniques	—	8.0	8.1	7.7	6.8
Product Development	—	9.3	4.8	11.5	6.8

The financial attributes were of more interest to higher organizational levels. The concern for the price-earnings ratio and growth pattern was confined to the executive officers and their immediate subordinates. The only element of the financial category which was of concern to lower levels was the ability and willingness of the corporation to serve as a source of funds.

The organizational category showed no clear-cut pattern. There was approximately equal concern for the organizational aspects at all levels of the company. The control system, the planning system, and the interest and skills of top management were not cited with any clearly identifiable pattern according to organizational level. These attributes were of importance to particular individuals for a variety of reasons identified with their job responsibility, such as planning vice-president or assistant controller. It is of interest to note, however, that some of the particular attributes cited among the organizational categories varied distinctly and predictably by level. The attributes of organizational form and standard operating procedures fit nicely with conventional wisdom. Table 4.8 shows that organizational form was a concern of higher management while standard operating procedures were a concern to primarily the lowest level of management.

The marketing category showed no clear pattern, other than a slight tendency for the attributes to be of more concern to the lower levels, three and four, than to the upper levels of management. The specific attributes exhibited no recognizable pattern.

TABLE 4.8   Concern for Organizational Attributes by Level of Responsibility (Percentage of All Responses at Each Level)

		Organizational Level			
	One	Two	Three	Four	Overall
Organizational Form	10.7%	2.7%	9.7%	—	5.8%
Standard Procedures	—	4.0	1.6	15.4	4.2

Another result of examining strengths and weaknesses by level is the apparent difference in perceptions of where a company is strong and where it may be weak according to the level of the evaluator within the company. Overall a pattern of greater optimism exists at higher organizational levels. One explanation for the trend is that the further down in an organization a manager is, the more levels there are above him to point to his mistakes and the weaknesses surrounding him. His comments reflect these evaluations.

The overall pattern of recognizing more strengths than weaknesses at higher levels was not consistent among all categories of attributes. Some categories were perceived differently at the different levels of management. The organizational elements were increasingly perceived as strengths the higher the level of the respondent. Marketing and financial attributes were perceived more positively by lower levels of management. Personnel and technical attributes also had slight tendencies toward more positive ratings by lower levels of management. Table 4.9 shows these results.

It appears that the manager's organizational level influences both his choice of which attributes to examine and his perception of them as either strengths or weaknesses. This effect is quite consistent across company boundaries, confirming the influence of the changing organizational perspective upon what is at least theoretically an objective exercise.

Strengths Were Judged Differently than Weaknesses

Managers utilize differing criteria in defining corporate strengths and weaknesses. The following three types of criteria seem to be in use.

Historical	Historical Experience of the Company
	Intracompany Comparisons
	Budgets
Competitive	Direct Competition
	Indirect Competition
	Other Companies
Normative	Consultant's Opinions
	Management's Understanding of Management Literature
	Rules of Thumb
	Opinion

The impact of the use of differing criteria is striking. Strengths are judged by different criteria than weaknesses. As shown in Table 4.10, 90 percent of historical criteria are used to identify a strength while only 21 percent of normative criteria are used to identify a strength.

The nature of the criteria determines whether they will be used for

TABLE 4.9   Percentage of Responses Identifying Category As a Strength at Each Organizational Level

Attributes	Organizational Level				
	One	Two	Three	Four	Overall
Organizational	85.7%	38.4%	83.3%	28.6%	42.9%
Personnel	66.7	58.8	27.3	50.0	51.2
Marketing	66.7	57.1	86.7	66.7	70.6
Technical	50.0	55.5	38.4	44.4	47.6
Financial	14.3	66.7	100.0	—	46.7

judging strengths or weaknesses. The utilization of the historical criteria for judging strengths occurs because managers are constantly searching for improvements in problem areas which they have previously identified. The base from which these improvements are made then becomes the standard by which the current attributes of the organization are judged. The converse is true with respect to weaknesses. The organization's current position is only a step on the way to where the managers wish it were. The gap is then measured between the current position and the goal which reflects a normative judgment of what ought to be. This relationship is depicted in Figure 4.3.

The same differentiation carries over to the relationship between the criteria employed and the attribute examined. It is evident that managers have developed models against which they test the strengths or weaknesses of their organization. These models reflect both the historical position and a normative sense of the possible.

This differentiation was especially critical for organizational questions. Every individual attribute within the organizational category was judged at least 50 percent of the time according to normative standards. The almost total absence of competitive judgment is noticeable. It seems apparent that the managers were not comfortable in comparing their companies' organizational attributes with other companies' characteristics. They contented themselves with comparisons to "what was in the past" or "what should

TABLE 4.10   The Association of Specific Criteria with Identification of Strengths and Weaknesses

	Strengths	Weaknesses
Historical	90%	10%
Competitive	67	33
Normative	21	79

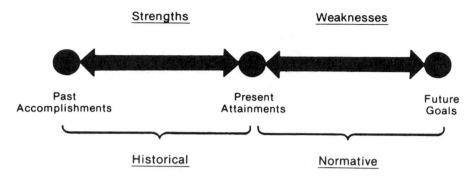

FIGURE 4.3   Criteria Used to Judge an Attribute

be." The specific use of the judgmental criteria for the individual organizational attributes is shown in Table 4.11.

Conclusions of the Study

The research study which this article presents was exploratory in the broadest sense of the word. The aim of the study was to provide insights and to develop understanding of a complex measurement process. No effort was made to test scientifically formulated propositions. Several generalizations emerge from the study.

Managers tend to treat strengths differently from weaknesses.

The underlying steps in the process of defining strengths and weaknesses are similar in all the companies studied. The particular

TABLE 4.11   The Relationship Between Specific Organizational Attributes and the Criteria Employed

Attributes	Criteria		
	Historical	Competitive	Normative
Organizational Form	27.3%	9.1%	63.6%
Top Management	50.0	—	50.0
Standard Procedures	25.0	—	75.0
Control System	9.1	—	90.9
Planning System	—	—	100.0
Overall	23.8%	2.4%	73.8%

(Row percentages sum to 100%.)

factors which are examined and the criteria for judgment vary according to the operational requirements of the business and its history.

The manager's position and responsibility in the organization are crucial influences on the way in which he carries out the process of defining strengths and weaknesses.

There is no single type of measurement or criterion relevant to the measurement of all attributes as strengths and weaknesses.

The results show that traditional notions about strengths and weaknesses are in need of further examination. The factors studied reflect upon the difficulty of establishing meaningful procedures for the transmission and evaluation of lower-level managers' analysis of strengths and weaknesses. The "adding of apples to oranges" syndrome is all too prevalent.

In addition to the procedural difficulties which emerged in the study of the process, several situational factors contributed to difficulties encountered by managers in implementing a program for defining corporate strengths and weaknesses. The factors resulted from general causes: the need for situational analysis, the need for self-protection, the desire to preserve the status quo, and the problems of definition and computational capacity. Each of these problems was observed not from statistical data but from analysis of anecdotal evidence.

The most common single complaint of managers who did not feel that the definition of strengths and weaknesses was meaningful was that they had to be defined in the context of a problem. One manager stated his opinion succinctly.

> I think that our people attempt to make honest appraisals of the organization's capability. We have some people who think that they can move fast and run any business and others who are committed to staying with the present course. Each honestly believes that he has made a realistic appraisal of the company's capabilities.
>
> As I see it, the only real value in making an appraisal of the organization's capabilities comes in the light of a specific deal — the rest of the time it is just an academic exercise. We have to ask ourselves if we have the marbles to put on the table when a deal is offered.

Although convinced of the need for evaluation and action this manager did not believe in the efficacy of a priori definitions which were not related to a specific situation.

Suggestions for Managers

The process of defining strengths and weaknesses should ideally require the manager to test his assumptions and to analyze the status quo in relationship to the requirements for future success given the competition and the changing environment. The analysis performed by managers is rarely so dispassionate. There is a great tendency toward inertia.

On other occasions, managers are faced with the necessity of recommending changes which include abolition of organizational subunits. There is tremendous pressure to identify the problem with personalities or environmental conditions rather than in a fashion which would prejudice the existence of a whole organizational subunit. Often the definition of the problem prescribes the solution. Managers are aware of this connection and shy away from making definitions which contribute to inevitable change.

Managers cannot and do not explore every existing or potential attribute in order to arrive at new evaluations of the corporation's strengths and weaknesses. They must make choices and decide when they are sufficiently certain. They can then examine areas about which there is less certainty or for which the payoff of an accurate assessment is larger.

The results of the study lead to suggestions for improvement of the process of defining strengths and weaknesses. The manager should:

- recognize that the process of defining strengths and weaknesses is primarily an aid to the individual manager in the accomplishment of his task,
- develop lists of critical areas for examination which are tailored to the responsibility and authority of each individual manager,
- make the measures and the criteria to be used in evaluation of strengths and weaknesses explicit so that managers can make their evaluations against a common framework,
- recognize the important strategic role of defining attributes as opposed to efficiency or effectiveness,
- understand the difference in the use of identified strengths and identified weaknesses.

Overall, the assessment of strengths and weaknesses is an important element of strategic planning. The actual items being evaluated are not specific occurrences; rather they are directions, strategies, overall policy commitments, and past practices. The conscious process of defining the strengths and weaknesses of a firm provides a key link in a feedback loop. It allows managers to learn from the success or failure of the policies which they initiate. According to Wiener:

> . . . feedback is a method of controlling a system by reinserting into it the results of its past performance. . . . If . . . the information which proceeds backward from the performance is able to change the general method and pattern of performance, we have a process which may well be called learning.[4]

Figure 4.4 illustrates a strategic planning system which emphasizes the feedback learning aspects of defining strengths and weaknesses. The fea-

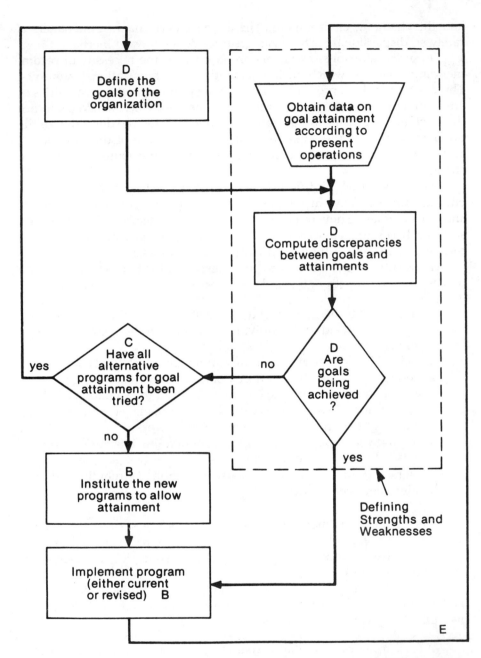

FIGURE 4.4   Feedback Learning Model of Defining Strengths and Weaknesses

tures of the model include: an input channel (A), output devices (B), a memory device (C), selection rules (D), and a channel for recycling (E) so that the system can receive inputs about its outputs. The comparison of attainments with goals using normative, competitive, or historical judgment criteria forms the central focus of the feedback loop.[5]

This system should be contrasted with the traditional strategic planning process shown earlier in Figure 4.1. In that system the definition of strengths and weaknesses was not part of a closed loop. It was an input, a hurdle goal which each new opportunity had to clear. Once past this initial barrier, the planning process left the definition of corporate strengths and weaknesses alone until a new opportunity was presented.

The research for this article shows that organizational acceptance of the necessity of a process of defining strengths and weaknesses depends on whether the information gathered can be integrated meaningfully into the manager's individual strategic planning efforts. Definitions of strengths and weaknesses generally applicable for whole organizations were not found. However, there appear to be definitions which can aid the individual manager in doing his own job. The use of a formal assessment program developed from the budgeting process seems unlikely to succeed because the information gathered at one organizational level is not directly additive with information from other levels. A program which carefully defines the relevant attributes to be examined and which imposes rigorous and consistent criteria may provide important assistance in the strategic planning process.

Notes

The work by these authors is listed in the References section immediately following.

1. See Selznick.
2. See Learned, Christensen, Andrews and Guth.
3. See Ansoff, Cordiner, Drucker, Golde, T. Leavitt and Simon, Smithburg and Thompson.
4. See Wiener.
5. For further discussion about the requirements of a learning system see H. Leavitt.

References

Ansoff, H. I. *Corporate Strategy*. New York: McGraw-Hill, 1956, p. 92.

Cordiner, R. J. *New Frontiers for Professional Managers*. New York: McGraw-Hill, 1956, pp. 95–98.

Drucker, P. *Managing for Results*. New York: Harper & Row, 1964, p. 313 *et seq.*

Golde, R. A. "Practical Planning for Small Businesses." *Harvard Business Review,*
   September–October 1964, p. 147.

Learned, E. P.; Christensen, C. R.; Andrews, K. R.; and Guth, W. D. *Business
   Policy: Text and Cases.* Homewood, Ill.: Richard D. Irwin, 1965, p. 21.

Leavitt, H. *Managerial Psychology.* Chicago: University of Chicago Press, 1964, p. 77
   et seq.

Leavitt, T. *Innovations in Marketing.* New York: McGraw-Hill, 1965, p. 176.

Selznick, P. *Leadership in Administration.* New York: Harper & Row, 1957, p. 143.

Simon, H. A.; Smithburg, D. W.; and Thompson, V. A. *Public Administration.* New
   York: Knopf, 1950, p. 24.

Wiener, N. *The Human Use of Human Beings: Cybernetics and Society,* Garden City,
   N.Y.: Doubleday & Company, 1954, p. 58.

5. Marketing Cost Analysis: A Modularized Contribution Approach

Patrick M. Dunne
Harry I. Wolk

In recent years, an increasing use of accounting information for planning, controlling, and evaluating the firm's marketing performance has been advocated in the literature.[1] Some of this published material is very sophisticated, and indeed there is almost no limit to how far one can go in analyzing the effectiveness of marketing operations by accounting techniques. At the same time, it is truly astounding that many marketing managers do not use even some of the more elementary accounting tools that are available.

The authors know of one company where Product X was generating an annual profit of $800,000, and Product Y was losing money at the rate of $600,000 per year — and management was totally unaware of the situation, just pleasantly happy to be making $200,000! They were simply astounded when a little accounting by product line revealed Product Y to be such a drain.

Not quite that elementary, but still well within the group of non-accounting trained managers, is the *modular contribution-margin income statement*. This technique spotlights the behavior of controllable costs and indicates each segment's contribution to profit and indirect fixed costs. It is a very useful tool for marketing managers who are concerned not only with the efficiency of the operation for which they are responsible, but also with

This article first appeared in *Journal of Marketing*, July 1977, pp. 83–94.

When this article was published, the authors were associate professor of marketing at Texas Tech University and professor of accounting at Drake University, respectively.

the profitability of the product, various territories, channels, types and sizes of customer, etc.

In order to generate accounting information for specific market segments, a detailed data base is a necessity. All transactions entering the system must be classified and coded so that costs can be matched with revenues at desired aggregation levels for different combinations of relevant factors. But the payoff is usually worth the effort. The modular contribution margin approach to marketing analysis enables management (a) to judge the profitability of a specific marketing mix in a specific area and (b) to decide whether or not to take action to change it.

Case Example

Consider the D-W Appliance Company, a small appliance manufacturer that produces blenders and mixers on separate production lines. The firm's marketing division is organized along territorial lines (East and West), and the products are sold by sales representatives through two marketing channels: (1) to wholesalers, who, in turn, distribute to small retailers, and (2) directly to large retailers. Order size is also important: channel costs are lower for orders of 100 units or more of either product.

If the Marketing Division Manager wanted to assess the profitability of his functional area, he might request an income statement. Under the full-cost approach to financial statements, costs would be separated according to function: cost of goods sold and operating expenses. A portion of the general expense of the company cost centers (accounting, corporate headquarters, etc.) would arbitrarily be allocated to the operating expense of the Marketing Division. (See Figure 5.1.)

This type of statement is, however, better suited to external reporting than to internal managerial planning and control, since it contains costs which do not directly affect decisions in the marketing area and which are not controllable by the Marketing Division Manager. Furthermore, in order to apply variance analysis to this kind of statement, comparing budgeted results with actual results for control purposes, the costs would first have to be separated by activity before the analysis could distinguish between cost changes in the level of an activity and those due to other causes.

The main advantage of the modular contribution margin approach as a managerial tool for planning and control is that it separates costs, by behavior, into variable and fixed costs.[2]

Variable costs are those costs which vary predictably with some measure of activity during a given time period. For example, commissions on sales for D-W are set at 10% of sales revenue. Total commission expense varies as sales vary.

Fixed costs, on the other hand, are costs which do not change in the short-run, e.g., the Marketing Division Manager's salary.

FULL-COST APPROACH

REVENUE
    Less: Cost of Goods Sold

GROSS MARGIN
    Less: Operating Expenses (Including the division's allocated share of company admin-
            istrative and general expenses.)

NET INCOME

CONTRIBUTION MARGIN APPROACH

REVENUE
    Less: Variable Manufacturing Costs
           Other Variable Costs directly traceable to the segment.

CONTRIBUTION MARGIN
    Less: Fixed Costs directly traceable to products.
           Fixed Costs directly traceable to the market segment.

SEGMENT NET INCOME

FIGURE 5.1   Income Statement Models

Cost Behavior and Controllability

The modular contribution margin model, which allows separation of costs by behavior, can be expanded to include separation of costs by controllability.

Controllable costs are those costs which originate in the particular organizational unit under consideration. Whether a cost is classified as controllable or uncontrollable obviously depends on the organizational segment under consideration. Territorial expenses in the statement for East Territory would be controllable costs for that territory and for the Marketing Division, but not for the West Territory.

As just suggested, controllability relates to the degree of influence over a cost by the relevant division manager. Labor costs that exceed standard costs for actual production in a particular department are a classic example of a cost for which the appropriate manager would be held accountable. However, even for this classification, a great deal of care must be exercised. Actual controllable labor costs may exceed standard because of many reasons beyond the manager's scope or control. For example, delivery time for shipments may be delayed by severe weather. Furthermore, controllability may be constrained by economic externalities. Selling costs would be a

Controllable Variable Costs	Controllable Fixed Costs
Uncontrollable Variable Costs	Uncontrollable Fixed Costs

controllable variable cost of the Marketing Division, while the manager probably has little, if any, influence over a price decline precipitated by a competitor's action.

Controllable fixed costs are rarely controllable in the very short run. Once a fixed asset is acquired, there is virtually no control over the annual depreciation charges. One may select the depreciation method, but no differences will arise between actual and budgeted costs except in those situations where depreciation can be calculated on usage. There are, however, some intermediate-term fixed costs (often called discretionary or programmed costs because they are determined annually on a budgetary basis) which may be highly controllable; i.e., actual costs may exceed budgeted costs. Advertising and R&D costs fall into this category.

Uncontrollable variable costs are variable costs which are not incurred in the segment under consideration. Therefore, the costs should be expressed as standard costs so that a manager will not be held responsible for the inefficiencies of another department. Variable manufacturing costs of blenders and mixers would be indirect variable costs for the Marketing Division, and should be expressed in the budget at standard costs.

Uncontrollable fixed costs are not included in segmental income statements since any basis of allocation to the segment would necessarily be arbitrary. Uncontrollable costs are often called common costs and for the Marketing Division would include a portion of those costs of the corporate headquarters and those manufacturing costs which couldn't be directly allocated to blenders and mixers, such as the plant manager's salary.

Segmental Analysis

Contribution margin income statements by department are useful for budgeting, performance analysis, short-run decision-making, pricing, and decisions between alternatives — e.g., whether to close down a warehouse or relocate it; whether to lease a fleet of trucks or own them. Market segment income statements are also useful for such marketing decisions as whether to drop a product line and whether to alter the physical distribution system; and they aid in the redirection of effort to the company's more profitable markets. The usual market segmentation is by product line, territory, channel, order size, and customer, but any of the segmentation bases of the marketing matrix of the firm's target markets could be used.

A modular data base also facilitates statements focusing on functional areas, depending on management's judgment about what information is relevant for decision-making and control. For example, if transportation is judged to be a crucial function in the case of blenders, then the expense for shipping blenders would be coded by that function and by the relevant variables (territory, channel, product, order size, customer, date). Revenue, in turn, would be coded at the time of each transaction.

Unless the company's information system is somewhat sophisticated, there is usually some initial difficulty in constructing accounting statements of functional/departmental areas.[3] Costs for a specific department must be broken out of the natural accounts via estimation techniques. (Since costs are usually accumulated in natural accounts, such as salary expense, the salary expense for the Marketing Division would have to be calculated.)

Under the modular contribution margin approach not all costs are allocated to segments. Rather, only those costs are considered which would disappear if the company were to drop that department or segment. Note that this is acceptable only for purposes of internal decision-making, and *not* for differential cost justification under the Robinson-Patman Act (as demonstrated in the Borden case) or for general financial reporting purposes (audited reports to stockholders, IRS returns, and SEC reports).

Allocation of Costs

Other refinements can be added to the modular contribution margin model. The charge for the specific assets used by the department (depreciation) could be based on the decline in the market value of the resources during the period. Or an interest charge on the working capital used by the department (based on the firm's actual cost of capital) could be included to give a clear picture of the department's operations and actual contribution.

Allocation, however, cannot be made arbitrarily on the basis of sales volume since that focus might overlook other relevant information. For example, how do you attach distribution expense to blenders and mixers for a mixed shipment of both products, when blenders are bulkier, heavier, and require more handling? Or if mixers are easy to sell to large retailers, while blenders require extensive sales effort, the entry of salesmen's expenses to blenders and mixers should reflect this difference.

If costs are based on a factor such as weight or space occupied, this may allow an equitable basis of cost assignment. This does not always happen, though, and so assigning costs to departments on the basis of weight can be highly misleading for analytical purposes. Suffice it to say that wherever variable costs are predictable and vary with a given base, standard costs should be used in budgeting for the Marketing Division.

The value of a modular contribution margin statement is the ability to match costs with revenues for the smallest market segments desired and then to aggregate these modules into statements for larger segments. Essentially, the modular data base provides management with the capability of transforming accounting information into two systems: one based on departments within the firm, the other based on market segments.

Useful Information

The flexibility and responsiveness of the modular contribution margin approach for market segments can be shown by applying it to the D-W Appliance Company. The first step is for management to decide on the relevant factors for examination. In this example, *product line* was chosen as the basic unit of interest, and the market was further segmented by territory, channel, and order size. (The modular data base could just as easily have provided for primary segmentation by territory or channel, or whatever.) The figures and tables which follow show the possible modular income statements that can be constructed.

Figure 5.2 shows the hierarchy and linkages among the segmental contribution margin income statements illustrated here.

Basic data for the illustration is shown in Figure 5.3, the Master Cost Data Sheet. Unit sales and channel of distribution costs are broken down by territory, product, and channel in Figure 5.4.

Income for the entire firm is shown in Figure 5.5. It is the only statement containing $430,000 of costs (territory costs, joint manufacturing costs, and corporate headquarters costs) which are joint to the product oriented segmental income statements shown in Figures 5.6 to 5.19.

Clues for Action

The loss at the corporate level (as shown in Figure 5.5) indicates that the firm should either strengthen, if possible, those segments which are weakest and/or reallocate more of its resources to those segments which are strongest.

In Figures 5.6 and 5.13, Total Income Statements for blenders and mixers, blenders are stronger than mixers in terms of Contribution Margin (32.7% versus 21.6%) although slightly less profitable after taking into account direct fixed costs (13.1% versus 14.8%). This may indicate that not enough programmed advertising costs are being budgeted to blenders. More advertising effort may be needed to effectively exploit higher Contribution Margin of blenders.

At the same time, the further breakdowns indicate that the Segment Income of the West Territory is lagging behind the East Territory for both blenders and mixers (see Figures 5.7, 5.10, 5.14, and 5.17). The biggest reason for this poor performance is the very low Segment Income of the Wholesaler Channels in the West Territory (Figures 5.11 and 5.18).

Action to improve the situation is especially called for in the Wholesaler Channel for blenders in the West Territory. Not only is the Segment Income percentage (6.5%) the lowest for any segment in the whole analysis, but the corresponding Contribution Margin is relatively strong (27.9%). The problem is one of spreading heavy fixed costs of manufacturing over more sales. The solution, again, would be to take advantage of the good contribution margin percentage through increased advertising effort or, perhaps in this case, by expanding the sales force.

As another indication of the revealing capability of this kind of analysis, consider the profitability of the two channels. If they had simply been compared in total (as a form of primary segmentation), the figures would have been:

CHANNEL	CONTRIBUTION MARGIN (%)	SEGMENT (%)	INCOME ($)
Wholesaler	26.3	12.9	212,588
Large Retailer	27.8	14.3	208,807

The two channels would have appeared to be very even in profitability. Yet recombining in various ways brings out still more information. Figure 5.20 shows that if the Wholesaler Channel in the West could be improved to match the Wholesaler Channel in the East, the total Wholesaler Channel would have outperformed the Large Retailer Channel.

Within the Large Retailer Channel, blenders and mixers in the East are relatively more profitable in terms of both Contribution Margin and Segment Income percentages than their counterparts in the West. However, Segment Income in total dollars for blenders and mixers in the East ($74,209) is barely half of that for the corresponding products in the West for the Large Retailer Channel ($134,598). Maybe the East Territory for Large Retailers needs a greater dosage of advertising dollars to exploit its relative advantage. Perhaps the whole Large Retailer Channel needs some kind of revamping — a need that otherwise would never have been revealed except through segmental analysis.

Another aspect of the problem lies in order size. Figure 5.21 reveals that this is most evident within the Large Retailer Channel in the West. Within that territory and channel, distribution costs for small order sizes of mixers are 50% greater per dollar of revenue than for large orders. Similarly, small orders of blenders in the West in the Large Retailer Channel are

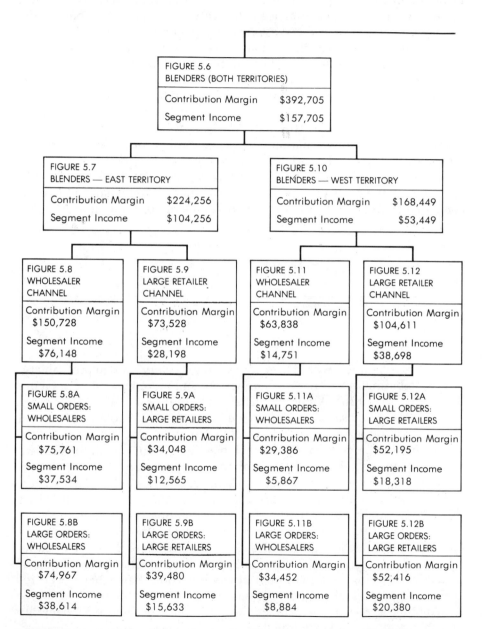

FIGURE 5.2   Segmental Contribution Income Statements: D-W Appliance
Company

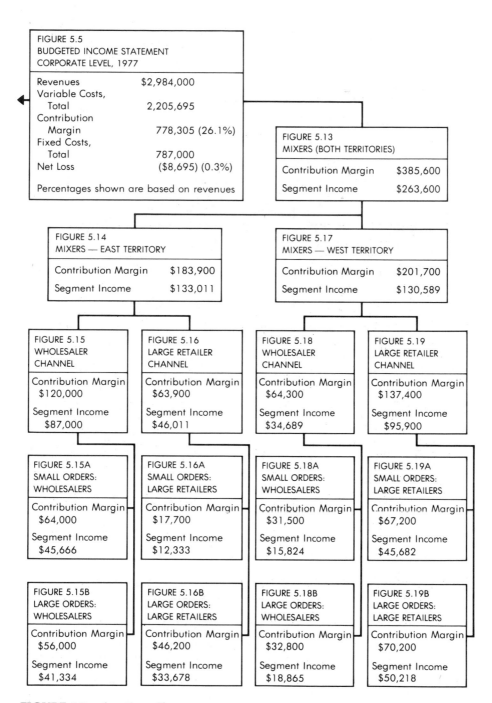

FIGURE 5.5
BUDGETED INCOME STATEMENT
CORPORATE LEVEL, 1977

Revenues	$2,984,000
Variable Costs,	
Total	2,205,695
Contribution	
Margin	778,305 (26.1%)
Fixed Costs,	
Total	787,000
Net Loss	($8,695) (0.3%)

Percentages shown are based on revenues

FIGURE 5.13
MIXERS (BOTH TERRITORIES)

| Contribution Margin | $385,600 |
| Segment Income | $263,600 |

FIGURE 5.14
MIXERS — EAST TERRITORY

| Contribution Margin | $183,900 |
| Segment Income | $133,011 |

FIGURE 5.17
MIXERS — WEST TERRITORY

| Contribution Margin | $201,700 |
| Segment Income | $130,589 |

FIGURE 5.15
WHOLESALER
CHANNEL

| Contribution Margin | $120,000 |
| Segment Income | $87,000 |

FIGURE 5.16
LARGE RETAILER
CHANNEL

| Contribution Margin | $63,900 |
| Segment Income | $46,011 |

FIGURE 5.18
WHOLESALER
CHANNEL

| Contribution Margin | $64,300 |
| Segment Income | $34,689 |

FIGURE 5.19
LARGE RETAILER
CHANNEL

| Contribution Margin | $137,400 |
| Segment Income | $95,900 |

FIGURE 5.15A
SMALL ORDERS:
WHOLESALERS

| Contribution Margin | $64,000 |
| Segment Income | $45,666 |

FIGURE 5.16A
SMALL ORDERS:
LARGE RETAILERS

| Contribution Margin | $17,700 |
| Segment Income | $12,333 |

FIGURE 5.18A
SMALL ORDERS:
WHOLESALERS

| Contribution Margin | $31,500 |
| Segment Income | $15,824 |

FIGURE 5.19A
SMALL ORDERS:
LARGE RETAILERS

| Contribution Margin | $67,200 |
| Segment Income | $45,682 |

FIGURE 5.15B
LARGE ORDERS:
WHOLESALERS

| Contribution Margin | $56,000 |
| Segment Income | $41,334 |

FIGURE 5.16B
LARGE ORDERS:
LARGE RETAILERS

| Contribution Margin | $46,200 |
| Segment Income | $33,678 |

FIGURE 5.18B
LARGE ORDERS:
WHOLESALERS

| Contribution Margin | $32,800 |
| Segment Income | $18,865 |

FIGURE 5.19B
LARGE ORDERS:
LARGE RETAILERS

| Contribution Margin | $70,200 |
| Segment Income | $50,218 |

FIGURE 5.2   (continued)

	East		West	
	Blenders	Mixers	Blenders	Mixers
Revenue (per unit)	$ 42.00	$ 26.00	$ 38.00	$ 24.00
Variable Manu-facturing Costs	$ 20.00	$ 15.00	$ 20.00	$ 15.00
Variable Selling Costs (10% of revenue)	4.20	2.60	3.80	2.40
Total	$ 24.20	$ 17.60	$ 23.80	$ 17.40
Contribution Margin Per Unit Before Channel Costs	$ 17.80	$ 8.40	$ 14.20	$ 6.60
Programmed Advertising Costs[a]	$20,000	$12,000	$15,000	$10,000
Budgeted Sales (units)	15,000	28,000	15,000	44,000

	Blenders	Mixers	East	West	Unal-located
Controllable Direct Manufacturing Costs	$200,000	$100,000			
Territorial Fixed Costs (joint to products)			$50,000	$30,000	
Joint Fixed Manufacturing Costs					$100,000
Corporate Headquarters Costs					$250,000

FIGURE 5.3   D-W Appliance Company Master Cost Data Sheet for 1977

[a]Programmed advertising costs are fixed costs that are reviewed each year through the budget process. (Therefore, they are not in a direct relationship with sales revenue or units sold. This could result from having a particular ad aimed at only one channel member or group of channel members. An example would be a trade magazine ad in a conference program for a Wholesalers Convention. Such an ad would not reach the retailer.)

	Wholesaler Small Order	Channel Large Order	Large Retailer Small Order	Channel Large Order
East:				
Blenders:				
Budgeted Sales (units)	5,119	4,868	2,381	2,632
Cost Per Unit	$3.00	$2.40	$3.50	$2.80
Total	$15,357	$11,683	$ 8,334	$ 7,370
Mixers:				
Budgeted Sales (units)	10,000	8,000	3,000	7,000
Cost Per Unit	$2.00	$1.40	$2.50	$1.80
Total	$20,000	$11,200	$ 7,500	$12,600
West:				
Blenders:				
Budgeted Sales (units)	2,881	3,132	4,619	4,368
Cost Per Unit	$4.00	$3.20	$2.90	$2.20
Total	$11,524	$10,022	$13,395	$ 9,610
Mixers:				
Budgeted Sales (units)	9,000	8,000	14,000	13,000
Cost Per Unit	$3.10	$2.50	$1.80	$1.20
Total	$27,900	$20,000	$25,200	$15,600

FIGURE 5.4   Budgeted Channel of Distribution Costs

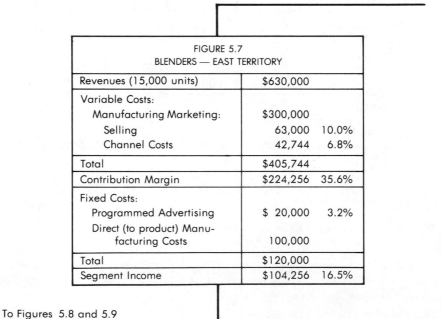

FIGURE 5.5		
CORPORATE LEVEL, 1977		
Revenues	$2,984,000	
Variable Costs:		
Manufacturing Marketing:	$1,680,000	
Selling	298,400	10.0%[1]
Channel Costs	227,295	7.6%
Total	$2,205,695	
Contribution Margin	$ 778,305	26.1%
Fixed Costs:		
Programmed Advertising	$ 57,000	1.9%
Direct (to product) Manu- facturing Costs	300,000	
Territory Costs	80,000	
Joint Manufacturing Costs	100,000	
Corporate Headquarters Costs	250,000	
Total	$ 787,000	
Net Loss	($8,695)	(.3%)

[1] Percentages shown are based upon revenues.

FIGURE 5.7		
BLENDERS — EAST TERRITORY		
Revenues (15,000 units)	$630,000	
Variable Costs:		
Manufacturing Marketing:	$300,000	
Selling	63,000	10.0%
Channel Costs	42,744	6.8%
Total	$405,744	
Contribution Margin	$224,256	35.6%
Fixed Costs:		
Programmed Advertising	$ 20,000	3.2%
Direct (to product) Manu- facturing Costs	100,000	
Total	$120,000	
Segment Income	$104,256	16.5%

To Figures 5.8 and 5.9

FIGURES 5.5 and 5.6–5.12   Total Income Statements

FIGURE 5.6 BLENDERS (BOTH TERRITORIES)		
Revenues (30,000 units)	$1,200,000	
Variable Costs:		
Manufacturing Marketing:	$ 600,000	
Selling	120,000	10.0%
Channel Costs	87,295	7.3%
Total	$ 807,295	
Contribution Margin	$ 392,705	32.7%
Fixed Costs:		
Programmed Advertising	$ 35,000	2.9%
Direct (to product) Manu-		
facturing Costs	200,000	
Total	$ 235,000	
Segment Income	$ 157,705	13.1%

FIGURE 5.10 BLENDERS — WEST TERRITORY		
Revenues (15,000 units)	$570,000	
Variable Costs:		
Manufacturing Marketing:	$300,000	
Selling	57,000	10.0%
Channel Costs	44,551	7.8%
Total	$401,551	
Contribution Margin	$168,449	29.6%
Fixed Costs:		
Programmed Advertising	$ 15,000	2.6%
Direct (to product) Manufac-		
turing Costs	100,000	
Total	$115,000	
Segment Income	$ 53,449	9.4%

To Figures 5.11 and 5.12

FIGURES 5.5 and 5.6–5.12   (continued)

From Figure 5.7 — *From Figure 5.7*

FIGURE 5.8 WHOLESALER CHANNEL						
	Small Order (5119 units)		Large Order (4868 units)		Total	
Revenues	$214,998		$204,456		$419,454	
Variable Costs:						
Manufacturing Marketing:	$102,380		$ 97,360		$199,740	
Selling	21,500	10.0%	20,446	10.0%	41,946	10.0%
Channel Costs	15,357	7.1%	11,683	5.7%	27,040	6.4%
Total	$139,237		$129,489		$268,726	
Contribution Margin	$ 75,761	35.2%	$ 74,967	36.7%	$150,728	35.9%
Fixed Costs:						
Programmed Advertising[1]	$ 4,100	1.9%	$ 3,900	1.9%	$ 8,000	1.9%
Direct (to product) Manufacturing Costs[2]	34,127		32,453		66,580	
Total	$ 38,227		$ 36,353		$ 74,580	
Segment Income	$ 37,534	(17.5%)	$ 38,614	18.9%	$ 76,148	18.2%

[1] Direct to the Large Retailer Channel and allocated in accordance with revenues. The same procedure is used for channel analysis in later exhibits.

FIGURE 5.9 LARGE RETAILER CHANNEL						
	Small Order (2381 units)		Large Order (2632 units)		Total	
Revenues	$100,002		$110,544		$210,546	
Variable Costs:						
Manufacturing Marketing:	$ 47,620		$ 52,640		$100,260	
Selling	10,000	10.0%	11,054	10.0%	21,054	10.0%
Channel Costs	8,334	8.3%	7,370	6.7%	15,704	7.5%
Total	$ 65,954		$ 71,064		$137,018	
Contribution Margin	$ 34,048	34.0%	$ 39,480	35.7%	$ 73,528	34.9%
Fixed Costs:						
Programmed Advertising[1]	$ 5,700	5.7%	$ 6,300	5.7%	$ 12,000	5.7%
Direct (to product) Manufacturing Costs[2]	15,783		17,547		33,330	
Total	$ 21,483		$ 23,847		$ 45,330	
Segment Income	$ 12,565	12.6%	$ 15,633	14.1%	$ 28,198	13.4%

[2] Allocated in proportion of number of units sold in each order size for this channel to total sales. The same procedure is used in later exhibits.

FIGURES 5.5 and 5.6–5.12   (continued)

FIGURE 5.11 WHOLESALER CHANNEL							
	Small Order (2881 units)		Large Order (3132 units)		Total		
Revenues	$109,478		$119,016		$228,494		
Variable Costs:							
Manufacturing Marketing:	$ 57,620		$ 62,640		$120,260		
Selling	10,948	10.0%	11,902	10.0%	22,850	10.0%	
Channel Costs	11,524	10.5%	10,022	8.4%	21,546	9.4%	
Total	$ 80,092		$ 84,564		$164,656		
Contribution Margin	$ 29,386	26.8%	$ 34,452	28.9%	$ 63,838	27.9%	
Fixed Costs:							
Programmed Advertising	$ 4,312	3.9%	$ 4,688	3.9%	$ 9,000	3.9%	
Direct (to product) Manufacturing Costs	19,207		20,880		40,087		
Total	$ 23,519		$ 25,568		$ 49,087		
Segment Income	$ 5,867	5.4%	$ 8,884	7.5%	$ 14,751	6.5%	

FIGURE 5.12 LARGE RETAILER CHANNEL							
	Small Order (4619 units)		Large Order (4368 units)		Total		
Revenues	$175,522		$165,984		$341,506		
Variable Costs:							
Manufacturing Marketing:	$ 92,380		$ 87,360		$179,740		
Selling	17,552	10.0%	16,598	10.0%	34,150	10.0%	
Channel Costs	13,395	7.6%	9,610	5.8%	23,005	6.7%	
Total	$123,327		$113,568		$236,895		
Contribution Margin	$ 52,195	29.7%	$ 52,416	31.6%	$104,611	30.6%	
Fixed Costs:							
Programmed Advertising	$ 3,084	1.8%	$ 2,916	1.8%	$ 6,000	1.8%	
Direct (to product) Manufacturing Costs	30,793		29,120		59,913		
Total	$ 33,877		$ 32,036		$ 65,913		
Segment Income	$ 18,318	10.4%	$ 20,380	12.3%	$ 38,698	11.3%	

From Figure 5.10

FIGURES 5.5 and 5.6–5.12   (continued)

FIGURE 5.13
MIXERS (BOTH TERRITORIES)

Revenues (72,000 units)	$1,784,000	
Variable Costs:		
Manufacturing Marketing:	$1,080,000	
Selling	178,400	10.0%
Channel Costs	140,000	7.8%
Total	$1,398,400	
Contribution Margin	$ 385,600	21.6%
Fixed Costs:		
Programmed Advertising	$ 22,000	1.2%
Direct (to product) Manufac-		
turing Costs	100,000	
Total	$ 122,000	
Segment Income	$ 263,600	14.8%

FIGURE 5.14
MIXERS — EAST TERRITORY

Revenues (28,000 units)	$728,000	
Variable Costs:		
Manufacturing Marketing:	$420,000	
Selling	72,800	10.0%
Channel Costs	51,300	7.0%
Total	$544,100	
Contribution Margin	$183,900	25.3%
Fixed Costs:		
Programmed Advertising	$ 12,000	1.6%
Direct (to product) Manu-		
facturing Costs	38,889	
Total	$ 50,889	
Segment Income	$133,011	18.3%

To Figures 5.15 and 5.16

FIGURES 5.5 and 5.13–5.19   Total Income Statements

FIGURE 5.5 CORPORATE LEVEL, 1977		
Revenues	$2,984,000	
Variable Costs:		
Manufacturing Marketing:	$1,680,000	
Selling	298,400	10.0%[1]
Channel Costs	227,295	7.6%
Total	$2,205,695	
Contribution Margin	$ 778,305	26.1%
Fixed Costs:		
Programmed Advertising	$ 57,000	1.9%
Direct (to product) Manu- facturing Costs	300,000	
Territory Costs	80,000	
Joint Manufacturing Costs	100,000	
Corporate Headquarters Costs	250,000	
Total	$ 787,000	
Net Loss	($8,695)	(.3%)

[1] Percentages shown are based upon revenues.

FIGURE 5.17 MIXERS — WEST TERRITORY		
Revenues	$1,056,000	
Variable Costs:		
Manufacturing Marketing:	$ 660,000	
Selling	105,600	$10.0%
Channel Costs	88,700	8.4%
Total	$ 854,300	
Contribution Margin	$ 201,700	19.1%
Fixed Costs:		
Programmed Advertising	$ 10,000	.9%
Direct (to product) Manufac- turing Costs	61,111	
Total	$ 71,111	
Segment Income	$ 130,589	12.4%

To Figures 5.18 and 5.19

FIGURES 5.5 and 5.13–5.19 (continued)

From Figure 5.14

FIGURE 5.15 WHOLESALER CHANNEL					
	Small Order (10,000 units)		Large Order (8,000 units)		Total
Revenues	$260,000		$208,000		$468,000
Variable Costs:					
Manufacturing Marketing:	$150,000		$120,000		$270,000
Selling	26,000	10.0%	20,800	10.0%	46,800	10.0%
Channel Costs	20,000	7.7%	11,200	5.4%	31,200	6.7%
Total	$196,000		$152,000		$348,000
Contribution Margin	$ 64,000	24.6%	$ 56,000	26.9%	$120,000	25.6%
Fixed Costs:					
Programmed Advertising	$ 4,445	1.7%	$ 3,555	1.7%	$ 8,000	1.7%
Direct (to product) Manufacturing Costs	13,889		11,111		25,000
Total	$ 18,334		$ 14,666		$ 33,000
Segment Income	$ 45,666	17.6%	$ 41,334	19.8%	$ 87,000	18.6%

FIGURE 5.16 LARGE RETAILER CHANNEL					
	Small Order (3,000 units)		Large Order (7,000 units)		Total
Revenues	$78,000		$182,000		$260,000
Variable Costs:					
Manufacturing Marketing:	$45,000		$105,000		$150,000
Selling	7,800	10.0%	18,200	10.0%	26,100	10.0%
Channel Costs	7,500	9.6%	12,600	6.9%	20,100	7.7%
Total	$60,300		$135,800		$196,100
Contribution Margin	$17,700	22.7%	$ 46,200	25.4%	$ 63,900	24.6%
Fixed Costs:					
Programmed Advertising	$ 1,200	1.5%	$ 2,800	1.5%	$ 4,000	1.5%
Direct (to product) Manufacturing Costs	4,167		9,722		13,889
Total	$ 5,367		$ 12,522		$ 17,889
Segment Income	$12,333	15.8%	$ 33,678	18.5%	$ 46,011	17.7%

FIGURES 5.5 and 5.13–5.19   (continued)

FIGURE 5.18 WHOLESALE CHANNEL							
	Small Order (9000 units)		Large Order (8000 units)		Total		
Revenues	$216,000		$192,000		$408,000		
Variable Costs:							
Manufacturing Marketing:	$135,000		$120,000		$255,000		
Selling	21,600	10.0%	29,200	10.0%	40,800	10.0%	
Channel Costs	27,900	12.9%	20,000	10.4%	47,900	11.7%	
Total	$184,500		$159,200		$343,700		
Contribution Margin	$ 31,500	14.6%	$ 32,800	17.1%	$ 64,300	15.8%	
Fixed Costs:							
Programmed Advertising	$ 3,176	1.5%	$ 2,824	1.5%	$ 6,000	1.5%	
Direct (to product) Manufacturing Costs	12,500		11,111		23,611		
Total	$ 15,676		$ 13,935		$ 29,611		
Segment Income	$ 15,824	7.3%	$ 18,865	9.8%	$ 34,689	8.5%	

From Figure 5.17

FIGURE 5.19 LARGE RETAILER CHANNEL							
	Small Order (14,000 units)		Large Order (13,000 units)		Total		
Revenues	$336,000		$312,000		$648,000		
Variable Costs:							
Manufacturing Marketing:	$210,000		$195,000		$405,000		
Selling	33,600	10.0%	31,200	10.0%	64,800	10.0%	
Channel Costs	25,200	7.5%	15,600	5.0%	40,800	6.3%	
Total	$268,800		$241,800		$510,600		
Contribution Margin	$ 67,200	20.0%	$ 70,200	22.5%	$137,400	21.2%	
Fixed Costs:							
Programmed Advertising	$ 2,074	.6%	$ 1,926	.6%	$ 4,000	.6%	
Direct (to product) Manufacturing Costs	19,444		18,056		37,500		
Total	$ 21,518		$ 19,982		$ 41,500		
Segment Income	$ 45,682	13.6%	$ 50,218	16.1%	$ 95,900	14.8%	

FIGURES 5.5 and 5.13–5.19   (continued)

Channel	Contribution Margin (%)	Segment %	Income $	Total
WHOLESALERS[a]	[26.3%][c]	[12.9%][c]		[$212,588][c]
West				
blenders	27.9%	6.5%	$14,751	
mixers	15.8%	8.5%	$34,689	
Subtotal				$ 49,440
East				
blenders	35.9%	18.2%	$76,148	
mixers	25.6%	18.6%	$87,000	
Subtotal				$163,148
LARGE RETAILERS[b]	[27.8%][c]	[14.3%][c]		[$208,807][c]
West				
blenders	30.6%	11.3%	$38,698	
mixers	21.2%	14.8%	$95,900	
Subtotal				$134,598
East				
blenders	34.9%	13.4%	$28,198	
mixers	24.6%	17.7%	$46,011	
Subtotal				$ 74,209

FIGURE 5.20   Aggregate Comparison of Wholesaler Channel and Large Retailer Channel

[a]Figures 5.8, 5.11, 5.15, and 5.18.
[b]Figures 5.9, 5.12, 5.16, and 5.19.
[c]Aggregate totals.

out of line relative to large orders (31% excess). Small order costs are also out of line relative to large orders for mixers in the East in both channels (39.1% and 42.6% for Large Retailers and Wholesalers). Efforts must be made to increase the size of Large Retailers' small orders, or the retailers responsible for these orders must be converted to buying from wholesalers.

Benefits of Segmentation

These are just a few of the possible areas where the use of the modular contribution margin income statement could improve management control and planning for the sake of greater profitability. In addition, actual results can be compared against the projected budget for each segment to analyze management's performance or the effect of uncontrollable factors on that performance.

Territory	Product	Large Order[1]	Small Order[1]	Relative Cost Excess[2]
LARGE RETAILERS				
West	Blenders	5.8%	7.6%	31.0%
West	Mixers	5.0%	7.5%	50.0%
East	Blenders	6.7%	8.3%	23.9%
East	Mixers	6.9%	9.6%	39.1%

Territory	Product	Large Order[2]	Small Order[3]	Relative Cost Excess[2]
WHOLESALERS				
West	Blenders	8.4%	10.5%	25%
West	Mixers	10.4%	12.9%	24%
East	Blenders	5.7%	7.1%	24.6%
East	Mixers	5.4%	7.7%	42.6%

FIGURE 5.21   Relative Distribution Costs by Order Size

[1]Channel costs as a percentage of revenues from Figures 5.9, 5.12, 5.16, and 5.19.
[2]Percentage is based on large order size; for example, 7.6% − 5.8% = 1.8% and 1.8%/5.8% = 31%.
[3]Channel costs as a percentage of revenues from Figures 5.8, 5.11, 5.15, and 5.18.

If segmental analysis had not been done at all, or if the segmentation had been conducted just by product (or just by territory, just by channel, or just by order size), many ideas for corrective action or expanded effort might not have been generated.

While the benefits of segmental statements must exceed costs of preparation, the power of the computer should lessen costs enough to make segmental analysis beneficial to an increasing number of companies.

Notes

1. For example, "Report of the Committee on Cost and Profitability Analyses for Marketing," *The Accounting Review Supplement* (1972), pp. 575–615; W. J. E. Crissy, Paul Fischer, and Frank H. Mossman, "Segmental Analysis: Key to Marketing Profitability," *Business Topics* (Spring 1973), pp. 42–49; V. H. Kirpalani and Stanley J. Shapiro, "Financial Dimensions of Marketing Management," *Journal of Marketing*, Vol. 37 No. 3 (July 1973), pp. 40–47; Leland L. Beik and Stephen L. Buzby, "Profitability Analysis by Market Segments," *Journal of Marketing*, Vol.

37 No. 3 (July 1973), pp. 48–53; Frank H. Mossman, Paul Fischer and W. J. E. Crissy, "New Approaches to Analyzing Marketing Profitability," *Journal of Marketing*, Vol. 38 No. 2 (April 1974), pp. 43–48; Merritt J. Davoust, "Analyzing a Client's Customer Profitability Picture," *Management Adviser*, May–June 1974, pp. 15–19; Harry I. Wolk and Patrick M. Dunne, "Modularized Contribution Margin Income Statements for Marketing and Physical Distribution Analysis," *Research Issues in Logistics*, James F. Robeson and John Grabner, eds. (Columbus: The Ohio State University, 1975), pp. 199–210; Stephen L. Buzby and Lester E. Heitger, "Profit Oriented Reporting for Marketing Decision Makers," *Business Topics*, Summer 1976, pp. 60–68; Richard L. Lewis and Leo G. Erickson, "Distribution System Costing: An Overview," *Distribution System Costing: Concepts and Procedures*, John R. Grabner and William S. Sargent, eds. (Columbus: The Ohio State University, 1972), pp. 1–30.

2. Sophisticated methods for separating fixed and variable costs are shown in William J. Baumol and Charles H. Sevin, "Marketing Costs and Mathematical Programming," *New Decision-Making Tools for Managers*, Edward C. Bursk and John F. Chapman, Eds. (New York: New American Library, Inc., 1963), pp. 247–65; and R. S. Gynther, "Improving Separation of Fixed and Variable Expenses," *Management Accounting*, June 1963, pp. 29–38.

3. Mossman, same as reference 1, p. 44.

6. The Marketing Audit Comes of Age

Philip Kotler
William Gregor
William Rogers

Comparing the marketing strategies and tactics of business units today versus ten years ago, the most striking impression is one of marketing strategy obsolescence. Ten years ago U.S. automobile companies were gearing up for their second postwar race to produce the largest car with the highest horsepower. Today companies are selling increasing numbers of small and medium-sized cars and fuel economy is a major selling point. Ten years ago computer companies were introducing ever-more powerful hardware for more sophisticated uses. Today they emphasize mini- and micro-computers and software.

It is not even necessary to take a ten-year period to show the rapid obsolescence of marketing strategies. The growth economy of 1950–1970 has been superseded by a volatile economy which produces new strategic surprises almost monthly. Competitors launch new products, customers switch their business, distributors lose their effectiveness, advertising costs skyrocket, government regulations are announced, and consumer groups attack. These changes represent both opportunities and problems and may demand periodic reorientations of the company's marketing operations.

Many companies feel that their marketing operations need regular reviews and overhauls but do not know how to proceed. Some companies simply make many small changes that are economically and politically feasible, but fail to get to the heart of the matter. True, the company develops an annual marketing plan but management normally does not take a deep and objective look at the marketing strategies, policies, organi-

This article first appeared in the *Sloan Management Review*, Winter 1977, pp. 25–44.
When this article was published, the authors were professor of marketing at Northwestern University and consultants with The Management Analysis Center, respectively.

zations, and operations on a recurrent basis. At the other extreme, companies install aggressive new top marketing management hoping to shake down the marketing cobwebs. In between there must be more orderly ways to reorient marketing operations to changed environments and opportunities.

Enter the Marketing Audit

One hears more talk today about the *marketing audit* as being the answer to evaluating marketing practice just as the public accounting audit is the tool for evaluating company accounting practice. This might lead one to conclude that the marketing audit is a new idea and also a very distinct methodology. Neither of these conclusions is true.

The marketing audit as an idea dates back to the early fifties. Rudolph Dallmeyer, a former executive in Booz-Allen-Hamilton, remembers conducting marketing audits as early as 1952. Robert J. Lavidge, President of Elrick and Lavidge, dates his firm's performance of marketing audits to over two decades ago. In 1959, the American Management Association published an excellent set of papers on the marketing audit under the title *Analyzing and Improving Marketing Performance,* Report No. 32, 1959. During the 1960s, the marketing audit received increasing mention in the lists of marketing services of management consultant firms. It was not until the turbulent seventies, however, that it began to penetrate management awareness as a possible answer to its needs.

As for whether the marketing audit has reached a high degree of methodological sophistication, the answer is generally no. Whereas two certified public accountants will handle an audit assignment using approximately the same methodology, two marketing auditors are likely to bring different conceptions of the auditing process to their task. However, a growing consensus on the major characteristics of a marketing audit is emerging and we can expect considerable progress to occur in the next few years.

In its fullest form and concept, a marketing audit has four basic characteristics. The first and most important is that it is *broad* rather than narrow in focus. The term "marketing audit" should be reserved for a *horizontal (or comprehensive) audit* covering the company's marketing environment, objectives, strategies, organization, and systems. In contrast a *vertical (or in-depth) audit* occurs when management decides to take a deep look into some key marketing function, such as sales force management. A vertical audit should properly be called by the function that is being audited, such as a sales force audit, an advertising audit, or a pricing audit.

A second characteristic feature of a marketing audit is that it is conducted by someone who is *independent* of the operation that is being evaluated. There is some loose talk about self-audits, where a manager follows a checklist of questions concerning his own operation to make sure that he is touching all the bases.[1] Most experts would agree, however, that the self-audit, while it is always a useful step that a manager should take, does not constitute a *bona fide* audit because it lacks objectivity and independence. Independence can be achieved in two ways. The audit could be an *inside audit* conducted by a person or group inside the company but outside of the operation being evaluated. Or it could be an *outside audit* conducted by a management consulting firm or practitioner.

The third characteristic of a marketing audit is that it is *systematic*. The marketing auditor who decides to interview people inside and outside the firm at random, asking questions as they occur to him, is a "visceral" auditor without a method. This does not mean that he will not come up with the very useful findings and recommendations; he may be very insightful. However, the effectiveness of the marketing audit will normally increase to the extent that it incorporates an orderly sequence of diagnostic steps, such as there are in the conduct of a public accounting audit.

A final characteristic that is less intrinsic to a marketing audit but nevertheless desirable is that it be conducted *periodically*. Typically, evaluations of company marketing efforts are commissioned when sales have turned down sharply, sales force morale has fallen, or other problems have occurred at the company. The fact is, however, that companies are thrown into a crisis partly because they have failed to review their assumptions and to change them during good times. A marketing audit conducted when things are going well can often help make a good situation even better and also indicate changes needed to prevent things from turning sour.

The above ideas on a marketing audit can be brought together into a single definition:

> A marketing audit is a *comprehensive, systematic, independent,* and *periodic* examination of a company's — or business unit's — marketing environment, objectives, strategies, and activities with a view of determining problem areas and opportunities and recommending a plan of action to improve the company's marketing performance.

What Is the Marketing Audit Process?

How is a marketing audit performed? Marketing auditing follows the simple three-step procedure shown in Figure 6.1.

Setting the Objectives and Scope

The first step calls for a meeting between the company officer(s) and a potential auditor to explore the nature of the marketing operations and the potential value of a marketing audit. If the company officer is convinced of the potential benefits of a marketing audit, he and the auditor have to work out an agreement on the objectives, coverage, depth, data sources, report format, and the time period for the audit.

FIGURE 6.1   Steps in a Marketing Audit

Consider the following actual case. A plumbing and heating supplies wholesaler with three branches invited a marketing consultant to prepare an audit of its overall marketing policies and operations. Four major objectives were set for the audit:

- determine how the market views the company and its competitors,
- recommend a pricing policy,
- develop a product evaluation system,
- determine how to improve the sales activity in terms of the deployment of the sales force, the level and type of compensation, the measurement of performance, and the addition of new salesmen.

Furthermore, the audit would cover the marketing operations of the company as a whole and the operations of each of the three branches, with particular attention to one of the branches. The audit would focus on the marketing operations but also include a review of the purchasing and inventory systems since they intimately affect marketing performance.

The company would furnish the auditor with published and private data on the industry. In addition, the auditor would contact suppliers of manufactured plumbing supplies for additional market data and contact wholesalers outside the company's market area to gain further information on wholesale plumbing and heating operations. The auditor would interview all the key corporate and branch management, sales and purchasing personnel, and would ride with several of those salesmen on their calls. Finally, the auditor would interview a sample of the major plumbing and heating contractor customers in the market areas of the two largest branches.

It was decided that the report format would consist of a draft report of conclusions and recommendations to be reviewed by the president and vice-president of marketing, and then delivered to the executive committee which included the three branch managers. Finally, it was decided that the audit findings would be ready to present within six to eight weeks.

Gathering the Data

The bulk of an auditor's time is spent in gathering data. Although we talk of a single auditor, an audit team is usually involved when the project is large. A detailed plan as to who is to be interviewed by whom, the questions to be asked, the time and place of contact, and so on, has to be carefully prepared so that auditing time and cost are kept to a minimum. Daily reports of the interviews are to be written up and reviewed so that the individual or team can spot new areas requiring exploration, while data are still being gathered.

The cardinal rule in data collection is not to rely solely for data and opinion on those being audited. Customers often turn out to be the key group to interview. Many companies do not really understand how their customers see them and their competitors, nor do they fully understand customer needs. This is vividly demonstrated in Table 6.1, which shows the results of asking end users, company salesmen, and company marketing personnel for their views of the importance of different factors affecting the user's selection of a manufacturer. According to the table, customers look first and foremost at the quality of technical support services, followed by prompt delivery, followed by quick response to customer needs. Company salesmen think that company reputation, however, is the most im-

TABLE 6.1   Factors in the Selection of a Manufacturer

FACTOR	ALL USERS RANK	COMPANY SALESMEN RANK	COMPANY NONSALES PERSONNEL RANK
Reputation	5	①	4
Extension of Credit	9	11	9
Sales Representatives	8	5	7
Technical Support Services	①	△3	6
Literature and Manuals	11	10	11
Prompt Delivery	[2]	4	5
Quick Response to Customer Needs	△3	[2]	△3
Product Price	6	6	①
Personal Relationships	10	7	8
Complete Product Line	7	9	10
Product Quality	4	8	[2]

SOURCE: *Marketing and Distribution Audit, A Service of Decision Sciences Corporation,* p. 32. Used with permission of the Decision Sciences Corporation.

portant factor in customer choice, followed by quick response to customer needs and technical support services. Those who plan marketing strategy have a different opinion. They see company price and product quality as the two major factors in buyer choice, followed by quick response to customer needs. Clearly, there is lack of consonance between what buyers say they want, what company salesmen are responding to, and what company marketing planners are emphasizing. One of the major contributions of marketing auditors is to expose these discrepancies and suggest ways to improve marketing consensus.

Preparing and Presenting the Report

The marketing auditor will be developing tentative conclusions as the data comes in. It is a sound procedure for him to meet once or twice with the company officer before the data collection ends to outline some initial findings to see what reactions and suggestions they produce.

When the data gathering phase is over, the marketing auditor prepares notes for a visual and verbal presentation to the company officer or small group who hired him. The presentation consists of restating the objectives, showing the main findings, and presenting the major recommendations. Then, the auditor is ready to write the final report, which is largely a matter of putting the visual and verbal material into a good written communication. The company officer(s) will usually ask the auditor to present the report to other groups in the company. If the report calls for deep debate and action, the various groups hearing the report should organize into subcommittees to do follow-up work with another meeting to take place some weeks later. The most valuable part of the marketing audit often lies not so much in the auditor's specific recommendations but in the process that the managers of the company begin to go through to assimilate, debate, and develop their own concept of the needed marketing action.

Marketing Audit Procedures for an Inside Audit

Companies that conduct internal marketing audits show interesting variations from the procedures just outlined. International Telephone and Telegraph, for example, has a history of forming corporate teams and sending them into weak divisions to do a complete business audit, with a heavy emphasis on the marketing component. Some teams stay on the job, often taking over the management.

General Electric's corporate consulting division offers help to various divisions on their marketing problems. One of its services is a marketing audit in the sense of a broad, independent, systematic look at the marketing picture in a division. However, the corporate consulting division gets few requests for a marketing audit as such. Most of the requests are for specific marketing studies or problem-solving assistance.

The 3M Company uses a very interesting and unusual internal marketing plan audit procedure. A marketing plan audit office with a small staff is located at corporate headquarters. The main purpose of the 3M marketing plan audit is to help the divisional marketing manager improve the marketing planning function, as well as come up with better strategies and tactics. A divisional marketing manager phones the marketing plan audit office and invites an audit. There is an agreement that only he will see the results and it is up to him whether he wants wider distribution.

The audit centers around a marketing plan for a product or product line that the marketing manager is preparing for the coming year. This plan is reviewed at a personal presentation by a special team of six company marketing executives invited by the marketing plan audit office. A new team is formed for each new audit. An effort is made to seek out those persons within 3M (but not in the audited division) who can bring the best experience to bear on the particular plan's problems and opportunities. A team typically consists of a marketing manager from another division, a national salesmanager, a marketing executive with a technical background, a few others close to the type of problems found in the audited plan, and another person who is totally unfamiliar with the market, the product, or the major marketing techniques being used in the plan. This person usually raises some important points others forget to raise, or do not ask because "everyone probably knows about that anyway."

The six auditors are supplied with a summary of the marketing manager's plan about ten days before an official meeting is held to review the plan. On the audit day, the six auditors, the head of the audit office, and the divisional marketing manager gather at 8:30 A.M. The marketing manager makes a presentation for about an hour describing the division's competitive situation, the long-run strategy, and the planned tactics. The auditors proceed to ask hard questions and debate certain points with the marketing manager and each other. Before the meeting ends that day, the auditors are each asked to fill out a marketing plan evaluation form consisting of questions that are accompanied by numerical rating scales and room for comments.

These evaluations are analyzed and summarized after the meeting. Then the head of the audit office arranges a meeting with the divisional marketing manager and presents the highlights of the auditor's findings and recommendations. It is then up to the marketing manager to take the next steps.

Components of the Marketing Audit

A major principle in marketing audits is to start with the marketplace first and explore the changes that are taking place and what they imply in the way of problems and opportunities. Then the auditor moves to examine the company's marketing objectives and strategies, organization, and systems. Finally he may move to examine one or two key functions in more detail that are central to the marketing performance of that company. However, some companies ask for less than the full range of auditing steps in order to obtain initial results before commissioning further work. The company may ask for a marketing environment audit, and if satisfied, then ask for a marketing strategy audit. Or it might ask for a marketing organization audit first, and later ask for a marketing environment audit.

We view a full marketing audit as having six major components, each having a semiautonomous status if a company wants less than a full marketing audit. The six components and their logical diagnostic sequence are discussed below. The major auditing questions connected with these components are gathered together in Appendix A at the end of this article.

Marketing Environment Audit

By marketing environment, we mean both the *macro-environment* surrounding the industry and the *task environment* in which the organization intimately operates. The macro-environment consists of the large-scale forces and factors influencing the company's future over which the company has very little control. These forces are normally divided into economic-demographic factors, technological factors, political-legal factors, and social-cultural factors. The marketing auditor's task is to assess the key trends and their implications for company marketing action. However, if the company has a good long-range forecasting department, then there is less of a need for a macro-environment audit.

The marketing auditor may play a more critical role in auditing the company's task environment. The task environment consists of markets, customers, competitors, distributors and dealers, suppliers, and marketing facilitators. The marketing auditor can make a contribution by going out into the field and interviewing various parties to assess their current thinking and attitudes and bringing them to the attention of management.

Marketing Strategy Audit

The marketing auditor then proceeds to consider whether the company's marketing strategy is well-postured in the light of the opportunities and problems facing the company. The starting point for the marketing strategy audit is the corporate goals and objectives followed by the marketing objectives. The auditor may find the objectives to be poorly stated, or he may find them to be well-stated but inappropriate given the company's resources and opportunities. For example, a chemical company had set a sales growth objective for a particular product line at 15 percent. However, the total market showed no growth and competition was fierce. Here the auditor questioned the basic sales growth objective for that product line. He proposed that the product line be reconsidered for a maintenance or harvest objective at best and that the company should look for growth elsewhere.

Even when a growth objective is warranted, the auditor will want to consider whether management has chosen the best strategy to achieve that growth.

Marketing Organization Audit

A complete marketing audit would have to cover the question of the effectiveness of the marketing and sales organization, as well as the quality of interaction between marketing and other key management functions such as manufacturing, finance, purchasing, and research and development.

At critical times, a company's marketing organization must be revised to achieve greater effectiveness within the company and in the marketplace. Companies without product management systems will want to consider introducing them, companies with these systems may want to consider dropping them, or trying product teams instead. Companies may want to redefine the role concept of a product manager from being a promotional manager (concerned primarily with volume) to a business manager (concerned primarily with profit). There is the issue of whether decision-making responsibility should be moved up from the brand level to the product level. There is the perennial question of how to make the organization more market-responsive including the possibility of replacing product divisions with market-centered divisions. Finally, sales organizations often do not fully understand marketing. In the words of one vice-president of marketing: "It takes about five years for us to train sales managers to think marketing."

Marketing Systems Audit

A full marketing audit then turns to examine the various systems being used by marketing management to gather information, plan, and control the marketing operation. The issue is not the company's marketing strategy or organization per se but rather the procedures used in some or all of the following systems: sales forecasting, sales goal and quota setting, marketing planning, marketing control, inventory control, order processing, physical distribution, new products development, and product pruning.

The marketing audit may reveal that marketing is being carried on without adequate systems of planning, implementation, and control. An audit of a consumer products division of a large company revealed that decisions about which products to carry and which to eliminate were made by the head of the division on the basis of his intuitive feeling with little information or analysis to guide the decisions. The auditor recommended the introduction of a new product screening system for new products and an improved sales control system for existing products. He also observed that the division prepared budgets but did not carry out formal marketing planning and hardly any research into the market. He recommended that the division establish a formal marketing planning system as soon as possible.

Marketing Productivity Audit

A full marketing audit also includes an effort to examine key accounting data to determine where the company is making its real profits and what, if any, marketing costs could be trimmed. Decision Sciences Corporation, for example, starts its marketing audit by looking at the accounting figures on sales and associated costs of sales. Using marketing cost accounting principles,[2] it seeks to measure the marginal profit contribution of different products, end user segments, marketing channels, and sales territories.

We might argue that the firm's own controller or accountant should do the job of providing management with the results of marketing cost analysis. A handful of firms have created the job position of marketing controllers who report to financial controllers and spend their time looking at the productivity and validity of various marketing costs. Where an organization is doing a good job of marketing cost analysis, it does not need a marketing auditor to study the same. But most companies do not do careful marketing cost analysis. Here a marketing auditor can pay his way by simply exposing certain economic and cost relations which indicate waste or conceal unexploited marketing opportunities.

Zero-based budgeting[3] is another tool for investigating and improving marketing productivity. In normal budgeting, top management allots to each business unit a percentage increase (or decrease) of what it got last time. The question is not raised whether that basic budget level still makes sense. The manager of an operation should be asked what he would basically need if he started his operation from scratch and what it would cost. What would he need next and what would it cost? In this way, a budget is built from the ground up reflecting the true needs of the operation. When this was applied to a technical sales group within a large industrial goods company, it became clear that the company had three or four extra technical salesmen on its payroll. The manager admitted to the redundancy but argued if a business upturn came, these men would be needed to tap the potential. In the meantime, they were carried on the payroll for two years in the expectation of a business upturn.

Marketing Function Audit

The work done to this point might begin to point to certain key marketing functions which are performing poorly. The auditor might spot, for example, sales force problems that go very deep. Or he might observe that advertising budgets are prepared in an arbitrary fashion and such things as advertising themes, media, and timing are not evaluated for their effectiveness. In these and other cases, the issue becomes one of notifying management of the desirability of one or more marketing function audits if management agrees.

Which Companies Can Benefit Most from a Marketing Audit?

All companies can benefit from a competent audit of their marketing operations. However, a marketing audit is likely to yield the highest payoff in the following companies and situations:

Production-Oriented and Technical-Oriented Companies. Many manufacturing companies have their start in a love affair with a certain product. Further products are added that appeal to the technical interests of management, usually with insufficient attention paid to their market potential. The feeling in these companies is that marketing is paid to sell what the company decides to make. After some failures with its "better mousetraps," management starts getting interested in shifting to a market orientation. But this calls for more than a simple declaration by top management to study and serve the customer's needs. It calls for a great number of organizational and attitudinal changes that must be introduced carefully and convincingly. An auditor can perform an important service in recognizing that a company's problem lies in its production orientation, and in guiding management toward a market orientation.

Troubled Divisions. Multidivision companies usually have some troubled divisions. Top management may decide to use an auditor to assess the situation in a troubled division rather than rely solely on the division management's interpretation of the problem.

High Performing Divisions. Multidivision companies might want an audit of their top dollar divisions to make sure that they are reaching their highest potential, and are not on the verge of a sudden reversal. Such an audit may also yield insights into how to improve marketing in other divisions.

Young Companies. Marketing audits of emerging small companies or young divisions of large companies can help to lay down a solid marketing approach at a time when management faces a great degree of market inexperience.

Nonprofit Organizations. Administrators of colleges, museums, hospitals, social agencies, and churches are beginning to think in marketing terms, and the marketing audit can serve a useful educational as well as diagnostic purpose.

What Are the Problems and Pitfalls of Marketing Audits?

While the foregoing has stressed the positive aspects of marketing audits and their utility in a variety of situations, it is important to note some of the problems and pitfalls of the marketing audit process. Problems can occur in the objective-setting step, the data collection step, or the report presentation step.

Setting Objectives

When the marketing audit effort is being designed by the auditor and the company officer who commissioned the audit, several problems will be encountered. For one thing, the objectives set for the audit are based upon the company officer's and auditor's best *a priori* notions of what the key problem areas are for the audit to highlight. However, new problem areas may emerge once the auditor begins to learn more about the company. The original set of objectives should not constrain the auditor from shifting his priorities of investigation.

Similarly, it may be necessary for the auditor to use different sources of information than envisioned at the start of the audit. In some cases this may be because some information sources he had counted on became unavailable. In one marketing audit, the auditor had planned to speak to a sample of customers for the company's electro-mechanical devices, but the company officer who hired him would not permit him to do so. In other cases, a valuable new source of information may arise that was not recognized at the start of the audit. For example, the auditor for an air brake system manufacturer found as a valuable source of market intelligence a long-established manufacturers' representatives firm that approached the company after the audit had begun.

Another consideration at the objective-setting stage of the audit is that the management most affected by the audit must have full knowledge of the purposes and scope of the audit. Audits go much more smoothly when the executive who calls in the auditor either brings the affected management into the design stage, or at least has a general introductory meeting where the auditor explains his procedures and answers questions from the people in the affected business.

Data Collection

Despite reassurances by the auditor and the executive who brought him in, there will still be some managers in the affected business who will feel threatened by the auditor. The auditor must expect this, and realize that an individual's fears and biases may color his statements in an interview.

From the onset of the audit, the auditor must guarantee and maintain confidentiality of each individual's comments. In many audits, personnel in the company will see the audit as a vehicle for unloading their negative feelings about the company or other individuals. The auditor can learn a lot from these comments, but he must protect the individuals who make them. The auditor must question interviewees in a highly professional manner to build their confidence in him, or else they will not be entirely honest in their statements.

Another area of concern during the information collection step is the degree to which the company executive who brought in the auditor will try to guide the audit. It will be necessary for this officer and the auditor to strike a balance in which the executive provides some direction, but not too much. While overcontrol is the more likely excess of the executive, it is possible to undercontrol. When the auditor and the company executive do not have open and frequent lines of communication during the audit, it is possible that the auditor may place more emphasis on some areas and less on others than the executive might have desired. Therefore, it is the responsibility of both the auditor and the executive who brought him in to communicate frequently during the audit.

Report Presentation

One of the biggest problems in marketing auditing is that the executive who brings in the auditor, or the people in the business being audited, may have higher expectations about what the audit will do for the company than the actual report seems to offer. In only the most extreme circumstances will the auditor develop surprising panaceas or propose startling new opportunities for the company. More likely, the main value of his report will be that it places priorities on ideas and directions for the company, many of which have already been considered by some people within the audited organization. In most successful audits, the auditor, in his recommendations, makes a skillful combination of his general and technical marketing background (e.g., designs of salesman's compensation systems, his ability to measure the size and potential of markets) with some opportunistic ideas that people in the audited organization have already considered, but do not know how much importance to place upon them. However, it is only in the company's implementation of the recommendations that the payoff to the company will come.

Another problem at the conclusion of the audit stems from the fact that most audits seem to result in organizational changes. Organizational changes are a common outcome because the audit usually identifies new tasks to be accomplished and new tasks demand people to do them. One thing the auditor and the executive who brought him in must recognize, however, is that organizational promotions and demotions are exclusively the executive's decision. It is the executive who has to live with the changes once the auditor has gone, not the auditor. Therefore, the executive should not be lulled into thinking that organizational moves are any easier because the auditor may have recommended them.

The final problem, and this is one facing the auditor, is that important parts of an audit may be implemented incorrectly, or not implemented at all, by the executive who commissioned the audit. Non-implementation of key parts of the audit undermines the whole effectiveness of the audit.

Summary

The marketing audit is one important answer to the problem of evaluating the marketing performance of a company or one of its business units. Marketing audits are distinguished from other marketing exercises in being *comprehensive, independent, systematic,* and *periodic.* A full marketing audit would cover the company's (or division's) external environment, objectives, strategies, organization, systems, and functions. If the audit covers only one function, such as sales management or advertising, it is best described as a marketing function audit rather than a marketing audit. If the exercise is to solve a current problem, such as entering a market, setting a price, or developing a package, then it is not an audit at all.

The marketing audit is carried out in three steps: developing an agreement as to objectives and scope; collecting the data; and presenting the report. The audit can be performed by a competent outside consultant or by a company auditing office at headquarters.

The possible findings of an audit include detecting unclear or inappropriate marketing objectives, inappropriate strategies, inappropriate levels of marketing expenditures, needed improvements in organization, and needed improvements in systems for marketing information, planning, and control. Companies that are most likely to benefit from a marketing audit include production-oriented companies, companies with troubled or highly vulnerable divisions, young companies, and nonprofit organizations.

Many companies today are finding that their premises for marketing strategy are growing obsolete in the face of a rapidly changing environment. This is happening to company giants such as General Motors and Sears as well as smaller firms that have not provided a mechanism for recycling their marketing strategy. The marketing audit is not the full answer to marketing strategy recycling but does offer one major mechanism for pursuing this desirable and necessary task.

Appendix A — Components of a Marketing Audit

The Marketing Environment Audit

I. Macro-Environment

Economic-Demographic
1. What does the company expect in the way of inflation, material short-ages, unemployment, and credit availability in the short run, inter-mediate run, and long run?
2. What effect will forecasted trends in the size, age distribution, and regional distribution of population have on the business?

Technology
1. What major changes are occurring in product technology? In process technology?
2. What are the major generic substitutes that might replace this product?

Political-Legal
1. What laws are being proposed that may affect marketing strategy and tactics?
2. What federal, state, and local agency actions should be watched? What is happening in the areas of pollution control, equal employment op-portunity, product safety, advertising, price control, etc., that is rele-vant to marketing planning?

Social-Cultural
1. What attitudes is the public taking toward business and toward prod-ucts such as those produced by the company?
2. What changes are occurring in consumer life-styles and values that have a bearing on the company's target markets and marketing methods?

II. Task Environment

Markets
1. What is happening to market size, growth, geographical distribution, and profits?
2. What are the major market segments? What are their expected rates of growth? Which are high opportunity and low opportunity segments?

Customers
1. How do current customers and prospects rate the company and its competitors, particularly with respect to reputation, product quality, service, sales force, and price?
2. How do different classes of customers make their buying decisions?

3. What are the evolving needs and satisfactions being sought by the buyers in this market?

Competitors
1. Who are the major competitors? What are the objectives and strategies of each major competitor? What are their strengths and weaknesses? What are the sizes and trends in market shares?
2. What trends can be foreseen in future competition and substitutes for this product?

Distribution and Dealers
1. What are the main trade channels bringing products to customers?
2. What are the efficiency levels and growth potentials of the different trade channels?

Suppliers
1. What is the outlook for the availability of different key resources used in production?
2. What trends are occurring among suppliers in their pattern of selling?

Facilitators
1. What is the outlook for the cost and availability of transportation services?
2. What is the outlook for the cost and availability of warehousing facilities?
3. What is the outlook for the cost and availability of financial resources?
4. How effectively is the advertising agency performing? What trends are occurring in advertising agency services?

Marketing Strategy Audit

Marketing Objectives
1. Are the corporate objectives clearly stated and do they lead logically to the marketing objectives?
2. Are the marketing objectives stated in a clear form to guide marketing planning and subsequent performance measurement?
3. Are the marketing objectives appropriate, given the company's competitive position, resources, and opportunities? Is the appropriate strategic objective to build, hold, harvest, or terminate this business?

Strategy
1. What is the core marketing strategy for achieving the objectives? Is it a sound marketing strategy?
2. Are enough resources (or too much resources) budgeted to accomplish the marketing objectives?

3. Are the marketing resources allocated optimally to prime market segments, territories, and products of the organization?
4. Are the marketing resources allocated optimally to the major elements of the marketing mix, i.e., product quality, service, sales force, advertising, promotion, and distribution?

Marketing Organization Audit

Formal Structure
1. Is there a high-level marketing officer with adequate authority and responsibility over those company activities that affect the customer's satisfaction?
2. Are the marketing responsibilities optimally structured along functional product, end user, and territorial lines?

Functional Efficiency
1. Are there good communication and working relations between marketing and sales?
2. Is the product management system working effectively? Are the product managers able to plan profits or only sales volume?
3. Are there any groups in marketing that need more training, motivation, supervision, or evaluation?

Interface Efficiency
1. Are there any problems between marketing and manufacturing that need attention?
2. What about marketing and R&D?
3. What about marketing and financial management?
4. What about marketing and purchasing?

Marketing Systems Audit

Marketing Information System
1. Is the marketing intelligence system producing accurate, sufficient, and timely information about developments in the marketplace?
2. Is marketing research being adequately used by company decision makers?

Marketing Planning System
1. Is the marketing planning system well-conceived and effective?
2. Is sales forecasting and market potential measurement soundly carried out?
3. Are sales quotas set on a proper basis?

Marketing Control System
1. Are the control procedures (monthly, quarterly, etc.) adequate to insure that the annual plan objectives are being achieved?
2. Is provision made to analyze periodically the profitability of different products, markets, territories, and channels of distribution?
3. Is provision made to examine and validate periodically various marketing costs?

New Product Development System
1. Is the company well-organized to gather, generate, and screen new product ideas?
2. Does the company do adequate concept research and business analysis before investing heavily in a new idea?
3. Does the company carry out adequate product and market testing before launching a new product?

Marketing Productivity Audit

Profitability Analysis
1. What is the profitability of the company's different products, served markets, territories, and channels of distribution?
2. Should the company enter, expand, contract, or withdraw from any business segments and what would be the short- and long-run profit consequences?

Cost-Effectiveness Analysis
1. Do any marketing activities seem to have excessive costs? Are these costs valid? Can cost-reducing steps be taken?

Marketing Function Audit

Products
1. What are the product line objectives? Are these objectives sound? Is the current product line meeting these objectives?
2. Are there particular products that should be phased out?
3. Are there new products that are worth adding?
4. Are any products able to benefit from quality, feature, or style improvements?

Price
1. What are the pricing objectives, policies, strategies, and procedures? To what extent are prices set on sound cost, demand, and competitive criteria?

2. Do the customers see the company's prices as being in line or out of line with the perceived value of its offer?

3. Does the company use price promotions effectively?

Distribution
1. What are the distribution objectives and strategies?
2. Is there adequate market coverage and service?
3. Should the company consider changing its degree of reliance on distributors, sales reps, and direct selling?

Sales Force
1. What are the organization's sales force objectives?
2. Is the sales force large enough to accomplish the company's objectives?
3. Is the sales force organized along the proper principle(s) of specialization (territory, market, product)?
4. Does the sales force show high morale, ability, and effort? Are they sufficiently trained and incentivized?
5. Are the procedures adequate for setting quotas and evaluating performances?
6. How is the company's sales force perceived in relation to competitors' sales forces?

Advertising, Promotion, and Publicity
1. What are the organization's advertising objectives? Are they sound?
2. Is the right amount being spent on advertising? How is the budget determined?
3. Are the ad themes and copy effective? What do customers and the public think about the advertising?
4. Are the advertising media well chosen?
5. Is sales promotion used effectively?
6. Is there a well-conceived publicity program?

Notes

1. Many useful checklist questions for marketers are found in C. Eldridge, *The Management of the Marketing Function* (New York: Association of National Advertisers, 1967).
2. See P. Kotler, *Marketing Management Analysis, Planning and Control* (Englewood Cliffs, N.J.: Prentice-Hall, Inc., 1976), pp. 457–462.
3. See P. J. Stonich, "Zero-Base Planning — A Management Tool," *Managerial Planning*, July–August 1976, pp. 1–4.

Concepts for Evaluating Strategic Market Opportunities

IN THE INTRODUCTORY SECTION, strategic marketing decisions were characterized as investment decisions — decisions concerning the allocation of resources across product-market alternatives to achieve a sustainable competitive advantage. Financial theory provides some classic capital budgeting methods for evaluating such investment opportunities. While these methods typically are applied to decisions concerning the purchase of revenue-producing assets, they can also be used to make strategic marketing decisions.

The capital budgeting approach, illustrated in Article 7 in this section, is conceptually appealing: if this approach is used to make investment decisions, the firm will realize its objective of maximizing stockholder wealth. However, the capital budgeting approach has some practical limitations, which have led to the consideration of additional factors in evaluating strategic opportunities. The remaining articles in this section discuss two of these factors: the experience curve and the importance of market share; and the product life cycle. In the following paragraphs, we review the traditional capital budgeting approach for evaluating investment opportunities. After discussing the limitations of this approach, we look at the concepts of the experience curve and the product life cycle.

Traditional Capital Budgeting

Strategic marketing decisions parallel the investment decisions encountered in capital budgeting.[1] A business faces a number of product-markets to which it can allocate resources. The business must decide the amount of resources to allocate to each product-market opportunity. The basis for making these decisions is the expected yield from the resources allocated.

Company Objective

Most financial theorists feel that the appropriate objective for a company, as it makes investment decisions, is to maximize stockholder wealth.[2] This objective was adopted because it is consistent with maximizing social welfare. James Van Horne described it this way: the use of any other objective by the firm "is likely to result in the sub-optimal allocation of funds and therefore leads to less than optimal capital formation and growth in the economy as well as less than optimal level of economic want satisfaction."[3]

The objective of maximizing stockholder wealth is superior to the traditional profit maximization objective because profit maximization fails to consider the timing of investments and returns; in addition, it is not characterized by a unique measure of profits, because different accounting procedures can produce a wide variety of profit levels.

Capital Budgeting Approach

The conventional method for allocating resources in a company is for individuals, typically at an operating level, to make investment proposals to a person or group in charge of capital budgeting. These proposals are accompanied by estimates of the investment required and the expected cash flows or profits to be generated. These proposals are then evaluated using a financial criterion, such as net present value. Based on this evaluation, funds are allocated to the promising proposals.

Evaluating Strategic Opportunities Using the CAPM

Article 7, "An Application of the Capital Asset Pricing Model to Divisional Required Returns" by James Van Horne, illustrates how risk can be incorporated into the net present value (NPV) calculation used to evaluate investment opportunities. While the specific example in the article deals with a capital expansion program, the technique can be easily applied to the evaluation of new product proposals, major sales force expansion decisions, changes in distribution channels, and other marketing strategies and tactics.

An interesting aspect of the CAPM (capital asset pricing model) approach outlined in this article concerns its implications for the diversification of a company's portfolio of product-market investments. The CAPM suggests that managers acting in the shareholders' interest should evaluate opportunities individually, adjusting the discount rate in accordance with each opportunity's level of systematic risk. Even though there is a popular notion that companies should invest in a diversified portfolio of product-market opportunities to reduce risk or uncertainty, the CAPM approach suggests that such diversification by the firm will not maximize stockholder wealth. Individual investors can diversify their portfolios more efficiently than the firm. Thus the manager should be simply concerned with achieving an appropriate return for a given risk level, and not with minimizing the risks of different projects.

The marketing strategy undertaken by the Kellogg Company is consistent with this approach. In 1978, 75 percent of Kellogg's revenues and 80 percent of its profits came from the cereal market. The market faced the following significant risks: consumer groups were denouncing the company's presweetened cereals; the FTC was mounting antitrust legislation against the company; and the proportion of children, the large cereal consumers, was declining in the population. Competitors General Mills and General Foods also faced this high risk environment and diversified into other foods and products. However, Kellogg's made the strategic decision to continue major investments in cereal products, and has out-performed the competition. Kellogg's was able to achieve a high return on their cereal investment strategy that was commensurate with the risks associated with this strategy.[4]

Drawbacks of the Capital Budgeting Approach

While the capital budgeting approach has strong theoretical support, some practical problems may arise when this approach is used as the sole guide for strategic investment decisions.[5] First, the procedure may limit the range of opportunities considered. In addition, the approach may result in focusing attention on a calculation rather than on the assumptions underlying the calculations. Finally, the capital budgeting approach tends to assume that the status quo will be maintained if a proposal is rejected, but this assumption may be unwarranted. The rejection of a new strategic direction may result in a gradual deterioration of the present position.

Limited Focus.   When a capital budgeting approach is used, the strategic proposals are typically generated by line managers, such as brand managers or sales managers. Proposals generated by these operating managers tend to be narrowly focusing on modifications to existing strategic directions. For example, a brand manager may propose a significant increase in support for his or her brand, without considering the positive or negative effects of such a proposal on other brands. It is unlikely that a brand manager would propose a major divestment of a group of brands because of a shift in the environment.

Lack of Attention to Assumptions.   To develop a capital budgeting proposal, all the benefits and costs associated with the proposed need to be quantified. The mere process of calculating a net present value for each opportunity may focus attention on selecting an alternative with the highest net present value rather than on questioning the assumptions on which the calculations are based. These assumptions are critical since there are significant uncertainties in forecasting investment levels, revenues, and costs over a long-term, strategic time period. In addition, there are likely to be biases in these forecasts when the proposals are generated by managers with a vested interest in the strategic decision.

Any manager can develop a proposal showing a positive net present value. The crucial question is not whether the NPV is positive but what justifies the positive NPV? What is the nature of the strategic investment opportunity that will result in a positive NPV? This question has led to the search for the critical factors that should be used to evaluate strategic opportunities. The remaining articles in this section examine two important factors — the experience that a company has acquired in a product-market and the life cycle stage of the product-market.

Experience Curves and Market Share

One of the major concepts used to evaluate strategic market opportunities is the experience curve. This concept suggests that the cost per unit of manufacturing and marketing a product declines as a function of the number of units produced — the cumulative production volume. This phenomenon was observed over forty years ago with respect to labor costs,[6] but the Boston Consulting Group has more recently extended the concept to all costs — direct labor, overhead, distribution, and selling. Article 8, Barry Hedley's "A Fundamental Approach to Strategy Development," provides evidence of the experience curve and discusses its implications.

The principal implication of the experience curve phenomenon concerns the setting of marketing objectives. As discussed in the Hedley article, since costs decline with accumulated experience, the company with the most accumulated experience will have the lowest costs, the highest margins, and the highest profits. The level of the market share is usually proportional to the level of accumulated experience. Thus, the profitability of a company relative to its competitors will be related to its relative market share. The company that dominates a product-market will make more money than its competitors. Hence market share becomes a key strategic objective.

The relationship between market share and profitability has been demonstrated empirically. Analyses of over 1,000 business units have shown a significant relationship among these elements: return on investment (ROI), relative market share, and absolute market share.[7] These findings, summarized in Figure 12.1 on page 232, clearly indicate that high share businesses are more profitable than low share businesses. Additional analyses suggest that high share businesses have lower costs. These findings support the experience curve explanation of the profitability–market share relationship, supplanting any explanation claiming that market power had permitted monopolistic pricing.

Is Market Share Really So Important?

The experience curve concept and market share play an important role in the strategic marketing planning models which we shall examine in Section IV of this book. These models were the cornerstone of strategic marketing in the 1970s; however, the role of market share is now being questioned:

> The sweeping downward arc of the experience curve hung like a guiding constellation over the business landscape of the 1970s. What's happening now, though, is that the curve is being consigned to a much reduced place in the firmament of strategic concepts. With it is going a good bit of the importance originally attached to market share.[8]

Some of the reasons for the revaluation of the role of market share[9] in strategy formulation are these: (1) the importance of shared costs, (2) the problems that exist in defining the relevant market, (3) the role of noncost factors in strategy development, (4) the costs of gaining market share, and (5) the low explained variance of the market share–ROI relationship.[10]

Shared Costs.   Frequently, a company's relative market share is not a good indicator of the company's cost advantage vis-à-vis present and potential competitors. For example, Bowmar was an early market leader in hand-held calculators. Although Bowmar had the highest market share and was furthest down the experience curve for hand-held calculators, Texas Instruments (TI) actually had the lowest manufacturing costs, even though it was a late entrant into the market. TI had this cost advantage because it had vast experience in manufacturing semiconductor components and component costs were low, not because it had an efficient manufacturing process. These components account for 80 percent of the cost of manufacturing calculators. Thus, when determining which manufacturer has the cost advantage, one discovers that relative market share does not provide enough information. It is necessary to consider also each competitor's related experience — the costs shared between the product of interest and other products manufactured and marketed by the firm. The existence of shared costs emphasizes the importance of selecting the appropriate definition of a product-market when drawing an experience curve or determining market share.

Definition of Relevant Market.   Clearly, many companies with low market shares are quite profitable. For example, Mercedes-Benz is a successful automobile manufacturer, but is hardly the market leader in automobiles. This example suggests that the relevant market for Mercedes-Benz may be just a segment of the automobile market — the luxury car market. We begin to see that considerable thought and creativity must be directed toward defining the relevant product-market for an experience curve and toward determining market position.

Overemphasis on Cost Advantage.   Another problem with establishing the experience curve as a cornerstone of marketing strategy is that the experience curve concept focuses attention on costs to the exclusion of other strategic factors. There are a number of noncost strategic advantages that a company can develop — such as patent protection, loyal distribution channels, and a consumer franchise.

By focusing solely on reducing costs, a firm can lose sight of market needs. There is no strategic benefit in being the lowest cost manufacturer of a product no one wants. Article 9, "Limits of the Learning Curve," indicates how excessive concern with the experience curve reduced the ability of the Ford Motor Company to adapt to a changing environment, leaving Ford vulnerable to domination by General Motors in the 1930s.

Cost of Gaining Market Share.   The evidence of the relationship between market share and ROI (see Figure 12.1) demonstrates the benefits associated with high market share. Companies with high share make more money. However, these results do not indicate conclusively whether companies should make investments to gain market share. Perhaps, the benefit of achieving a high market share does not justify the level of investment in the development and promotion of a product that is needed to achieve the position. For example, *Fortune* reports that Du Pont cut prices for years to achieve a dominant position in the manufacture of Nylon, however, Du Pont was never able to make significant profits.[11]

Electronic Calculators: An Illustration

The experience curve concept emphasizes that managers should examine the cost advantage of their business in a product-market relative to their competition. It is important to realize that product-markets evolve over time. Changes in the nature of a product-market may be caused by a wide variety of factors, such as new customer needs and product technologies. When these changes arise, the relative importance of the various cost elements in a product also may change. Since the nature of shared costs among competitors differs, the relative cost advantage of competitors will differ as major cost elements become more or less important. The electronic calculator market, described in Table III.1, illustrates how different cost elements and competitors prevail during the evaluation of the product market.

TABLE III.1   The Changing Competitive Balance in the Electronic Calculator Market

	MAJOR COST ELEMENTS	DOMINANT COMPETITORS
Phase 1	Semiconductors (discrete devices)	U.S. (e.g., Wang)
Phase 2	Component assembly	Overseas (e.g., Sharp and Casio)
Phase 3	Integrated circuits (high hourly labor costs not significant)	U.S. (e.g., Texas Instruments)
Phase 4	(A) Sophisticated: integrated circuit consti- tutes much of value-added	U.S. (e.g., Texas Instruments and Hewlett-Packard)
	(B) Simple (4-function): keyboard assembly is large part of value-added	Overseas production
Phase 5	Assembly, distribution, and product differentiation	Unresolved

From Table III.1 we can learn that the evolutionary phase of a product-market is an important consideration in evaluating strategic market opportunity. For example, a key ingredient for success in the electronic calculator market during Phase 2 was the capability to assemble discrete semiconductors at low cost. However, a technological change, the availability of integrated circuits, shifted the product-market to Phase 3. A competitive advantage in low-cost assembly was no longer an important consideration in evaluating this product-market opportunity. The key consideration became capability in integrated circuit design, fabrication, and production. Product life cycle analyses is one method for anticipating the evolution of product markets.

Product Life Cycle

The product life cycle (PLC) is a concept used to describe and predict product-market evolution, such as the evolution of the electronic calculator market described previously.[12] In fact Charles Hofer makes this suggestion: "The most fundamental variable in determining an appropriate strategy is the stage of the product life cycle."[13] J. E. Smallwood wrote Article 10, "The Product Life Cycle: A Key to Strategic Marketing Planning," in which he presents the PLC concept and discusses how the strategic allocation of resources should vary over the life cycle.

From a strategic perspective, the PLC concept proposes that product-markets go through an inevitable evolution from introduction (birth)

through growth and maturity to decline (death). The effectiveness of marketing variables changes across the stages because of differences in consumer knowledge, market structure, and competitive behavior at the various stages. The PLC concept suggests that if strategic investments are made during the introductory and early growth phases, returns will accrue during the late growth and maturity phases. Investments are discouraged during the maturity phase because intense competition during this phase will not permit the firm to achieve appropriate returns. In contrast to the PLC concept presented in the Smallwood article, the final article in this section, Article 11, is "Forget the Product Life Cycle Concept," in which N.K. Dhalla and S. Yuspeh question the very existence of life cycles.

The contrasting views presented in these two articles reflect the diversity of views marketers hold concerning the usefulness of the PLC concept. These differences arise because marketers have different theories of product demand and different definitions of a product category.

Determinants of Product Demand[14]

The PLC concept purports to represent the demand for a product over time, but there is no well-defined theory of product demand to support the PLC. Even though the classic PLC curve has been observed in a number of product-markets, the factors causing the shape of the curve have not been clearly articulated. The application of a biological model to the PLC would suggest that the demand for a product, like the activity of a living organism, goes through inevitable, preordained changes over time. This perspective suggests that product demand is predictable over time and is beyond the control of marketers. Accordingly, while marketers need to alter the nature of their tactical marketing programs during the various stages, they cannot affect the basic demand for the product by marketing efforts. Clearly, this biological analogy begins to look inappropriate. We know that a wide variety of PLC shapes have been observed. Thus, we can see that product demand is not highly predictable or beyond the control of marketers.

Research on the diffusion of innovation has also been used to explain the evolutionary nature of product demand and the PLC.[15] This research suggests that the S-shaped curve of the introductory, growth, and maturity phases represents the rate at which consumers adopt new products or concepts: demand remains at a low level in the introductory stage while innovators and early adopters become familiar with the new concept; growth in demand accelerates when the early adopters spread the information about the new concept; finally, demand levels off in the maturity stages when all potential adopters of the new concept have been exposed to it.

In addition, theories on the diffusion of innovations suggest that the specific shape of the S-shaped curve is determined by the nature of the product, the consumer's adoption decision, and the communication efforts concerning the products. The diffusion process will occur sooner (the introductory and growth stages will be shorter) when the product benefits can be communicated easily, when the product is simple, when consumers can try the product with low risk, and so on.

Thus, the research on diffusion of innovation indicates that product demand and the PLC is determined by the nature of the product and the marketing efforts concerning the product. However, the diffusion of innovation explains only the factors causing the first three stages in the PLC. The decline phase cannot be explained by the diffusion of the innovation process. Thus, a fully developed PLC theory needs to supplement the diffusion of innovation explanation with a mechanism accounting for the decline in demand.

The decline in product demand typically represents a shift in demand from the product of interest to a different product. Such shifts arise when new technology gives rise to products that will satisfy customer needs better or when new customer needs develop in response to changes in societal values. At this time, we do not have adequate theories to account for the advent of new technologies or new social values.

In conclusion, we can say that the following elements are determinants of the nature of product demand and the PLC.

1. The nature of the customer adoption decision.
2. Characteristics of the product.
3. Marketing efforts.
4. The availability of substitutes arising from new technologies.
5. The degree to which customer needs satisfied by the product are changing.

The relative importance of these factors is determined, in part, by how the product is defined.

Definition of Product in the PLC

Traditionally, the product in product life cycles is defined at one of the following three hierarchical levels of aggregation: (1) product class, such as passenger automobiles; (2) product form, such as sports cars; and (3) brand, such as Datsun 280ZX. The discussion in Article 10 (by Smallwood) focuses on the product class and form while the discussion in the Dhalla and Yuspeh article (Article 11) concentrates on the brand level.

When one considers the difference in product definition, the perspective of Smallwood and that of Dhalla and Yuspeh are not so contradictory as one might at first suppose. Perhaps, at the brand level, marketing activities are the most important element causing product demand. Since marketing activities cause the brand-level product life cycle, the life cycle concept may not be useful in making strategic resource allocation decisions at the brand level. At the product form or class level, product demand may be determined primarily by forces largely outside the control of firms — forces such as societal values, technology, and competitive activity. Thus the life cycle of the product form or class may be more meaningful for strategic analysis than that of a brand. Such analysis would enable the business to cope more effectively with the largely uncontrollable environment facing product forms and classes.

The Level of Aggregation for PLC Analysis[16]

A problem that confronts all strategy analysis is determining the appropriate level of aggregation. Should the unit of analysis be the brand, the product form, the product class, the market segment, or the industry. The previous discussion of the two articles on the PLC demonstrates that when analyses are made at different levels — the brand versus the product form — the conclusions can be dramatically different. Based on their analyses at the brand level, Dhalla and Yuspeh reject the PLC concept, while Smallwood accepts the PLC concept on the basis of his analysis at the product form level.

The key question is: Which level of aggregation best captures the changing nature of the environment to which marketing strategies must respond? George Day, building on the work of Derek Abell, suggests that a useful level of aggregation is

> the application of a distinct technology to the provision of a particular function for a specific customer group. Only when there is a change along one or more of these dimensions that involves a sharp departure from the present strategies of the participating competitors is a separate life cycle needed.[17]

An analysis of the PLC for nylon illustrates how this heuristic approach is applied. In a classic article, Ted Levitt discussed how Du Pont extended the PLC for nylon by sequentially marketing the product for different applications.[18] After an initial effort directed toward parachute cords, the marketers undertook applications to women's hosiery, tire cords, and carpeting.

Should the marketing strategist consider one extended PLC for nylon or separate PLCs for each application? The previously stated heuristic suggests that separate PLCs are appropriate because each application is characterized by a different function and customer group; and each application represents a separate strategic market opportunity and should be considered individually in the development of a marketing strategy.

Readings in Section III

The readings in this section discuss three concepts used to evaluate strategic market opportunities. In the first article, Article 7, James Van

Horne demonstrates how strategic investment opportunities can be evaluated using capital budgeting techniques. This article extends the classic financial evaluation method to include the risk associated with an investment in the evaluation.

The experience curve concept is examined in the next two articles. Article 8 by Barry Hedley outlines the nature of experience curves and the implications of experience curve analysis for developing marketing strategies. Article 9 by William Abernathy and Kenneth Wayne discusses some dangers in overreliance on experience curve analysis.

Articles 10 and 11 in this section are devoted to the product life concept. These articles illustrate both the usefulness of this concept for evaluating opportunities and the difficulties in defining the appropriate unit for strategic analysis.

Notes

1. An excellent and more detailed presentation of the concepts in this section can be found in Paul F. Anderson, "Marketing Investment Analysis," in *Research in Marketing*, vol. 4, ed. J.N. Sheth (Greenwich, Conn: JAI Press, 1980). Materials from this article were used in developing this section and the next section. A more advanced and complete treatment of capital budgeting can be found in Thomas E. Copeland and J. Fred Weston, *Financial Theory and Corporate Policy*, (Reading, Mass.: Addison-Wesley, 1979), chaps. 2 and 3.
2. Eugene Fama and Merton H. Miller, *The Theory of Finance* (Hinsdale, Ill.: Dryden Press, 1972).
3. James C. Van Horne, *Financial Management and Policy*, 4th ed. (Englewood Cliffs, N.J.: Prentice-Hall, 1977), p. 98. Alternatives to this perspective concerning the theory of the firm can be found in Paul F. Anderson, "Marketing, Strategic Planning, and the Theory of the Firm," *Journal of Marketing* 42 (Spring 1982): 15–26.
4. "Kellogg Still the Cereal People," *Business Week*, 26 November 1979, pp. 80–93.
5. Seymour Tilles, "Strategies for Allocating Funds," *Harvard Business Review*, January–February 1966, pp. 72–80.
6. See Louis E. Yelle, "The Learning Curve: Historical Review and Comprehensive Survey," *Decision Sciences* 10 (1979): 302–328.
7. R.D. Buzzell, B.T. Gale, and R.G.M. Sullen, "Market Share—A Key to Profitability," *Harvard Business Review*, January–February 1975, pp. 97–106; and R.D. Buzzell and F.D. Wiersema, "Successful Share Building Strategies," *Harvard Business Review*, January–February 1981, pp. 133–144.
8. Walter Kiechel III, "The Decline of the Experience Curve," *Fortune*, 5 October 1981, p. 139.
9. For a review of the concepts, research findings, and problems associated with the role of market share in strategic planning, see Yoram Wind and Vijay Mahajan, "Market Share: Concepts, Findings, and Directions for Future Research" in *Review of Marketing 1981*, ed. B. Enis and K. Roering (Chicago: American Marketing Association, 1981), pp. 31–42.
10. Additional limitations of the experience curve are discussed in George Day's

"Diagnosing the Product Portfolio," Article 15 in this book; and in George Day, "Analytical Approaches to Strategic Market Planning," in Enis and Roering eds., *Review of Marketing 1981*, pp. 92–94; and in George Day and David Montgomery, "Diagnosing the Experience Curves" (Research Paper No. 641, Stanford Graduate School of Business, 1982).

11. Kiechel, "Decline of the Experience Curve," p. 140.

12. For a review of research concerning the product life cycle, see D.R. Rink and J. Swan, "Product Life Cycle Research: A Literature Review," *Journal of Business Research*, September 1979, pp. 219–242.

13. C.W. Hofer, "Toward a Contingency Theory of Business Strategy," *Academy of Management Journal*, December 1975, p. 785.

14. The Fall 1981 issue of the *Journal of Marketing* contains a special section on the product life cycle. Articles in this section review the recent conceptual thinking and empirical results concerning the PLC.

15. See E.V. Roger and F.F. Shoemaker, *Communication of Innovations* (New York: Collier McMillian, 1971) and T.S. Robertson, *Innovative Behavior and Communication* (New York: Holt, Rinehart, & Winston, 1971).

16. This discussion draws heavily on George S. Day, "The Product Life Cycle: Analysis and Applications Issues," *Journal of Marketing*, 45 (Fall 1980): 60–67.

17. Ibid. p. 61.

18. Theodore Levitt, "Exploiting the Product Life Cycle," *Harvard Business Review* 43 (November–December 1965): 81–94.

7. An Application of the Capital Asset Pricing Model to Divisional Required Returns

James C. Van Horne

Introduction

Few topics have captured so much interest in the academic literature as the capital asset pricing model (CAPM). In recent years, the model has been extended to corporate finance decisions, particularly those dealing with capital investments. Despite this interest, we have few examples of the actual application of the model by a corporation. This absence may be because the model is not yet widely used in corporate finance and/or due to the fact that when usage does occur it is not reported. This paper describes the recent application of the CAPM by Finnigan Corporation, a high technology company. My knowledge of the application stems from my acquaintance with several principal officers and directors. I have not advised the company, nor have I been otherwise involved in the implementation of this concept. In what follows, I describe the application of the CAPM at Finnigan Corporation and some of its effect on management. The study was based on interviews with management and review of various memoranda and documents provided by the Chairman and President. I have tried to report the experiences of this company as accurately as possible without making any normative judgments.

Description of the Company

Finnigan Corporation was begun in 1967 by Dr. Robert E. Finnigan to produce a gas or liquid chromatograph/mass spectrometer system. This

This article first appeared in *Financial Management*, Spring 1980, pp. 14–19.

When this article was published, the author was the A.P. Giannini professor of finance and associate dean at the Graduate School of Business at Stanford University.

device is used to analyze complex organic compounds. In succeeding years, many improvements have been made in the system, and it has found rather wide application in environmental control, health sciences, forensic science (crime laboratories), and industrial process and quality control. The system ranges in price from $50,000 to $200,000, depending upon the features. The market is felt to be growing at about a 21% annual rate; Finnigan currently enjoys about a 40% market share.

In 1969, a small company called Disc Instruments, Inc., was acquired. This wholly-owned subsidiary produces encoders, which convert rotary or linear motion into electrical or light pulses. In essence, encoders allow the conversion of analog information into digital information. Applications are found in machine tools, production automation equipment, computer peripherals, medical and scientific instruments, and in military and communication systems. Encoders range in price from about $30 to $1,500. The market is felt to be growing at an annual rate of about 20 to 25%. Finnigan currently has about a 20% market share.

Thus, Finnigan Corporation has two major product lines: spectrometers and encoders. In 1978, Finnigan Institute Division was formed to offer courses to train users of analytical instruments, one of which is the spectrometer. This "stand-alone" division is educational in orientation and to date is small in revenue and negligible in profits. Finnigan Corporation is headquartered in Sunnyvale, California, with three major organizational components. The Instrument Division produces spectrometers in the Sunnyvale plant; the Disc Subsidiary produces encoders in a plant in Costa

TABLE 7.1   Finnigan Corporation Consolidated Balance Sheet, December 31, 1978 and 1977

	1978	1977
	(000)	
Assets		
Current assets:		
Cash	$ 787	$ 566
Accounts receivable net of		
$190,000 allowance for doubtful accounts		
($88,000 in 1977)	9,144	7,756
Inventories		
Finished goods	1,427	1,319
Work in process	3,361	1,146
Components	2,696	1,856
	7,484	4,321
Prepaid income taxes	735	190
Other prepaid expenses	99	108
Total current assets	18,249	12,941

TABLE 7.1 (continued)

	1978	1977
	(000)	
Equipment and improvements, at cost		
Machinery and equipment	2,034	1,757
Leasehold improvements	688	504
	2,722	2,261
Less accumulated depreciation and amortization	1,217	943
Net equipment and improvements	1,505	1,318
Other assets	753	805
	$20,507	$15,064
Liabilities and Stockholders' Equity		
Current liabilities:		
Accounts payable	$ 2,763	$1,766
Accrued income taxes	1,280	1,122
Accrued payroll and related benefits	1,222	726
Other accrued liabilities	1,637	959
Notes payable — banks	1,087	1,157
Total current liabilities	7,989	5,730
Long-term debt	3,200	2,400
Deferred income taxes	480	
Stockholders' equity		
Common stock; 4,000,000 shares authorized.		
1,585,000 shares issued and		
outstanding (1,554,000 shares in 1977)	5,034	4,809
Retained earnings	3,804	2,125
Total stockholders' equity	8,838	6,934
	$20,507	15,064

Rent expense and lease commitments:
  Rent expense was $686,000 in 1978 and $512,000 in 1977.
  The Company is obligated under noncancellable building and equipment leases. The aggregate annual rental commitment under the leases is as follows: 1979 — $660,000; 1980 — $411,000; 1981 — $293,000; 1982 — $280,000; 1983 — $219,000; 1984–1988 — $627,000; 1989 and beyond — $106,000.
  There were no significant capitalized financing leases at December 31, 1978 and 1977.

Mesa, California; and the Institute operates from offices in Cincinnati, Ohio. All facilities are leased, so fixed assets are confined to equipment and leasehold improvements. Balance sheets at December 31, 1978, and 1977, are shown in Table 7.1 and a summary of operations for the five-year period 1974–1978 is shown in Table 7.2. Of the $30 million in sales in 1978,

TABLE 7.2   Finnigan Corporation: Summary of Operations 1974–1978

FOR THE YEAR:	1978	1977	1976	1975	1974
		(in 000's except per share amounts)			
Net sales	$29,987	$22,374	$16,097	$15,630	$12,907
Cost of sales	15,243	11,003	8,405	8,197	6,554
Research and development	2,045	1,902	1,405	1,435	1,126
Selling, general, and admin-					
istrative expenses	8,928	6,869	5,352	5,116	3,766
Interest expense	282	315	230	242	247
Income before income taxes					
and extraordinary					
item	3,489	2,285	705	640	1,214
Provision for income taxes	1,810	1,195	365	329	646
Income before extraordinary					
item	1,679	1,090	340	311	568
Extraordinary item			90	48	72
Net income	$ 1,679	$ 1,090	$ 430	$ 359	$ 640
Per common and common					
equivalent share:					
Income before extraordinary					
item	$ 1.04	$ .70	$ .22	$ .21	$ .43
Extraordinary item			$ .06	$ .03	$ .05
Net income	$ 1.04	$ .70	$ .28	$ .24	$ .48

$25.5 million were in spectrometer products and services, whereas $4.5 million were in encoders. Operating profits were $3.7 million and $0.9 million, respectively, for these two lines of business. The philosophy of management is to develop new markets for these two product lines, not to develop entirely new products or acquire other companies. This philosophy is particularly suited to the use of the CAPM.

While initially a venture capital situation, Finnigan had an initial public offering of shares in 1972. A second offering occurred in 1974. Currently there are 1.6 million shares outstanding held by approximately 500 stockholders. The stock is traded over-the-counter on the NASDAQ system. Because of its rapid growth, the company pays no dividend on its stock, nor is it likely to do so in the near future.

Instigating Required Rates of Return

In 1977, Mr. T. Z. Chu, Chairman and President, changed the goals of the company to a return on assets standard instead of a return on sales and growth standard. He became interested in some of the concepts of modern finance and, in particular, in the implications of the CAPM for required rates of return. This led to establishment of investment hurdle rates for the company as a whole, as well as for the Instruments Division and the Disc Subsidiary. In late 1977, the company formulated for the first time a statement of company objectives prominently featuring return on asset standards.

How Required Rates Were Estimated

Return on asset standards were the result of estimating debt and equity costs, where the latter was based on the CAPM. A working assumption was that Finnigan's long-term capitalization would be one-third debt and two-thirds equity. The marginal cost of debt, including compensating balance requirements, was estimated at 9.2% before taxes at the time of the study. The after-tax cost of debt, using a 52% tax rate, was

$$R_d = .092(1 - .52) = 4.4\%. \tag{1}$$

The cost of equity capital for the firm as a whole was estimated using a variation of the familiar capital asset pricing model formula:

$$R_e = i + (\bar{R}_m - i)\beta + e \tag{2}$$

where i is the risk-free rate, $\bar{R}_m$ is the expected return on the market portfolio, β is the beta coefficient for the stock in question, and e is the return requirement associated with residual risk. The beta measures the responsiveness of returns for the stock to returns for the market portfolio, as represented by Standard & Poor's 500-stock index. The greater the beta, the greater the systematic or unavoidable risk of the stock. A beta of 1.00, of course, indicates that the stock has the same systematic risk as the market as a whole, whereas a beta greater than 1.00 means the stock has more systematic risk than the market, and a beta less than 1.00 means the stock has less systematic risk. The last term, e, reflects the residual risk of the stock in question, which is the result of factors unique to the particular company involved.

For the risk-free rate, Finnigan used the rate of return on one-year Treasury bills. At the time, bills of this maturity were yielding 6%. For the expected return on the market portfolio, the company used an estimate developed by Wells Fargo Bank which, at the time, was approximately 13%. The beta for Finnigan's stock, based on monthly data for the preceding 60 months, was 1.70. This coefficient indicates that Finnigan has considerably more systematic risk than the typical stock in the market. In addition to these variables, Mr. Chu felt that residual risk was a factor for a company of Finnigan's size because bankruptcy costs were important to investors in Finnigan's stock. As a result, he wished to make some adjustment for the company's unique business risk. No precise quantification of residual risk was possible. Based on his assessment of the possibility of insolvency, Mr. Chu felt 1.5% to be a reasonable adjustment for residual risk. However, he is quick to admit that the estimate was subjective and without much in the way of foundation.

Putting all these factors together, the required rate of return on Finnigan's stock was found to be

$$R_e = .06 + (.13 - .06)\ 1.7 + .015 = 19.4\% \tag{3}$$

Using the weights indicated above for debt and equity, the required rate of return for the company as a whole was found to be

$$R_{d+e} = .33\ (.044) + .67\ (.194) = 14.5\% \tag{4}$$

which was rounded to 15% for internal purposes.

While the overall required rate of return for Finnigan was important, Mr. Chu was more interested in establishing separate rates of return for the two divisions. The Instruments Division was felt to be more risky than the Disc Subsidiary, so it was anticipated that different required rates of return would be used. Mr. Chu collected beta-type information on various companies that were similar to each of the two components of Finnigan. The idea was to identify publicly-held companies that were similar to the particular component of Finnigan. While a number of proxy companies were identified for the Instrument Division, far fewer could be identified for the Disc Subsidiary, because most electromechanical component companies are divisions of larger companies. The proxy companies used in both situations are listed in Table 7.3.

While the financial performance and betas of these companies varied, Mr. Chu settled on a required return on equity of 23% for the Instrument Division. Again, a risk-free rate of 6% and an expected return on the market portfolio of 13% were assumed. In effect, beta information on the proxy companies was used as a guide for estimating the required return for

TABLE 7.3   Proxy Companies Used in Connection with Finnigan Organizational Components

INSTRUMENTS DIVISION		DISC SUBSIDIARY
Baird Atomic	Nicolet Instrument	Dynamic Research Corporation
Beckman Instruments	Perkin-Elmer	Electrocraft
Fisher Scientific	Orion Research	Sierracin
Gilford Instrument	Spectra Physics	
Instrumentation Laboratory	Spex Industries	
Kratos	Water Associates	

the division. Because of the variability of the betas as well as the fact that the Instrument Division was felt by Mr. Chu to be riskier than the typical proxy company, an average beta for the proxy companies was not employed. The estimate of the required return on equity for the division embraced both systematic risk, as reflected by the betas of the proxy companies, and unsystematic risk. Here the 1.5% premium for residual risk was employed. It is important to point out again that the final estimate of the required return on equity represented a judgment by Mr. Chu as opposed to any precise quantification.

For the Disc Subsidiary, the required return on equity was estimated to be 18%. This lower estimate was based on the lower betas of the proxy companies as well as on the greater cash flow and earnings stability of the encoder business, as evidenced by internal accounting data. It also embodied an adjustment for residual risk, presumably 1.5%. However, the final required return on equity estimate again was subjective.

For the required returns for the two components of the company, it was assumed that one-third debt and two-thirds equity would be employed. In other words, no allowance was made for the components having different debt capacities. The desired debt-equity ratio for Finnigan as a whole was simply used in both cases. As a result, the following required rates of return were derived:

Disc: $R = .33(.044) + .67(.18) = 13.5\%$

Instrument: $R = .33(.044) + .67(.23) = 16.8\%$

which were rounded to 14% and 17%, respectively. These two rates then served as required hurdle rates for the two divisions when evaluating investment projects on a discounted cash flow basis.

Emphasis on Asset Management

More important from the standpoint of the company was the fact that these rates were treated as minimal rates of return that investors expected each of the two organizational components to earn on assets employed. In other words, in addition to using the rates as hurdle rates for new investments, the company used them also to judge overall return performance in each division. Mr. Chu identified this shift in emphasis to balance sheet and asset management as opposed to an emphasis on growth in an internal memo:

> We are interested in maximizing our shareholders', and incidentally our own, wealth. We can accomplish this by effecting a *sustainable* increase in the market valuation of Finnigan stock and by issuing dividends. Since our cash needs will likely be so great, as not to permit granting of dividends for some time, we must concentrate our efforts on improving the market valuation of our stock.

> . . . To me, all the important characteristics that are under our control can be boiled down to one thing — effective assets management. . . . Beginning in 1978, we will concentrate our efforts on improving return on assets!

Given this new emphasis, managers of the various operations were held accountable for the return on assets employed as opposed to a growth in sales. As the company leases all its buildings, particular stress was placed on the efficient management of receivables and inventories. In addition, an emphasis was placed on investments involving increased efficiency.

As described by various members of management, the principal benefit of the CAPM approach was a change in attitude rather than implementation of a precise way for judging capital investments. In addition, compensation incentive plans for management were stated in terms of the return on assets.

For the first time, the overall company was viewed in terms of its different elements. The Disc Subsidiary was now considered safer, requiring lower rates of return than the Instrument Division. Disc Subsidiary personnel seemed to feel that "the company cared about them and would put capital in them." The CAPM approach established that different operations of the company would be permitted to show different returns.

As the company leases its buildings, equipment purchases and leasehold improvements are the only capital assets. These amounted to only 7% of total assets of the company at the end of 1978, and acquisitions here are infrequent as well as relatively small. While new capital investments are judged in relation to the required rate of return of the division, intuition and judgment still come into play in the actual decision, according to management. From Exhibit 1, it is seen that the principal investments of the company involve growth in receivables and inventories. As a result, the main use of the CAPM at Finnigan Corporation has been to establish a target return on assets and on increments to such assets.

The notion of setting target returns based on an external evaluation of risk appears now to be well established in management thinking. For instance, an investment proposal to start new analytical service laboratories that would provide testing services to outsiders represented a departure from the existing business of Finnigan. One question asked was what was an acceptable return for other companies already in this business? This question was never asked before.

In summary, we have examined a high technology company that recently implemented a capital asset pricing model approach to target rates of return for two separate divisions. While the approach has not revolutionized capital allocation decisions at Finnigan Corporation, it nonetheless has had an important effect in establishing performance targets and management incentives based on return on assets as opposed to sales growth.

8. A Fundamental Approach to Strategy Development

Barry Hedley

In the face of continuing economic and environmental uncertainty, an increasing number of companies are rejecting traditional approaches to long range planning. These approaches were frequently "extrapolative" in nature, and in the absence of smooth economic trends it seems right that they should be discarded. Yet there is considerable confusion concerning what should take their place.

It is, however, possible to specify the requirements which must be satisfied by any approach to strategy development which can hope to be successful in today's changeable world. First, the approach must provide a means for identifying the underlying factors which are critical for long term success at the individual business level, and which are sufficiently fundamental that their effects can be expected to persist indefinitely in the face of continual general environmental change. Secondly, the framework must offer a way of establishing the implications of these factors for the allocation of limited resources — and especially of cash — within a company which is comprised of a number of businesses. This allocation must take place in such a way that the performance of the multi-business company *overall* can be optimized.

These are in fact the same problems companies have always faced in trying to develop sound corporate strategy. What has happened is simply that changes in the environment have brought the requirements into sharper focus, made the constraints more severe. Indeed it could be argued that the recent crises of inflation and recession may yet have at least one beneficial effect: under sheer fear for survival they could force companies to focus carefully on the *fundamentals* for the first time. It is not an exaggeration to say that, properly directed, this focus could convert the crisis into a

This article first appeared in *Long Range Planning*, December 1976, pp. 2–11.

When this article was published, the author was director of The Boston Consulting Group Ltd.

149

real opportunity for more effective corporate strategy development in the future.

The remainder of this article is devoted to a description of a suitable approach for identifying the fundamental strategic factors at the level of the individual business. In the subsequent article in the February edition of *Long Range Planning* the approach will be extended to the process of overall strategy development for the multi-business company.

Strategy for Individual Businesses

At its most basic, long term strategic success in an individual business depends on a company's ability to achieve a position such that its costs incurred in making the product concerned and delivering it to the relevant market are as low or lower than its competitors'. Since all competitors in a given business will tend to enjoy similar price levels for their products, having lower costs than competition will naturally result in superior profitability. This will be true regardless of general fluctuations in economic conditions and indeed the lower cost competitor should enjoy both superior and more stable profitability, as illustrated schematically in Figure 8.1. Developing sound strategy for an individual business thus requires a good understanding of the factors influencing long run costs.

The Experience Curve Effect

It has long been recognized that the labor input required to manufacture a product tends to decline systematically with increases in accumulated pro-

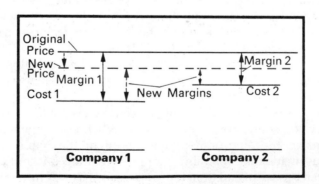

Company 1 has lower costs than Company 2 in the same business. It thus enjoys superior profitability. Should economic conditions change adversely, as represented by the price fall indicated by the broken line, Company 1's margins will drop proportionately less than Company 2's (by roughly one-third versus one-half in the diagram as indicated).

FIGURE 8.1   The Benefits of Lower Costs (Schematic)

duction.[1] The Boston Consulting Group has found that the type of relationship involved — originally called the 'learning curve' — frequently applies also to the *total cost* involved in manufacturing, distributing and selling a product. The relationship can be expressed simply as follows: each time the accumulated experience of manufacturing a particular product doubles, the total unit cost in real terms (i.e., in 'constant money', net of GDP inflation) can be made to decline by a characteristic percentage. The decline is normally in the region of 20–30 percent.

The fundamental nature of this relationship — note especially that it deliberately factors out the influence of inflation — makes it a particularly useful tool for product management and strategy development. The relationship has now been explored in a broad range of industries in many different countries, and it has been found to apply extremely widely. It is best illustrated by plotting real unit cost against cumulative production volume (a quantitative measure of "accumulated experience"). If logarithmic scales are used, a straight line normally results, as shown in the actual examples in Figure 8.2. This line typically has a slope such that the real unit cost drops to around 70–80 percent of its former value for each

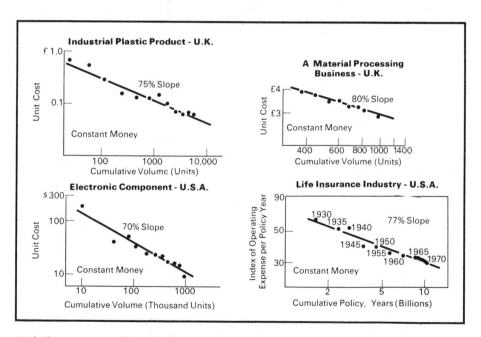

With the exception of the Life Insurance example which is derived from published data, the other curves were derived for products of clients in the course of consulting assignments performed by The Boston Consulting Group. The curves are therefore presented anonymously.

FIGURE 8.2 Some Examples of Cost Experience Curves

doubling of cumulative volume, and is usually referred to as an "experience curve."[2]

There are a variety of factors which contribute to the cost reduction performance implicit in the experience curve effect. These include:

- productivity improvement due to technological change and/or "learning" effects leading to adoption of new production methods,
- economies of scale and of specialization,
- displacement of less efficient factors of production, especially investment for cost reduction and capital-for-labor substitution,
- modifications and redesign of product for lower costs.

For present purposes, however, it is less important to catalogue all the means by which real costs can be reduced than it is to note the key strategic implications of the experience curve:

- failure to reduce costs along an appropriate experience curve slope (i.e., equivalent to that achieved by competitors) will lead to an uncompetitive cost position,
- failure to grow as rapidly as competitors will lead to an uncompetitive cost position: the competitor with the largest market share and hence, over time, the largest accumulated experience, should have the lowest costs and thus the highest profitability.

Achieving Real Cost Reduction in Practice

With respect to the first of these, it is by no means unusual to find managers who are skeptical about the possibility of achieving continuous real cost reductions over long periods of time. Indeed in our consulting practice we do occasionally find companies whose real cost performance has been on an upward, rather than a downward trend. This raises an important point: cost reductions are not *automatic*. Real costs have to be aggressively managed downwards. Poor control of operations; lack of investment in new methods enabling cost reduction; allowing an excessive build-up of nonproductive overhead: these can all lead to adverse real cost performance. The overwhelming evidence is, however, that given good management real costs *can* be made to decline *forever*. After all, this simply means that over time, and as a function of experience, we should get better (in real terms) in making and selling things — that we do not "un-learn" as experience builds. This is hardly counterintuitive!

It is often easiest to find means for real cost reduction in high growth businesses. Production scale is expanding, and there is plenty of scope for the introduction of new technology and labor-saving production methods without redundancy programs (the latter is often a problem in low growth U.K. industries). Under these conditions alert management will find many opportunities for reducing the level of "laggards" in the overall cost mix. In experience curve terms, the growth is simply resulting in rapidly expanding accumulated experience, and rapid progress is made along the cost curve. The rates of real cost decline which result can easily outstrip inflation, so that costs even decline when expressed in current money terms.

An Example: Electronic Calculators

Electronic calculators, which in the space of a few years have been transformed from expensive luxuries into every day items, provide a very good example of this. Events in the calculator market also illustrate the strategic need for management to understand the dynamics of experience curve cost reduction if they are to remain effective competitors. A simplified history of the development of solid state electronic calculators is outlined in Table 8.1. Electronic calculators first appeared on the scene around the beginning of the 1960s, various rival firms claiming their invention. In the very early days it seems that the major element of cost was that of the discrete semiconductor devices (transistors, diodes) from which the calculators were made. The leading competitors were probably those based in the U.S.A. close to the best source of solid state components and technology.

At this time the calculators were extremely expensive. As a result the market was limited to those few applications for which they were cost effective. Meanwhile, however, tremendous expansion was taking place in solid state electronics in general: the market for solid state diodes, for example, regularly expanded in unit volume at a rate in excess of 50 percent per annum during the early and mid 1960s. This rapid growth engendered correspondingly rapid experience curve based cost and price de-

TABLE 8.1 Electronic Calculators (Solid State)

	Major Cost Elements	Dominant Competitors
Phase 1	Semiconductors (Discrete Devices)	Americans (e.g. Wang)
Phase 2	Assembly	Japanese (e.g. Sharp, Casio) S.E. Asia
Phase 3	Integrated Circuits	Americans (e.g. Texas Instruments)
Phase 4	Assembly Plus **Distribution**	? (Unresolved) (Tesco, Woolworth, Boots)

clines in discrete devices: for example, between 1960 and 1965 the price of the average germanium diode in the U.S.A. fell by a factor of seven in real terms as illustrated in the price curves in Figure 8.3. Before long, the main concern in calculator costs became the labor costs, largely related to assembly.

As a result of this, during the mid 1960s the advantage passed to the low labor cost countries, including — at that time — Japan. Japanese companies had assumed virtual control of the market by the end of the

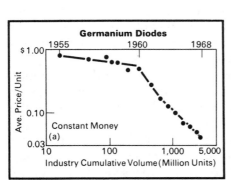

FIGURE 8.3a

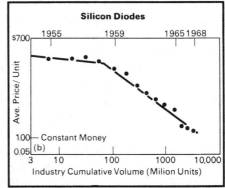

FIGURE 8.3b

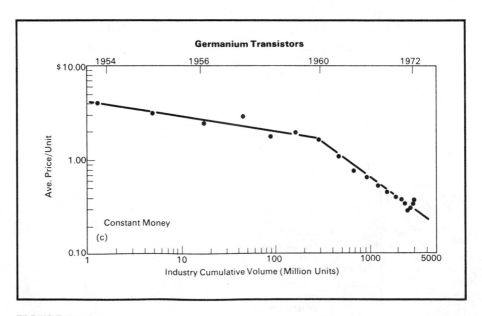

FIGURE 8.3c

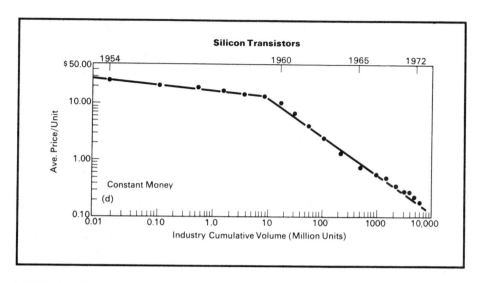

FIGURE 8.3d

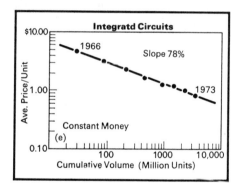

FIGURE 8.3e

FIGURE 8.3   Price Experience Curves for Semiconductors

Notes on Price Patterns: The very steep price declines at certain times in some of these curves resulted from a competitive "shakeout" in which intense competitive activity was following a previous price "umbrella" period in which price reductions were not matching underlying experience curve cost decreases. This rapid decline normally only abates when one or more competitors relinquish their fierce attack on the market (or defenders relinquish their hold on market share) and stability returns. The alternative is stable pricing (parallel to costs) throughout. This appears to have been the pattern with integrated circuits. These price patterns are repeated in many different businesses.

SOURCE: *Perspective on Experience,* The Boston Consulting Group Inc., Boston 1968, 1970, 1972.

decade. Costs continued to come down on an experience curve basis and the market expanded as prices dropped lower and lower, bringing electronic calculators within the range of more pockets. The overall size of the market was now beginning to look very attractive and in the early 1970s the American semiconductor manufacturers themselves entered the market. They realized that with the use of integrated circuits — the so-called LSI ("large scale integration") chips — many assembly operations could be made unnecessary. The overall cost advantage thus lay with the integrated circuit manufacturers themselves, and these companies entered the market in a big way, most notably Texas Instruments, who clearly set out to dominate the business.

Calculators were now at price levels such that they were becoming a consumer item. Growth was large: the annual market for consumer (as opposed to desk-top) calculators expanded from only 2 million units in 1972 to almost 20 million units by the end of 1974. Prices dropped dramatically, both as a result of experience curve cost reductions and also under the influence of aggressive competition for market shares: a "shakeout" was occurring, rather as had happened in discrete semiconductor devices themselves early in the 1960s. This shakeout is not yet complete, and in cost experience curve terms there are some interesting considerations for the protagonists to bear in mind.

First, under the influence of the experience curve, the cost structure of making calculators must unquestionably be changing again: the integrated circuits and displays will be becoming a smaller part of the total cost. Labor costs and assembly in particular will be resuming their relative importance. This could well return the advantage to the low labor cost countries unless overall volume and experience have now reached a level at which highly automated assembly methods can be used enabling cost-effective manufacture in the U.S.A. and other advanced countries. The other consideration is the relative importance of distribution costs now that calculators themselves are so cheap. This encourages the distribution of calculators through mass merchandizing outlets such as those indicated in Table 8.1 rather than through speciality business machine stores. The manufacturers who win in the end may well be those with the best distribution links. Meanwhile, costs and prices continue to decline. Prices are probably declining even more rapidly than costs, for some competitors at least: Bowmar, the second largest U.S.A. manufacturer, quit the business in mid 1975 and filed for reorganization under U.S.A. bankruptcy laws. Texas Instruments, the largest manufacturer — not even in the business at the start of the decade — appears to be prepared to tolerate heavy losses in order to make the market its own. The competitive struggle continues.

The story of calculators is, of course, a dramatic tale of rapid growth and spectacular cost and price declines. A clear understanding of experience curve effects is obviously necessary for effective strategic management in that business. Electronic watches will undoubtedly be the next significant market to undergo similar dynamic changes as a result of high growth compounding the effects of the experience curve.

Low Growth Businesses

It should not be thought that, based on this extensive discussion of the calculator business, the experience curve is only relevant in high growth businesses. In low growth businesses too real cost reductions are possible, but at a lower rate given the slower rate of accumulation of experience. This is indicated by the examples in Figure 8.4. Thus even in a mature business, any competitor who is not achieving the appropriate experience curve cost reductions can expect to be in profit trouble over the long term.

This is the first simple and fundamental strategic message of the experience curve: never relax on cost control. In many growth businesses, U.S. companies actually control cost monthly on an experience curve basis. All companies, in all businesses, should at least ensure that their real costs are not rising on trend. Analysis often reveals that companies who pride themselves on good cost control are not in fact as tough as this in practice. They should be: the experience curve shows it can be done in the majority of cases.

Profitability and Market Share

The second of the two strategic implications listed earlier has an even more far-reaching significance, which certainly applies in both high and low growth businesses. This implication suggests that — even given good experience curve cost control — profitability, over the long term, will be directly related to market share. It is interesting that extensive independent business research — of which perhaps the best-known example is the recent 'PIMS' study — is also confirming the ubiquitous nature of this relationship.[3] Market share of the acquired firm has also been identified as the critical success requirement in a recent study of European acquisitions.[4] Only rarely is it possible to find explicit cost data for a number of competitors in a single business in order to verify directly the fact that the experience curve effect is at the root of this profit/market share relationship. One example is, however, given by the cost data made public in the U.S.A. in anti-trust hearings concerning the business of manufacturing steam turbine electricity generators.

These data are displayed on an experience curve basis in Figure 8.5. General Electric, the largest competitor, at any point in time had the lowest unit costs. All three competitors tended to move in step over time down a common experience curve. While the market shares remained stable, relative cost levels stayed stable. General Electric was consistently more profitable than Westinghouse who in turn was more profitable than Allis

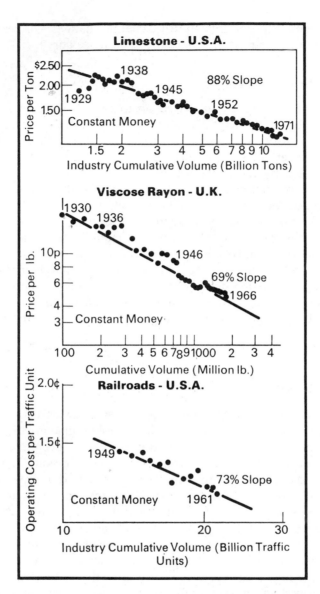

The curves for limestone and viscose rayon are for price; the curve for U.S. railroads is for cost.

FIGURE 8.4   Some Experience Curves in Mature Businesses

Chalmers. Despite making real cost reductions on trend over time, Allis Chalmers could never catch up with the leaders unless the relative market share positions were changed. And indeed it looks as though Allis Chalmers even failed to secure real cost reductions on trend over the last 5 to 6

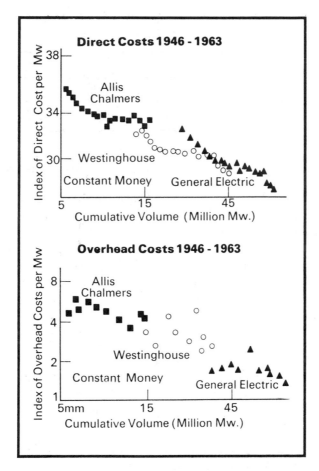

FIGURE 8.5 U.S. Steam Turbine Generators: Competitive Cost Comparison

SOURCE: Antitrust Hearings.

years of the period. It is perhaps not surprising that this has been a perennial problem business for Allis Chalmers.

Incidentally, it is worth noting that the slope of the experience curve relating the three companies' direct costs to each other is closer to 90 percent than to 70–80 percent. This is not uncommon for such "cross-sectional" experience curves and can arise from a variety of factors such as: equal raw material costs for all competitors; commonly available elements of production technology; tendency for the larger share competitor to spend more per unit on marketing to stabilize his higher share; and so forth. The slope is nevertheless sufficiently steep to lead to very marked profitability differences: at a price level yielding Allis Chalmers no margin

TABLE 8.2   The U.K. Cellophane Industry

	1970/1971		1972/1973	
	Sales (£m.)	PBIT/Sales (per cent)	Sales (£m.)	PBIT/Sales (per cent)
British Cellophane	41	10·0	68	14·9
British Sidac	15	3·1	19	7·8
Transparent Paper	8	(2·1)	11	5·6

above direct costs, General Electric's margin on these costs would be in excess of 20 percent.

This type of profitability/market share relationship is exhibited in a large range of effectively "single business" industries. An example from the U.K. is illustrated in Table 8.2.

This example — a low physical growth industry — is particularly interesting since it clearly shows the effects of market share on both absolute levels of profitability and stability of profitability: Transparent Paper, the marginal competitor, swung from loss to profit between 1970 — a depressed year for the business — and 1973. British Cellophane, the largest competitor, was consistently the most profitable and experienced a less wild swing in performance between the two years. It is interesting that despite the fact that at a detailed level it is obviously an oversimplification to regard these as "single business" companies, and indeed there is obviously a degree of non-comparability between the three — differing degrees of participation in converting, for example — the overall results of the experience curve effect are quite clearly to be seen.

An Example: The Motor Industry

Perhaps the best known example of the profit/market share relationship is in another low growth business: the motor industry. GM, Ford, Chrysler and American Motors form a very clear pecking order in terms of size and profits. What may be less well known is the closely similar pattern displayed by the higher growth Japanese motor industry, as shown in Figure 8.6.

Despite very active competition at an "operational" level between these companies, the experience curve effect indicates that they cannot achieve long term changes in profitability without changes in market share and hence, over time, relative experience and costs. The strategy implications for a low share competitor, such as American Motors or Chrysler, must include resignation to low profitability as long as market share remains low. This may well seem like a hopeless situation, given that gaining share in a major way against GM would probably be a long and extremely costly task, virtually impossible to fund given the lower present profitability of the companies.

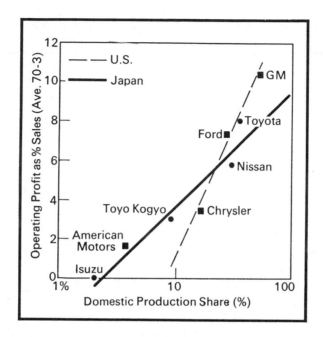

FIGURE 8.6 The U.S. and Japanese Motor Companies

The Need for "Segmentation"

There is, however, an alternative. Curiously, a guide to the solution can be found in the British motor industry, a cursory analysis of which would appear initially to refute the experience curve effect. As shown in Table 8.3 the profit relationship between Ford, Vauxhall and Chrysler is much as one would predict from the experience curve. British Leyland, however, which is almost twice the size of Ford in turnover, has been significantly less profitable on trend. The likely reason for this apparent anomaly is revealed on more detailed examination.

In Table 8.4, the basic product offerings of the U.K. motor companies

TABLE 8.3 The British Motor Industry

	Average 1970–1973	
	Sales (£m.)	Op. Profit Margin (per cent)
British Leyland	1261	4·1
Ford (U.K.)	716	4·8
Vauxhall	262	0·3
Chrysler (U.K.)	249	0·6

TABLE 8.4   U.K. Car Manufacturers Base Product Offerings (Mid-1975)

Leyland	Ford	Vauxhall	Chrysler
Allegro	Escort	Viva	Imp
Maxi	Cortina	Chevette	Avenger
1800/2200	Capri	Victor	Hunter
MG Midget	Consul/Granada		
MGB			
Mini			
Marina			
Rover Saloon			
Range Rover			
Triumph Spitfire			
Toledo/Dolomite			
2000/2500 Saloon			
TR 6			
TR 7			
Stag			
Jaguar XJ6 12			
V12 Open E-Type			
(Daimler Limousine)			
(Taxi)			

are listed. The tremendous breadth of Leyland's product line relative to the other manufacturers is startling. This is, of course, partly a legacy of the way Leyland was put together by merger. Yet undoubtedly a detailed experience curve analysis would show that the main determinant of cost in an individual car model is production scale of that basic model, although the potential cost level is also likely to be influenced by the overall accumulated experience of the firm as a whole. Clearly Leyland's average volume *per model* is in fact lower than Ford's, and this will put a strategic limitation on the cost level which Leyland can attain even given the good labor relations, smooth production operations, and competitive manning which the CPRS study of the industry showed to be so necessary.[5]

Any future for Leyland in popular cars must surely lie at least in part in the direction of a strategy developing greater volume per model, either through increased market share, increased rationalization or specialization, or some combination of the two. The same could be said of Chrysler in either the U.K. or, indeed, the U.S.A., though here the degree of focus would need to be even greater. Again, this conclusion would tend to be supported by the findings of the CPRS study. It is certainly true, however, that huge overall size is not essential for profitability in the car industry: Rolls Royce Motors, with a turnover of the order of £50–60m., shows a before tax return on capital of almost 20 percent; Group Lotus, with a turnover of around £10m., has even higher profitability. Of course, seeking profitability by specialized *segment* based dominance can be risky, as other specialty car manufacturers have discovered from time to time (e.g., Jensen, Aston Martin). But this is the only approach for a small manufacturer if he is to have any chance of profitable survival.

At the other end of the scale, the most secure approach to profitability is to dominate the industry both overall *and* on a segment basis: in the U.S.A., GM is not only the largest manufacturer overall, it also offers the

TABLE 8.5   U.S. Car Manufacturers: Volume by Model (1974)

Company	Total Volume	Base Body Types		Engine Types	
		No. Offered	Vol. per Type	No. Offered	Vol. per Type
GM	4440	6	740	4	1110
Ford	2300	5	460	4	580
Chrysler	1270	4	320	3	420
American Motors	260	4	65	2	130

The manufacturing approach adopted by the U.S. manufacturers is such that quite a broad range of superficially different vehicles can be produced on a few identical chassis.

broadest product range. Unlike Leyland, however, its overall volume is such that it is still the largest manufacturer in terms of unit volume per basic model type, whether one is talking about body types or engines (Table 8.5). As a result it should enjoy superior costs (though even GM has suffered from specialist volume-based European and Japanese competition in small cars), and *hence* the higher profitability noted previously in Figure 8.6, which is now seen to be an oversimplification of the way the experience curve effect applies in this particular industry.

The motor industry example is particularly useful, since it demonstrates the need for explicit examination of business segmentation before applying the experience curve concept for purposes of strategy development. Most broad business areas do in fact break down into a number of business segments which have fairly distinct economics. However, the process of developing an understanding of the basis on which a strategic segmentation should be made is often very complex. It normally involves making a detailed examination of each major element of cost and value addition in the business, and exploring the possible basis on which an experience based advantage relative to competition could exist within each element.

It is not possible within the scope of this article to go into the process of segmentation in great depth. It is in any case a process which is difficult to describe in general terms. The motor industry example does, however, give a feel for some of the issues which can be raised concerning production costs. Frequently there are also important segmentation issues in the marketing area as well. For example, this is undoubtedly a further dimension which would actually need to be considered in practice in the motor industry before strategy could be finally determined. The reason American Motors lies so much above the profit trend of the other three U.S.A. manufacturers undoubtedly results to a significant degree from a market segmentation approach on their part (e.g., focus on smaller cars).

The overall aim of segmentation can be summarized, then, as the identification of product–market segments which are sufficiently distinct, economically and competitively, that it is meaningful to develop strategy for them separately as "individual businesses."[6] The segmentation process must also identify clearly the experience curve basis on which a superior cost position can be developed in the business segment, to enable competitive strategy to be properly developed. In some cases simple relative market share in the segment may not be the sole determinant: all elements of cost do not always have the same experience base, also, some cost elements may share in experience with other business segments. In these cases, it may be necessary to focus directly on likely relative costs by synthesizing a view of the effects of the company's varying position in the different experience bases into its implications for overall costs.

Summary

The Experience Curve and Individual Business Strategy

It is in practice at the more detailed business segment level that the concept of the value of relative scale and market share is applicable. The basic strategic message of the experience curve can thus be summarized as follows:

> The largest competitor in a particular business area should have the potential for the lowest unit costs and hence greatest profits. If it is unprofitable it is probably either being 'out-segmented' by more focused competition, or it is defective in experience curve cost control.

> Smaller competitors in a business area are likely to be unprofitable, and they will remain so unless a strategy can be devised for gaining dominant market share at reasonable cost. If achieving overall dominance is not feasible, then the smaller competitor should seek to identify an economically distinct segment of the business in which he can dominate the relevant experience bases sufficiently to attain a viable cost position overall. If this is not feasible, then the smaller competitor must resign himself to inadequate profitability forever. Under these circumstances the business should really be phased out.

These are the fundamental rules of individual business strategy. They focus on position *relative to competitors*. Relative competitive position thus provides the required simple and unchanging objective towards which strategy development efforts should be single-mindedly focused. This objective will remain valid in spite of unpredictable changes in the economic environment. Come inflation or deflation, boom or bust, the superior business performers will be those in strong market positions relative to competition in the relevant business segment. Strategic planning must concentrate on achieving dominance as its primary object. Any efforts directed towards environmental forecasting or extrapolative long range planning are really only useful in so far as they contribute to this goal.

These conclusions at the individual business level imply that in any multibusiness company, the best performers over the long term will tend to be those businesses in which the company has a superior market share; "problem" businesses or divisions will tend to be those where market shares are marginal. This simple observation, coupled with an appreciation of the effect and value of long-term growth, leads to an extremely useful integrated approach to overall strategy development for the multibusiness company.

References

1. One of the earliest references to this phenomenon was Wright, T.P., "Factors Affecting the Cost of Airplanes," *J. Aeron. Sci.* 3, 122–128, February (1936).
2. For a full description of the experience curve effect and further examples of its application in practice see The Boston Consulting Group, *Perspectives on Experience*, 1968, 1970, 1972.
3. A concise report of the main findings of the PIMS study is given in Robert D. Buzzell, Bradley T. Gale, and Ralph G. M. Sultan, "Market Share: Key to Profitability," *Harvard Business Review*, January–February 1975.
4. John Kitching, "Winning and Losing with European Acquisitions," *Harvard Business Review*, March–April 1974.
5. The Central Policy Review Staff, *The Future of the British Car Industry*, Her Majesty's Stationery Office, London (1975).

9. Limits of the Learning Curve

William J. Abernathy
Kenneth Wayne

Many companies have built successful marketing and production strategies around the learning curve — the simple but powerful concept that product costs decline systematically by a common percentage each time that volume doubles. The learning-curve relationship is important in planning because it means that increasing a company's product volume and market share will also bring cost advantages over the competition.

However, other results that are not planned, foreseen, or desired may grow out of such a market penetration/cost reduction progression. Reduced flexibility, a loss of innovative capability, and higher overhead may accompany efforts to cut costs.

A manager failing to consider the possible outcome of following a cost-minimizing strategy may find himself with few competitive options once he reaches the point where decelerating volume expansion prevents him from obtaining further significant cost reduction.

But if he can identify the likely consequences in advance, he can either anticipate them in his plans or choose an alternative strategy. In this article we analyze those consequences and conclude that management cannot expect to receive the benefits of cost reduction provided by a steep learning-curve projection and at the same time expect to accomplish rapid rates of product innovation and improvement in product performance. Managers should realize that the two achievements are the fruits of different strategies.

Proponents of the learning curve have developed the relationships between volume growth and cost reduction through the use of two distinct but related approaches:

This article first appeared in the *Harvard Business Review*, September–October 1974, pp. 109–119.

When this article was published, the authors were associate professor of business administration and research assistant/doctoral student at the Harvard Business School, respectively.

166

1. The learning curve (also called the progress function and start-up function) shows that *manufacturing costs* fall as volume rises. It has typically been developed for standardized products like airframes and cameras.
2. The experience curve traces declines in the *total costs* of a product line over extended periods of time as volume grows. Typically, it includes a broader range of costs that are expected to drop than does the learning curve, but disregards any product or process design changes introduced during the period of consideration. Gas ranges and facial tissues are two major product lines on which experience curves have been developed.

The two approaches are sufficiently similar for many purposes of planning and analysis. As we shall demonstrate in due course, however, changes in pricing policy and product design can create significant discrepancies. Care must be exercised in choosing between the two related approaches.

Hard Strategic Questions

Evidence on cost decreases in a wide range of products, including semiconductors, petrochemicals, automobiles, and synthetic fibers, supports the notion that total product costs, as well as manufacturing costs, decline by a constant and predictable percentage each time volume doubles. Because this volume/cost relationship is reliable and quantifiable, it has appeal as a strategic planning tool for use in marketing and financial planning, as well as in production. Moreover, a strategy that seeks the largest possible market share at the earliest possible date can gain not only market penetration but also advantages over competitors who have failed to reach equal volume.

Examples of the economic effects of the learning curve can be found everywhere. The price of ferromagnetic memory cores for computers plunged from 5 cents per bit (unit of memory) in 1965 to less than a half cent in 1973, thereby significantly reducing the costs of computers. In less than two decades of production DuPont reduced the cost of rayon fiber from 53 cents a pound to 17 cents (values not adjusted for inflation). Airframe costs can drop more than 50% per pound during the three to five years of a high-volume production run if the manufacturer can control the rate of modification and sustain volume production.

In considering examples of independent action by one corporation, the most important is that of the Ford Motor Company in its early years. (The Ford example actually shows an experience curve, but the point it makes is equally valid for a learning-curve situation.) During an initial period of less than two years, the average price of a Ford automobile was reduced from more than $5,000 to about $3,000 through the introduction of a dominant product, the Model T. Then, as Figure 9.1 shows on a logarithmic scale, the company cut the price of the Model T to less than $900 following an 85% experience curve. (To underline the contrasts in price, all the figures are translated into 1958 dollars.)

During this time span wages were increased more than threefold, the working day reduced by fiat from ten hours to eight, the moving assembly line invented, and one of the nation's largest industrial complexes (River Rouge) created entirely out of retained earnings. We shall return to the Ford case shortly.

The frequency with which this cost reduction/volume increase pattern is found in practice sometimes leads to the incorrect impression that the learning-curve effect just happens. On the contrary, product design, marketing, purchasing, engineering, and manufacturing must be carefully coordinated and managed. The producer cuts costs with a combination of effects; these include spreading overhead over larger volume, reducing inventory costs as the process becomes more rational and throughput time drops, cutting labor costs with process improvements, achieving greater division of labor, and improving efficiency through greater familiarity with the process on the part of the work force and management. The impetus toward lower costs and higher volume is fragile, however, and if any one of the necessary conditions is removed, a discontinuous return to higher costs may result.

The question management must ask in undertaking such a strategy is whether it fully anticipates or desires the implications that accompany results or that follow execution of the strategy. After the start-up phase, doubling of volume has tremendous implications for the organization. Not all the changes it undergoes may be desirable. Management must anticipate the consequences so that it can plan for them, or else it should reject the strategy from the beginning. Some of the questions that it must ask itself are:

> What is the practical limit to volume/cost reduction? Much of the empirical evidence that has been presented in support of the experience and learning curves ignores their limits, implicitly suggesting that cost reductions go on forever. How long can benefits be expected?

> What pattern of changes in the organization accompanies progress along the learning curve? Clearly, a long sequence of cost reduction has implications for the organization. How must it be changed to bring such cost reductions about? What happens to overhead, the rate of innovation, manufacturing technology, inventory, the work force, and the investment in plant and equipment?

> What happens when the practical limits of cost reduction are reached? At this point, can the organization change its strategy from cost minimizing to product-performance maximizing? Or has the or-

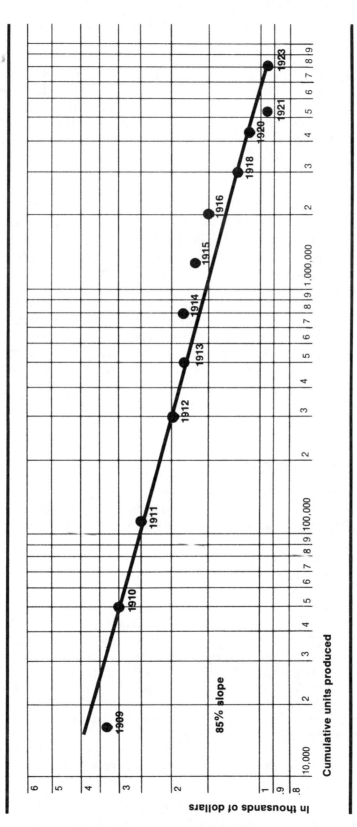

FIGURE 9.1 Price of Model T, 1909–1923 (Average List Price in 1958 Dollars)

ganization so changed itself that it loses the vitality, flexibility, and capability for innovation it needs for quick response? In more specific terms, have the quality of the manufacturing technology, the fixed and variable cost structures, and the innovative powers of the work force and management deteriorated so much that the organization cannot make a strategy change?

To explore these questions, we shall consider Ford's early experience, particularly with the Model T. Then we shall examine other manufacturing cases — such as TV picture tubes, electronic components, and office equipment. The evidence suggests that with those products whose performance can be improved significantly — typically involving complex manufacturing processes such as use of electronic equipment machinery — the incidence of product innovation establishes the limit to the learning curve.

The consequence of intensively pursuing a cost-minimization strategy is a reduced ability to make innovative changes and to respond to those introduced by competitors — although the amount of loss seems to depend on the degree to which the manufacturer follows such a strategy, and its intensity. The problem of strategy choice, then, is balancing the hoped-for advantages from varying degrees of cost reduction against a consequent loss in flexibility and ability to innovate.

From Model T to Model A

At Ford, the experience curve did not continue indefinitely; it governed only the Model T era. Then Ford abandoned it for a performance-maximizing strategy by which the company tried to improve performance year by year at an even higher product price. The product was the Model A. However, Ford's long devotion to the experience-curve strategy made the transition to another strategy difficult and very costly.

Figure 9.2 shows volume and average prices of the Ford line for some 60 years in an experience-curve format. (The scale of the top part is chronological; the bottom part is logarithmic.) Data on retail price trends, displayed by the two curves, are related to both product-line diversity and the rate of product change. Data on the variety of wheel bases and engines, the horsepower range offered, and the average vehicle weight illustrate how the number of options expanded, contracted, and expanded again. An indicator of the changes in models appears at the top of the exhibit. Taking these three types of information together — product line diversity, the rate of model change, and price trends — one can see that they changed concurrently, whether price is defined on a per-vehicle basis (the upper trend line) or on a per-pound basis (the lower).

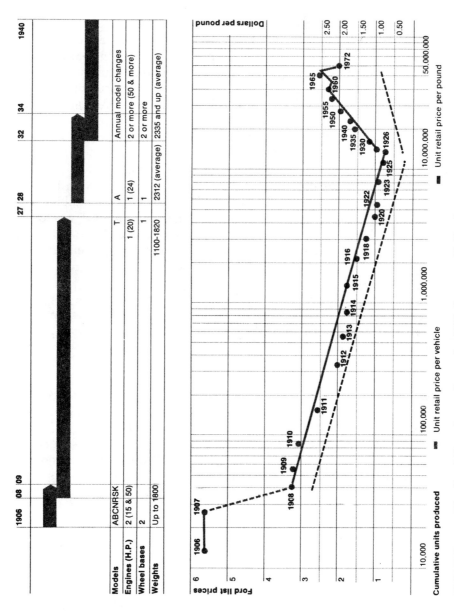

FIGURE 9.2   The Ford Experience Curve (in 1958 Constant Dollars)

Because manufacturing costs vary directly with weight, a comparison of the two trend lines in different periods is revealing. After the Model T was discontinued in 1927, Ford raised the price of its car from year to year, in contrast to the earlier period. The increases were due mainly to design changes which were made to enhance comfort, performance, and safety, but which required more and more expensive materials and caused the price per pound to rise steadily. Considered over a number of years, these systematic annual changes represent a trade-off in favor of size, weight, and performance, as opposed to price.

As Figure 9.2 shows, after an initial period in which several models were offered at the same time, the product line was consolidated in 1909 to the Model T. Ford's objective was to reduce the price of the automobile and thereby increase volume and market share. Before the Model T was conceived, when the least expensive Ford car was priced at $850 and tires alone cost more than $60 a set, Henry Ford announced plans to sell autos at $400 — although, he told reporters, "It will take some time to figure what we can do."

By 1907, after the death of the former company president and the expulsion of dissident stockholder-managers who advocated high-priced cars, attention turned to product cost reduction. The company felt confident in taking this step because of its success with the relatively inexpensive Model N in 1907 and later with the Model T, which was clearly a superior product.[1]

The company accomplished savings by building modern plants, extracting higher volume from the existing plant, obtaining economies in purchased parts, and gaining efficiency through greater division of labor. By 1913 these efforts had reduced production throughput times from 21 days to 14. Later, production was speeded further through major process innovations like the moving assembly line in motors and radiators and branch assembly plants. At times, however, labor turnover reportedly ran as high as 40% per month.[2]

Up to this point, Ford had achieved economies without greatly increasing the rate of capital intensity. To sustain the cost cuts, however, the company embarked on a policy of backward and further forward integration in order to reduce transportation and raw materials costs, improve reliability of supply sources, and control dealer performance. The rate of capital investment showed substantial increases after 1913, rising from 11 cents per sales dollar that year to 22 cents by 1921. The new facilities that were built or acquired included blast furnaces, logging operations and saw mills, a railroad, weaving mills, coke ovens, a paper mill, a glass plant, and a cement plant.

Throughput time was slashed to four days[3] and the inventory level cut in half, despite the addition of large raw materials inventories. The labor hours required of unsalaried employees per 1,000 pounds of vehicle delivered fell correspondingly some 60% during this period, in spite of the additions to the labor force resulting from the backward integration thrust and in spite of substantial use of Ford employees in factory construction.

Constant improvements in the production process made it more integrated, more mechanized, and increasingly paced by conveyors. Consequently, the company felt less need for management in planning and control activities. The percentage of salaried workers was cut from nearly 5% of total employment for 1913 to less than 2% by 1921; These reductions in Ford personnel enabled the company to hold in line the burgeoning fixed-cost and overhead burden.

The strategy of cost minimization single-mindedly followed with the Model T was a spectacular success. But the changes that accompanied it carried the seeds of trouble that affected the organization's ability to vary its product, alter its cost structure, and continue to innovate.

Cost of Transition

In its effort to keep reducing Model T costs while wages were rising, Ford continued to invest heavily in plant, property, and equipment. These facilities even included coal mines, rubber plantations, and forestry operations (to provide wooden car parts). By 1926, nearly 33 cents in such assets backed each dollar of sales, up from 20 cents just four years earlier, thereby increasing fixed costs and raising the break-even point.

In the meantime, the market was changing. In the early 1920s, consumer demand began shifting to a heavier, closed body and to more comfort. Ford's chief rival, General Motors, quickly responded to this shift with new designs. Ford's response was to add features to the Model T which gradually increased the weight; between 1915 and 1925 the weight of the car actually gained by nearly 25%, while engine power remained the same.

But the rate of product improvement halted the steady reduction of costs. Nevertheless, to maintain market growth Ford further cut the list price along the experience-curve formula. This created a severe margin squeeze, particularly when unit sales began falling after 1923. As the rate of design changes accelerated and wage levels continued to rise, manufacturing costs loomed ever larger in the retail price. In 1926, the manufacturing costs of some models reached 93% of list price, and some models were actually sold to dealers at prices below costs. (See Table 9.1 for sales, manufacturing, and other data on Ford during the critical two decades.) Ford, unbeatable at making one product efficiently, was vulnerable to GM's strategy of quality and competition via superior vehicle performance. As Alfred Sloan, architect of GM's strategy, later wrote:

> Mr Ford . . . had frozen his policy in the Model T, . . . preeminently an open-car design. With its light chassis, it was unsuited to the heavier closed body, and so in less than two years [by 1923] the closed body made the already obsolescing design of the Model T noncompetitive as an engineering design. . . .

TABLE 9.1   Ford Vital Statistics, 1910–1931

Year	Motor vehicles sales (in thousands of units)	% of market share	% of employees salaried	Labor rate (in $ per hour)	Manufacturing cost as % of list price*	Direct labor hours per vehicle*†	Fixed assets per $ sales	Labor hours per vehicle	Profit (loss) (in millions of dollars)‡
1910	32	10.7%	6.9%	$0.25				232	$ 15
1911	70	20.3	3.5	0.23				265	21
1912	170	22.1	5.5	0.23			$0.10	95	40
1913	203	39.6	4.9	0.27	41%	65	0.11	152	75
1914	308	48.0	5.7	0.55	40	42	0.15	79	90
1915	501	43.4	4.5	0.55			0.19	72	74
1916	735	38.6	4.4	0.55			0.15	84	178
1917	664	46.1	3.2	0.61	79	47	0.16	106	51
1918	498	43.5	3.5	0.66			0.22	133	95
1919	941	46.9	3.0	0.76			0.26	100	140
1920	463		2.9	0.84	70	49	0.27	267	64
1921	971	55.4	1.9	0.87			0.22	102	125
1922	1,307		1.4	0.82	60	31	0.20	125	237
1923	2,019	47.5	1.1	0.85			0.19	125	193
1924	1,929		1.2	0.83	62	35	0.25	140	214
1925	1,920	41.5	1.2				0.27	160	219
1926	1,563		1.4	0.87	93	69	0.33	178	132
1927	424	10.6	1.5	0.87			0.81	475	(65)
1928	750		2.0				0.84	375	(143)
1929	1,870	32.0	2.1	0.92	86	80	0.40	182	175
1930	1,432		2.8				0.54	210	113
1931	731	26.2	4.0		69	40	1.06	290	(97)

*For Model T Touring Car 1913–1926, Model A Tudor 1929 and 1931.

†Computed from direct labor cost for models specified above and from Ford labor rates.

‡In constant 1958 dollars.

Sources: Ford Archives; Federal Trade Commission, *Report on the Motor Vehicle Industry*, 76th Congress, First Session (1940), House Document 468. Missing figures are not available.

The old [GM] strategic plan of 1921 was vindicated to a "T," so to speak, but in a surprising way as to the particulars. The old master had failed to master change. . . . His precious volume, which was the foundation of his position, was fast disappearing. He could not continue losing sales and maintain his profits. And so, for engineering and market reasons, the Model T fell. . . . In May 1927 . . . he shut down his great River Rouge plant completely and kept it shut down for nearly a year to retool, leaving the field to Chevrolet unopposed and opening it up for Mr. Chrysler's Plymouth. Mr. Ford regained sales leadership again in 1929, 1930, and 1935, but, speaking in terms of generalities, he had lost the lead to General Motors.[4]

A company that had developed and introduced eight new models during a four-year period, before undertaking the cost-minimization strategy, had subsequently so specialized its work force, process technology, and management that it consumed nearly a year in model development and changeover. As an illustration of its specialization, in the course of the model change Ford lost $200 million, replaced 15,000 machine tools and rebuilt 25,000 more, and laid off 60,000 workers in Detroit alone.

So we see that when costs could not be reduced as fast as they were added through design changes, the experience-curve formula became inoperative. While this sequence should give pause to managers who wish to apply the experience curve to make product-line changes, it does not invalidate the principle of the learning curve, which assumes a standardized product.

Decline of Innovation

The sequence of evolutionary development in product and process during the period of the cost-minimization strategy and the subsequent strategy transition is paralleled in the pattern of major Ford innovations. Figure 9.3 plots the frequency and significance of Ford-initiated innovations by type of application: product innovation, process innovation, and transfer of process technology to or from associated industries. The new methods and designs are those claimed by Ford. For our analysis, four independent industry experts evaluated the importance of each one and rated it on a scale of 1 to 5. The innovations range in significance from the introduction of the plastic steering wheel (index average of 1) in 1921 to the invention of the power-driven final assembly line (index of 5) in 1914. The vertical axis in Figure 9.3 provides a sum of the average points assigned to significant developments by two-year intervals in Ford's history.

Figure 9.3 indicates that the intensity of innovative activity is closely related to major events in the unfolding of the cost-minimization strategy. During the Model T period the activity shows a ripple effect. Installation of new product applications occurs in clusters with new model development and then declines in frequency as the design is standardized, efficiency is refined, and the process is integrated into operations. Process innovations

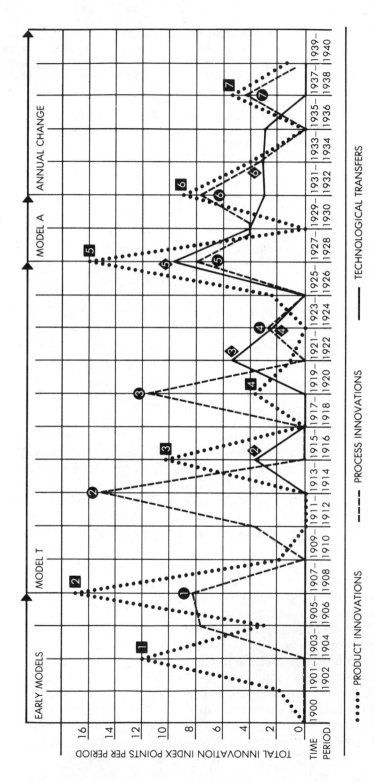

FIGURE 9.3   Innovation and Process Change at Ford

rise to a peak after the period of product innovation, as the manufacturer rationalizes the process and reduces costs. (Compare the peak designated circled 1 with the peak designated squared 1, circled 2 with squared 2, and so on.) As the manufacturer works out these problems, he transfers process technology following the thrust into backward integration, and a third peak of activity occurs (triangled 2, triangled 3, and so on).

The figure suggests not only that the nature of innovation changes, but also that the intensity of innovative activity diminishes. Ford produced only one new product application or process technique during the seven years after 1932 that rated as high on the scale as 4 — the development of transfer machines. This step toward further automation took place in 1937.

The changes introduced to trim costs altered the innovative activity in two ways. First, after 1926 the types of innovation peaked coincidentally. As operations became more elaborate and systemslike, product and process change developed intimate linkages; many different elements had to be altered simultaneously to introduce change. This relationship implies a high cost of change. Secondly, the nature of product innovation shifted. In the early years, a new model meant a complete transformation involving major innovation. Later, model change became an annual affair, and innovation centered on new features available across model lines rather than on new models. For instance, the V-8 engine, whose development appears as a substantial cluster of innovations in Figure 9.3, was produced without substantial alterations for 18 years.

Not surprisingly, the third class of innovation, technology transfers, increased in frequency through the period under consideration. This class had particularly long-term value at Ford since it improved the manufacturing capability. Many of these transfers were accomplished in Ford's newly integrated feeder operations, such as one where technology was applied to produce plate glass continuously.

Ford's experience demonstrates the important link between innovation and strategy. Innovation is not the pacing element; it is part of the strategy. Ford's choice of strategy made innovation more costly and a more serious organizational problem. Unfortunately, the cost-cutting drives also led to weakening of the resources (the salaried employees) needed to initiate and carry out innovation. It is not surprising that the company took nearly a year to change over to the Model A.

With its new model, Ford rose again. Combining the old philosophy of cost reduction with the appeal of an entirely new car boasting demonstrably high performance, the company wrestled the major market share from GM in 1930. But its market share fell once more. Indeed, Chrysler, a distinct third among auto makers during the 1920s, held second place ahead of Ford during most of the Depression.

As it turned out, the company's highly specialized production process lacked the balance to handle the new product; for example, the company had overcapacity in wood (the Model T had many wooden parts) but undercapacity in glass and body parts manufacturing. Moreover, as indicated by the data in Table 9.1, Ford never regained the high levels of labor and capital productivity of its heyday. Despite extensive investments in new plant and equipment, even in the highest volume year for the Model A (1929), 40 cents in plant and equipment assets were required per dollar of sales, and nearly 80 hours of direct labor were required per vehicle.

Ford did not improve on these figures until the late 1940s, when new management restructured the company and made heavy plant investments. From the time it introduced the Model A, Ford was compelled to compete on the basis of product quality and performance — a strategy in which it was not skilled.

Airframes, Computers, and so on

The Ford case provides a spectacular example of one company's action in pursuing a cost-minimization strategy to its end. Although this is an extreme case in terms of strategy choices and investment magnitudes, the same forces and consequences can be found at stake in other industries. In some cases these forces and consequences are evident when a rapid rate of product change retards the inauguration of the learning curve, and in other cases the difficulties terminate the downward trend. Consider:

> Douglas Aircraft, once an extremely successful, high-volume aircraft manufacturer, was forced into a merger in 1967 with the McDonnell Company by financial problems whose roots lay in poor control of airframe production costs under fast-shifting conditions. On the assumption that it could reduce the costs of its new jet model following a learning-curve formula, Douglas had made certain commitments on delivery dates and prices to airline customers. But continued modification of its plans disrupted, as *Fortune* put it, "the normal evolution of the all-important learning curve."[5]
>
> International Business Machines' schedules to deliver its new 360 series of computers a decade ago were thrown out of kilter. IBM's 1965 annual report described the situation this way: "Although our production of System/360 is building up rapidly and equipment shipped has been performing well, we had problems. . . . As a result we found it necessary in October to advise customers of delays from our originally planned delivery schedules. The basic building blocks in the System/360 circuitry are advanced new microelectronic circuit modules requiring totally new manufacturing concepts." The snag was attributable to the company's efforts to attain high-volume production while it was undertaking major product innovation.
>
> The price of TV picture tubes followed the experience-curve pat-

tern from the introduction of television in the late 1940s until 1963, the average unit price dropping from $34 to $8 (in terms of 1958 dollars). The advent of color TV ended the pattern, as the price for both black-and-white and color TV tubes shot up to $51 by 1966. Then the experience curve reasserted itself; the price dropped to $48 in 1968, $37 in 1970, and $36 in 1972. The transition was less traumatic than is sometimes the case because the innovation was foreseen and the new product was sufficiently similar to the old one that manufacturers could apply their established techniques and facilities in making the color tube.

In some cases radically new technology or the cost of transition has forced many of the "old" manufacturers out of the business. Such has been the case in the shift from vacuum tubes to transistors, from manual to electric typewriters, and from mechanical calculators to electronic machines. The major producers of textile machinery for rug manufacturing, like Lansdowne and Crompton & Knowles, found their markets taken from them by the advent of the new tufting technology in carpets.

The contrary relationship between product innovation and efficiency does not exist only in instances where the impetus for change comes about after a long and successful production run, as in the Ford case and in that of Volkswagen more recently. It can also be found when the change is an unintended continuation of uncertainty following new model introduction, as happened in the foregoing airframe and computer examples.

Common Elements of Change

To consider the sort of changes that can accompany a cost-minimizing strategy, it is useful to abstract that aspect of the Ford case. The kinds of changes that took place can be grouped into six categories — product, capital equipment and process technology, task characteristics and process structure, scale, material inputs, and labor.

Product. Standardization increases, models change less frequently, and the product line offers less diversity. As the implementation of the strategy continues, the total contribution improves with acceptance of lower margins accompanying larger volume.

Capital Equipment and Process Technology. Vertical integration expands and specialization in process equipment, machine tools, and facilities increases. The rate of capital investment rises while the flexibility of these investments declines.

Task Characteristics and Process Structure. The throughput time improves and the division of labor is extended as the production process is rationalized and oriented more toward a line-flow operation. The amount of direct supervision decreases as the labor input falls.

Scale. The process is segmented to take advantage of economies of scale. Facilities offering economies of scale, such as engine plants, are centralized as volume rises, while others, like assembly plants, are dispersed to trim transportation costs. Spreading the higher overhead over larger volume gains savings.

Material Inputs. Through either vertical integration or capture of sources of supply, material inputs come under control. Costs are reduced by forcing suppliers to develop materials that meet process needs and by directly reducing processing costs.

Labor. The heightening rationalization of the process leads to greater specialization in labor skills and may ultimately lessen workers' pride in their jobs and concern for product quality. Process changes alter the skills requirements from the flexibility of the craftsman to the dexterity of the operative.

The same pattern of change in the six categories that characterizes the Ford history also describes periods of major cost reduction in other industries. For example, as light-bulb manufacturing progressed from a manual process to an almost entirely automated one, a similar pattern of product development, process elaboration, increase in capital intensity, and so on, was evident.[6] In areas as diverse as furniture manufacturing and commercial building construction, the problems of improving productivity and achieving innovation often hinge on changes similar in thrust to those at Ford. Life-cycle studies of international trade in many products, such as chemicals and petrochemicals, demonstrate a coordinated pattern of change involving product characteristics, scale, and price competition that is consistent with the Ford case.

Studies of manufacturing technology yield a common finding for electronics, chemical, and metal-working companies, among others, that certain conditions in a company, like its supervisory structure, product-line diversity, and utilization of technology, relate to characteristics of the manufacturing process. More specifically, manufacturers with more efficient line flows have different ratios of supervisory personnel to the work force, different levels of authority, less product diversity, and greater product standardization than manufacturers with more flexible production process structures.

Risks of Success

In analyzing the difficulties of Ford and other companies, we are not arguing that the pursuit of a cost-minimization strategy is inappropriate. The failure of many companies, particularly small, innovative ones, can be traced to their inability to make the transition to high volume and cost efficiency. Nevertheless, management needs to recognize that conditions stimulating innovation are different from those favoring efficient, high-volume, established operations.

While there must be a theoretical limit to the amount by which costs can ultimately be reduced, a manufacturer reaches the practical limit first. However, the practical limit is not reached because he has exhausted his means of cutting costs; it is rather determined by the market's demand for product change, the rate of technological innovation in the industry, and competitors' ability to use product performance as the basis for competing.

In determining how the learning-curve strategy should be pursued, management must realize that the risk of misjudging the limit rises directly with the successful continuation of the strategy. There are two reasons for this seemingly paradoxical development: first, the market becomes increasingly vulnerable to performance competition and second, attempts to continue reducing costs diminish the organization's ability to respond to this kind of competition.

The market becomes more vulnerable to performance competition because the company must stake out an ever-larger market share to maintain a constant, significant rate of cost cutting. Demand must be doubled each time in order to realize the same proportional cost reduction. As the market expands, it becomes harder to hold together and the competition is better able to segment it "from the top," with a superior product or customized options. Once this action is taken, the company on the learning curve must either abandon the all-important volume bases of scale or introduce a major product improvement. Either step, or both, ends the cost-reduction sequence.

The unfortunate implication is that product innovation is the enemy of cost efficiency, and vice versa. To make the learning curve evolve successfully, the manufacturer needs a standard product. Under conditions of rapid product change, he cannot slash unit output costs.

Managing Technology

The role expected of technology is critical in the formulation of manufacturing strategy. Many a company has sailed into the unknown, trailing glowing reports about the R&D under way in its laboratories and the new products it is developing. Yet too often the promises in annual reports to stockholders and in news releases are never realized. The problem hinges on difficulties in recognizing that a shift in strategy has a pervasive effect *across* the organization's functional areas. The production department cannot follow a program of cost reduction along the learning curve at the same time that R&D or the marketing people are going full steam ahead into new ventures that change the nature of the product.

When a new product born of technology fails, management is often chided because it marketed the product poorly. The problem may have come, however, from management's failure to realize that its capabilities to handle innovation had weakened. Foresight is a matter of judging the challenge in terms of altered capabilities as well as technological changes and market forces. In the Ford case the difficulties arose as much from what the organization did to itself as from GM's actions. The ability to switch to a different strategy seems to depend on the extent to which the organization has become specialized in following one strategy and on the magnitude of change it must face. An extreme in either factor can spell trouble.

Very little is known about how to plan for this type of technological change. But we can point to two courses of action that some major companies have followed in avoiding the problems we have described. One is to maintain efforts to continue development of the existing high-volume product lines. This requires setting the industry pace in periodically inaugurating major product changes while stressing cost reduction via the learning curve between model changes. This course of action — which IBM has followed in computers — is obviously a costly option which only companies with large resources should undertake. It amounts to a decision to maintain comparatively less efficient operations overall.

The second course of action is to take a decentralized approach in which separate organizations or plants in the corporate framework adopt different strategies within the same line of business. Several corporations in high-technology industries have taken this approach with success. One organization in the company will pursue profits with a traditional product, like rayon, to the limit of the experience curve. At the same time a new, different organization will undertake the development of innovative (perhaps even competitive) products or processes, such as nylon. In taking this tack, some companies have shut down old plants and started up new ones instead of mingling different capabilities that are at various stages of their development.[7]

Neither of these courses of action will suit the needs of every organization, but some means of dealing with the issue of technological change and strategy transitions should be included in strategic planning.

Notes

1. Allan Nevins, *Ford: The Times, the Man, the Company* (New York: Scribner, 1954), Chapter 12.

2. Keith Sward, *The Legend of Henry Ford* (New York: Rinehart, 1948), p. 51.
3. See *Factory Facts From Ford* (Detroit: Ford Motor Company, 1924).
4. Alfred P. Sloan, Jr., *My Years With General Motors* (New York: Doubleday, 1964), pp. 162–163.
5. John Mecklin, "Douglas Aircraft's Stormy Flight Plan," *Fortune*, December 1966, p. 258.
6. See James R. Bright, *Automation and Management* (Boston: Division of Research, Harvard Business School, 1958).
7. For more on this approach, see Wickham Skinner, "The Focused Factory," *Harvard Business Review*, May–June 1974, p. 113.

10. The Product Life Cycle: A Key to Strategic Marketing Planning

John E. Smallwood

Modern marketing management today increasingly is being supported by marketing information services of growing sophistication and improving accuracy. Yet the task remains for the marketing manager to translate information into insights, insights into ideas, ideas into plans, and plans into reality and satisfactory programs and profits. Among marketing managers there is a growing realization of the need for concepts, perspectives, and for constructs that are useful in translating information into profits. While information flow can be mechanized and the screening of ideas routinized, no alternative to managerial creativity has yet been found to generate valuable marketing ideas upon which whole marketing programs can be based. The concept of the product life cycle has been extremely useful in focusing this creative process.

The product life cycle concept in many ways may be considered to be the marketing equivalent of the periodic table of the elements concept in the physical sciences; like the periodic table, it provides a framework for grouping products into families for easier predictions of reactions to various stimuli. With chemicals — it is a question of oxidation temperature and melting point; with products — it is marketing channel acceptance and advertising budgets. Just as like chemicals react in similar ways, so do like products. The product life cycle helps to group these products into homogeneous families.

The product life cycle can be the key to successful and profitable product management, from the introduction of new products to profitable disposal of obsolescent products. The fundamental concept of the product life cycle (PLC) is illustrated in Figure 10.1.

This article first appeared in *MSU Business Topics*, Winter 1973, pp. 29–35.

When this article was published, the author was director of economic and marketing research at Whirlpool Corporation.

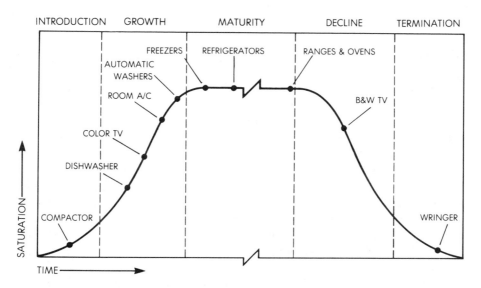

FIGURE 10.1. Life Cycle Stages of Various Products

In application, the vertical scale often is measured in saturation of the product (percentage of customer units using), while the horizontal scale is calibrated to represent the passage of time. Months or years are usually the units of time used in calibration, although theoretically, an application along the same concept of much shorter or longer durations (milliseconds in physical sciences, millennia in archaeology) might be found. In Figure 10.1 the breakdown in the time scale is shown by stages in the maturity of product life. The saturation scale, however, is a guide only and must be used accordingly. When comparing one product with another, it is sometimes best treated by use of qualitative terms, not quantitative units. It is important to the user of the product life cycle concept that this limitation be recognized and conceptual provisions be made to handle it. For example, if the basic marketing unit chosen is "occupied U.S. households," one cannot expect a product such as room air conditioners to attain 100 percent saturation. This is because many households already have been fitted with central air conditioning; thus, the potential saturation attainment falls well short of 100 percent of the marketing measurement chosen.

To overcome this difficulty, marketing managers have two basic options. They can choose a more restrictive, specific marketing unit such as "all occupied U.S. households that do not have forced air heating"; homes without forced air heating are unlikely candidates for central air conditioning. It can be anticipated that room air conditioners will saturate not only *that* market, but portions of other markets as well. On the other hand, on the basis of informed judgment, management can determine the *potential* saturation of total households and convert the PLC growth scale to a measurement representing the degree of attainment of potential saturation in U.S. households. The author has found the latter approach to be the more useful one. By this device, automatic washers are considered to be at 100 percent saturation when they are at their full potential of an arbitrarily chosen 80 percent.

Consider Figure 10.1, where various products are shown positioned by life cycle stages: the potential saturations permit the grouping of products into like stages of life cycle, even when their actual saturation attainments are dissimilar. One can note that in Figure 10.1 automatic washers (which are estimated at 58 percent saturation) and room air conditioners (30 percent) are positioned in the same growth stage in Figure 10.1; freezers (29 percent) and refrigerators (99 percent), on the other hand, are in the maturity stage. This occurs because, *in our judgment,* freezers have a potential of only about one-third of "occupied households" and thus have attained almost 90 percent of that market. Automatic clothes washers, however, have a potential of about four-fifths of the occupied households and at about 70 percent of their potential still show some of the characteristics of the growth stage of the PLC. General characteristics of the products and their markets are summarized in Table 10.1.

The product life cycle concept is illustrated as a convenient scheme of product classification. The PLC permits management to assign given products to the appropriate stages of acceptance by a given market: *introduction,*

TABLE 10.1   Product Life Cycle

	INTRODUCTION	GROWTH	MATURITY	DECLINE	TERMINATION
MARKETING					
Customers	Innovative/ High income	High income/ Mass market	Mass market	Laggards/ Special	Few
Channels	Few	Many	Many	Few	Few
Approach	Product	Label	Label	Specialized	Availability
Advertising	Awareness	Label superiority	Lowest price	Psychographic	Sparse
Competitors	Few	Many	Many	Few	Few
PRICING					
Price	High	Lower	Lowest	Rising	High
Gross Margins	High	Lower	Lowest	Low	Rising
Cost Reductions	Few	Many	Slower	None	None
Incentives	Channel	Channel/ Consumer	Consumer/ Channel	Channel	Channel
PRODUCT					
Configuration	Basic	Second generation	Segmented/ Sophisticated	Basic	Stripped
Quality	Poor	Good	Superior	Spotty	Minimal
Capacity	Over	Under	Optimum	Over	Over

growth, maturity, decline, and termination. The actual classification of products by appropriate stages, however, is more art than science. The whole process is quite imprecise; but unsatisfactory as this may be, a useful classification can be achieved with management benefits that are clearly of value. This can be illustrated by examining the contribution of the PLC concept in the following marketing activities: sales forecasting, advertising, pricing, and marketing planning.

Applications of the PLC to Sales Forecasting

One of the most dramatic uses of the PLC in sales forecasting was its application in explaining the violent decline in sales of color TV during the credit crunch recession of 1969–70. This occurred after the experience of the 1966–67 mini-recession which had almost no effect on color TV sales that could be discerned through the usual "noise" of the available product flow data. A similar apparent insensitivity was demonstrated in 1958, in 1961, and again in 1966–67, with sales of portable dishwashers. However, it too was followed by a noticeable sales reduction in the 1969–71 period, with annual factory shipments as shown in Figure 10.2.

In early 1972 sales of both portable dishwashers and color TV sets showed a positive response to an improving economic climate, raising the question as to why both products had become vulnerable to economic contractions after having shown a great degree of independence of the business cycle during previous years. The answer to the question seems to lie in their stage in the product life cycle. In comparing the saturation of color TV and dishwashers, as shown in Figure 10.2, consider first the case of color TV sales.

We can ascertain that as late as 1966, saturation of color TV was approximately 8 percent. By late in 1969, however, saturation had swiftly increased to nearly 40 percent.

The same observation is true in the case of dishwashers — considered a mass market appliance only since 1965. This is the key to the explanation of both situations. At the early, introductory stages of their life cycles, both appliances were making large sales gains as the result of being adopted by consumers with high incomes. Later, when sales growth depended more upon adoption by the less affluent members of the mass market whose spending plans are modified by general economic conditions, the product sales began to correlate markedly to general economic circumstances.

It appears that big ticket consumer durables such as television sets and portable dishwashers tend to saturate as a function of customer income. This fact is illustrated by the data displayed in Figure 10.3, concerning refrigerators and compactors, where one can note the logical relationship between the two products as to the economic status of their most important customers and as to their position in the product life cycle. The re-

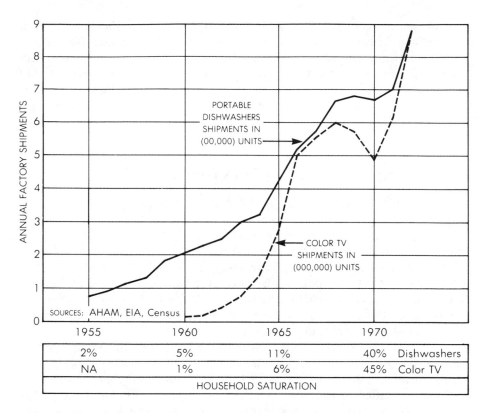

FIGURE 10.2   Effect of Recession on Product Sales

frigerator is a mature product while the compactor is the newest product in the major appliance family.

The refrigerator once was in the introduction stage and had marketing attributes similar to the compactor. The refrigerator's present marketing characteristics are a good guide to proper expectations for the compactor as it matures from the *introductory* stage through *growth* to *maturity*. One can anticipate that the compactor, the microwave oven, and even nondurables such as good quality wines will someday be included in the middle income consumption patterns, and we will find their sales to be much more coincident with general economic cycles.

Product Life Stages and Advertising

The concept of a new product filtering through income classes, combined with long-respected precepts of advertising, can result in new perspectives for marketing managers. The resulting observations are both strategic and tactical. New advertising objectives and new insights for copy points and

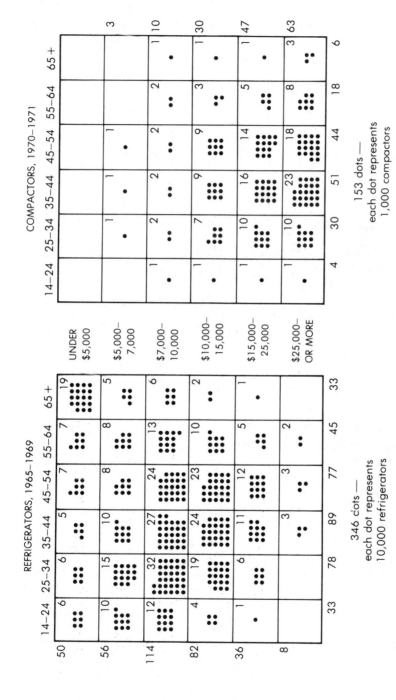

FIGURE 10.3 Purchase Patterns by Age and Income of Households

media selection may be realized. Consider the advertising tasks by the following phases:

Phase 1.   Introduction

The first objective is to make the best customer prospects aware that the new product or service is now available; to tell him what it does, what are the benefits, why claims are to be believed, and what will be the conditions of consumption.

Phase 2.   Growth

The next objective is to saturate the mass market with the same selling points as used in Phase 1. In addition, it is to recognize that a particular brand of the product is clearly superior to other "inferior" substitutes while, at the same time, to provide a rationalization that this purchase is not merely a wasteful, luxury indulging activity, but that it will make the consumer a better *something*, a better husband, mother, accountant, driver, and so forth.

Phase 3.   Maturity

A new rationalization, respectability, is added, besides an intensification of brand superiority ("don't buy substitutes; get the real XYZ original, which incidentally, is *new* and *improved* . . ."). To a great extent, the *product* registration is dropped. Respectability is a strong requisite of the American lower class, which in this phase is the economic stratum containing the most important opportunities for sales gains. Companies do not abandon higher income customers, but they now match advertising to a variety of market segments instead of concentrating on only one theme for the market. Several distinct advertising programs are used. All elements of the marketing mix — product, price, sales promotion, advertising, trading and physical distribution channels — are focused on specific market segments.

Phase 4.   Decline

Superior substitutes for a product generally will be adopted first by the people who before were the first to adopt the product in consideration. These people usually are from the upper economic and social classes. Advertising themes reflect this situation when they concentrate on special market segments such as West Coast families or "consumption societies" such as beer drinkers or apartment dwellers.

Product Life Stages and Pricing

As a product progresses through all five stages of the life cycle shown in Figure 10.1, the price elasticity can be expected to undergo dramatic changes. Generally speaking, price elasticity of a relatively simple product will be low at first. Thus, when customers are drawn from the higher income classes, demand is relatively inelastic. Later, when most customers are in the lower income categories, greater price elasticity will exist.

Of course, increased price elasticity will not automatically lower prices during the growth stage of the PLC. It is in this growth stage, however, that per unit costs *are* most dramatically reduced because of the effect of the learning curve in engineering, production, and marketing. Rising volume and, more important, the *forecasts* of higher volumes, justifies increased capital investments and higher fixed costs, which when spread over a larger number of units thereby reduce unit costs markedly. New competitors surface with great rapidity in this stage as profits tend to increase dramatically.

Pricing in the mature phase of the PLC usually is found to be unsatisfactory, with no one's profit margins as satisfactory as before. Price competition is keener within the distribution channel in spite of the fact that relatively small price differences seldom translate into any change in aggregate consumer activity.

Product Planning and the PLC

Curiously enough, the very configuration of the product takes on a classical pattern of evolution as it advances through the PLC. At first, the new device is designed for function alone; the initial design is sometimes crude by standards that will be applied in the future. As the product maturation process continues, performance sophistication increases. Eventually the product develops to the point where competitors are hardpressed to make meaningful differences which are perceptible to consumers.

As the product progresses through the product life cycle these modifications tend to describe a pattern of metamorphosis from "the ugly box" to a number of options. The adjustment cycle includes:

Part of house: the built-in look and function. Light fixtures, cooking stoves, wall safes, and furnaces are examples.

Furniture: a blending of the product into the home decor. This includes television, hi-fi consoles, radios, clocks, musical instruments, game tables, and so forth.

Portability: a provision for increased *presence* of the product through provisions for easier movement (rollers or compactness), or multiple unit ownership (wall clocks, radios, even refrigerators), or miniaturization for portability. Portability and *personalization*, such as the pocket knife and the wristwatch, can occur.

System: a combination of components into one unit with compatible uses and/or common parts for increased convenience, lower cost, or less space. Home entertainment centers including television, radio, hi-fi, refrigerator-freezers, combination clothes washer-dryers, clock radios, pocket knife-can-and-bottle openers are illustrative.

Similar changes can also be observed in the distribution channel. Products often progress from specialty outlets in the introductory stage to mass distribution outlets such as discount houses and contract buyers during the "maturity" and "decline" phases of the PLC. Interestingly enough, the process eventually is reversed. Buggy whips can still be found in some specialty stores and premium prices are paid for replicas of very old products.

Conclusion

The product life cycle is a useful concept. It is the equivalent of the periodic table of the elements in the physical sciences. The maturation of production technology and product configuration along with marketing programs proceeds in an orderly, somewhat predictable course over time with the merchandising nature and marketing environment noticeably similar between products that are in the same stage of their life cycle. Its use as a concept in forecasting, pricing, advertising, product planning, and other aspects of marketing management can make it a valuable concept, although considerable amounts of judgment must be used in its application.

11. Forget the Product Life Cycle Concept!

Nariman K. Dhalla
Sonia Yuspeh

Not long ago, a leading manufacturer was promoting a brand of floor wax. After a steady period of growth, the sales of the product had reached a plateau. Marketing research suggested that an increase in spot television advertising, backed by a change in copy, would help the brand to regain its momentum. Feeling that the funds could be better spent in launching a new product, management vetoed the proposal.

But the new product failed to move off the shelf despite heavy marketing support. At the same time, the old brand, with its props pulled out from under it, went into a sales decline from which it never recovered. The company had two losers on its hands.

This experience is not atypical among the nation's corporations. Many strongly believe that brands follow a life cycle and are subject to inevitable death after a few years of promotion. Like so many fascinating but untested theories in economics, the product life cycle concept (PLC) has proved to be remarkably durable, and has been expounded eloquently in numerous publications. In fact, its use in professional discussions seems to add luster and believability to the insistent claim that marketing is close to becoming a science.

The PLC concept, as developed by its proponents, is fairly simple. Like human beings or animals, everything in the marketplace is presumed to be mortal. A brand is born, grows lustily, attains maturity, and then enters

Reprinted by permission of the *Harvard Business Review*, January–February 1976, pp. 102–112. Copyright © 1976 by the President and Fellows of Harvard College; all rights reserved.

When this article was published, the authors were associate research director for economic and econometric research, and senior vice president and director of research planning, respectively, at J. Walter Thompson Company.

declining years, after which it is quietly buried. Figure 11.1 shows profit-volume relationships that are supposed to prevail in a typical PLC.

Even a cursory analysis shows flaws in this picture. In the biological world the length of each stage in the cycle is fixed in fairly precise terms; moreover, one stage follows another in an immutable and irreversible sequence. But neither of these conditions is characteristic of the marketing world. The length of different stages tends to vary from product to product. Some items move almost directly from introduction to maturity and have hardly any growth stage. Other products surge to sudden heights of fashion, hesitate momentarily at an uneasy peak, and then quickly drop off into total oblivion. Their introductory and maturity stages are barely perceptible.

What is more, it is not unusual for products to gain "second lives" or even "reincarnation." Thanks to brilliant promotion, many brands have gone from the maturity stage not to decline and death but to a fresh period of rapid growth. Later in this article we shall examine a few examples of the unlifelike and noncyclical behavior of products.

Despite the lack of correspondence between the marketing and the biological worlds, PLC advocates continue to remain dogmatic and proclaim that their concept has wide applications in different areas of planning and policy formulation. Table 11.1 gives a bird's-eye view of the four stages of the PLC and the type of marketing action that, according to proponents, is suitable for each stage. While there is no unanimity among PLC advo-

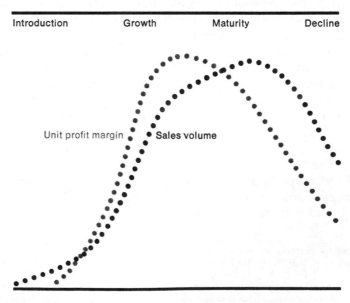

| Introduction | Growth | Maturity | Decline |

Unit profit margin   Sales volume

FIGURE 11.1   Generalized PLC Pattern for Sales and Profits

TABLE 11.1 How PLC Advocates View the Implications of the Cycle for Marketing Action

Effects and responses	Stages of the PLC — Introduction	Growth	Maturity	Decline
Competition	None of importance	Some emulators	Many rivals competing for a small piece of the pie	Few in number with a rapid shakeout of weak members
Overall strategy	Market establishment; persuade early adopters to try the product	Market penetration; persuade mass market to prefer the brand	Defense of brand position; check the inroads of competition	Preparations for removal; milk the brand dry of all possible benefits
Profits	Negligible because of high production and marketing costs	Reach peak levels as a result of high prices and growing demand	Increasing competition cuts into profit margins and ultimately into total profits	Declining volume pushes costs up to levels that eliminate profits entirely
Retail prices	High, to recover some of the excessive costs of launching	High, to take advantage of heavy consumer demand	What the traffic will bear; need to avoid price wars	Low enough to permit quick liquidation of inventory
Distribution	Selective, as distribution is slowly built up	Intensive; employ small trade discounts since dealers are eager to store	Intensive; heavy trade allowances to retain shelf space	Selective; unprofitable outlets slowly phased out
Advertising strategy	Aim at the needs of early adopters	Make the mass market aware of brand benefits	Use advertising as a vehicle for differentiation among otherwise similar brands	Emphasize low price to reduce stock
Advertising emphasis	High, to generate awareness and interest among early adopters and persuade dealers to stock the brand	Moderate, to let sales rise on the sheer momentum of word-of-mouth recommendations	Moderate, since most buyers are aware of brand characteristics	Minimum expenditures required to phase out the product
Consumer sales and promotion expenditures	Heavy, to entice target groups with samples, coupons, and other inducements to try the brand	Moderate, to create brand preference (advertising is better suited to do this job)	Heavy, to encourage brand switching, hoping to convert some buyers into loyal users	Minimal, to let the brand coast by itself

cates on details of this pattern, the basic relationships have been described repeatedly by authorities.[1]

Most writers present the PLC concept in qualitative terms, in the form of idealization without any empirical backing. Also, they fail to draw a clear distinction between product class (e.g., cigarettes), product form (e.g., filter cigarettes), and brand (e.g., Winston). But, for our purposes, this does not matter. We shall see that it is not possible to validate the model at any of these levels of aggregation.

Myths of Class and Form

Many product classes have enjoyed and will probably continue to enjoy a long and prosperous maturity stage — far more than the human life expectancy of three score years and ten. Good examples are Scotch whisky, Italian vermouth, and French perfumes. Their life span can be measured, not in decades, but in centuries. Almost as durable are such other product classes as automobiles, radios, mouthwashes, soft drinks, cough remedies, and face creams. In fact, in the absence of technological breakthroughs, many product classes appear to be almost impervious to normal life cycle pressures, provided they satisfy some basic need, be it transportation, entertainment, health, nourishment, or the desire to be attractive.

As for product form, it tends to exhibit less stability than does product class. Form is what most PLC advocates have in mind when they speak of a generalized life cycle pattern for a "product." Even here the model is not subject to precise formulation. Theoretically, it presumes the existence of some rules indicating the movement of the product from one stage to another. However, when one studies actual case histories, it becomes clear that no such rules can be objectively developed.

For evidence of this conclusion, consider Figure 11.2, which gives examples of life cycles of product forms in four diverse product classes: cigarettes, make-up bases, toilet tissues, and cereals. In order to present a realistic picture, the sales (whether in dollars or units) have been adjusted to a common base in the light of varying annual consumer expenditures on nondurable goods. In this way, it becomes possible to remove changes that do not reflect life cycle patterns, e.g., population growth, inflationary pressures, and cyclical economic fluctuation.

Unpredictable Variations

Although in most cases it is not feasible to go back far enough to get a complete birth-to-death portrayal, certain facts are obvious from Figure 11.2:

With the exception of nonfilter cigarettes, year-to-year variations make it difficult to predict when the next stage will appear, how long it will last, and to what levels the sales will reach.

One cannot often judge with accuracy in which phase of the cycle the product form is.

The four major phases do not divide themselves into clean-cut compartments. At certain points, a product may appear to have attained maturity when actually it has only reached a temporary plateau in the growth stage prior to its next big upsurge.

One of the most thorough attempts to validate the PLC concept for product classes and product forms was carried out a few years ago by the Marketing Science Institute.[2] The authors examined over 100 product categories in the food, health, and personal-care fields, and measured the number of observations that did not follow the expected sequence of introduction, growth, maturity, and decline. They compared these actual inconsistent observations with simulated sequences of equal length generated with the aid of random numbers. The hypothesis developed was that the PLC concept had some "raison d'être" only if it was capable of explaining sales behavior better than a chance model could.

The outcome of this test was discouraging. Only 17% of the observed sequences in product classes and 20% of the sequences in product forms were significantly different from chance (at the confidence level of 99 times out of 100). The authors reached the following conclusion:

> After completing the initial test of the life cycle expressed as verifiable model of sales behavior, we must register strong reservations about its general validity, even stated in its weakest, most flexible form. In our tests of the model against real sales data, it has not performed uniformly well against objective standards over a wide range of frequently purchased consumer products, nor has it performed equally well at different levels of product sales aggregation. . . . Our results suggest strongly the life cycle concept, when used without careful formulation and testing as an explicit model, is more likely to be misleading than useful.[3]

No Life Cycles for Brands

When it comes to brands, the PLC model has even less validity. Many potentially useful offerings die in the introductory stage because of inadequate product development or unwise market planning, or both. The much-expected ebullient growth phase never arrives. Even when a brand survives the introductory stage, the model in most cases cannot be used as a planning or a predictive tool.

Figure 11.3 shows the life cycle trends of certain brands in the product forms earlier discussed. The evidence for the PLC concept is discouraging. With the exception of nonfilter cigarettes, the brands tend to have different

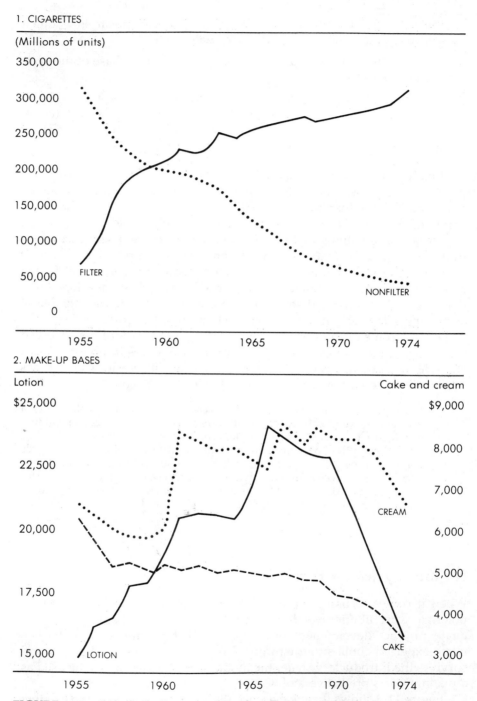

FIGURE 11.2   Life Cycle Patterns of Product Forms in Four Product Classes

NOTE: Dollar sales figures are in thousands of dollars. Both unit and dollar sales are adjusted to a common base of consumer nondurable goods expenditures.

3. TOILET TISSUES: MAJOR NATIONAL BRANDS ONLY

4. CEREALS

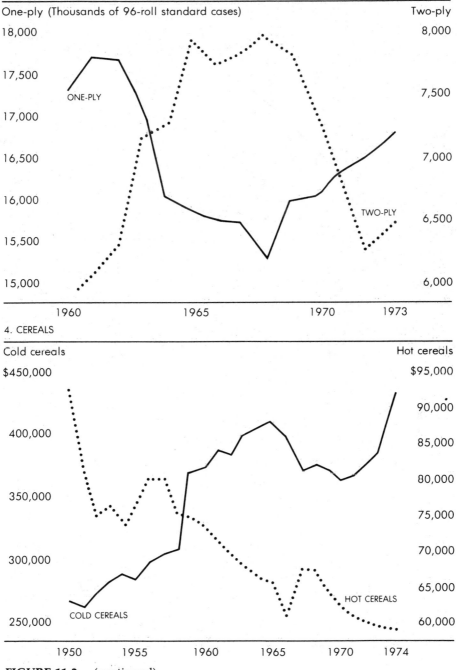

FIGURE 11.2 (continued)

SOURCES: For 1, *Advertising Age;* for 2 and 4, *Supermarketing and Food Topics;* for 3, J. Walter Thompson research.

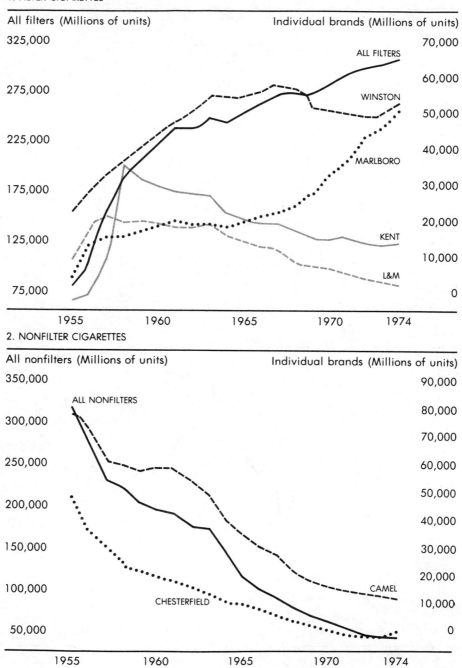

FIGURE 11.3   Life Cycle Patterns of Brands Compared with Product Forms

NOTE: All sales figures are adjusted to a common base of consumer nondurable goods expenditures.

3. ONE-PLY TOILET TISSUES

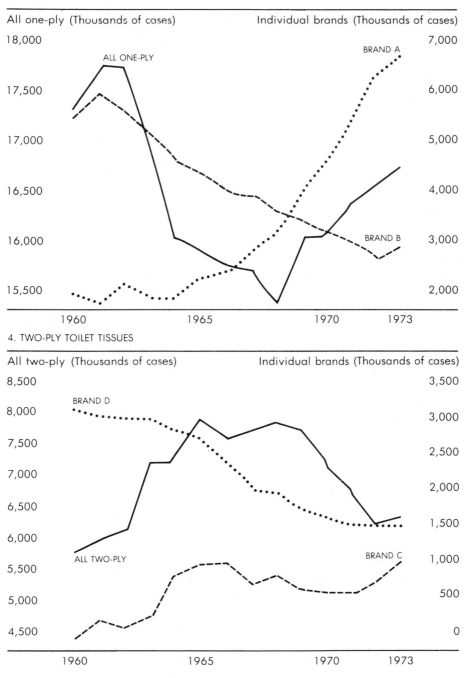

FIGURE 11.3 (continued)

SOURCE: For cigarettes, *Advertising Age*; for toilet tissues, J. Walter Thompson research.

sales patterns, and the product-form curves throw no light on what the sales would be in the future. All that can be said is that if a product form (e.g., nonfilter cigarettes) is truly in a final declining stage, it is very difficult for a brand (e.g., Chesterfield) to reverse the trend. However, with respect to the first three stages of the PLC, no firm conclusions can be drawn about brand behavior from the product-form curve.

Some PLC advocates have tried to salvage their theory by introducing different types of curves to fit different situations. For instance, one authority, in a study of 258 ethical drug brands, suggests six different PLC curves[4]; another develops no less than nine variants: marketing specialties, fashion cycle, high-learning products, low-learning products, pyramided cycles, instant busts, abortive introductions, straight fads, and fads with significant residual markets.[5]

Such efforts at curve fitting leave much to be desired. From the standpoint of practical marketing, they are sterile exercises in taxonomy. It would be better to admit that the whole PLC concept has little value in the world of brands. Clearly, the PLC is a *dependent* variable which is determined by marketing actions; it is not an *independent* variable to which companies should adapt their marketing programs. Marketing management itself can alter the shape and duration of a brand's life cycle.

Of course, a company may not be able to extend the maturity phase indefinitely. When a brand passes "over the hill" in sales, no marketing strategies are effective anymore. Such a drop may be due to changes in consumer tastes and values, or to the fact that users have shifted their preference to a new and improved competitive product. In these instances, euthanasia has to be quietly performed so that the company's capital resources can be used profitably in other ventures.

Blunders Due to PLC Blinders

Unfortunately, in numerous cases a brand is discontinued, not because of irreversible changes in consumer values or tastes, but because management, on the basis of the PLC theory, believes the brand has entered a dying stage. In effect, a self-fulfilling prophecy results.

Suppose a brand is acceptable to consumers but has a few bad years because of other factors — for instance, poor advertising, delisting by a major chain, or entry of a "me-too" competitive product backed by massive sampling. Instead of thinking in terms of corrective measures, management begins to feel that its brand has entered a declining stage. It therefore withdraws funds from the promotion budget to finance R&D on new items. The next year the brand does even worse, panic increases, and new products are hastily launched without proper testing. Not surprisingly, most of the new products fail. Thus management has talked itself into a decline by relying solely on the PLC concept.

The annals of business are full of cases of once strong and prosperous brands that have died — if not with a bang, at least with a whimper — because top management wore PLC blinders. A good example is the case of Ipana. This toothpaste was marketed by a leading packaged-goods company until 1968, when it was abandoned in favor of new brands. In early 1969, two Minnesota businessmen picked up the Ipana name, concocted a new formula, but left the package unchanged. With hardly any promotion, the supposedly petrified demand for Ipana turned into $250,000 of sales in the first seven months of operation. In 1973, a survey conducted by the Target Group Index showed that, despite poor distribution, the toothpaste was still being used by 1,520,000 adults. Considering the limited resources of the owners, the brand would have been in an even stronger position had it been retained by its original parent company and been given appropriate marketing support.

Planning Without PLC

In a slightly different vein, there are several cases of companies that have ignored the PLC concept and achieved great success through imaginative marketing strategies. The classic example of the 1940s and 1950s is Du-Pont's nylon. This product, whose original uses are primarily military (parachutes, rope, and so on), would have gradually faded into oblivion had the company believed that the declining sales curve signaled death. Instead, management boldly decided to enter the volatile consumer textile market. Women were first induced to switch from silk to nylon stockings. The market was later expanded by convincing teenagers and subteens to start wearing hosiery. Sales grew even further when the company introduced tinted and patterned hosiery, thereby converting hosiery from a neutral accessory to a central element of fashion.

Here are other brands whose productive lives have been stretched many decades by sound planning:

> Listerine Antiseptic has succeeded in retaining its lion's share of the mouthwash market despite heavy competitive pressures and the introduction of strongly supported new brands.

> Marlboro is fast edging up to top place in the highly segmented filter-cigarette market by focusing on the same basic theme — only developing different variations of it.

> Seven-up, whose growth had been impeded because of its image strictly as a mixer, now has more room to expand as a result of taking the "Uncola" position against Coke and Pepsi.

This list could be expanded considerably. The following are ten other leading brands that have been around for a long time but are still full of vitality because of intelligent marketing: Anacin analgesic, Budweiser beer, Colgate toothpaste, Dristan cold remedy, Geritol vitamin-mineral supplement, Jell-o gelatin, Kleenex facial tissue, Maxwell House coffee, Planter's peanuts, and Tide detergent.

The importance of a proper marketing effort is further illustrated in Figure 11.4. Here are comparisons of rival brands in various product forms. In 1961, the brands in each pairing had approximately the same share of usage. However, by 1973 one of each two was able to move up substantially, while the other took a reverse turn. Had the PLC forces played an all-important role during this 12-year span, both brands in each pair would have gone downhill. This exhibit demonstrates that the judicious use of

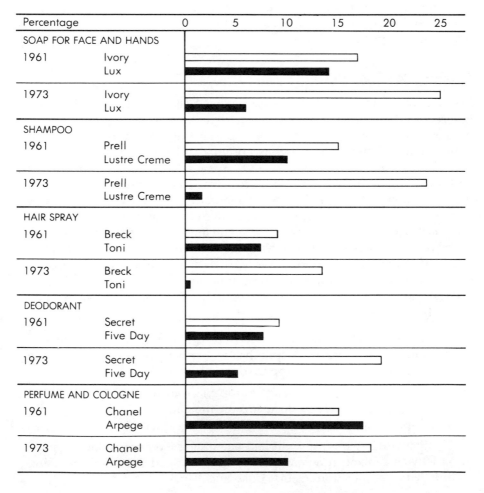

FIGURE 11.4   Growth and Decline of Brand Usage Share Within Product Forms, 1961 and 1973

SOURCE: For 1961, "Beauty Secrets," *Good Housekeeping;* for 1973, *Target Group Index Reports* for 1974.

advertising and other marketing tools can check the erosion of a consumer franchise. If a brand is widely available at a competitive price, and has certain benefits which are meaningful to a large segment of the population, then well-conceived and properly directed marketing communications will produce the right response at the checkout counter. This is true regardless of whether the brand has been in existence for two years or twenty.

Capitalizing on Today's Products

A major disservice of the PLC concept to marketing is that it has led top executives to overemphasize new product introduction. This route is perilous. Experience shows that nothing seems to take more time, cost more money, involve more pitfalls, or cause more anguish than new product programs.

Actual statistics are hard to come by, but it is generally believed in business circles that the odds are four to one against a new product becoming a winner. Yet, like a new baby in the house, the new product too often gets all the attention while the older brands are pretty much neglected.

The point is not that work on new products should be halted. Obviously work should continue, for new products are vital to the future. Yet it is today's products that are closest to the cash register; the company's chances of generating greater profits normally depend on them. It is foolish for a corporation to invest millions of dollars to build goodwill for a brand, then walk away from it and spend additional millions all over again for a new brand with no consumer franchise.

In these days of inflation, shortages, and slow economic growth, industry can ill afford a system that pushes brand proliferation too far. The challenge to management lies in avoiding market fragmentation and in building up large national franchise for a few key brands through heavy and intelligent marketing support.

An Effective System

How can such support be given? Management needs an approach that will help it to position the brand to a large segment of the population, evaluate different options, and foresee opportunities or dangers that lie ahead. Such an approach can be put together by combining strategic research and tracking studies with marketing and communications models. Let us now consider one example from the snack food industry.

Getting Started.   A branded drink had a small, select group of loyal users who liked its strong, bitter taste. But sales for some time had been gradually declining. Despite the advice of some PLC-oriented marketing consultants, management was opposed to discontinuing the line and to bringing out ways of increasing that franchise among the large body of nonusers. The results indicated that the brand could be best positioned against one segment of the market — nutrition-conscious housewives who took their role as custodians of family health and well-being very seriously.

Although never mentioned before in advertising, it so happened that the tangy bitterness of the brand was mainly due to the addition of certain "natural" ingredients. Also, this benefit was distinctive and not generic to the whole product category. Hence the company had a clear edge over competition.

New advertising was prepared around nutrition, wholesomeness, and the added ingredients. At the same time, in order to retain loyal users, management continued the old 30-second TV spots emphasizing strong taste. On the research side, arrangements were made to obtain from consumer panels and tracking studies quarterly information on the brand's "share of mind" and share of market. The emphasis in the tracking research was on the target groups, namely, housewives who were (1) fond of the taste, and (2) neutral toward taste but health conscious.

Building an Effective Model.   After three years, it was felt that sufficient data had been collected to start building a marketing-communications model that would bring relevant variables, both controllable and uncontrollable, into a coherent, unified picture. Using this picture, management could examine the effects of its marketing policies on two key consumer targets.

The basic format of the model can be seen at a glance in Figure 11.5. The mathematical details are discussed at length in the Appendix.

Once the system was in operation, it was frequently used to predict likely changes in sales as a result of certain actions planned by the company. For example, when preparing his budget for the next quarter, the marketing manager wanted to know what would happen if he kept the price unchanged but augmented advertising from $3.30 million to $3.55 million. As described in the Appendix, the model indicated that an increase of this magnitude would theoretically raise the brand share by 0.3 percentage point. Similar projections could be made for other types of changes contemplated in the marketing mix.

The model was of great value in another way. At one point, discrepancies began to appear between actual and estimated attitude changes. The higher advertising levels were not able to generate better attitudinal ratings, as predicted by the equation. Some part of the system apparently had broken down. Further investigation revealed that the advertising campaign was wearing thin. This problem was solved by developing a fresh program built around the same basic strategy.

Thus, because management had a "radar set" beamed on the marketplace, it was in a position to initiate remedial measures before there was a sharp drop in sales.

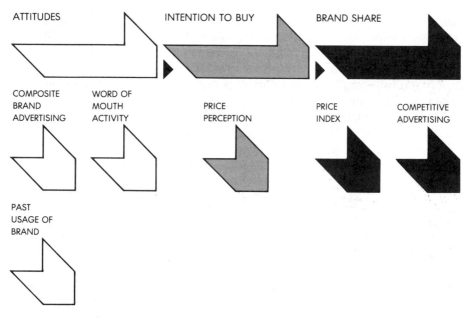

FIGURE 11.5 Model Showing Relationships of Different Variables to Brand Share

A model of this type can also aid management in distinguishing between irreversible sales declines and those which are controllable through a marketing effort. Suppose a brand has taken an irreversible turn for the worse, with the scores on attitudes and intentions continuing to decline and consumer research indicating a fundamental change in consumer tastes and values. Then it is advisable to discontinue the brand and embark upon other profitable ventures. Such drastic action can be justified if based on a careful study of the marketplace rather than on blind faith in the PLC concept.

Conclusion

The PLC concept has little validity. The sequence of marketing strategies typically recommended for succeeding stages of the cycle is likely to cause trouble. In some respects, the concept has done more harm than good by persuading top executives to neglect existing brands and place undue emphasis on new products.

The 1960s were a period of growing affluence, cheap energy, limitless supplies, and rising public expectations. This decade saw brand proliferation, product parity, and market segmentation carried to an extreme. The scenario now has changed. Inflation, shortages, and slow economic growth characterize the 1970s. As a result, aggressive brand proliferation no longer makes sense. The emphasis should shift from spouting out new "me-too" products to prolonging the productive life of existing brands through sound and solid marketing support.

Marketing-communications models can be of great help. They measure quantitatively the influence of different elements on sales, permit the evaluation of different options, and provide advance warning signals so that remedial action can be taken before a crisis occurs. The management that uses them will not be misled by minor sales aberrations into believing erroneously that a brand has entered a declining stage.

Appendix

Model building in the field of marketing and consumer behavior is complex. At the early stages, it is desirable to run a sufficient number of cross-lagged and partial correlations in order to determine the true causal path among the variables under study. The equations, when formulated, should be checked for biases such as multicollinearity and autocorrelation. If a simultaneous-equation model is developed, the parameters should be estimated through two-stage least squares, or through limited or full-information maximum likelihood techniques.

The purpose of this section is not to go into mathematical details but to show how management can make use of the model, assuming that all statistical requirements have been satisfied.

To simplify exposition, the equations for the snack drink brand discussed in the text are presented in the linear form, though actually non-linear and interactive relationships are more realistic. Here are three equations in a specific marketing-communications model:

$$ATT_t = -3.49 + 1.05 \text{ ADV-BR}_t + 1.50 \text{ WOM}_t + 0.88 \text{ BS}_{t-1}$$

$$INT_t = 5.13 + 0.74 \text{ ATT}_t - 0.44 \text{ PR-PER}_t$$

$$BS_t = 129.57 + 1.03 \text{ INT}_{t-1} - 0.94 \text{ PR-IND}_t - 0.90 \text{ ADV-COM}_t$$

The symbols in this equation are defined below. The data source for each symbol is shown in parentheses, with TS standing for tracking studies, CP for consumer panels, and AA for advertising agency:

- ATT (TS)
  Attitudes (sum of ratings on nutrition, natural ingredients, and liking for taste)

- ADV-BR (AA)
  Advertising expenditures on the brand, in millions of dollars (composite figure)

- WOM (TS)
  Word of mouth (percent of respondents who talk about the brand
    with friends, neighbors, or relatives)
- BS (CP)
  Brand share
- INT (TS)
  Intention to buy the brand at the time of next purchase
- PR-PER (TS)
  Price perception (percent of respondents who regard the brand as
    high priced)
- PR-IND (CP)
  Ratio of brand's price to the average price of all competitors (100
    means the brand price is the same as the average for competition)
- ADV-COM (AA)
  Advertising expenditures of major competitors in millions of dollars
- $t, t - 1$
  Time period, t for current quarter and $t - 1$ for preceding quarter.

The variables are self-explanatory, except for ADV-BR (Equation 1),
which takes into account the lagged effects of advertising. At the preliminary stages of model building, it was found that 80% of the impact was felt
almost immediately and 20% was felt in the subsequent quarter. These
weights were employed in computing the composite figure.

The following illustration shows how the model could be used to predict likely changes in brand share. Suppose the marketing manager is faced
with the following problem: What would be the increase in brand share
from the current level of 12.2%, if he keeps the price unchanged but aug-
ments advertising from $3.3 million to $3.55 million between the first and
the second quarter? (The input in the model for the second quarter would
be $3.5 million $-$ 3.55 $\times$ 0.8 + 3.3 $\times$ 0.3.) Much would depend on the
accuracy with which he could forecast the four variables that are beyond
the company's control — word of mouth (WOM), price perception (PR-
PER), the price index (PR-IND), and competitive advertising (ADV-COM).

Assume that the marketing manager is able to prepare the following
estimates based on past trends and opinions of some experts in the field:

- WOM (2d quarter)   6.5%
- PR-PER (2d quarter)   11.6%
- PR-IND (3d quarter)   105.5
- ADV-COM (3d quarter) $37.4 million

The three equations in the model can now be used to predict the brand
share two quarters ahead. The computations are as follows:

$$ATT_{t+1} = -3.49 + 1.05\ ADV\text{-}BR_{t+1} + 1.50\ WOM_{t+1} + 0.88\ BS_t$$

$$= -3.49 + (1.05)(3.5) + (1.50)(6.5) + (0.88)(12.2)$$

$$= 20.67$$

$$INT_{t+1} = 5.13 + 0.74\ ATT_{t+1} + 0.44\ PR\text{-}PER_{t+1}$$

$$= 5.13 + (0.74)(20.67) - (0.44)(11.6) = 15.32$$

$$BS_{t+2} = 129.57 + 1.03\ INT_{t+1} - 0.94\ PR\text{-}IND_{t+2}$$
$$- 0.90\ ADV\text{-}COM_{t+2}$$

$$= 129.57 + (1.03)(15.32) - (.94)(105.5)$$
$$- (.90)(37.4) = 12.52$$

Thus a planned increase of $250,000 in advertising in the next quarter would lead to a theoretical brand share of 12.52% in the subsequent quarter, compared to the current share of 12.2%.

The model described has been tailor-made for a particular company. Naturally, the effect of outside influences on corporate efforts would differ from product category to product category and from brand to brand.

Notes

1. See, for example, David J. Luck, *Product Policy and Strategy* (Englewood Cliffs, N.J.: Prentice-Hall, 1972); Arch Patton, *Top Management's Stake in a Product's Life Cycle* (New York: McKinsey & Co., Inc., June 1959), Thomas A. Staudt and Donald A. Taylor, *A Managerial Introduction to Marketing*, 2nd ed. (Englewood Cliffs, N.J.: Prentice-Hall, 1970); and Chester R. Wasson, *Product Management* (St. Charles, Ill.: Challenge Books, 1971).
2. See Rolando Polli and Victor J. Cook's "A Test of the Product Life Cycle as a Model of Sales Behavior," *Market Science Institute Working Paper*, November 1967, p. 43, and also their "Validity of the Product Life Cycle," *The Journal of Business*, October 1969, p. 385.
3. See Polli and Cook, "A Test of the Product Life Cycle," p. 61.
4. See William E. Cox, "Product Life Cycles as Marketing Models," *The Journal of Business*, October 1967, p. 375.
5. See Wasson's *Product Management*.

Strategic Marketing Models for Allocating Resources

THE ARTICLES IN THIS SECTION discuss normative models that are used by managers to develop marketing strategies.[1] These models — the PIMS model, the BCG market growth/market share matrix, and the market attractiveness/competitive capabilities matrix — are used both to evaluate product-market alternatives and to determine the level of investment that should be directed toward the product-markets. The financial analysis, product life cycle, and experience curve concepts discussed in the previous section provide a foundation for these strategic planning models.

The PIMS Project

In the introduction to the previous section, we discussed the use of traditional financial analysis to evaluate product market opportunities. Although financial analysis is theoretically appealing, it does not provide insight into the factors that make an opportunity attractive. Why do some strategic alternatives have a high ROI while other alternatives have a low ROI? The PIMS project described in the first article in this section was established to address this shortcoming of traditional financial analysis.

The principal objective of the PIMS (Profit Impact of Market Strategy) project is to determine empirically the factors that lead to business unit profitability. As a first step toward the realization of this objective, the 200 member corporations of the Strategic Planning Institute (SPI) provided data on the performance, operation, financial structure, and environment of individual business units. Then, this data base was used to discover empirical generality concerning factors that related to business unit performance and to assist managers in evaluating the performance of, and developing strategies for, their specific business units.

Factors Related to Profitability

Early results of analyzing the PIMS data base indicated that profitability and cash flow are related to nine strategic factors. These nine influences account for almost 80 percent of the determination of business success or failure. In approximate order of importance, they are the following:

1. *Investment intensity.*   Technology and the chosen way of doing business govern how much fixed capital and working capital are required to produce a dollar of sales or a dollar of value added in the business. Investment intensity generally produces a negative impact on percentage measures of profitability or net cash flow; i.e., businesses that are mechanized or automated or inventory-intensive generally show lower returns on investment and sales than businesses that are not.

2. *Productivity.*   Businesses producing high value added per employee are more profitable than those with low value added per employee. (Definition: "value added" is the amount by which the business increases the market value of the raw materials and components it buys.)

3. *Market position.*   A business's share of its served market (both absolute and relative to its three largest competitors) has a positive impact on its profit and net cash flow. (The "served market" is the specific segment of the total potential market — defined in terms of products, customers, or areas — in which the business actually competes.)

4. *Growth of the served market.*   Growth is generally favorable to dollar measures of profit, indifferent to percent measures of profit, and negative to all measures of net cash flow.

5. *Quality of the products or services offered.*   Quality, defined as the customers' evaluation of the business's product/service package as compared to that of competitors, has a generally favorable impact on all measures of financial performance.

6. *Innovation/differentiation.*   Extensive actions taken by a business in the areas of new product introduction, R&D, marketing effort, and so on, generally produce a positive effect on its performance if that business has strong market position to begin with. Otherwise, usually not.

7. *Vertical integration.*   For businesses located in mature and stable markets, vertical integration (i.e., make rather than buy) generally has a favorable effect on performance. In markets that are rapidly growing, declining, or otherwise changing, the opposite is true.

8. *Cost push.*   The rates of increase of wages, salaries, and raw material prices, and the presence of a labor union, have complex impacts on profit and cash flow — depending on how the business is positioned to pass along the increase to its customers or to absorb the higher costs internally.

9. *Current strategic effort.*   The current direction of change of any of the

above factors has effects on profit and cash flow that are frequently opposite to that of the factor itself. For example, having strong market share tends to increase net cash flow, but getting share drains cash while the business is making that effort.

Additionally — There is such a thing as being a good or a poor "operator." A good operator can improve the profitability of a strong strategic position or minimize the damage of a weak one; a poor operator does the opposite. The presence of a management team that functions as a good operator is therefore a favorable element of a business; it produces a financial result greater than one would expect from the strategic position of the business alone.[2]

Some additional findings are discussed in the first article of this section, Article 12.

Recent research using the PIMS data base is directed toward elaborating on these basic relationships. Attention now is being directed toward uncovering contingencies and qualifications that must be considered when using the basic PIMS findings. For example, Buzzell and Wiersema[3] examined the relationship between changes in marketing mix variables and changes in market share. They found that increased new product activity and increased expenditures in sales force, advertising, and sales promotion were related to increases in market share; cutting price, they found, had little effect on share.[4]

PIMS Models for Strategic Analysis

The general strategic principles developed through research on the PIMS data base are of interest to managers and scholars, but the SPI has also developed a Par ROI and a Par cash flow model to help individual business unit managers evaluate the performance of their units and make strategic decisions. These models are linear equations derived through regression analysis. With these models, managers can determine what ROI and cash flow would normally be expected from a business unit in a similar strategic situation with average management and luck. This normal or Par ROI and cash flow are determined by simply substituting the values describing the specific unit into the regression equation derived by analyzing all business units in the data base. An example of a Par ROI report is shown in Table IV.1.

Based on this Par ROI report, managers can assess the performance of their business. Are their businesses above or below expected profits? What strategic factors are responsible for abnormal performance? What would the Par ROI be if specific changes were made in strategic factors such as market share, marketing expenditures, or product quality? By using the Par cash flow model, managers also can determine the typical cash flow that would result from making specific strategic changes. Thus the Par

TABLE IV.1   Par ROI Report (Impact of ROI-Influencing Factors: A Diagnosis of Strategic Strengths and Weaknesses)

		PIMS MEAN	THIS BUSINESS	IMPACT	SENSITIVITY A CHANGE OF	SENSITIVITY CHANGES IMPACT BY
	ATTRACTIVENESS OF ENVIRONMENT			0.6		
1	Purchase Amount — Immediate Costs	5.2	4.0	1.8	0.20	−0.31
2	Real Market Growth, Short Run	8.2	−4.1	−0.6	2.00	0.20
3	Industry (SIC) Growth, Long Run	9.1	6.8	−0.5	1.00	0.02
4	Selling Price Growth Rate	6.8	0.5	−0.1	1.00	0.00
	COMPETITIVE POSITION			0.2		
5	Market Position			−2.9		
	Market Share	23.7	15.0		5.00	3.05
	Relative Market Share	61.7	34.8			
6	Industry Concentration Ratio	56.5	51.0	−0.2	5.00	0.19
7	Employees Unionized (%)	48.3	0.0	2.6	5.00	−0.25
8	Immediate Customer Fragmentation	12.2	25.0	0.2	2.00	0.04
9	Market Share Growth Rate	3.3	8.1	0.7	2.00	0.31
10	Market Share Instability	4.0	1.2	−0.3	0.50	0.06
	DIFFERENTIATION FROM COMPETITORS			2.8		
11	Relative Product Quality	25.9	34.3	0.8	5.00	0.75
12	Price Relative to Competition	103.5	100.3	0.1	1.00	−0.08
13	Standard Products/Services?		Yes	0.5		
14	Relative Compensation	100.9	102.0	0.0	1.00	−0.10
15	New Product Sales/Total Sales	11.9	0.0	1.3	5.00	−0.49
	EFFECTIVENESS OF INVESTMENT USE			5.0		
16	Investment Intensity Index			7.3		
	Investment/Sales	56.1	33.0		5.00	−2.71
	Investment/Value Added	96.7	65.6			
17	Value Added per Employee ($)	30.0	23.8	−1.7	5.00	1.67
18	Vertical Integration	58.8	51.9	−0.8	2.00	0.37
19	Relative Integration Backward		Less	−0.9		
20	Relative Integration Forward		Same	−0.3		

TABLE IV.1 (continued)

		PIMS MEAN	THIS BUSINESS	IMPACT	SENSITIVITY A CHANGE OF	SENSITIVITY CHANGES IMPACT BY
21	Fixed Capital Intensity	52.3	42.4	0.5	5.00	−0.36
22	Capacity Utilization	79.6	76.3	−0.4	5.00	0.30
23	Investment per Employee ($)	30.4	15.6	0.4	5.00	−0.12
24	Inventory/Sales	18.8	10.7	1.0	2.00	−0.34
25	FIFO Valuation?		No	0.0		
26	Newness of P&E (NBV/GBV)	55.0	52.0	0.0	2.00	0.27
	DISCRETIONARY BUDGET EXPENDITURES			1.4		
27	Marketing Expense/Sales	10.8	7.7	1.5	2.00	−1.27
28	R&D Expense/Sales	2.4	2.5	−0.1	0.50	−0.23

1. Par ROI is the sum of the five category impacts added to the all-PIMS average ROI:

Attractiveness of Environment	0.6%
Competitive Position	0.2
Differentiation from Competitors	2.8
Effectiveness of Investment Use	5.0
Discretionary Budget Expenditures	1.4
Sum of Impacts	9.9%
+ Average Return on Investment	22.1
"Par" Return on Investment	32.0%

2. While useful insights may be gained by looking at individual factor impacts, attention should be focussed on the aggregate (categorical) impacts when individual factors are interrelated.
3. Interpretation of Purchase Amount Immediate Customers:
    4 = from $100 up to $999

SOURCE: Reprinted from Bradley T. Gale, Donald F. Heany, and Donald J. Swire, "The Par ROI Report: Explanation and Commentary," *The Strategic Planning Institute*, 1977, pages 8–9.

reports are used to evaluate strategic alternatives in terms of the expected ROI and investment level (cash flows) associated with achieving the ROI.

Limitations of the PIMS Model

Article 13, "PIMS: A Reexamination," deals with some problems and limitations with the PIMS project. Criticism of the PIMS model center around the specification of the Par models and the interpretation of the results.

Model Specification. Specification problems focus on whether important variables have been omitted from the model and whether the structure of the model is appropriate. A critical issue that has not been resolved is whether one complex model can be used to describe the performance of a wide diversity of businesses. Perhaps, it would be more appropriate to develop separate regression models for homogeneous groups of businesses, such as raw material, industrial product, consumer product, and service businesses.

Another issue is the choice of dependent and independent variables. Is ROI the best measure of business unit performance? Should not managerial intentions and environmental characteristics be incorporated in the model?

A final issue concerns the estimation bias resulting from a confounding of the dependent and independent variables. In the Par ROI model, the investment, revenue, and cost terms are on both sides of the model equation. Investment is the denominator of ROI (the dependent variable), and it is also the numerator of investment intensity (an independent variable). Sales and costs are also components of both the dependent and independent variables. Profits (sales minus costs) are the numerator of ROI (the dependent variable) and part of investment intensity and marketing expenditure (the independent variables). The net result of this problem is that the high explanatory power of the Par models (80 percent of the variance explained) may be due in part to the tautological nature of the model.

Interpretation of Results.   Perhaps the most serious problem with the PIMS models is the implication that the relationships in the model are causal. The Par models describe static relationships between variables at a specific time. Owing to the cross-section nature of the analysis, one cannot infer that changes in the independent variables will cause changes in the dependent variable — the ROI or cash flow. For example, even though relative market share is significantly related to ROI, an increase in market share may not lead to a higher ROI — because the cost of increasing market share may be greater than the benefit realized.

Summary — the PIMS Model

While there are many problems with the PIMS models, the PIMS project is one of the few strategy research efforts based on empirical research: most observations on strategy are based on management experience, simple rules of thumb, and case studies. Thus, the PIMS model provides a unique source of information for making strategic decisions.

Portfolio Models

The remaining articles in this section deal with two portfolio classification models: the BCG market growth/market share model and the market attractiveness/competitive capabilities model. These models represent the two types of portfolio classification models that have been virtually synonymous with strategic market planning since the early 1970s.[5] On the basis of an extensive survey, Phillippe Haspeslagh estimates that, as of 1979, 36 percent of the Fortune 1000 and 45 percent of the Fortune 500 industrial companies use, to some extent, the portfolio planning approach associated with these models.[6]

When using these portfolio classification models, one must first undertake the following three steps:

1. Define the strategic product-market opportunities. The considerations associated with defining these strategic opportunities are discussed in Section II of this book.
2. Plot each product-market opportunity on a two-dimensional grid. Classify the opportunity on the basis of its position in this grid.
3. Assign a classification to the product-market opportunity, thereby determining the strategic objective for the opportunity and the level of resources to be allocated so that the objective can be realized.

The market growth/market share and market attractiveness/competitive position models differ in terms of variables used to classify opportunity. However, there are strong similarities between these models in terms of objectives and resource allocation patterns associated with positions on the grid.

Market Growth/Market Share Model

The market growth/market share model, developed by the Boston Consulting Group, is described in Article 14, "Strategy and the Business Portfolio." The two dimensions used to classify strategic opportunities in this model are related to the product life cycle and experience curve concepts discussed in Section II of this book. The vertical axis, long-term market growth, divides the opportunities into those in the introductory/growth stage of the product life cycle and those in the mature/decline stage of the product life cycle. The horizontal dimension uses relative market share as a surrogate for relative position on the experience curve. Using this dimension, opportunities are classified by whether or not they have dominant market share opportunities. Opportunities with a dominant share have the most experience and hence the lowest cost.

Classification in Terms of the Model.   Using these two dimensions, each strategic opportunity is classified as one of these: star, cash cow, dog, or problem. The strategy for the product-market is determined by the classification. Note that the potential strategies can be ordered in terms of the resources to be allocated to the product-market.

Investment Level	Strategy	Objective	Classification
+ +	invest	gain share	problem
+	maintain	hold share	star
−	harvest	lose share	problem, dog
− −	milk	maintain share	cash cow

It is important to realize that product-market opportunities are classified in terms of their long-term growth rate and relative market share — *not* in terms of their profitability or cash generation. Thus, a product-market with high growth and low relative share is classified as a problem, even if it is generating a high positive cash flow. The cash generation may be due to a harvesting strategy, an improper definition of the market, or improper long-term management of the unit.

Criticism of the Market Growth/Market Share Matrix. The market growth/market share matrix has certainly received substantial acceptance and has spawned a new vocabulary for marketing strategy; but it is not universally accepted. Two articles in this section — "Diagnosing the Product Portfolio" and "Strategic Marketing: Betas, Boxes, or Basics" — raises some concerns about the validity of the model. These concerns center around the following premises basic to the model:

1. *Relative market share and long-term market are the most important considerations for making strategic marketing decisions.* By focusing on these two factors, the BCG product portfolio approach ignores a number of factors empirically related to profitability that were found in the PIMS studies and theoretically related to performance in financial models, such as risk.

2. *Cash flow is a function of relative market share.* The experience curve is the conceptual foundation for the horizontal dimension of the BCG portfolio. Article 8 provides some empirical support for the notion that a business with the most cumulative experience in a product market will have the lowest cost. However, there are a number of product markets in which experience effects are quite weak. In addition, there are situations in which market share is a poor indicator of relative cost. For example, Apple has the largest market share in personal computers, but IBM may have the lowest cost due to share experience gained through manufacturing larger computers.

3. *It is "easier" to gain share in high growth markets.* This premise is based on the idea that competitive reaction is greater in a mature market. On this assumption, the prescriptions of the market growth/market share matrix indicate that strategic investments should be restricted to high growth product-markets (stars or problems). But there is little evidence to support this premise. Many managers are wary of restricting investments to high growth markets. Roy Ash followed a course of investing in high growth, high technology businesses when he was CEO of AM International. This

strategy resulted in the near-collapse of AM. Richard Black, who replaced Ash,

> . . . favors a slower, more methodical growth strategy. He sees great appeal in businesses that operate in markets growing at a 3 percent to 5 percent annual rate. "If you've got a 30 percent to 40 percent growth business, you've got everybody looking at the business and jumping in," he explains. "I have nothing against high technology, but why do I want to get into a put-limit poker game [such as word processing] with giant companies that have money coming out of their ears? . . ."[7]

4. *A business should be in cash balance.* While the market growth/market share model does not preclude raising cash externally, there is an implied assumption that cash must be generated from some product-market (cash cows) to fund growth and share-gaining activities in other product markets (problems and stars). Thus the portfolio of product-market opportunities needs to be balanced between problems, stars, and cash cows. However, many businesses have made strategic investments with funds raised externally rather than generated internally.

5. *Interdependencies between product-markets is limited to the generation and use of cash.* Basically, the product portfolio approach treats each strategic alternative as an independent unit. The business unit manager manages a portfolio of product-markets just as a mutual fund manager manages a portfolio of stocks. This perspective ignores potential synergies between product-markets, such as shared experience. Such synergies form the basis of unique competitive advantages that determine why one business is successful in a product-market and another is not.

Article 15, "Diagnosing the Product Portfolio," emphasizes that there are a number of problems associated with implementing strategies based on the BCG product portfolio. First, it is often difficult to define the unit of analysis and measure its position. Then, too, there are administrative problems in aligning the rewards of managers to the objective for the product manager. Clearly, the manager of a cash cow should not be rewarded on the basis of growth and the manager of a problem should not be rewarded on the basis of profitability. Such reward structures would result in managerial decisions counter to the generation of cash or the achievement of a dominant market position. (This issue is addressed in Article 26.) Finally, the labels assigned to product-markets may lead to a self-fulfilling prophecy, precluding the investigation of new directions that might alter the long-term prospects in the product-market.

Market Attractiveness/Competitive Capabilities Model

An article in this section, "The Directional Policy Matrix — a Tool for Strategic Planning," describes procedures for considering a broader array of variables for positioning strategic opportunities on a grid. The principal difference between this portfolio approach and the BCG approach discussed previously is the use of multiple factors to assess each dimension rather than a single factor. When using the market attractiveness/ competitive capabilities model, the market size, market profitability, and environmental factors are considered in addition to long-term market growth to assess the position of product market on the market attractiveness dimension. Similarly, the assessment of position on the competitive capabilities dimension considers technological, financial, and managerial capabilities in addition to relative market share and the associated experience curve cost advantages.

It is true that more factors are considered when using the market attractiveness/competitive capabilities matrix, but it is also true that the assessment of position is highly subjective. In fact, the strategic insight provided by this approach may be limited to a rather mundane conclusion that a business should invest heavily in attractive product-market opportunities for which the business possesses a strong competitive advantage.

Identifying and Exploiting Competitive Advantage — Back to Basics

The final article in this section, Article 17, is "Strategic Marketing: Betas, Boxes, or Basics," which reviews the two portfolio approaches and concludes that these models offer limited insight and may even provide misleading guidance in some situations. Its author, Robin Wensley, suggests that a return to basics, the search for sustainable competitive advantage, would provide more meaningful guidance for strategic decision modeling. This basic principle was incorporated in our definition of marketing strategy that was presented in the introduction to Section I.

Focusing on building sustainable competitive advantage means that managers should evaluate strategic alternatives primarily in terms of the strengths and weaknesses of business. Opportunities are attractive when they build on unique competitive capabilities possessed by the business. Obviously, these unique capabilities give the business an advantage over competition in the product-market. Such capabilities reflect synergies between the core activities of the business unit and the strategic alternatives that are being considered.

H. Igor Ansoff's growth vector matrix, shown in Figure IV.1 is a useful, analytical tool for assessing the competitive advantage and synergy that a business can bring to a product-market opportunity.[8] The dimensions of this matrix are the similarity or synergy between the core marketing and production/technological capabilities of a business and the capabilities it needs to be successful in each product opportunity being considered. Clearly, a

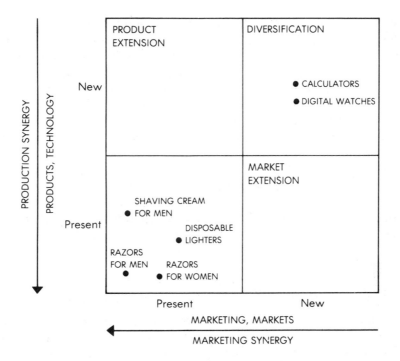

FIGURE IV.1 Assessing Relative Competitive Advantage

business has its greatest competitive advantage in product-markets very similar to its core business activities; and the business will not have an advantage in product markets requiring new and different marketing and technological capabilities.

The usefulness of the Ansoff matrix can be illustrated by examining strategic opportunities considered by Gillette.[9] Gillette's core business was razors and razor blades for men. As Gillette explored growth opportunities, some of the strategic investments they made were in razors for women (Daisy), shaving cream for men, disposable lighters (Cricket), digital watches, and pocket calculators. The manufacture of razors for women requires that a similar product be delivered to a new market, but there is a high degree of synergy between the core business and this new opportunity. The marketing and production of razors for men and women are quite similar. Making shaving cream for men is another example of a highly synergistic strategic opportunity. The Gillette brand name is useful in developing a consumer franchise. Shaving cream is purchased in the same location as razors, and thus Gillette's distribution network for razors can be used for shaving cream. On the other hand, new production capabilities, technologies, and marketing skills are needed to be successful in digital watches and pocket calculators. These opportunities do not exploit Gillette's unique manufacturing or marketing capabilities. Digital watches and pocket calculators have a low degree of synergy with Gillette's core capabilities; and, predictably, Gillette was unsuccessful in these ventures.

We can see that shaving cream and women's razors are obviously synergistic to Gillette's core business; however, we find that an assessment of Gillette's capabilities in disposable lighters is not as straightforward at first glance. Disposable lighters and razors and razor blades do not appear to be very similar. However, an examination of Gillette's unique capabilities reveals substantial synergy: Gillette's unique capabilities are the mass production of low-cost products utilizing precision plastic molded parts and the marketing of low cost, disposable, brand name, consumer products through mass distribution. Even though the Gillette brand name may not be useful in marketing disposable lighters, Gillette's manufacturing and marketing skills give Gillette a competitive advantage in this product-market.

Readings in Section IV

The readings in this section discuss three models for setting objectives and allocating resources to product-market opportunities. The PIMS project and Par models are described in Article 12 and critically evaluated in Article 13. The next two articles (14 and 15) describe the market growth/market share matrix developed by the Boston Consulting Group. The market attractiveness/competitive capabilities matrix is illustrated in Article 16. A fourth model for allocation of resources, the ROI financial model, was discussed in Section III. Article 17 compares financial and marketing approaches to resource allocation.

Notes

1. For a complete review of analytical methods for strategic design making, see George S. Day, "Analytical Approaches to Strategic Market Planning," in *Review of Marketing 1981*, eds. Ben Enis and Kenneth Roering (Chicago: American Marketing Association, 1981), pp. 89–105.
2. Sidney Schoeffler, "Nine Basic Findings on Business Strategy," *PIMS Letter*, No. 1, The Strategic Planning Institute, 1977.
3. Robert D. Buzzell and Frederik D. Wiersema, "Successful Share-Building Strategies," *Harvard Business Review*, January–February 1981, pp. 135–144.
4. Some other studies that have utilized the PIMS data base are Robert Buzzell, "Are There Natural Market Structures?" *Journal of Marketing*, Winter 1981, pp. 89–101; Paul Farris and Robert Buzzell, "Why Advertising and Promotion Costs Vary: Some Cross-Sectional Analysis," *Journal of Marketing*, Fall 1979, pp. 112–122; Paul Farris and David J. Reibstein, "How Prices, Ad Expenditures and Profits are Linked," *Harvard Business Review*. November–December 1978, pp. 173–184; Bradley T. Gale, "Can More Capital Buy Higher Productivity?" *Harvard*

Business Review, July–August 1980, pp. 78–86; Bradley T. Gale and Ben Branch, "Strategic Determinants of Cash Flow," *Harvard Business Review*, July–August 1981, pp. 131–136; Hans B. Thorelli and Stephen C. Burnett, "The Strategic Significance of Product Life Cycles for Industrial Goods Business," *Journal of Marketing*, Fall 1981; and Carolyn Y. Woo and Arnold C. Cooper, "Strategies of Effective Low Share Businesses," *Strategic Management Journal* 2(July–September 1981): 301–318.

5. For a description of additional portfolio models, Yoram Wind and Vijay Mahajan, "Designing Product and Business Portfolios," *Harvard Business Review*, January–February 1981, pp. 155–165.

6. Phillippe Haspeslagh, "Portfolio Planning: Uses and Limits," *Harvard Business Review*, January–February 1982, pp. 58–81.

7. *Business Week*, January 25, 1982, p. 63.

8. H. Igor Ansoff, *Corporate Strategy: An Analytic Approach to Business Policy for Growth and Expansion* (New York: McGraw-Hill, 1965).

9. *Business Week*, "Gillette: After the Diversification That Failed," February 28, 1977, pp. 58–62.

12. Planning for Profit

Bradley T. Gale

One hundred and ninety of the world's largest and most diversified companies have added a new capability to their arsenal of planning tools. They have tapped into a new and unique collection of strategic experiences of product-line businesses now maintained by The Strategic Planning Institute (SPI). Member companies use information derived from this data base as one additional input to:

- identify key success factors,
- quantify a business's strengths and weaknesses,
- establish ROI benchmarks,
- estimate probable consequences of alternative strategic moves,
- review portfolios at the group or company level,
- screen acquisition candidates,
- size up competitors.

This article offers a brief overview of The PIMS (Profit Impact of Market Strategy) Program of SPI. It describes a multi-company effort to develop a factual, scientific basis for strategic planning. It also indicates how SPI's member companies capitalize upon this new basis in order to enhance their return on investment and their cash flow.

Financial Performance of Business in a Comparable Situation

Often, the task of explaining why low-profit businesses fail seems more difficult than trying to explain why profitable businesses succeed. Poor

This article first appeared in *Planning Review* 6, no. 1 (January 1978), pp. 4–7, 30–32.

When this article was published, the author was director of research for the Strategic Planning Institute and a member of the economics faculty of the University of Massachusetts at Amherst.

225

profits may result from a variety of factors, including too much specialized equipment in the production process, or attaining only a small market share in a high-growth market, or spending too much on marketing, or producing a non-differentiated product. While the decision to initiate most of these ill-fated strategies may have seemed sensible, each of these actions increases the chances of bad financial performance.

The tap root of these planning mistakes is that the experiences of many businessmen are excessively narrow. Experience will tell a businessman which factors are critical for his particular industry. For example, electronics manufacturers appreciate how important it is to keep a careful watch on research and development expenditures and new-product introductions. Soap companies learn the importance of monitoring their competitors' advertising campaigns. Distribution businesses focus on the flow of sales per square foot of store or warehouse space.

While knowledge gained from one's own industry can be very helpful, it can, at the same time, be incomplete or even misleading. For example, it may well be a mistake for a business which is ranked number two or three in the industry to follow the strategies of the industry leader, who could be twice as large. Rather, one should search the strategic experiences of businesses in other industries to discover empirical evidence as to how a number two can compete against a much larger number one and make profits in the process. The trick is to examine the strategy experiences of businesses outside one's industry that have similar characteristics and face a comparable competitive situation.

Practical Guidance Is Now Available

Evolution of PIMS

Until a few years ago it was nearly impossible to obtain empirical data on the successful and unsuccessful experiences of businesses outside one's own industry. Such data had not been systematically assembled and analyzed. Planners were forced to work with highly aggregated data collected by government agencies or trade associations. During the last five years, however, The PIMS Program has assembled a unique business data base, and has developed a research program and planning service specifically designed to help corporate managers and planners select and implement strategies that promise a higher return on investment. This data base is cross-sectional, i.e., it comes from product-line businesses in many industries.

The PIMS data base was developed in response to economic pressures of the time period.[1] During the 1960's, some diversified manufacturing companies were confronted with severe cash-flow problems, which forced them to be very selective as to which of their businesses to expand. Unfortunately, many top-management teams did not have first-hand experience in each product-line business. Others felt that their experience was not relevant to their future environment. Managers began to search for a systematic way to analyze the strategic options advanced by their different operating units. This basic need for factual information on individual business units was intensified by the general cash-flow crunch which hit many companies during the early 1970's.

In 1972, The PIMS Program was established as a developmental project at the Harvard Business School.[2] Three dozen large, diversified companies agreed to contribute the strategy experiences of some of their product-line businesses to a new and shared data base. The intent was to discover in this cross-sectional data base the "laws" of the marketplace. Next, PIMS was to produce reports for the managers and planners of each business unit in the data base which they can use as a basis for decision making.

PIMS Now

By 1975, more companies had joined The PIMS Program. The data base contained almost 600 product-line businesses. Many of the participating companies wished to broaden the range of planning services available from researchers on the PIMS staff. Accordingly, The Strategic Planning Institute was formed in 1975 as the permanent home of The PIMS Program. It is a non-profit, tax-exempt corporation governed by its member companies in the U.S.A., Canada, Europe and South America. Thus, The PIMS Program is now a multi-company, multi-country activity. Its primary goal is unchanged, namely, to provide a factual basis for the business-planning efforts of its participants.[3]

As of this date, the PIMS data base contains detailed information on the strategy experiences of more than one thousand product-line businesses. These businesses are owned and operated by a diverse group of companies operating in many different industries. The PIMS staff analyzes these experiences to discover the general "laws" that determine what business strategy, in what kind of competitive environment, produces what profit results. The findings are made available to member companies in a form useful to their business planning.

The PIMS research program has identified about thirty factors which, taken together, can explain about 75% of the differences in profitability reported by these businesses.

It is interesting to note that these factors do not include the name of the product, industry, or technology. Rather, they pertain to (1) the structural characteristics of the industry (e.g., the rate of growth, the degree of customer and seller concentration), (2) the business's competitive position within its industry (market share, product quality relative to leading competitors), and (3) the productivity of capital and labor, regardless of what they produce.

PIMS research findings of this type are disseminated to member companies in two forms. First, they are issued as general reports on the principles of business strategy. A few examples are included at the end of this article. Second, PIMS produces specific reports on each business in the data base, that is, PIMS applies the general findings to a particular business. It diagnoses the complex relationships between key factors and financial performance. Each business receives a detailed analysis of its strategic position based on what one would expect from other similar businesses (that is, those with the same business characteristics, though not necessarily those operating in the same field of goods and services). This analysis helps to insure that strategic decisions are made neither on a hunch, nor solely on the basis of an individual company's past practice in one industry, but with the knowledge of what other managers have achieved with businesses having similar characteristics.

But My Business Is Different

When first introduced to PIMS concepts, a general manager will insist that his business is different or unique. He imagines that experiences of businesses in other industries are irrelevant to his strategic planning. It is true that each business has a particular market share, a particular industry growth rate, a particular level of marketing expenses, and a particular investment base. Yet one must also recognize that businesses in other industries may have the same market share. Thus, while each business is unique, one can gain strategic insight by focusing on the factors which are common across businesses rather than on differences. It is the relative importance of each of these common factors that is unique. Recall that some thirty factors explain about seventy-five percent of the variability in profit performance. Other things which make a business unique explain only about twenty-five percent. Indeed, PIMS research indicates that much of this unexplained twenty-five percent is due to transitory factors.

Medical practitioners would find the above methodology quite familiar. They appreciate that each patient is unique. Yet they insist on focusing on characteristics which are common to all individuals (pulse rate, blood pressure, body temperature, weight relative to height, smoker versus nonsmoker, and so on).

How Member Companies Use PIMS

Identify Key Success Factors

Member companies use SPI reports and resources for a variety of planning purposes. Most begin by using PIMS concepts to provide a common language for discussion of business strategy. They review research findings to isolate key factors which influence profitability and cash flow. During their first year with SPI, most companies use PIMS as a vehicle to generate key questions about the current position and future prospects of their businesses.

Par Report: Quantify Strengths and Weaknesses, Set ROI Benchmarks

Each business receives a set of reports based on its own characteristics. The "Par" ROI Report specifies the return on investment that is normal (or "Par") for a business, given its market attractiveness, competitive position, degree of differentiation from competitors, and its production structure. The report also quantifies individual strategic strengths and weaknesses, as indicated by the impacts of key profit-influencing factors. These strengths and weaknesses explain why the Par ROI is high or low. The Cash Flow Par Report provides similar information, but with a focus on factors that influence cash flow (expressed as a percentage of investment).

Some companies use PIMS Par Reports to establish reasonable objective profit or cash-flow benchmarks for each of their businesses. Others use these reports to diagnose major strategic strengths and weaknesses. For example, what factors tend to drain cash, or produce large profits? In some cases, the strategic weaknesses far outweigh the strengths. Although inputs to a divestment decision come from many sources, PIMS reports appear to have clinched the difficult decision to exit in several cases.

Estimate Probable Consequences of Alternative Strategic Moves

SPI's Strategy Report offers a product-line business a computational pre-test of several possible strategic moves in the business. It indicates the normal short- and long-term consequences of each such move, based on the experiences of other businesses that have made similar moves, from similar starting points, in similar business environments in the past. The report answers the following questions: (1) If this business continues on its current track, what will its future operating results be? (2) What changes in market share, investment intensity, and vertical integration are likely to produce better results?

Member companies also use SPI's Strategy Report to estimate the future consequences of specific strategies under management consideration. For example, when management is getting ready to make a strategic decision for a particular business, there will frequently be a flurry of activity to generate strategy reports based on several different sets of strategic moves and different scenarios about the future market environment.

SPI's Optimum Strategy Report nominates that combination of market-share, investment-intensity and vertical-integration moves which promises to optimize a given performance measure (e.g., discounted cash flow over 10 years, return on investment for the next 5 years, or short-term dollar earnings). This nomination is also based upon the experiences of other businesses operating under similar circumstances. Some companies use the Optimum Strategy Report as a catalyst to nominate strategies with a better yield than the current business plan for detailed exploration.

Portfolio Review

A recent capability has been developed by SPI researchers. Member companies can now assess the strengths and weaknesses of portfolios of businesses. This analysis can be done for the entire company, a group, or a division. Using PIMS research findings, an assessment of the strengths and weaknesses of a portfolio can begin with an examination of the portfolio's position with respect to several key profit determinants. In some cases a key weakness such as heavy investment intensity or low product quality may affect the entire portfolio of businesses.

Companies analyzing portfolios use PIMS to answer the following kinds of questions:

- Has the strategic position of the portfolio improved over the last few years?
- Is the portfolio performing well or badly given its strategic position?
- Will proposed business plans strengthen the portfolio? How much?
- Which plans deserve the most detailed review?
- Which businesses are potential divestment candidates?

Special Topics

While the bulk of PIMS' activity focuses on the major businesses of member companies, PIMS has also developed tools to help managers address specialized planning problems in other areas. For example, the Start-Up Business project has assembled a new data base to provide a factual basis for planning decisions pertaining to new business ventures. Member companies use SPI's Start-Up Business Report to help decide whether to continue, alter, or close down a start-up business. SPI has also developed a tool for screening acquisition candidates and sizing up competitors. This limited information tool is used in circumstances when it is difficult to assemble detailed information. A recent probe has been launched to discover strategic or tactical remedies for businesses in profit trouble.

Interface Between SPI and Member Companies

To help member companies make effective use of these planning tools, SPI assigns a staff member to each participating company (as a service coordinator). The service coordinator works with member companies to plan their PIMS activity, explain general research findings, define business units, interpret reports on individual businesses, organize presentations, and perform a variety of other service tasks.

Each member company designates an individual to act as the liaison between their business unit and SPI. In many cases, this individual represents the corporate planning staff. Typically, division-line people know more about their particular industry than the planner. By drawing on the PIMS data base, however, the planner can usually provide additional information and strategic insights which complement the hands-on knowledge of division managers.

Some Research Findings

The PIMS staff has built a number of empirical models to explain why profitability and cash flow differ from business to business. These models contain factors which affect financial performance. Some representative findings are summarized in the following exhibits. PIMS participants find these exhibits especially interesting when they imagine the position of a particular business, or a portfolio of business, in the exhibit.

Marketing Share Helps Profitability

It is now widely recognized that one of the main determinants of business profitability is market share.[4] Under most circumstances, businesses that have achieved a high share of the markets they serve are considerably more profitable than their small-share competitors. Figure 12.1 shows average ROI (pre-tax) for groups of businesses in The PIMS Program, highlighting their profit enhancement from successively larger shares of their markets.

There are several reasons why a high share of the market causes high profitability. First, large-share businesses usually enjoy scale economies in working capital, marketing, research and development, and in certain other cost components. Second, they also enjoy economies of cumulative volume which reduce unit costs via the experience-curve effect, and by spreading set-up costs over a longer production run. Third, those anxious to minimize the risk of making a wrong choice may favor a large-share business. This customer behavior gives dominant suppliers a share-based product-differentiation advantage. Finally, large-share businesses often have greater bargaining power over customers and suppliers, and frequently they are able to take the initiative over their competitors.

Unionization Reduces the Effect of Share on ROI

While the PIMS data base clearly demonstrates a strong general relationship between ROI and market share, it also indicates that the importance of

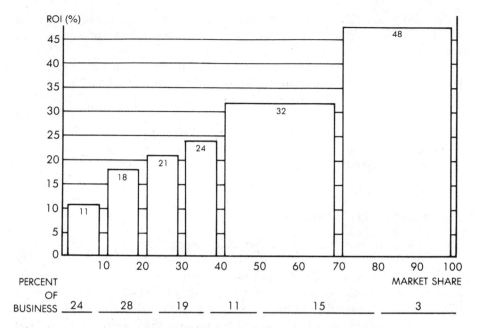

FIGURE 12.1   Market Share Helps Profitability

share can be amplified or attenuated by other factors. For example, when a large fraction of a business's labor force is unionized, the effect of market share on ROI is reduced (Figures 12.2 and 12.3). In Figure 12.2 (and in Figures 12.4 and 12.5), the PIMS sample of businesses is divided into three approximately equal groups on the basis of two factors. The figure shown in each of the nine boxes represents the average ROI of the businesses in that subgroup. Figure 12.3 is a plot of the information in the top and bottom rows of Figure 12.2.

ROI (%)

MARKET SHARE

	LO	(13)	(28)	HI
LO	16	22	37	
(40)				
UNIONIZATION	14	21	27	
(70)				
HI	16	20	25	

FIGURE 12.2   Share, Unionization, and ROI

ROI (%)
40
30
20
10
0
13
28
LOW UNIONIZATION
HIGH UNIONIZATION

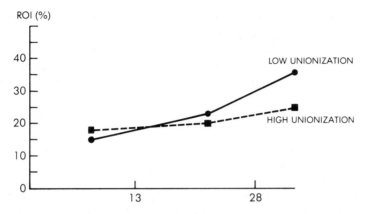

FIGURE 12.3 Unionization Reduces the Effect of Share on ROI

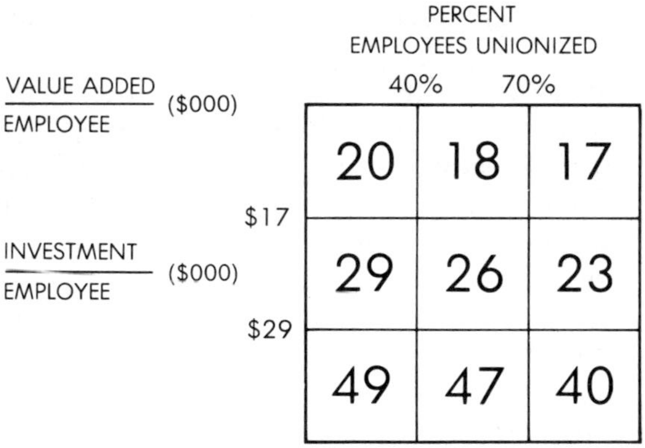

PERCENT
EMPLOYEES UNIONIZED
40%
70%
VALUE ADDED / EMPLOYEE ($000)
INVESTMENT / EMPLOYEE ($000)
$17
$29
20 18 17
29 26 23
49 47 40

FIGURE 12.4 Unionization Hurts Productivity

MARKET SHARE
GROWTH RATE
−1%
4.4%
CASH FLOW / INVESTMENT (%)
MARKET SHARE
13%
28%
1 0 −8
−2 2 0
11 7 0

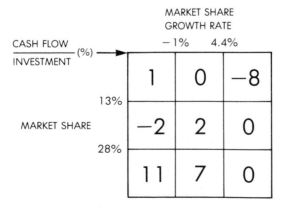

FIGURE 12.5 High Market Share Generates Cash, but Building Share Absorbs Cash

Market share is more important to businesses that are not unionized than it is to unionized businesses. Put differently, unionization hurts ROI when market share is high. Unions appear to dissipate much of the potential unit-cost advantage of large-share businesses. This failure to achieve lower unit costs may occur (1) because of the restrictive work rules which reduce productivity, or (2) because union bargaining results in a larger fraction of value added ending up as wages and a smaller fraction as profits.

Strong businesses have a high ROI potential, so they can tolerate some restrictive work rules and practices or concede some bargaining points and still earn an ROI sufficiently above average to satisfy corporate management. Small-share businesses have a low ROI potential. They cannot and apparently are not forced to tolerate cost-inflating work rules and practices, as shown by the insignificant profit difference between low and high unionization when market share is low. Of course, the data reflect only those businesses which had both small share and high unionization and survived.

These research findings suggest that large-share businesses should be especially concerned about the adverse effects of becoming unionized. Strong businesses which are already unionized should seek union cooperation to avoid work rules and practices that may reduce productivity, raise unit costs or dissipate a potential cost advantage. For businesses with a small or medium level of market share, the profit benefits of obtaining a large market share are greater if the industry (or business itself) is not unionized. But competition for share and the cost of building share may also be greater for the non-unionized businesses.

Part of the reason why unionization reduces the profitability of large-share businesses appears to be the negative effect of unionization on productivity. Specifically, Figure 12.4 shows the joint effect of unionization and investment per employee on value added per employee. As one would expect, productivity (as measured by "value added per employee") increases dramatically as investment per employee increases. By contrast, value added declines as unionization increases.[5]

Gaining Market Share Tends to Drain Cash

High-share businesses generate more cash than low-share businesses, but the process of building market share absorbs cash. Figure 12.5 shows the joint effect of market share and market-share growth rate on the ratio of cash flow to investment.

Cash flow in a particular year is defined as cash generated by after-tax earnings minus cash absorbed by any increase in working capital or by an increase in net investment in plant equipment. The ratio shown in Figure 12.5 is average cash flow (1971–1974) expressed as a percentage of the average level of investment tied up in the business during this four-year time period. Investment is defined as the level of net book value of plant and equipment plus working capital.

Small-share businesses which are gaining share absorb a good deal of cash because their profitability tends to be low and because they are building their productive capacity. By contrast, large-share businesses which are losing share tend to generate vast amounts of cash.

Figure 12.5 reports cash flow before dividends. With an after-tax ROI of about 10% and a payout ratio of 50%, the after-dividends pattern of cash flow would be about five points less than the figure in Figure 12.5. Such an after-dividends pattern of cash flow dramatizes the cash crunch faced by many businesses.

Summary

Before the advent of diversified companies, competition in the marketplace determined which businesses were shaken out of the industry. In a modern, multi-business company, management must decide which businesses to liquidate and which to expand. Managers can serve both their companies and society at large by making investment decisions which reduce the probability of wasting scarce investment resources. To make these decisions, managers need detailed information on the competitive position and the expected financial performance of each business in their portfolio. They also need to know what strategic and tactical courses of action typically succeed and which typically fail. Given such information, they can minimize the risk of making investments in unproductive areas.

The PIMS Program has developed a strategic planning service designed to satisfy these management needs. Information on strategic actions, market and industry situations, and results achieved has been compiled and organized into a multi-purpose data base. The analysis of this data base has shown which business characteristics are the important determinants of profitability and other success measures. Executives of the participating companies are using SPI findings, reports, and services in a variety of ways to develop and appraise strategic plans for individual business units and to balance their portfolios of product-line businesses.

Glossary of Factors

Return on Investment (ROI): pre-tax net income, including special non-recurring costs, minus corporate overhead costs, as a percent of average investment including fixed and working capital at book value, but excluding corporate investment not particular to this business.

Market Share: dollar sales of business in a given time period as a percentage of the total market sales volume.

Unionization: the percent of total employees of this business that is unionized.

Value Added per Employee: value added, expressed in thousands of dollars, per employee. Value added is net sales, including lease revenues, minus total purchases (which include the cost of raw materials, energy, components, assemblies, supplies and/or services purchased or consumed).

Investment per Employee ($000): average investment, expressed in thousands of dollars, per employee.

Market Share Growth Rate: the annual growth rate of market share, expressed as a percent.

Cash Flow/Investment: cash generated by after-tax earnings minus cash absorbed by any increase in working capital or by any increase in net investment in plant and equipment, expressed as a percentage of average investment.

Notes

1. Prior factual, scientific programs had also been developed in response to the economic pressures of their time periods. The depression of the 1930's led to the development of macroeconomic theory, national income accounting data and macroeconomic models and forecasts. World War II brought about supply bottlenecks caused by dramatic changes in the composition of final demand by industry in the U.S. This led to detailed input-output data (information on interindustry sales and purchases) and the estimation of output targets by industry.

2. From 1972 to 1974 PIMS was located at the Marketing Science Institute, a research organization affiliated with the Harvard Business School.

3. For an overview of PIMS during its developmental period see Sidney Schoeffler, Robert D. Buzzell, and Donald F. Heany, "Impact of Strategic Planning on Profit Performance", *Harvard Business Review*, March–April, 1974.

4. For additional empirical evidence on the share-ROI relation see Bradley T. Gale, "Market Share and Rate of Return", *Review of Economics and Statistics*, November, 1972; and Robert D. Buzzell, Bradley T. Gale, and Ralph G. M. Sultan, "Market Share — A Key To Profitability", *Harvard Business Review*, January–February, 1975.

5. Unionization is especially damaging to productivity when investment per employee is high.

13. PIMS: A Reexamination

Carl R. Anderson
Frank T. Paine

A major thrust in current policy research has been development of predictive models which enhance analysis of various strategic alternatives. In the forefront of this model development are studies undertaken in conjunction with the PIMS (Profit Impact of Market Strategies) project. Since its initial development at General Electric and eventual transfer to the Strategic Planning Institute (SPI), the PIMS program has generated considerable interest in the business and academic community. Because it was designed as a program for analyzing strategic moves based on extensive use of confidential data from many businesses (including direct competitors), a minimum of actual data has been made available to the academic community concerning its operation and results. Within the last few years, sufficient information has become available to allow at least a general critique of the PIMS approach.

Background

Begun in 1960 by Schoeffler and associates at General Electric, the project has since moved to SPI, enabling considerable expansion of the original data base. In 1977, over 1,000 "businesses" are contained in the PIMS data base. A "business" is congruent with the term "strategic business unit (SBU)" and is defined as an operating unit which sells a distinct set of products to an identifiable group of customers in competition with a w ‴ defined set of competitors. The most publicized use of the PIMS data i. regression model which contains 37 independent variables and predicts 80 percent of the criterion variable, return on investment (ROI) (2, 28, 29).

This article first appeared in the *Academy of Management Review,* July 1978, pp. 602–612. Portions of this article were presented at the 37th Annual Meeting of the National Academy of Management, Orlando, Florida, August 1977.

When this article was published, the authors were associate professor and professor of management and organizational behavior, respectively, at the University of Maryland.

This model is used to diagnose strategic variables at the level of the SBU. In conjunction with this diagnosis, several reports are routinely generated during PIMS analysis.

The *PAR Report* is concerned with ROI and cash flow which is normal for the combination of circumstances which a particular business faces (market share, competition, market position, production process, capital/ cost structure). The generated ROI figure is based on past performance of real businesses under "comparable" conditions and assumes that managerial skills and decision abilities are at "average" levels.

The *Strategy Report* analyzes short and long term effects of strategic changes on ROI. Usual strategic changes analyzed include changes in market share, changes in degree of vertical integration, and changes in capital intensity. The report summarizes the effect of these changes in several financial areas, including ROI.

The *Optimum Strategy Report* is concerned with isolating a particular combination of strategic moves which optimize a particular criterion (including profit, cash, or growth), again judging by the past experiences of others in similar situations.

SPI argues for this approach on the grounds of learning about strategy from experience for which diversity is required. From this diverse experience they derive "principles" which are usually expressed in the form of a 3 × 3 matrix (3 levels of each of 2 variables) with ROI as the criterion (see Tables 13.2 and 13.3).

The following sections express general observations based on our evaluation of publicly available data concerning the PIMS approach. Hopefully, these observations will lead to further improvement and refinement of the technique.

Basic Assumptions and Philosophy

> Observation 1: *PIMS achieves its primary usefulness in the analysis and diagnostic appraisal phase of the policy formation process. Problem finding and solution generating phases are deemphasized.*

A number of broad issues describe the basic approach taken by SPI in constructing the PIMS program. First, the PIMS program is not a total strategy concept but is useful primarily as an analysis and diagnostic appraisal device. In this sense, it does not deal with the problem finding and solution generating phase, which still requires a great deal of managerial creativity, nor with the set of objectives likely to arise from individual and interpersonal decision making within the organization. It assumes a single objective (maximization of ROI) in much of its analysis. It is useful through its various reports as a method for evaluating a particular strategy based on comparisons with other firms and for suggesting factors that should be examined in selecting one particular strategy.

Observation 2: *The complexity of the PIMS model may lead to problems of interpretation and understanding and to a tendency for the user to rely on the "exactness" of the technique.*

The PIMS model is described as a complex rather than a simplistic model of strategy. On one hand, the rationale for this approach is based on the assumption that complex models are more likely to be right than simplistic models. On the other hand, they introduce problems of understanding and interpretation which may hinder their usefulness. Although SPI cautions against this, there may be a tendency for the user to rely on the generated figures as exact measures or forecasts of future performance, an especially important problem with regard to the generated Strategy Reports.

Observation 3: *Current analysis of the PIMS data is largely a retrospective approach to strategy formulation.*

By this we mean that, generally, future possibilities or opportunities which result from changed environmental conditions are largely ignored in analysis of effects of planned strategies. Rather, what other organizations have done in the *past* serves as the basis for analysis. "Organizational retrospection," as we have termed this framework, may be a suitable approach for firms operating in relatively stable situations, but it cannot be applied with validity to all environmental conditions, especially those where significant discontinuities occur or change is rampant. These require a more sophisticated analysis/forecasting technique and/or flexibility strategies for preparedness and readiness (2).

Observation 4: *Positive (or negative) effects of synergy are deemphasized in the PIMS approach.*

The PIMS approach concentrates on the isolation of relatively independent SBUs as the basic unit of analysis. While this has become accepted practice in recent years for analysis of business-level strategy, it has an inherent weakness in that effects of synergy are ignored for the organization as a whole—interaction among SBUs may create substantial benefits or negative contributions for the entire organization. For example, goodwill on one product line may have substantial carryover to other lines. This "partialling out" of strategies requires a more sophisticated analysis with the total system in mind. The PIMS program might be modified to conduct such an analysis in the future (13).

Suitability of ROI as a Criterion

Observation 5: *The ROI criterion employed in the PIMS program may not be a suitable global criterion for the measurement of strategic performance.*

A number of sources (15, 16, 32) have criticized use of ROI as a measure of organizational performance. In general, these criticisms have centered around ROI which may inhibit long-term goal attainment, especially
investment in plant and equipment and similar capital spending; there is
an unwillingness to take growth related risks, since ROI is usually
measured in the short-term. Strategic decisions which may result from the
use of ROI include analysis of and possible elimination of marginal products or product groups, price adjustments for low return items, and decreasing inventories to improve returns. New investment is particularly
neglected since these investments may not produce a significant return for
several years, thereby leading to poor performance ratings for the manager. Problems resulting from these decisions may include long-term unemployment, capacity shortages, and diminished sales growth. In summary, one original purpose of PIMS was to provide a yardstick to
counteract enthusiasm (unwarranted) which often enters at the conclusion
of the planning cycle. We feel that the criterion may be overly conservative
and short-sighted.

Cross-Sectional Data Base

Observation 6: *The cross-sectional data base employed by PIMS has
certain identifiable, inherent weaknesses which can lead to erroneous conclusions.*

For a number of years, critics of policy research pointed to a lack of
empirical data as a major weakness in development of policy as a field of
study. To date, PIMS has been the only attempt to overcome this major
weakness through collection of accurate data on a large scale. The method
and rationale for this collection has been criticized (12, 30). The PIMS
approach is based on data from many firms which are pooled and then
treated as being from the same population. Researchers have pointed to a
better methodology which would involve time series (trends) on every firm
as well as cross-sectional comparisons. The lack of time-series analysis to
date is probably due to the newness of the PIMS data base rather than to
the oversight of this obviously rich analytical field.

There are some important considerations for the time series approach
which may discount validity of current conclusions derived from the cross-
sectional analysis. First, the goals—strategies employed by an organization—change over time, and these changes must be documented and compared to results. To date this has not been done. Further, the environmental variables analyzed vary over time for each firm in an industry
(and across industries). For example, changes in competitive postures over
time must be considered. Finally, in the current data, the number of observations of any particular environment is limited; thus, the variation due to

that environment may not be picked up in the model. PIMS reports similar factors influencing performance across obviously different environmental sectors (see Observation 16). A longitudinal analysis of any particular sector should pick up these changes.

Incorporation of Goal Structures

> Observation 7: *PIMS analysis has not identified intended goals— strategies for which performance was measured. In the future, goal structures should be added to the data base.*

Both Kirchoff (15) and Hatten and Schendel (12) point to the need for identifying goals of organizations under study in the PIMS project (what were they trying to do when performance was measured?). Paine (20) goes one step further in suggesting the use of goal structures or hierarchies as a means of identifying the particular strategy (and level of implementation) for the organization.

In a broader sense, the PIMS data base consists of mostly interval data; nominal and ordinal data are neglected for either statistical (the regression model and associated assumptions) or definitional reasons. Several researchers have pointed to this factor as a deficiency in the data which may lead to erroneous or simplistic conclusions through omission of important nominal or ordinal variables including goals. Apparently use of non-interval data is not completely rejected because of statistical reasons since certain noninterval data are currently incorporated in the model.

Methodology

> Observation 8: *Analysis of independent variables in the absence of remaining model variables may lead to erroneous conclusions primarily due to problems of multicollinearity.*

A number of criticisms of PIMS research methodology especially concern the regression model. As noted in the introduction, the major use of PIMS data is the association between ROI and 37 independent variables incorporated in a linear regression model. As part of the explanation of their strategic findings, SPI presents a series of 3×3 matrices which relate variables two at a time to ROI. Many difficulties have been noted with this approach. Rumelt (27) criticizes the analysis of these associations in the absence of the remaining variables (or if they were held constant). Fruhan (8) concurs with this conclusion especially concerning the relationship between market share and ROI (see Contingency Factors). In general, when there is a great deal of multicollinearity in the independent variable set (28), this becomes a valid criticism. One can expect changes in the magnitude of the relationships or, more seriously, sign changes in the direction of the relationship.

Observation 9: *Omission of key strategic variables from the model may lead to erroneous conclusions.*

In the case of high multicollinearity, the researcher must be extremely careful to specify as exactly as possible the independent variable set. Omission of a variable which has an important impact on the dependent variable or specified independent variables can result in changes in both sign and magnitude of coefficients. This problem may occur in PIMS analysis due to omission of goals and strategies and related decision-making variables. One analysis undertaken to date (18) appears to provide substantial evidence for both Observations 8 and 9.

Observation 10: *The standard error of the estimate for the regression model should be specified.*

Kirchoff (15) points out that the accuracy claims of SPI (80 percent predictability of ROI) may be magnified since they do not report the standard error of the estimate for their model. Kirchoff suggests that the error may be in excess of ± 12 percent. When predicting an average ROI of 17 percent, this magnitude of error certainly questions the accuracy of the prediction. A partial test of the model by the Carnegie group seems to support this contention (18).

Observation 11: *The PIMS data base represents the most reliable and accurate data relevant to strategy formulation currently available.*

It would be easy to criticize the accuracy (quality) of the PIMS data collection process. For example, some accounting judgments must be made in reporting certain variables; but given the overwhelming superiority of PIMS data to other sources in quantity, number of measured variables, timeliness, conscientious attempt to minimize potential sources of input error through the collection of valid data, and the qualitative nature of our science, we feel that criticism here is unwarranted at present.

"Similar Businesses Under Similar Conditions"

Observation 12: *Criteria for selection of "similar" businesses appear arbitrary. In addition, relevant ranges which determine the degree of "similarity" are not specified.*

Since the basis of the Par report is comparison of the particular business being analyzed with "similar businesses under similar circumstances," it is important to specify the conditions necessary for a business to be classified as similar. PIMS claims that similarities are not necessarily confined to industry categories. It would appear that the basis of comparison is market share, competition, market position, production process, and capital/cost structure. We could find no specific definitions for some of these variables, and no relevant ranges were specified within which a business could fall and be considered similar.

Given these unspecified factors, it is difficult for the researcher (or the user) to arrive at generalizable conclusions for selection of "similar" businesses. It is a particular problem for practitioners since they are responsible for selection of comparison businesses. As indicated in future directions for research, recent advances in organizational and strategic theory can make a significant contribution in this area.

Causality Assumptions

The most critical fault with PIMS approach is its supposition of causal relationships with little theoretical or statistical basis. The problem occurs most frequently with the construction of and relationships among the 37 independent variables used to predict ROI. The following discussion centers on a number of causal inconsistencies which may influence PIMS results, including directly and indirectly controllable factors, theoretical relationships among variables, and variable construction inconsistencies.

Observation 13: *Differences in management controllability exist among the 37 independent variables. These differences suggest a causal sequence.*

Significant differences exist among PIMS independent variables regarding the degree of controllability which management may exercise over them. Table 13.1 presents a categorization of the variables according to whether they are directly controllable by management, partially controllable, or largely uncontrollable (environmental). As the table indicates, about 50 percent of the variables are at least partially beyond the direct control of management, thus impacting generally on business strategy as situational factors (constraints, threats, or opportunities). Several authors (14, 19) suggest that these variables may impact on one another (the apparently high degree of correlation among the variables discussed in the methodology section provides a statistical indication that this may be the case). For example, a decision to increase product quality through investment in research and development, upgrading of manufacturing costs, and higher inventory turnover (controllable factors) has an impact on short run market growth as well as on long run growth of the industry (uncontrollable factors). A number of authors (21, 23, 31) have suggested causal sequences which may be useful in further defining the nature of the relationships among these factors. For example, the current state of environmental uncertainty (Where are we now?) could first be defined in terms of the uncontrollable factors. This serves to define the current and past posi-

TABLE 13.1   Categorization of PIMS Independent Variables According to the Degree to Which They May Be Controlled by Management

DIRECTLY CONTROLLABLE BY MANAGEMENT (GOALS-STRATEGIES)	PARTIALLY CONTROLLABLE BY MANAGEMENT	LARGELY UNCONTROLLABLE BY MANAGEMENT (ENVIRONMENTAL)
Market position	Instability of market share	Industry long-run growth
Price relative to competition	Relative pay scale[a]	Short-run market growth
Product quality	Capacity utilization[b]	Industry exports
New product sales	Corporate size	Sales direct to end user
MFG costs/Sales	Change in market share	Share of four largest firms
Receivables/Sales	Change in selling price index	Buyer fragmentation index
Vertical integration	Change in vertical integration	Investment intensity[c]
Inventory/Purchases	Market position impact	Fixed capital intensity[c]
Sales/Employee		Competitive market activity
Marketing less sales force expenses/Sales		Change in capital activity
R&D expenses/Sales		Investment intensity impact
Corporate payout		
Degree of diversification		
Growth of sales		
Change in product quality		
Change in advertising and promotion/Sales		
Change in sales force expenses/Sales		
Change in return on sales		

[a] Only controllable by increasing.
[b] Only controllable in the short run.
[c] Only controllable at the entry level.

tion of the organization with respect to key environmental variables. As a second step, we suggest a closer examination of the controllable and partially controllable factors to determine the consistency between environment, strategy, and capabilities. Such an analysis should be undertaken in the future as part of the PIMS research program.

Observation 14: *Theoretical frameworks from strategic management and organization theory suggest causal relationships among the independent variable set.*

Other advances in strategic management and organization theory (1, 2, 10, 11, 12, 13, 21, 23, 26) suggest that causal relationships may exist among many variables included in the PIMS model. Examples include the effect of environmental uncertainty on the organization's structure and decision making. For example, high growth, highly fragmented buyers, low degree of capital intensity, and highly active competitors (see Table 13.1) should lead to a different mix of controllable factors than the opposite set of conditions. In addition, several variables measured in the PIMS data base are not included in the analysis; they have significant impact on the firm according to organization theory (see Future Directions). Examples include frequency of product and technological change.

Observation 15: *Some variables included in the PIMS regression model may have an impact due to their construction rather than to a "true" causal impact.*

There must be a sharp distinction drawn between variables used as predictors and those used to extend causal theory. Some variables included in the PIMS model to predict ROI apparently do so through the method of construction. Examples include investment intensity and various expense items. Since ROI is defined as:

$$\frac{Sales - (certain)\ Expenses}{Investment,}$$

investment intensity naturally would be expected to show an inverse relationship to ROI and in fact does so (see Table 13.2). Similarly, market expense tends to depress ROI as its level increases (see Table 13.3). In other words, rationale for the relationship may be unjustified as presented by the SPI group (29).

Finally, some causal relationships assumed in the PIMS analysis are unjustified for several previously cited reasons. Foremost is the conclusion that firm performance above the level of Par ROI is due to management

TABLE 13.2   Impact of Strategic Planning on Profit Performance: Investment Intensity and Market Share

INVESTMENT INTENSITY	MARKET SHARE		
	UNDER 12%	12%–26%	OVER 26%
Under 45%	21.2%	26.9%	34.6%
45%–71%	8.6	13.1	26.2
Over 71%	2.0	6.7	15.7

PIMS Conclusion: Low market share plus high investment intensity equals disaster.

SOURCE: Schoeffler, S., R. D. Buzzell, and D. F. Heany, "Impact of Strategic Planning on Profit Performance," *Harvard Business Review* (March–April 1974), 137–145.

TABLE 13.3   Impact of Strategic Planning on Profit Performance: Product Quality and Ratio of Marketing Expenditures to Sales

PRODUCT QUALITY	RATIO OF MARKETING EXPENDITURES TO SALES		
	LOW UNDER 6%	AVERAGE 6%–11%	HIGH OVER 11%
Inferior	15.4%	14.8%	4.7%
Average	17.8	16.9	14.2
Superior	25.2	25.5	19.8

PIMS Conclusion: A high marketing expenditure damages profitability when quality is low.

SOURCE: Schoeffler, S., R. D. Buzzell, and D. F. Heany, "Impact of Strategic Planning on Profit Performance," *Harvard Business Review* (March–April 1974), 137–145.

effectiveness. Model error and environmental (contingency) factors may contribute equally to this result.

Contingency Factors

Although certain aspects of the PIMS analysis define factors upon which selected strategies are contingent, many aspects of the analysis do not utilize currently accepted contingency factors or prescribe strategy influencing actions on a "principle" basis (4, 5, 21, 29). (The Strategy Report, for example, makes "most likely environment" assumptions based on industry sales growth, change in selling price, change in wage rates, and change in various cost factors.)

> Observation 16: *Conclusions derived from the PIMS analysis may be misleading due to omission of certain contingency factors including inconsistencies across industries and neglect of relevant ranges for variables.*

The PIMS conclusions with regard to market share have been criticized most heavily because of their neglect of contingencies (3, 4, 7, 8). PIMS concludes that increasing market share is a key factor which influences profitability and supports this contention with several explanatory tables (see Table 13.2). Fruhan (8) questions such a conclusion on the basis that the analysis ignores factors such as adequacy of financial resources, viability of position if the effort to increase market share fails, and influence of environmental factors in allowing the company to pursue the chosen strategy.

Bloom and Kotler (4) attack PIMS' results with regard to market share on the basis of specification of relevant range for their results:

. . . the PIMS study does not reveal whether profitability eventually turns down at very high market-share levels. The study lumps together all market shares above 40%; therefore the behavior of ROI in response to still higher market shares is undisclosed. Consequently, a high market-share company must itself analyze whether profitability will fall with further gains in market share (4, p. 65).

The relevant range problem can be further extended to other variables in the analysis. Table 13.2, for example, suggests that decreasing investment intensity leads to higher profit levels. Extension of this concept would require liquidation of all plant and equipment, an obvious case for specifying the turnaround point. A similar argument can be advanced for marketing in Table 13.3.

Contingencies which exist across various industries present further problems in the PIMS analysis. Much work in the area of organization theory, beginning with the pioneering efforts of Lawrence and Lorsch (17), has identified those factors which differentiate one industry from another. Among the more important variables which have been documented are size (24), degree of technological intensity (25, 33), uncertainty of the environment (6, 7), and degree of centralization (9). It is not our purpose to review this large body of literature here other than to suggest that future research with the PIMS data base should concentrate on developing and testing this important theoretical area. The next section examines some variables available in the PIMS data which can prove useful in testing several suggested hypotheses.

Future Dimensions

The previous 16 observations suggest a number of improvements which can be made in the PIMS system, both to enhance its applicability to the practitioner and to aid in the testing and construction of policy related theories. First, and most importantly, it seems necessary to classify the PIMS variables into categories which reflect the causal relationships among them. This will enable the practitioner to better evaluate the strategies under consideration, since the current situation can be more exactly compared to that defined in the PIMS model. Improved variable specification also will enhance development of consistent theories of strategy and policy analysis; without additional specification, the model cannot be adequately compared to those model developments undertaken in the past and those which will be developed in the future.

Second, it appears necessary to examine additional data which are available in the PIMS data base but which are not now included in the model. Many of these data are related to suggested relationships from organization theory and are discussed in the following paragraphs. Further, although many of these data may not have a strong *direct* relationship (which appears to be the criterion for selection of those variables included in the model), the indirect relationships in a further specified model may be quite strong. Examples of variables which are available and should be tested include the following. In particular, these serve to define further the turbulence or uncertainty of the environment, a factor given increased importance in recent policy and strategy models (1, 7, 14):

1. Frequency of product changes.
2. Technological change.
3. Development time for new products.
4. Change in market in terms of end users.
5. Capacity and supply problems.
   a. Scarcity of materials, personnel, energy, plant capacity.
   b. Alternate sources of supply available.

These variables and the associated performance measures provide an obviously rich source of information concerning recent hypotheses generated in the strategy field. As an example, the following hypothesis taken from Khandwalla (14) could easily be tested using the PIMS data base:

> The more turbulent the external environment, the more strategically important to management are uncertainty absorption and avoidance mechanisms like market research, forecasting, advertising, and vertical integration (14, p. 335).

Further, hypotheses proposed by Anderson and Paine (1) are subject to PIMS data evaluation. In particular the following type of hypothesis is relevant:

> The more uncertain the external environment, the more management is likely to undertake search for advance information, especially through market research and technological R&D.

An outgrowth of these hypothesis tests would be corroboration of the various models recently proposed for evaluation of strategic decisions. Looking further ahead, several writers have pointed to the difficulty of defining what is meant by the term "strategy" (or "policy"). The PIMS program is in a position to provide such a definition since it is currently the only source for verification of conclusions with varied, accurate empirical data.

Conclusions

The PIMS program probably is the most substantial empirical attempt yet in the policy field. Generally the program has succeeded to a large degree in accomplishing its lofty goals; it is the most comprehensive analysis system currently in use. However, if a number of its weaknesses were removed, its usefulness to both the practitioner and to those interested in advancing the theoretical base of policy and strategy formulation would be enhanced.

One major outgrowth of the PIMS program is its initiation of thought about the true nature of the relationships among those variables incorporated in strategy. Obviously, the practitioner must deal with these relationships on a daily basis, but attempts at conceptualizing these relationships by the theorist have been lacking. Perhaps the major function of the PIMS program in the future will be to serve as a catalyst to further sophistication of these models and as a measure of their true applicability in the real world.

References

1. Anderson, C. R., and F. T. Paine. "Managerial Perceptions and Strategic Behavior," *Academy of Management Journal*, Volume 18, Number 4 (December 1975), pp. 811–823.
2. Ansoff, H. I. *Corporate Strategy: An Analytic Approach to Business Policy for Growth and Expansion.* (New York: McGraw-Hill, 1965).
3. Ansoff, H. I. *Business Strategy* (New York: Penguin, 1970).
4. Bloom, P. N., and P. Kotler. "Strategies for High Market-Share Companies," *Harvard Business Review* (November–December 1975), 63–72.
5. Buzzell, R. D., T. G. Bradley, and R. G. M. Sultan. "Market Share—A Key to Profitability," *Harvard Business Review* (January–February 1975), 97–106.
6. Downey, H. K., and J. W. Slocum, Jr. "Uncertainty Measures, Research, and Sources of Variation," *Academy of Management Journal*, Vol. 18 (1975), 562–578.
7. Duncan, R. "Characteristics of Organizational Environments and Perceived Environmental Uncertainty," *Administrative Science Quarterly*, Vol. 17 (1972), 313–327.
8. Fruhan, W. E., Jr. "Pyrrhic Victories in Fights for Market Share," *Harvard Business Review* (September–October 1972), 100–107.
9. Galbraith, J. *Designing Complex Organizations.* (Reading, Mass.: Addison-Wesley, 1973).
10. Glueck, W. F. *Business Policy: Strategy Formation and Management Action* (New York: McGraw-Hill, 1976).
11. Hatten, K. J. "Strategic Models in the Brewing Industry" (Ph.D. dissertation, Purdue University, 1974).
12. Hatten, K. J., and D. E. Schendel. "Strategy's Role in Policy Research," *Journal of Economics and Business*, Vol. 28 (1975–1976), 196–202.
13. Hofer, C. W. "Toward a Contingency Theory of Business Strategy," *Academy of Management Journal*, Vol. 18, No. 4 (December 1975), 184–210.
14. Khandwalla, P. N. *The Design of Organizations* (New York: Harcourt, Brace, Jovanovich, 1977).
15. Kirchoff, B. A. "Discussant's Response to Strategy Evaluation: The State of the Art and Future Directions," Business Policy and Planning Research State of the Art Workshop, Pittsburgh, May 1977.

16. Kirchoff, B. A. "Organization Effectiveness Measurement and Policy Research," *Academy of Management Review*, Vol. 2, No. 3 (July 1977), 347–355.

17. Lawrence, P. R., and J. W. Lorsch. *Organization and Environment* (Boston: Harvard Business Review, Division of Research, 1967).

18. Magid, W., J. Roman, and R. Santoski. "Critical Analysis of PIMS." Working paper prepared for C. Kriebel (Pittsburgh: Carnegie-Mellon University, 1977).

19. Montanari, J. "An Expanded Theory of Structural Determination: An Empirical Investigation of the Impact of Managerial Discretion on Organizational Structure," (Ph.D dissertation, University of Colorado, 1976).

20. Paine, F. T. "Towards an Integrated Contingency Theory of Strategy." Business Policy and Planning Research State of the Art Workshop, Pittsburgh, May 1977.

21. Paine, F. T., and C. R. Anderson. "Contingencies Affecting Strategy Formulation and Effectiveness: An Empirical Study." *Journal of Management Studies*, Vol. 14, No. 2 (May 1977), 147–158.

22. Paine, F. T., and C. R. Anderson. "Strategic Management: an Intervention Approach," *Proceedings of the National Academy of Management* (Orlando, Florida: August 1977).

23. Patton, R. A. "A Simultaneous Equation Model of Corporate Strategy: The case of the U.S. Brewing Industry," (Ph.D. dissertation, Purdue University, 1976).

24. Porter, L. W. *Organizational Patterns of Managerial Job Attitudes* (New York: American Foundation for Management Research, 1964).

25. Pugh, D. S., D. J. Hickson, and C. R. Hinings. "An Empirical Taxonomy of Structures of Work Organizations," *Administrative Science Quarterly*, Vol. 14 (1969), 115–126.

26. Rumelt, R. P. *Strategy, Structure, and Economic Performance* (Boston: Division of Research, Harvard University, Graduate School of Business Administration, 1974).

27. Rumelt, R. P. "Strategy Evaluation: The State of the Art and Future Directions," Business Policy and Planning State of the Art Workshop, Pittsburgh, May, 1977.

28. Schoeffler, S. "Cross-Sectional Study of Strategy, Structure, and Performance: Aspects of the PIMS Program," in H. B. Thorelli (Ed.), *Strategy + Structure = Performance: The Strategic Planning Imperative* (Bloomington, Ind.: Indiana University Press, 1977).

29. Schoeffler, S., R. D. Buzzell, and D. F. Heany. "Impact of Strategic Planning on Profit Performance," *Harvard Business Review* (March–April 1974), pp. 137–145.

30. Utterback, J. M. "Environmental Analysis and Forecasting," Business Policy and Planning State of the Art Workshop, Pittsburgh, May, 1977.

31. Winn, D. N. *Industrial Market Structure and Performance 1960–1968* (Ann Arbor, Michigan: Division of Research, Graduate School of Business Administration, University of Michigan, 1975).

32. Winter, Ralph E. "Stress and Fast Profits Called A Key Deterrent to Capital Spending," *The Wall Street Journal* (June 10, 1977), p. 1.

33. Woodward, J. *Industrial Organization: Theory and Practice* (London: Oxford University Press, 1965).

14. Strategy and the "Business Portfolio"

Barry Hedley

All except the smallest and simplest companies comprise more than one business. Even when a company operates within a single broad business area, analysis normally reveals that it is, in practice, involved in a number of product-market segments which are distinct economically. These must be considered separately for purposes of strategy development.

[It has been] shown [in Article 8] that the fundamental determinant of strategy success for each individual business segment was relative cost position. As a result of the experience curve effect the competitor with high market share in the segment relative to competition should be able to develop the lowest cost position and hence the highest and most stable profits. This will be true regardless of changes in the economic environment. Hence relative competitive position in the appropriately defined business segment forms a simple but sound strategic goal. Focusing on this goal provides a basis for effective long range planning even in the face of considerable environmental uncertainty.

Almost invariably, any company which reviews its various businesses carefully in this light will discover that they occupy widely differing relative competitive positions. Some businesses will be competitively strong already, and may appear to present no strategic problem; others will be weak, and the company must face the question of whether it would be worthwhile to attempt to improve their position, making whatever investments might be required to achieve this; if this is not done, the company can only expect poor performance from the business and the best option economically will be divestment.

Even in quite small companies, the total number of possible combina-

Reprinted with permission from *Long Range Planning*, 10, (February 1977): 9–15. Copyright 1977, Pergamon Press, Ltd.

When this article was published, Mr. Hedley was a director of The Boston Consulting Group Ltd.

tions of individual business strategies can be extremely large. The difficulty of making a firm final choice on strategy for each business is normally compounded by the fact that most companies must operate within constraints established by limited resources, particularly cash resources. This is an especially vital concern in times of high inflation or recession such as have been experienced in recent years.

An effective solution to this problem requires the development of a framework enabling the selection of the optimum combination of individual business strategies from the spectrum of possible alternatives and opportunities open to the company, while at the same time remaining within the boundaries set by the company's overall constraints. The purpose of this article is to discuss an approach to doing this, which has evolved considerably in the course of its regular application in consulting assignments. The approach hinges on the integration of the implications of the experience curve effect for profit performance at the individual business level with an understanding of the nature of the strategy alternatives open to each business as a function of its overall growth rate. Final decisions on strategy for each business are then taken within the context of the company viewed explicitly as a portfolio of individual businesses. Hence the approach has come to be termed the product or *business portfolio* today. However, there seems to be some confusion in practice as to exactly what it is and how it is meant to be applied. It is hoped that this article will help clarify the nature of the approach and its power as an aid to effective strategy development.

The Business Portfolio Concept[1]

The Effect and Value of Growth

At its most basic level, the importance of growth in shaping strategy choice is twofold. First, the growth of a business is a major factor influencing the likely ease — and hence cost — of gaining market share. In low growth businesses, any market share gained will tend to require an actual volume reduction in competitors' sales. This will be very obvious to the competitors and they are likely to fight to prevent the throughput in their plants dropping. In high growth businesses, on the other hand, market share can be gained steadily merely by securing the largest share of the *growth* in the business: expanding capacity earlier than the competitors, ensuring product availability and effective selling support despite the strains imposed by the growth, and so forth. Meanwhile competitors may even be unaware of their share loss because their actual volume of throughput has been well maintained. Even if aware of their loss of share, the competitors may be unconcerned by it given that their plants are still well loaded. This is particularly true of competitors who do not understand the strategic importance of market share for long term profitability resulting from the experience curve effect.

An unfortunate example of this is given by the history of the British motorcycle industry. British market share was allowed to erode in motorcycles worldwide for more than a decade, throughout which the British factories were still fairly full: British motorcycle production volumes held up at around 80,000 units per year throughout the sixties; in sharp contrast, Japanese export volumes leapt from only about 60,000 in 1960 to 2.5 million in 1973; their total production volumes roughly tripled in the same period. The long term effect was that while Japanese real costs were falling rapidly British costs were not: somewhat oversimplified, this is why the British motorcycle industry faced bankruptcy in the early seventies.[2]

The second important factor concerning growth is the opportunity it provides for investment. Growth businesses provide the ideal vehicles for investment, for ploughing cash into a business in order to see it compound and return even larger amounts of cash at a later point in time. Of course this opportunity is also a need: the faster a business grows, the more investment it will require just to maintain market share. Yet the experience curve effect means that this is essential if its profitability is not to decline over time.

Importance of Relative Competitive Position for Cash Generation

While these growth considerations affect the rate at which a business will *use* cash, the relative competitive position of the business will determine the rate at which the business will *generate* cash: the stronger the company's position relative to its competitors the higher its margins should be, as a result of the experience curve effect. The simplest measure of relative competitive position is, of course, relative market share. A company's relative market share in a business can be defined as its market share in the business divided by that of the largest other competitor. Thus only the biggest competitor has a relative market share greater than one. All the other competitors should enjoy lower profitability and cash generation than the leader.

The Growth–Share Matrix

Individual businesses can have very different financial characteristics and face different strategic options depending on how they are placed in terms of growth and relative competitive position. Businesses can basically fall into any one of four broad strategic categories, as depicted schematically in the growth-share matrix in Figure 14.1.

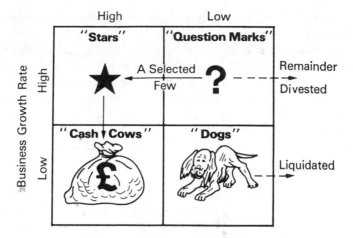

Relative Competition Position (Market Share)

FIGURE 14.1   The Business Portfolio or Growth-Share Matrix

Stars — high growth, high share — are in the upper left quadrant. Growing rapidly, they use large amounts of cash to maintain position. They are also leaders in the business, however, and should generate large amounts of cash. As a result, *star* businesses are frequently roughly in balance on net cash flow, and can be self-sustaining in growth terms. They represent probably the best profit growth and investment opportunities available to the company, and every effort should therefore be made to maintain and consolidate their competitive position. This will sometimes require heavy investment beyond their own generation capabilities and low margins may be essential at times to deter competition, but this is almost invariably worthwhile for the longer term: when the growth slows, as it ultimately does in all businesses, very large cash returns will be obtained if share has been maintained so that the business drops into the lower left quadrant of the matrix, becoming a *cash cow*. If *star* businesses fail to hold share, which frequently happens if the attempt is made to net large amounts of cash from them in the short and medium term (e.g., by cutting back on investment and raising prices, creating an "umbrella" for competitors), they will ultimately become *dogs* (lower right quadrant). These are certain losers.

Cash cows — low growth, high share — should have an entrenched superior market position and low costs. Hence profits and cash generation should be high, and because of the low growth reinvestment needs should be light. Thus large cash surpluses should be generated by these businesses. *Cash cows* pay the dividends and interest, provide the debt capacity, pay for the company overhead *and* provide the cash for investment elsewhere in the company's portfolio of businesses. They are the foundation on which the company rests.

Dogs — low growth, low share — represent a tremendous contrast. Their poor competitive position condemns them to poor profits. Because the growth is low, there is little potential for gaining sufficient share to achieve a viable cost position at anything approaching a reasonable cost. Unfortunately, the cash required for investment in the business just to maintain competitive position, though low, frequently exceeds that generated, especially under conditions of high inflation. The business therefore becomes a "cash trap" likely to absorb cash *perpetually* unless further investment in the business is rigorously avoided. The colloquial term term *dog* describing these businesses, though undoubtedly pejorative, is thus rather apt. A company should take every precaution to minimize the proportion of its assets that remain in this category.

Question marks — high growth, low share — have the worst cash characteristics of all. In the upper right quadrant, their cash needs are high because of their growth, but their cash generation is small because of their low share. If nothing is done to change its market share, the *question mark* will simply absorb large amounts of cash in the short term and later, as the growth slows, become a *dog*. Following this sort of strategy, the *question mark* is a cash loser throughout its existence. Managed this way, a *question mark* becomes the ultimate 'cash trap'.

In fact there is a clear choice between only two strategy alternatives for a *question mark*, hence the name. Because growth is high, it should be easier and less costly to gain share here than it would be in a lower growth business. One strategy is therefore to make whatever investments are necessary to gain share, to try to fund the business to dominance so that it can become a *star* and ultimately a *cash cow* when the business matures. This strategy will be very costly in the short term — growth rates will be even higher than if share were merely being maintained, and additional marketing and other investments will be required to make the share actually change hands — but it offers the only way of developing a sound business from the *question mark* over the long term. The only logical alternative is divestment. Outright sale is preferable; but if this is not possible, then a firm decision must be taken not to invest further in the business and it must be allowed simply to generate whatever cash it can while none is reinvested. The business will then decline, possibly quite rapidly if market growth is high, and will have to be shut down at some point. But it will produce cash in the short term and this is greatly preferable to the error of sinking cash into it perpetually without improving its competitive position.

Some Examples

These then, are the four basic categories to which businesses can belong. Some companies tend to fit almost entirely into a single quadrant. General Motors and English China Clays are examples of predominantly *cash cow* companies. Chrysler, by comparison, is a *dog* which compounded its fundamental problem of low share in its domestic U.S. market by acquiring further mature low share competitors in other countries (e.g., Rootes which became Chrysler U.K.). IBM in computers, Xerox in photocopiers, and BSR in low cost record autochangers are all examples of predominantly *star* businesses. Xerox's computer operation XDS was clearly a *question mark* and it is not surprising that Xerox effectively gave it away free to Honeywell, and considered itself lucky to escape at that price! When RCA closed down its computer operation, it had to sustain a write-off of about $490 million. *Question marks* are costly.

Portfolio Strategy

Most companies have their portfolio of businesses scattered through all four quadrants of the matrix. It is possible to outline quite briefly and simply what the appropriate overall portfolio strategy for such a company should be. The first goal should be to maintain position in the *cash cows*, but to guard against the frequent temptation to reinvest in them excessively. The cash generated by the *cash cows* should be used as a first priority to maintain or consolidate position in those *stars* which are not self sustaining. Any surplus remaining can be used to fund a *selected* number of *question marks* to dominance. Most companies will find they have inadequate cash generation to finance market share-gaining strategies in all their *question marks*. Those which are not funded should be divested either by sale or liquidation over time.

Finally, virtually all companies have at least some *dog* businesses. There is nothing reprehensible about this, indeed on the contrary, an absence of *dogs* probably indicates that the company has not been sufficiently adventurous in the past. It is essential, however, that the fundamentally weak strategic position of the *dog* be recognized for what it is. Occasionally it is possible to restore a *dog* to viability by a creative business segmentation strategy, rationalizing and specializing the business into a small niche which it can dominate. If this is impossible, however, the only thing which could rescue the *dog* would be an increase in share taking it to a position comparable to the leading competitors in the segment. This is likely to be unreasonably costly in a mature business, and therefore the only prospect for obtaining a return from a *dog* is to manage it for cash, cutting off all investment in the business. Management should be particularly wary of expensive "turn around" plans developed for a *dog* if these do not involve a significant change in fundamental competitive position. Without this, the *dog* is a sure loser. An indictment of many corporate managements is not the fact that their companies have *dogs* in the portfolio, but rather that these *dogs* are not managed according to logical strategies. The decision to liquidate a business is usually even harder to take than that of entering a

new business. It is essential, however, for the long term vitality and performance of the company overall that it be prepared to do *both* as the need
arises.

Thus the appropriate strategy for a multibusiness company involves
striking a balance in the portfolio such that the cash generated by the *cash
cows*, and by those *question marks* and *dogs* which are being liquidated, is
sufficient to support the company's *stars* and to fund the selected *question
marks* through to dominance. This pattern of strategies is indicated by the
arrows in Figure 14.1. Understanding this pattern conceptually is, however, a far cry from being able to implement it in practice. What any
company should do with its own specific businesses is of course a function
of the precise shape of the company's portfolio, and the particular opportunities and problems it presents. But how can a clear picture of the
company's portfolio be developed?

The Matrix Quantified

Based on careful analysis and research it is normally possible to divide a
company into its various business segments appropriately defined for purposes of strategy development. Following this critical first step, it is usually
relatively straightforward to determine the overall growth rate of each
individual business (i.e., the growth of the *market*, not the growth of the
company within the market), and the company's size (in terms of turnover
or assets) and relative competitive position (market share) within the business.[3]

Armed with these data it is possible to develop a precise overall picture
of the company's portfolio of businesses graphically. This can greatly facilitate the identification and resolution of the key strategic issues facing the
company. It is a particularly useful approach where companies are large,
comprising many separate businesses. Such complex portfolios often defy
description in more conventional ways.

The nature of the graphical portfolio display is illustrated by the example in Figure 14.2. In this chart, growth rate and relative competitive
position are plotted on continuous scales. Each circle in the display represents a single business or business segment, appropriately defined. To
convey an impression of the relative significance of each business, size is
indicated by the area of the circle, which can be made proportional to either
turnover or assets employed. Relative competitive position is plotted on a
logarithmic scale, in order to be consistent with the experience curve effect,
which implies that profit margin or rate of cash generation differences
between competitors will tend to be related to the *ratio* of their relative
competitive positions (market shares). A linear axis is used for growth, for
which the most generally useful measure is *volume* growth of the business
concerned. In general, rates of cash use should be directly proportional to
growth.

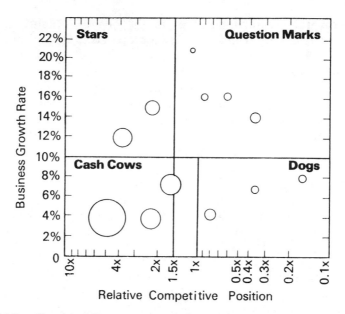

FIGURE 14.2   Graphical Representation of the Portfolio

Circle area is proportional to size of business concerned, e.g., turnover or assets.

The lines dividing the portfolio into four quadrants are inevitably somewhat arbitrary. "High growth," for example, is taken to include all businesses growing in excess of 10 percent per annum in volume terms. Certainly, above this growth rate market share tends to become fairly fluid and can be made to change hands quite readily. In addition many companies have traditionally employed a figure of 10 percent for their discount rate in times of low inflation, and so this also tends to be the growth rate above which investment in market share becomes particularly attractive financially.[4]

The line separating areas of high and low relative competitive position is set at 1.5 times. Experience in using this display has been that in high growth businesses relative strengths of this magnitude or greater are necessary in order to ensure a sufficiently dominant position that the business will have the characteristic of a *star* in practice. On the other hand, in low growth businesses acceptable cash generation characteristics are occasionally, but not always, observed at relative strengths as low as 1 times; hence the addition of a second separating line at 1 times in the low growth area to reflect this. These lines should, of course, be taken only as approximate guides in characterizing businesses in the portfolio as *dogs* and *question marks, cash cows* and *stars*. In actuality, businesses cover a smooth spectrum across both axes of the matrix. There is obviously no "magic" which transforms a *star* into a *cash cow* as its growth declines from 10.5 to 9.5 percent. It is undeniably useful, however, to have some device for broadly indicating where the transition points occur within the matrix, and the lines suggested here have worked well in practical applications of the matrix in a large number of companies.

Portfolio Approaches in Practice

The company shown in Figure 14.2 would be a good example of a potentially well balanced portfolio. With a firm foundation in the form of two or three substantial *cash cows*, this company has some well placed *stars* to provide growth and to yield high cash returns in the future when they mature. The company also has some *question marks* at least two of which are probably sufficiently well placed that they offer a good chance of being funded into *star* positions at a reasonable cost, not out of proportion to the company's resources. The company is not without *dogs*, but properly managed there is no reason why these should be a drain on cash.

The Sound Portfolio, Unsoundly Managed

Companies with an attractive portfolio of this kind are not rare in practice. In fact Figure 14.2 is a disguised version of a representation of an actual U.K. company analysed in the course of a Boston Consulting Group assignment. What is much rarer, however, is to find that the company has made a clear assessment of the matrix positioning and appropriate strategy for each business in the portfolio.

Ideally, one would hope that the company in Figure 14.2 would develop strategy along the following lines. For the *stars*, the key objectives should be the maintenance of market share; current profitability should be accorded a lower priority. For the *cash cows*, however, current profitability may well be the primary goal. *Dogs* would not be expected to be as profitable as the *cash cows*, but would be expected to yield cash. Some *question marks* would be set objectives in terms of increased market share; others, where gaining dominance appeared too costly, would be managed instead for cash.

The essence of the portfolio approach is therefore that strategy objectives must vary between businesses. The strategy developed for each business must fit its own matrix position *and* the needs and capabilities of the company's overall portfolio of businesses. In practice, however, it is much more common to find all businesses within a company being operated with a common overall goal in mind. "Our target in this company is to grow at 10 percent per annum and achieve a return of 10 percent on capital." This type of overall target is then taken to apply to every business in the company. *Cash cows* beat the profit target easily, though they frequently miss on growth. Nevertheless, their managements are praised and they are normally rewarded by being allowed to plough back what only too frequently amounts to an *excess* of cash into their "obviously attractive" businesses — attractive businesses, yes, but *not* for growth investment. *Dogs* on the other hand rarely meet the profit target. But how often is it accepted that it is in fact unreasonable for them *ever* to hit the target? On the contrary, the most common strategic mistake is that major investments are made in *dogs* from time to time in hopeless attempts to turn the business around without actually shifting market share. Unfortunately, only too often *question marks* are regarded very much as *dogs*, and get insufficient investment funds ever to bring them to dominance. The *question marks* usually do receive some investment, however, possibly even enough to maintain share. *This is throwing money away into a cash trap.* These businesses should either receive enough support to enable them to achieve segment dominance, *or none at all.*

These are some of the strategic errors which are regularly committed even by companies which have basically sound portfolios. The result is a serious suboptimization of potential performance in which some businesses (e.g., *cash cows*) are not being called on to produce the full results of which they are actually capable, and resources are being mistakenly squandered on other businesses (*dogs, question marks*) in an attempt to make them achieve performance of which they are intrinsically incapable without a fundamental improvement in market share. Where mismanagement of this kind becomes positively dangerous is when it is applied within the context of a basically unbalanced portfolio.

The Unbalanced Portfolio

The disguised example in Figure 14.3 is another actual company. This portfolio is seriously out of balance. As shown in Figure 14.3(a), the company has a very high proportion of *question marks* in its portfolio, and an inadequate base of *cash cows*. Yet at the time of investigation this company was in fact taking such cash as was being generated by its mature businesses and spreading it out amongst all the high growth businesses, only one of which was actually receiving sufficient investment to enable it even to maintain share! Thus the overall relative competitive position of the portfolio was on average declining. At the same time, the balance in the portfolio was shifting: as shown in the projected portfolio in Figure 14.3(b), because of the higher relative growth of the *question marks* their overall weight in the portfolio was increasing, making them even harder to fund from the limited resources of the mature businesses. If the company continued to follow the same strategy of spreading available funds between all the businesses, then the rate of decline could only increase over time leading ultimately to disaster.

This company was caught in a vicious circle of decline. To break out of the circle would require firm discipline and the strength of will to select

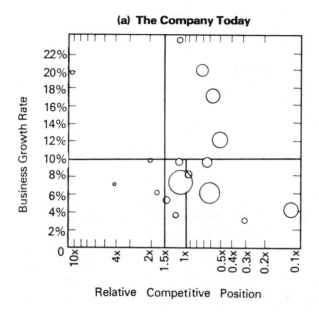

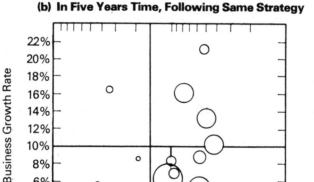

FIGURE 14.3 An Unbalanced Portfolio

only one or two of the *question marks* and finance those, whilst cutting off investment in the remainder. Obviously the choice of which should receive investment involves rather more than selection at random from the portfolio chart. It requires careful analysis of the actual nature of the businesses concerned and particularly the characteristics and behavior of the competitors faced in those businesses. However, the nature of the strategic choice facing the company is quite clear, when viewed in portfolio terms. Without the clarity of view provided by the matrix display, which focuses on the real fundamentals of the businesses and their relationships to each other within the portfolio, it is impossible to develop strategy effectively in any multibusiness company.

Implications for Strategy Development Today

The need for an approach of this kind is more acute than ever today. In recent times business managers and planners have had to adapt to a new norm of continual change and unpredictability in economic affairs. The difficulty of adapting has been compounded over the last few years by persistent pressures of inflation and recession. Inflation, of course, results in pressure on profits — certainly on "real" profits — and even more importantly on cash. More cash is required for the same physical stocks, net debtors inflate and, of course, investment in plant and equipment becomes much more costly in cash terms. Apparent profits can normally be increased in inflationary times, though taxes and dividends take their share. The net result, however, especially in a climate of price and marginal control, is that cash available for reinvestment is insufficient to finance real growth at anything like historic rates. Introduction of accounting changes, spearheaded by the provision of tax relief on "stock profits," helps the situation but is by no means a complete solution in itself. The influence of recession, superimposed on the inflation, has been to increase further the pressure on profits. In a few instances, recession may have reduced cash needs as working capital needs declined and short-term capacity expansion requirements were revised downwards. But that has been cold comfort, at best.

The Predictable Reactions

How are companies reacting to these pressures? It is, of course, difficult and dangerous to generalize. It appears, however, that the most common corporate response has been simply a general "tightening of the belt." The call has gone out to all businesses both to generate more profits in the short-term, and to control cash tightly. The results have been predictable. Prices have been increased as much as is legally possible. Expenditures which look "postponable" have been eliminated. This has covered everything from company cars and office painting to more important expenditures — such as plant overhaul, market research, product research and development — which may produce only "intangible" short-term benefits. Cash has been conserved both by tight stock control, and by energetically trying to take increased supplier credit at the same time as reducing the level of one's own debtors. Significantly, investments in plant and equipment have frequently been refused, unless they offered a very high return and rapid payback. And perhaps most importantly of all, these measures tend to have been applied virtually across the board, affecting all the businesses within large multibusiness companies more or less equally.

Actions such as these are understandable reflex managerial responses. They have alleviated the pressures to which companies have been exposed. Unfortunately, however, they are only acceptable in the short-term. They must not be continued now even if the pressures which originally stimulated them persist into the longer term. It is particularly important that they be discontinued if the maximum benefit is to be taken of any near term improvement in trading conditions. If these "across the board" measures *are* continued, then severe and lasting damage will be done in some businesses for which they are wholly inappropriate long term.

Many companies have been living from day to day for too long. Clear and explicit consideration of long range strategy must be restored to our business consciousness and decision making, or we shall find that we have mortgaged the future irretrievably. Relative competitive position within the context of the portfolio concept can provide the simple and sound individual business objectives which are needed for any company to optimize its strategic opportunities.

Notes

1. A number of discussions of the business portfolio concept have appeared previously at various times in publications by The Boston Consulting Group. These include: *Perspectives*, The Product Portfolio (1970); *Commentary*, Growth and Financial Strategies (1971); and *Perspectives*, The Growth Share Matrix (1973).

2. The Boston Consulting Group Ltd., *Strategy Alternatives for the British Motorcycle Industry*, A Report prepared for the Secretary of State for Industry, HMSO (1975).

3. Frequently the ratio of the market share of the company in the business relative to that of the largest competitor can be used for the latter measure. In some business segments with more complex economics, different cost elements may have differing experience curve bases for cost reduction. In such cases a simple measure of overall relative competitive position is given by the weighted average of the company's relative position in each of these separate experience curve bases. The weights to be used in computing the average are the proportion of the total cost or value added accounted for by the cost element related to each experience base. The average relative share thus still represents an experience curve based proxy for relative cost position in this complex situation, just as it does in the simpler case where all costs in the business segment are simply a reflection of accumulated experience in that segment alone.

4. It is an interesting mathematical fact that if the market were expected to grow in excess of the discount rate *forever*, the discounted present value of increased market share would actually be infinite!

15. Diagnosing the Product Portfolio

George S. Day

The product portfolio approach to marketing strategy formulation has gained wide acceptance among managers of diversified companies. They are first attracted by the intuitively appealing concept that long-run corporate performance is more than the sum of the contributions of individual profit centers or product strategies. Secondly a product portfolio analysis suggests specific marketing strategies to achieve a balanced mix of products that will produce the maximum long-run effects from scarce cash and managerial resources. Lastly the concept employs a simple matrix representation which is easy to communicate and comprehend. Thus it is a useful tool in a headquarters campaign to demonstrate that the strategic issues facing the firm justify more centralized control over the planning and resource allocation process.

With the growing acceptance of the basic approach has come an increasing sensitivity to the limitations of the present methods of portraying the product portfolio, and a recognition that the approach is not equally useful in all corporate circumstances. Indeed, the implications can sometimes be grossly misleading. Inappropriate and misleading applications will result when:

- the basic **assumptions** (especially those concerned with the value of market share dominance and the product life cycle) are violated,
- the **measurements** are wrong, or
- the **strategies** are not feasible.

This article identifies the critical assumptions and the measurement and application issues that may distort the strategic insights. A series of questions are posed that will aid planners and decision-makers to better understand this aid to strategic thinking, and thereby make better decisions.

Reprinted from *Journal of Marketing*, April 1977, pp. 29–38, published by the American Marketing Association.

When this article was published, George S. Day was professor of marketing at the University of Toronto.

What Is the Product Portfolio?

Common to all portrayals of the product portfolio is the recognition that the competitive value of market share depends on the structure of competition and the stage of the product life cycle. Two examples of this approach have recently appeared in this journal.[1] However, the earliest, and most widely implemented is the cash quadrant or share/growth matrix developed by the Boston Consulting Group.[2] Each product is classified jointly by rate of present or forecast **market growth** (a proxy for stage in the product life cycle) and a measure of **market share dominance.**

The arguments for the use of market share are familiar and well documented.[3] Their basis is the cumulation of evidence that market share is strongly and positively correlated with product profitability. This theme is varied somewhat in the BCG approach by the emphasis on relative share —measured by the ratio of the company's share of the market to the share of the largest competitor. This is reasonable since the strategic implications of a 20% share are quite different if the largest competitor's is 40% or if it is 5%. Profitability will also vary, since according to the experience curve concept the largest competitor will be the most profitable at the prevailing price level.[4]

The product life cycle is employed because it highlights the desirability of a variety of products or services with different present and prospective growth rates. More important, the concept has some direct implications for the cost of gaining and/or holding market share:

> During the **rapid growth stage,** purchase patterns and distribution channels are fluid. Market shares can be increased at "relatively" low cost by capturing a disproportionate share of incremental sales (especially where these sales come from new users of applications rather than heavier usage by existing users).

> By contrast, the key-note during the **maturity stage** swings to stability and inertia in distribution and purchasing relationships. A substantial growth in share by one competitor will come at the expense of another competitor's capacity utilization, and will be resisted vigorously. As a result, gains in share are both time-consuming and costly (unless accompanied by a breakthrough in product value or performance that cannot be easily matched by competition).

Product Portfolio Strategies

When the share and growth rate of each of the products sold by a firm are jointly considered, a new basis for strategy evaluation emerges. While there are many possible combinations, an arbitrary classification of prod-

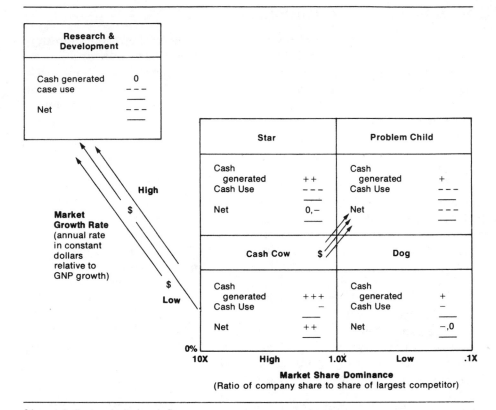

FIGURE 15.1   The Cash Quadrant Approach to Describing the Product
Portfolio[a]

ucts into four share/growth categories (as shown in Figure 15.1) is sufficient
to illustrate the strategy implications.

Low Growth/Dominant Share (Cash Cows)

These profitable products usually generate more cash than is required to
maintain share. All strategies should be directed toward maintaining market dominance — including investments in technological leadership. Pricing decisions should be made cautiously with an eye to maintaining price
leadership. Pressure to over-invest through product proliferation and market expansion should be resisted unless prospects for expanding primary
demand are unusually attractive. Instead, excess cash should be used to
support research activities and growth areas elsewhere in the company.

High Growth/Dominant Share (Stars)

Products that are market leaders, but also growing fast, will have substantial reported profits but need a lot of cash to finance the rate of growth. The appropriate strategies are designed primarily to protect the existing share level by reinvesting earnings in the form of price reductions, product improvement, better market coverage, production efficiency increases, etc. Particular attention must be given to obtaining a large share of the new users or new applications that are the source of growth in the market.

Low Growth/Subordinate Share (Dogs)

Since there usually can be only one market leader and because most markets are mature, the greatest number of products fall in this category. Such products are usually at a cost disadvantage and have few opportunities for growth at a reasonable cost. Their markets are not growing, so there is little new business to compete for, and market share gains will be resisted strenuously by the dominant competition.

The slower the growth (present or prospective) and the smaller the relative share, the greater the need for positive action. The possibilities include:

1. Focusing on a specialized segment of the market that can be dominated, and protected from competitive inroads.
2. Harvesting, which is a conscious cutback of all support costs to some minimum level which will maximize the cash flow over a foreseeable lifetime — which is usually short.
3. Divestment, usually involving a sale as a going concern.
4. Abandonment or deletion from the product line.

High Growth/Subordinate Share (Problem Children)

The combination of rapid growth and poor profit margins creates an enormous demand for cash. If the cash is not forthcoming, the product will become a "Dog" as growth inevitably slows. The basic strategy options are fairly clear-cut; either invest heavily to get a disproportionate share of the new sales or buy existing shares by acquiring competitors and thus move the product toward the "Star" category or get out of the business using some of the methods just described.

Consideration also should be given to a market segmentation strategy, but only if a defensible niche can be identified and resources are available to gain dominance. This strategy is even more attractive if the segment can provide an entrée and experience based from which to push for dominance of the whole market.

Overall Strategy

The long-run health of the corporation depends on having some products that *generate* cash (and provide acceptable reported profits), and others that *use* cash to support growth. Among the indicators of overall health are the size and vulnerability of the "Cash Cows" (and the prospects for the "Stars," if any), and the number of "Problem Children" and "Dogs." Particular attention must be paid to those products with large cash appetites. Unless the company has abundant cash flow, it cannot afford to sponsor many such products at one time. If resources (including debt capacity) are spread too thin, the company simply will wind up with too many marginal products and suffer a reduced capacity to finance promising new product entries or acquisitions in the future.

The share/growth matrix displayed in Figure 15.2 shows how one company (actually a composite of a number of situations) might follow the strategic implications of the product portfolio to achieve a better balance of sources and uses of cash. The *present* position of each product is defined by the relative share and market growth rate during a representative time

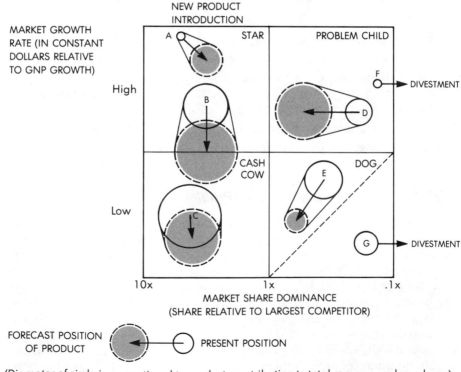

(Diameter of circle is proportional to products contribution to total company sales volume)

FIGURE 15.2   Balancing the Product Portfolio

period. Since business results normally fluctuate, it is important to use a time period that is not distorted by rare events. The *future* position may be either (a) a momentum forecast of the results of continuing the present strategy, or (b) a forecast of the consequences of a change in strategy. It is desirable to do both, and compare the results. The specific display of Figure 15.2 is a summary of the following strategic decisions.

- Aggressively **support** the newly introduced product A, to ensure dominance (but anticipate share declines due to new competitive entries).
- Continue present strategies of products B and C to ensure **maintenance** of market share.
- Gain share of market for product D by investing in **acquisitions.**
- Narrow and modify the range of models of product E to **focus** on one segment.
- **Divest** products F and G.

Pitfalls in the Assumptions

The starting point in the decision to follow the implications of a product portfolio analysis is to ask whether the underlying assumptions make sense. The most fundamental assumptions relate to the role of market share in the businesses being portrayed in the portfolio. Even if the answers here are affirmative one may choose to not follow the implications if other objectives than balancing cash flows take priority, or there are barriers to implementing the indicated strategies.

What Is the Role of Market Share?

All the competitors are assumed to have the same overhead structures and experience curves, with their position on the experience curve corresponding to their market share position. Hence market share dominance is a proxy for the *relative* profit performance (e.g., GM vs. Chrysler). Other factors beyond market share may be influential in dictating *absolute profit performance (e.g., calculators versus cosmetics).*

The influence of market share is most apparent with high value-added products, where there are significant barriers to entry and the competition consists of a few, large, diversified corporations with the attendant large overheads (e.g., plastics, major appliances, automobiles, and semiconductors). But even in these industrial environments there are distortions under conditions such as:

One competitor has a significant technological advantage which can be protected and used to establish a steeper cost reduction/ experience curve.

The principal component of the product is produced by a supplier who has an inherent cost advantage because of an integrated process. Thus Dupont was at a cost disadvantage with Cyclohexane vis-à-vis the oil companies because the manufacture of the product was so highly integrated with the operations of an oil refinery.[5]

Competitors can economically gain large amounts of experience through acquisitions or licensing, or shift to a lower (but parallel) cost curve by resorting to off-shore production or component sourcing.

Profitability is highly sensitive to the rate of capacity utilization, regardless of size of plant.

There are many situations where the positive profitability and share relationship becomes very tenuous, and perhaps unattainable. A recent illustration is the building industry where large corporations — CNA with Larwin and ITT with Levitt — have suffered because of their inability to adequately offset their high overhead charges with a corresponding reduction in total costs.[6] Similar problems are also encountered in the service sector, and contribute to the many reasons why services which are highly labor-intensive and involve personal relationships must be approached with extreme caution in a product portfolio analysis.[7]

There is specific evidence from the Profit Impact of Market Strategies (PIMS) study[8] that the value of market share is not as significant for consumer goods as for industrial products. The reasons are not well understood, but probably reflect differences in buying behavior, the importance of production differentiation and the tendency for proliferation of marginally different brands in these categories. The strategy of protecting a market position by introducing line extensions, flankers, and spin-offs from a successful core brand means that product class boundaries are very unclear. Hence shares are harder to estimate. The individual brand in a category like deodorants or powdered drinks may not be the proper basis for evaluation. A related consequence is that joint costing problems multiply. For example, Unilever in the U.K. has 20 detergent brands all sharing production facilities and marketing resources to some degree.

When Do Market Shares Stabilize?

The operating assumption is that shares tend toward stability during the maturity stage, as the dominant competitors concentrate on defending their existing position. An important corollary is that gains in share are easier and cheaper to achieve during the growth stage.

There is scattered empirical evidence, including the results of the PIMS project, which supports these assumptions. Several qualifications must be made before the implications can be pursued in depth:

While market share *gains* may be costly, it is possible to mismanage a dominant position. The examples of A&P in food retailing, and British Leyland in the U.K. automobile market provide new benchmarks on the extent to which strong positions can erode unless vigorously defended.

When the two largest competitors are of roughly equal size, the share positions may continue to be fluid until one is finally dominant.

There are certain product categories, frequently high technology oriented, where a dominant full line/full service competitor is vulnerable if there are customer segments which do not require all the services, technical assistance, etc., that are provided. As markets mature this "sophisticated" segment usually grows. Thus, Digital Equipment Corp. has prospered in competition with IBM by simply selling basic hardware and depending on others to do the applications programming.[9] By contrast, IBM provides, for a price, a great deal of service backup and software for customers who are not self-sufficient. The dilemma for the dominant producer lies in the difficulty of serving both segments simultaneously.[10]

What Is the Objective of a Product Portfolio Strategy?

The strategies emerging from a product portfolio analysis emphasize the balance of cash flows by ensuring that there are products that use cash to sustain growth and others that supply cash.

Yet corporate objectives have many more dimensions that require consideration. This point was recognized by Seymour Tilles in one of the earliest discussions of the portfolio approach.[11] It is worth repeating to avoid a possible myopic focus on cash flow considerations. Tilles' point was that an investor pursues a balanced combination of risk, income, and growth when acquiring a portfolio of securities. He further argued that "the same basic concepts apply equally well to product planning." The problem with concentrating on cash flow to maximize income and growth is that strategies to balance risks are not explicitly considered.

What must be avoided is excessive exposure to a specific threat from one of the following areas of vulnerability:

- the economy (e.g., business downturns)
- social, political, environmental pressures
- supply continuity
- technological change
- unions and related human factors

It also follows that a firm should direct its new product search activities into several different opportunity areas to avoid intensifying the degree of vulnerability. Thus, many companies in the power equipment market, such as Brown Boveri, are in a quandary over whether to meet the enormous resource demands of the nuclear power equipment market, because of the degree of vulnerability of this business compared to other possibilities such as household appliances.

The desire to reduce vulnerability is a possible reason for keeping, or even acquiring, a "Dog." Thus, firms may integrate backward to assure a supply of highly leveraged materials.[12] If a "Dog" has a high percentage of captive business, it may not even belong as a separate entity in a portfolio analysis.

A similar argument could be used for products which have been acquired for intelligence reasons. For example, a large Italian knitwear manufacturer owns a high-fashion dress company selling only to boutiques to help follow and interpret fashion trends. Similarly, because of the complex nature of the distribution of lumber products, some suppliers have acquired lumber retailers to help learn about patterns of demand and changing end-user requirements. In both these cases the products/businesses were acquired for reasons outside the logic of the product portfolio, and should properly be excluded from the analysis.

Can the Strategies Be Implemented?

Not only does a product portfolio analysis provide insights into the long-run health of a company; it also implies the basic strategies that will strengthen the portfolio. Unfortunately, there are many situations where the risks of failure of these strategies are unacceptably high. Several of these risks were identified in a recent analysis of the dangers in the pursuit of market share.[13]

One danger is that the company's financial resources will not be adequate. The resulting problems are enormously compounded should the company find itself in a vulnerable financial position if the fight were stopped short for some reason. The fundamental question underlying such dangers is the likelihood that competitors will pursue the same strategy, because they follow the same logic in identifying and pursuing opportunities. As a result, there is a growing premium on the understanding of competitive responses, and especially the degree to which they will be discouraged by aggressive action.

An increasingly important question is whether government regulations will permit the corporation to follow the strategy it has chosen. Antitrust regulations — especially in the U.S. — now virtually preclude acquisitions undertaken by large companies in related areas. Thus the effort by ITT to acquire a "Cash Cow" in Hartford Fire and Indemnity Insurance was nearly aborted by a consent decree, and other moves by ITT into Avis, Canteen Corp., and Levitt have been divested by court order at enormous cost. Recent governmental actions — notably the *ReaLemon* case — may even make it desirable for companies with very large absolute market share to consider reducing that share.[14]

There is less recognition as yet that government involvement can cut both ways; making it difficult to get in *or out of* a business. Thus, because of national security considerations large defense contractors would have a difficult time exiting from the aerospace or defense businesses. The problems are most acute in countries like Britain and Italy where intervention policies include price controls, regional development directives and employment maintenance which may prevent the replacement of out-moded plants. Unions in these two countries are sometimes so dedicated to protecting the employment status quo that a manager may not even move employees from one product line to another without risking strike activity.

The last implementation question concerns the viability of a niche strategy, which appears at the outset to be an attractive way of coping with both "Dogs" and "Problem Children." The fundamental problem, of course, is whether a product or market niche can be isolated and protected against competitive inroads. But even if this can be achieved in the long-run, the strategy may not be attractive. The difficulties are most often encountered when a full or extensive product line is needed to support sales, service and distribution facilities. One specialized product may simply not generate sufficient volume and gross margin to cover the minimum costs of participation in the market. This is very clearly an issue in the construction equipment business because of the importance of assured service.

Pitfalls in the Measures

The "Achilles' Heel" of a product portfolio analysis is the units of measure; for if the share of market and growth estimates are dubious, so are the interpretations. Skeptics recognize this quickly, and can rapidly confuse the analysis by attacking the meaningfulness and accuracy of these measures and offering alternative definitions. With the present state of the measurements there is often no adequate defense.

What Share of What Market?

This is not one, but several questions. Each is controversial because they influence the bases for resource allocation and evaluation within the firm:

- Should the definition of the product-market be broad (reflecting the generic need) or narrow?
- How much market segmentation?
- Should the focus be on the total product-market or a portion served by the company?
- Which level of geography: local versus national versus regio-centric markets?

᠊   The answers to these questions are complicated by the lack of defensible procedures for identifying product-market boundaries. For example, four-digit SIC categories are convenient and geographically available but may have little relevance to consumer perceptions of substitutability which will influence the long-run performance of the product. Furthermore, there is the pace of product development activity which is dedicated to combining, extending, or otherwise obscuring the boundaries.

Breadth of Product-Market Definition?   This is a pivotal question. Consider the following extremes in definitions:

- intermediate builder chemicals for the detergent industry *or* Sodium Tri-polyphosphate
- time/information display devices *or* medium-priced digital-display alarm clocks
- main meal accompaniments *or* jellied cranberry

Narrow definitions satisfy the short-run, tactical concerns of sales and product managers. Broader views, reflecting longer-run, strategic planning concerns, invariably reveal a larger market to account for (a) sales to untapped but potential markets, (b) changes in technology, price relationships, and supply which broaden the array of potential substitute products, and (c) the time required by present and prospective buyers to react to these changes.

Extent of Segmentation?   In other words, when does it become meaningful to divide the total market into sub-groups for the purpose of estimating shares? In the tire industry it is evident that the OEM and replacement markets are so dissimilar in behavior as to dictate totally different marketing mixes. But how much further should segmentation be pushed? The fact that a company has a large share of the high-income buyers of replacement tires is probably not strategically relevant.

In general the degree of segmentation for a portfolio analysis should be limited to grouping those buyers that share situational or behavioral characteristics that are strategically relevant. This means that different marketing mixes must be used to serve the segments that have been identified, which will be reflected in different cost and price structures. Other manifestations of a strategically important segment boundary would be a discontinuity in growth rates, share patterns, distribution patterns and so forth when going from one segment to another.

These judgments are particularly hard to make for geographic boundaries. For example, what is meaningful for a manufacturer of industrial equipment facing dominant local competition in each of the national markets in the European Economic Community? Because the company is in each market, it has a 5% share of the total EEC market, while the largest regional competitor has 9%. In this case the choice of a regional rather than

national market definition was dictated by the *trend* to similarity of product requirements throughout the EEC and the consequent feasibility of a single manufacturing facility to serve several countries.

The tendency for trade barriers to decline for countries within significant economic groupings will increasingly dictate regio-centric rather than nationally oriented boundaries. This, of course, will not happen where transportation costs or government efforts to protect sensitive industry categories (such as electric power generation equipment), by requiring local vendors, creates other kinds of barriers.

Market Served Versus Total Market?

Firms may elect to serve only just a part of the available market; such as retailers with central buying offices or utilities of a certain size. The share of the market served is an appropriate basis for tactical decisions. This share estimate may also be relevant for strategic decisions, especially if the market served corresponds to a distinct segment boundary. There is a risk that focusing only on the market served may mean overlooking a significant opportunity or competitive threat emerging from the unserved portion of the market. For example, a company serving the blank cassette tape market only through specialty audio outlets is vulnerable if buyers perceive that similar quality cassettes can be bought in general merchandise and discount outlets.

Another facet of the served market issue is the treatment of customers who have integrated backward and now satisfy their own needs from their own resources. Whether or not the captive volume is included in the estimate of total market size depends on how readily this captive volume can be displaced by outside suppliers. Recent analysis suggests that captive production — or infeeding — is "remarkably resilient to attack by outside suppliers."[15]

What Can Be Done?

The value of a strategically relevant product-market definition lies in "stretching" the company's perceptions appropriately — far enough so that significant threats and opportunities are not missed, but not so far as to dissipate information gathering and analysis efforts on "long shots." This is a difficult balance to achieve, given the myriads of possibilities. The best procedure for coping is to employ several alternative definitions, varying specificity of product and market segments. There will inevitably be both points of contradiction and consistency in the insights gained from portfolios constructed at one level versus another. The process of resolution can be very revealing, both in terms of understanding the competitive position and suggesting strategy alternatives.[16]

Market Growth Rate

The product life cycle is justifiably regarded as one of the most difficult marketing concepts to measure — or forecast.

There is a strong tendency in a portfolio analysis to judge that a product is maturing when there is a forecast of a decline in growth rate below some specified cut-off. One difficulty is that the same cut-off level does not apply equally to all products or economic climates. As slow growth or level GNP becomes the reality, high absolute growth rates become harder to achieve for all products, mature or otherwise. Products with lengthy introductory periods, facing substantial barriers to adoption, may never exhibit high growth rates, but may have an extended maturity stage. Other products may exhibit precisely the opposite life cycle pattern.

The focus in the product portfolio analysis should be on the long-run growth rate forecast. This becomes especially important with products which are sensitive to the business cycle, such as machine tools, or have potential substitutes with fluctuating prices. Thus the future growth of engineered plastics is entwined with the price of zinc, aluminum, copper and steel; the sales of powdered breakfast beverages depends on the relative price of frozen orange juice concentrate.

These two examples also illustrate the problem of the self-fulfilling prophecy. A premature classification as a mature product may lead to the reduction of marketing resources to the level necessary to defend the share in order to maximize net cash flow. But if the product class sales are sensitive to market development activity (as in the case of engineered plastics) or advertising expenditures (as is the case with powdered breakfast drinks) and these budgets are reduced by the dominant firms then, indeed, the product growth rate will slow down.

The growth rate is strongly influenced by the choice of product-market boundaries. A broad product type (cigarettes) will usually have a longer maturity stage than a more specific product form (plain filter cigarettes). In theory, the growth of the individual brand is irrelevant. Yet, it cannot be ignored that the attractiveness of a growth market, however defined, will be diminished by the entry of new competitors with the typical depressing effect on the sales, prices, and profits of the established firms. The extent of the reappraisal of the market will depend on the number, resources, and commitment of the new entrants. Are they likely to become what is known in the audio electronics industry as "rabbits," which come racing into the market, litter it up, and die off quickly?

Pitfalls from Unanticipated Consequences

Managers are very effective at tailoring their behavior to the evaluation system, *as they perceive it*. Whenever market share is used to evaluate per-

formance, there is a tendency for managers to manipulate the product-market boundaries to show a static or increasing share. The greater the degree of ambiguity of compromise in the definition of the boundaries the more tempting these adjustments become. The risk is that the resulting narrow view of the market may mean overlooking threats from substitutes or the opportunities within emerging market segments.

These problems are compounded when share dominance is also perceived to be an important determinant of the allocation of resources and top management interest. The manager who doesn't like the implications of being associated with a "Dog" may try to redefine the market so he can point to a larger market share or a higher than average growth rate. Regardless of his success with the attempted redefinition, his awareness of how the business is regarded in the overall portfolio will ultimately affect his morale. Then his energies may turn to seeking a transfer or looking for another job, and perhaps another prophecy has been fulfilled.

The forecast of market growth rate is also likely to be manipulated, especially if the preferred route to advancement and needed additional resources is perceived to depend on association with a product that is classified as "Star." This may lead to wishful thinking about the future growth prospects of the product. Unfortunately the quality of the review procedures in most planning processes is not robust enough to challenge such distortions. Further dysfunctional consequences will result if ambitious managers of "Cash Cows" actually attempt to expand their products through unnecessary product proliferation and market segmentation without regard to the impact on profits.

The potential for dysfunctional consequences does not mean that profit center managers and their employees should not be aware of the basis for resource allocation decisions within the firm. A strong argument can be made to the effect that it is worse for managers to observe those decisions and suspect the worst. What will surely create problems is to have an inappropriate reward system. A formula-based system, relying on achievement of a target for return on investment or an index of profit measures, that does not recognize the differences in potential among businesses, will lead to short-run actions that conflict with the basic strategies that should be pursued.

Alternative Views of the Portfolio

This analysis of the share/growth matrix portrayal of the product portfolio supports Bowman's contention that much of what now exists in the field of corporate or marketing strategy can be thought of as contingency theories. "The ideas, recommendations, or generalizations are rather dependent (contingent) for their truth and their relevance on the specific situational factors."[17] This means that in any specific analysis of the product portfolio there may be a number of factors beyond share and market growth with a much greater bearing on the attractiveness of a product-market or business; including:

- the contribution rate
- barriers to entry
- cyclicality of sales
- the rate of capacity utilization
- sensitivity of sales to change in prices, promotional activities, service levels, etc.
- the extent of "captive" business
- the nature of technology (maturity, volatility, and complexity)
- availability of production and process opportunities
- social, legal, governmental, and union pressures and opportunities

Since these factors are situational, each company (or division) must develop its own ranking of their importance in determining attractiveness.[18] In practice these factors tend to be qualitatively combined into overall judgments of the attractiveness of the industry or market, and the company's position in that market. The resulting matrix for displaying the positions of each product is called a "nine-block" diagram or decision matrix.[19]

Although the implications of this version of the product portfolio are not as clear-cut, it does overcome many of the shortcomings of the share/growth matrix approach. Indeed the two approaches will likely yield different insights. But as the main purpose of the product portfolio analysis is to help guide — but not substitute for — strategic thinking, the process of reconciliation is useful in itself. Thus it is desirable to employ both approaches and compare results.

Summary

The product portfolio concept provides a useful synthesis of the analyses and judgments during the preliminary steps of the planning process, and is a provocative source of strategy alternatives. If nothing else, it demonstrates the fallacy of treating all businesses or profit centers as alike, and all capital investment decisions as independent and additive events.

There are a number of pitfalls to be avoided to ensure the implications are not misleading. This is especially true for the cash quadrant or share/growth matrix approach to portraying the portfolio. In many situations the basic assumptions are not satisfied. Further complications stem from uncertainties in the definitions of product-markets and the extent and timing of competitive actions. One final pitfall is the unanticipated consequences of adopting a portfolio approach. These may or may not be undesirable depending on whether they are recognized at the outset.

Despite the potential pitfalls it is important to not lose sight of the concept; that is, to base strategies on the perception of a company as an interdependent group of products and services, each playing a distinctive and supportive role.

Notes

1. Bernard Catry and Michel Chevalier, "Market Share Strategy and the Product Life Cycle," *Journal of Marketing,* Vol. 38 No. 4 (October 1974), pp. 29–34; and Yoram Wind and Henry J. Claycamp, "Planning Product Line Strategy: A Matrix Approach," *Journal of Marketing,* Vol. 40, No. 1 (January 1976), pp. 2–9.

2. Described in the following pamphlets in the *Perspectives* series, authored by Bruce D. Henderson, "The Product Portfolio" (1970), "Cash Traps" (1972) and "The Experience Curve Reviewed: The Growth-Share Matrix or the Product Portfolio." (Boston Consulting Group, 1973). By 1972 the approach had been employed in more than 100 companies. See "Mead's Technique to Sort Out the Losers," *Business Week* (March 11, 1972), pp. 124–30.

3. Sidney Schoeffler, Robert D. Buzzell and Donald F. Heany, "Impact of Strategic Planning on Profit Performance," *Harvard Business Review* Vol. 52 (March–April 1974), pp. 137–45; and Robert D. Buzzell, Bradley T. Gale and Ralph G. M. Sultan, "Market Share — A Key to Profitability," *Harvard Business Review,* Vol. 53 (January–February 1975), pp. 97–106.

4. Boston Consulting Group, *Perspectives on Experience* (Boston: 1968 and 1970), and "Selling Business a Theory of Economics," *Business Week,* September 8, 1974, pp. 43–44.

5. Robert B. Stobaugh and Philip L. Towsend, "Price Forecasting and Strategic Planning: The Case of Petrochemicals," *Journal of Marketing Research,* Vol. XII (February 1975), pp. 19–29.

6. Carol J. Loomis, "The Further Misadventures of Harold Geneen," *Fortune,* June 1975.

7. There is incomplete but provocative evidence of significant share-profit relationships in the markets for auto rental, consumer finance, and retail securities brokerage.

8. Same as reference 3 above.

9. "A Minicomputer Tempest," *Business Week,* January 27, 1975, pp. 79–80.

10. Some argue that the dilemma is very general, confronting all pioneering companies in mature markets. See Seymour Tilles, "Segmentation and Strategy," *Perspectives* (Boston: Boston Consulting Group, 1974).

11. Seymour Tilles, "Strategies for Allocating Funds," *Harvard Business Review,* Vol. 44 (January–February 1966), pp. 72–80.

12. This argument is compelling when $20,000 of Styrene Monomer can affect the production of $10,000,000 worth of formed polyester fiberglass parts.

13. William E. Fruhan, "Pyrrhic Victories in Fights for Market Share," *Harvard Business Review,* Vol. 50 (September–October 1972), pp. 100–107.

14. See Paul N. Bloom and Philip Kotler, "Strategies for High Market-Share Companies," *Harvard Business Review,* Vol. 53 (November–December 1975), pp. 63–72.

15. Aubrey Wilson and Bryan Atkin, "Exorcising the Ghosts in Marketing," *Harvard Business Review,* Vol. 54 (September–October 1976), pp. 117–27. See also,

Ralph D. Kerkendall, "Customers as Competitors," *Perspectives* (Boston: Boston Consulting Group, 1975).

16. George S. Day and Allan D. Shocker, *Identifying Competitive Product-Market Boundaries: Strategic and Analytical Issues* (Boston: Marketing Science Institute, 1976).

17. Edward H. Bowman, "Epistemology, Corporate Strategy, and Academe," *Sloan Management Review* (Winter 1974), pp. 35–50.

18. The choice of factors and assessment of ranks is an important aspect of the design of a planning system. These issues are described in Peter Lorange, "Divisional Planning: Setting Effective Direction," *Sloan Management Review* (Fall 1975), pp. 77–91.

19. William E. Rothschild, *Putting It All Together: A Guide to Strategic Thinking* (New York: AMACOM, 1976).

16. The Directional Policy Matrix — Tool for Strategic Planning

S. J. Q. Robinson
R. E. Hichens
D. P. Wade

In diversified business organizations one of the main functions of the management is to decide how money, materials and skilled manpower should be provided and allocated between different business sectors in order to ensure the survival and healthy growth of the whole. Good management allocates resources to sectors where business prospects appear favorable and where the organization has a position of advantage.

In a reasonably stable economic environment the normal method of comparing the prospects of one business sector with another, and for measuring a company's strengths and weaknesses in different sectors, is to use historical and forecast rates of return on capital employed in each sector to provide a measure of the sector's prospects or the company's strength. This is because a sector where business prospects are favorable and the company's position is strong tends to show higher profitability than one in which business prospects are less attractive and the company's position is weak. But records and forecasts of profitability are not sufficient yardsticks for guidance of management in corporate planning and allocation of resources.

The main reasons are:

(a) They do not provide a systematic explanation

    (1) Why one business sector has more favorable prospects than another.

This article first appeared in *Long Range Planning* 11, No. 3 (June 1978): 8–15.

When this article was published, the authors were, respectively, in the Corporate Planning Division of Shell Chemical UK, Ltd; with Shell International Chemical Co., Ltd; and in the Planning and Economics Division of Shell International Chemical UK.

(2) Why the company's position in a particular sector is strong or weak.

(b) They do not provide enough insight into the underlying dynamics and balance of the company's individual business sectors and the balance between them.

(c) When new areas of business are being considered, actual experience, by definition, cannot be consulted. Even when entry to a new area is to be achieved by acquiring an existing business the current performance of the existing business may not be reliable as a guide to its future.

(d) World-wide inflation has severely weakened the validity and credibility of financial forecasts, particularly in the case of businesses which are in any way affected by oil prices.

Corporate managements which recognize these shortcomings bring a variety of other qualitative and quantitative considerations to bear on the decision-making process in addition to the financial yardsticks. These are described in the following sections.

Outline of Technique

In building up a corporate plan, a company will normally have available a number of plans and investment proposals for individual business sectors. These will include historical data on the company's past financial performance in the sector, and financial projections embodying the future investment plans. Such projections will reflect the expectations of those responsible for the company's business in that particular sector in relation to:

(a) Market growth;

(b) Industry supply/demand balance;

(c) Prices;

(d) Costs;

(e) The company's future market shares;

(f) Manufacturing competitiveness;

(g) Research and development strength;

(h) The activities of competitors; and

(i) The future business environment.

The basic technique of the Directional Policy Matrix is to identify:

(a) the main criteria by which the prospects for a business sector may be judged to be favorable or unfavorable; and

(b) those by which a company's position in a sector may be judged to be strong or weak.

Favorable in this context means with high profit and growth potential for the industry generally.

These criteria are then used to construct separate ratings of "sector prospects" and of "company's competitive capabilities" and the ratings are plotted on a matrix. It is convenient to divide the matrix into three columns and three rows, but other layouts are equally feasible. The ratings can be plotted in various ways. Figure 16.1 displays the position of a number of different sectors in a hypothetical company's portfolio. Alternatively, the matrix can be used to display all the competitors in one particular business sector, since the method lends itself to evaluating competitors' ratings as well as those of one's own company.

Details of Technique

Scope of the Analysis

The detailed techniques have been developed by reference to the petro-leum-based sector of the chemical industry, but the general technique is applicable to almost any diversified business with separately identifiable sectors. It could be applied to a diversified shipping company where the

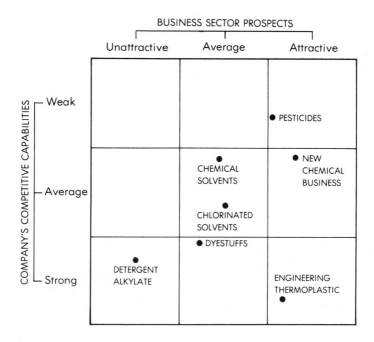

FIGURE 16.1   Positions of Business Sectors in a Hypothetical Company's Portfolio

separate business sectors might be different types of cargo, or to an engineering company offering a range of products and services. In most cases there is no difficulty in identifying a logical business sector to analyze. In the chemical industry business sectors can generally be identified with product sectors, since these form distinct businesses with well defined boundaries and substantial competition within the boundaries.

Any particular geographical area may be defined for study. For the majority of petroleum-based chemicals it has been found most convenient to consider economic blocs (e.g., Western Europe) since there is generally greater movement of chemicals within these blocs than between them.

The time scale of assessment is the effective forecasting horizon. This will vary according to the business growth rate and the lead time needed to install new capacity or develop new uses. For most petroleum-based chemicals a time scale of 10 years has been found appropriate.

Analysis of Business Sector Prospects

There are four main criteria by which the profitability prospects for different sectors of the petroleum-based chemical business may be judged. These are:

(a) Market growth rate;
(b) Market quality;
(c) Industry feedstock situation; and
(d) Environmental aspects.

Some of these criteria are not applicable to other industries and other criteria have to be introduced. Industry feedstock situation, for example, would not be of significance in evaluating sectors of the engineering industry. Market growth and market quality, however, are fundamental to any analysis of business sector prospects.

The significance of these four criteria and the way in which they are rated is as follows.

Market Growth.   Sectors with high market growth are not always those with the greatest profit growth. Nevertheless market growth is a necessary condition for growth of sector profits even if it is not a sufficient condition. It has therefore been included in the rating of sector prospects on the basis of an appropriate scale. For sector analysis in the chemical industry the scale given below is the one used in Shell chemical companies. The center point, or average rating, corresponds roughly with the five-year average growth rate predicted for the heavy organic chemical industry in Western Europe. A star rating system gives more visual impact than a display of numerals.

Sector Growth Rate Per Year	Market Growth Rating
0–3 percent	* (minimum)
3–5 percent	**
5–7 percent	*** (average)
7–10 percent	****
10 percent and over	***** (maximum)

When applying this rating system to another industry it would be necessary to construct a different scale with a center point appropriate to the average growth rate for that industry.

The other criteria are used to qualify the basic forecast of growth of demand so far as their effect on growth of profits is concerned.

Market Quality.   Certain sectors of the chemical industry show a consistent record of higher and/or more stable profitability than others. These differences can be ascribed in part to differences in the quality of the markets which the various sectors serve. For example, in some sectors, notably those of a commodity type, profitability can be highly variable as profit margins contract and expand over a wide range as market conditions swing between under- and over-supply. This problem is often most severe in the case of commodity type products with a large number of producers. Again some sectors may have a chronically poor profitability record because the market is dominated by a small group of powerful customers who are able to keep prices down.

Other sectors remain profitable even in depressed periods of the economic cycle. This may be due to a variety of causes. For example, the market may be supplied by a few well entrenched producers who are content to let sales fall when demand goes down, rather than reduce prices. Or it may be that the consuming industry, able to add a high value, and having a prospect of further substantial growth accepts the need for suppliers to earn a reasonable living. Or, again, the determining factor may be the high technical content of the product, the performance of which has been carefully tailored to the needs of the consumer.

Market quality is difficult to quantify; in order to arrive at a sector rating it is necessary to consider a number of criteria in relation to the sector and try to assess their impact. The following are some of the more important questions:

(a) Has the sector a record of high, stable profitability?

(b) Can margins be maintained when manufacturing capacity exceeds demand?

(c) Is the product resistant to commodity pricing behavior?

(d) Is the technology of production freely available or is it restricted to those who developed it?

(e) Is the market supplied by relatively few producers?

(f) Is the market free from domination by a small group of powerful customers?

(g) Has the product high added value when converted by the customer?

(h) In the case of a new product, is the market destined to remain small enough not to attract too many producers?

(i) Is the product one where the customer has to change his formulation or even his machinery if he changes supplier?

(j) Is the product free from the risk of substitution by an alternative synthetic or natural product?

A sector for which the answers to all or most of these questions are yes would attract a four or five star market quality rating.

Industry Feedstock Situation.   Normally in the chemical industry, expansion of productive capacity is often constrained by uncertainty of feedstock supply. If this is the case, or if the feedstocks for the sector in question have a strong pull towards an alternative use, or are difficult to assemble in large quantities, this is treated as a plus for sector prospects and attracts a better than average rating.

Conversely if the feedstock is a by-product of another process, and consumption of the main product is growing faster than the by-product, pressure may arise, either from low prices or direct investment by the by-product producer, to increase its consumption. This would attract a lower than average rating.

Environmental (Regulatory) Aspects.   Sector prospects can be influenced by the extent of restrictions on the manufacture, transportation or marketing of the product. In some cases the impact of such restrictions is already quantifiable and has been built into the forecasts of market growth. If it has not, it must be assessed if there is a strongly positive or negative environmental or regulatory influence to be taken into account for the product.

Analysis of a Company's Competitive Capabilities

Three main criteria have been identified by which a company's position in a particular sector of the chemical business may be judged strong, average or weak. With suitable adaption they can probably be applied to the analysis of companies' positions in almost any business sector. The three criteria are:

(a) Market position;

(b) Production capability; and

(c) Product research and development.

The significance of these criteria and the ways in which they are rated are shown below. In general it is convenient to review the position of one's own company in relation to that of all the significant competitors in the sector concerned as this helps to establish the correct relativities.

Normally the position being established is that of the companies *today*. Other points can be plotted for one's own company to indicate possible future positions which might result from implementing alternative investment proposals and product strategies.

Market Position. The primary factor to consider here is percentage share of the total market. Supplementary to this is the degree to which this share is secured. Star ratings are awarded against the following guidelines:

***** Leader. A company which, from the mere fact of its pre-eminent market position, is likely to be followed normally accompanied by acknowledged technical leadership. The market share associated with this position varies from case to case. A company with 25 percent of West European consumption in a field of ten competitors may be so placed. A company with 50 percent in a field of two competitors will not be.

**** Major Producer. The position where, as in many businesses, no one company is a leader, but two to four competitors may be so placed.

*** A company with a strong viable stake in the market but below the top league. Usually when one producer is a leader the next level of competition will be three star producers.

** Minor market share. Less than adequate to support R&D and other services in the long run.

* Current position negligible.

Production Capability. This criterion is a combination of process economics, capacity of hardware, location and number of plants, and access to feedstock. The answers to all the following questions need to be considered before awarding a one to five star production capability rating:

Process economics. Does the producer employ a modern economic production process? Is it his own process or licensed? Has he the research and development capability or licensing relationships that will allow him to keep up with advances in process technology in the future?

Hardware. Is current capacity, plus any new capacity announced or building, commensurate with maintaining present market share? Does the producer have several plant locations to provide security to his customers against breakdown or strike action? Are his delivery arrangements to principal markets competitive?

Feedstock. Has the producer secure access to enough feedstocks to sustain his present market share? Does he have a favorable cost position on feedstock?

Product Research and Development. In the case of performance products this criterion is intended to be a compound of product range, product quality, a record of successful development in application, and competence in technical service. In other words, the complete technical package upon which the customer will pass judgment. In awarding a one to five star rating, judgment should be passed on whether a company's product R&D is better than, commensurate with, or worse than its position in the market.

In the case of commodity products, this criterion is not relevant and is not rated.

Assignment of Ratings — Plotting the Matrix

The most straightforward method of assigning ratings for each of the criteria is discussion by functional specialists. They should be drawn from the particular sector of the company's business which is being studied and assisted by one or two non-specialists to provide the necessary detached viewpoint and comparability with other sector assessments.

Although members of the group may differ in the initial ratings which they assign, it is usually possible to arrive at a set of consensus ratings. Where there are still unresolved differences, a representative rating can generally be obtained by averaging. More sophisticated methods of sampling opinion have been designed, using computer techniques, but experience shows that the group discussion method was to be preferred as the end result is reached by a more transparent series of steps which make it more credible both to those participating and to management.

Simplified System

In the simplified form of the technique each of the main criteria is given an equal weighting in arriving at an overall rating for business sector prospects and for company's competitive capabilities. This system of equal weighting may be open to question in comparing certain business sectors but has been found to give good results when applied to a typical chemical product portfolio.

In converting star ratings into matrix positions it is necessary (in order to avoid distortion) to count one, two, three, four and five stars as zero, one, two, three, four points respectively. One star is thus equivalent to a nil rating and a three star rating scores two points out of four and occupies a midway position where three points out of five would not.

It is also convenient in practice to quantify the criteria in half star increments so that there are effectively eight half star graduations between one star and five star. Half stars are shown as: (*).

The working of the system is illustrated by the hypothetical example in Table 16.1. In this, the technique is being used to assess the competitors in a particular business sector. In general it is desirable to record the arguments and supporting data in considerable detail but in this case the results of the matrix analysis are summarized in highly abbreviated form.

Weighting System

In certain businesses it is unrealistic to suppose that each factor is equally important, in which case an alternative method of analyzing company's competitive capabilities can be used, introducing objectively determined weightings.

An example of such weightings is given in Table 16.2. This is taken from a particular study on specialty chemicals, in which the four functions were considered to be the most important.

(a) Selling and distribution;

(b) Problem solving;

(c) Innovative research and development; and

(d) Manufacturing.

In addition to giving a more refined approach to the company competitive axis, the set of weighting factors is useful in its own right, indicating what sort of organizational culture is most apt in this particular business.

Interpretation of Matrix Positions

The results of the hypothetical example in Table 16.1 can be plotted on the matrix as shown in Figure 16.2.

Since the various zones of the matrix are associated with different combinations of sector prospects and company strength or weakness, different product strategies are appropriate to them. These are indicated by the various key words which suggest the type of strategy or resource allocation to be followed for products falling in these zones.

The zones covered by the various policy key words are not precisely defined by the rectangular subdivision arbitrarily adopted for the matrix. Experience suggests that:

(a) The zones are of irregular shape;

(b) They do not have hard and fast boundaries but shade into one another; and

(c) In some cases they are overlapping.

The most appropriate boundaries can only be determined after further practical experience of comparing business characteristics with positions plotted in the matrix.

TABLE 16.1   Examples of Simplified Weighting System

Product sector: Product X is a semi-mature thermoplastic suitable for engineering industry applications. There are two existing producers in Western Europe and a third producer is currently building plant.

SECTOR PROSPECTS ANALYSIS (WESTERN EUROPE, 1975–1980)

		STARS	POINTS
Market growth	15–20% per year forecast	*****	4
Market quality			
Sector profitability record?	Above average.		
Margins maintained in over-capacity?	Some price-cutting has taken place but product has not reached commodity status.		
Customer to producer ratio?	Favorable. Numerous customers; only two producers so far.		
High added value to customer?	Yes. The product is used in small scale, high value, engineering applications.		
Ultimate market limited in size?	Yes. Unlikely to be large enough to support more than three or four producers.		
Substitutability by other products?	Very limited. Product has unique properties.		
Technology of production restricted?	Moderately. Process is available under license from Eastern Europe.		
Overall market quality rating:	Above average.	****	3
Industry feedstock	Product is manufactured from an intermediate which it-self requires sophisticated technology and has no other outlets.	****	3
Environmental aspects	Not rated separately.	—	—
Overall sector prospects rating			10

TABLE 16.1 (continued)

COMPANIES COMPETITIVE CAPABILITIES ANALYSIS (COMPETITORS A, B AND C)

	A	B	C	A	B	C
Market position						
Market share	65%	25%	10%	*****	***	***
Production capability						
Feedstock	Manufactures feedstock by slightly outdated process from bought-in precursors	Has own precursors. Feedstock manufactured by third party under process deal	Basic position in precursors. Has own second process for feedstock			
Process economics	Both A and B have own "first generation" process supported by moderate process R&D capacity		C is licensing "second generation" process from Eastern Europe			
Hardware	A and B each have one plant sufficient to sustain their respective market shares		None as yet. Market product imported from Eastern Europe			
Overall production capability ratings				****	***	**(*)
Product R&D (in relation to market position)	Marginally weaker	Comparable	Stronger	****	***	**(*)
Overall competitors' ratings				10/12	6/12	4/12

TABLE 16.2   Example of Weightings on Company's Competitive Capabilities Axis

| | BUSINESSES | | | |
	W	X	Y	Z
Selling and distribution	2	3	6	3
Problem solving	2	4	3	1
Innovative R&D	4	1	0	1
Manufacturing	2	2	1	5
	10	10	10	10

Matrix Positions in the Right Hand Column

Leader.   Competitor A, the largest producer with the lowest unit costs and a commanding technical situation, is in the highly desirable position of leader in a business sector with attractive prospects. His indicated strategy is to give absolute priority to the product with all the resources necessary to

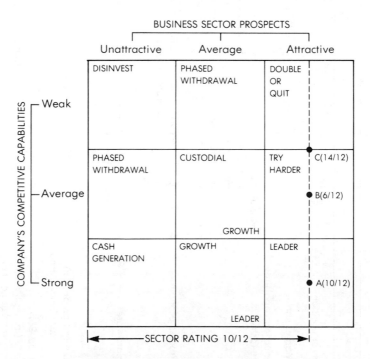

FIGURE 16.2   Comparison of Competitive Capabilities — Product X

hold his market position. This being a fast growing sector he will, before long, need to install extra capacity. Although in all probability he is already earning satisfactory profits from Product X his current cash flow from this source may not be sufficient to finance a high rate of new investment. In that case the cash must be found from another sector of his business. Later, as the growth rate slows down Product X should be able to finance its own growth and eventually to become a net generator of cash.

However, in this hypothetical example, competitor A's position on process and feedstock economics is threatened by second generation processes. This suggests that he may need to strengthen his process R&D. A production capability of one star below market position reflects A's slight weakness in this area.

Try Harder. Competitor B is in this position. It implies that products located in this zone can be moved down towards at least an equality position by the right allocation of resources. However competitor B does not appear to have any very special advantages in this sector and unless he can strengthen his position by, for example, licensing one of the new processes, he may be condemned to remain No. 2. This is not necessarily an unacceptable position in the short term but is likely to become increasingly vulnerable with the passage of time.

Double or Quit.   This is the zone of the matrix from which products that are destined to become the future high fliers should be selected. A company should not normally seek to diversify into any new sector unless the prospects for it are judged to be attractive. Only a small number of the most promising should be picked for doubling and the rest should be abandoned. Competitor C, on the strength of his successful feedstock process development and his licensing relationships with Eastern Europe for the X process, has already decided to double, i.e., invest in a commercial plant. He is therefore on the borderline of the Double or Quit and Try Harder zones: his production capability and product R&D ratings are both higher than his present market rating. Competitor C faces a more uncertain prospect of reaching a viable position in this sector than if he had been first in the field like competitor A.

Matrix Positions in the Middle Column

Business sectors falling in the middle column of the matrix are in general those in which market growth has fallen to around the average for the industry. In many cases they are the high growth sectors of a decade or two previously which have now reached maturity. Sector prospects can range, however, from 0.33 (below average) to 0.66 (above average) according to market quality, industry feedstock situation and environmental considerations. The significance of the key words in this column is as follows:

Growth.   Products will tend to fall in this zone for a company which is one of two to four major competitors (four star market position) backed up by commensurate production capability and product R&D. In this situation no one company is in a position to be a leader and the indicated strategy for the companies concerned is to allocate sufficient resources to grow with the market in anticipation of a reasonable rate of return.

Products in this zone will in general be earning sufficient cash to finance their own (medium) rate of expansion.

Custodial.   A product will fall in the custodial zone of the matrix when the company concerned has a position of distinct weakness either in respect of market position (below three star), process economics, hardware, feedstock or two or more of these in combination. Typically, custodial situations apply to the weaker brethren in sectors where there are too many competitors. The indicated strategy in these situations is to maximize cash generation without further commitment of resources.

Experience shows that for any individual company's portfolio there tend to be more products in the center box of the matrix than in any other, and that these products do not just fall into the custodial and growth zones but also occupy intermediate positions between the two. In such cases the matrix gives less clear cut policy guidance but the relative positions of the sectors still enable a ranking to be drawn up for resource allocation.

Matrix Positions in the Left Hand Column

Business sectors falling in this column are those in which a growth rate below the average for the industry as a whole is combined with poor market quality and/or weaknesses in the industry feedstock situation and environmental outlook. A typical case would be a sector in which the product itself is obsolescent and is being replaced by a quite different product of improved performance and environmental acceptability or one in which the product is serving a customer-dominated industry which has fallen into a low rate of growth.

Cash Generation.   A company with a strong position in such a sector can still earn satisfactory profits and for that company the sector can be regarded as a cash generator. Needing little further finance for expansion it can be a source of cash for other faster growing sectors.

Phased Withdrawal.   A company with an average-to-weak position in a low-growth sector is unlikely to be earning any significant amount of cash and the key word in this sector is phased withdrawal. This implies that efforts should be made to realize the value of the assets and put the money to more profitable use. The same policy would apply to a company with a very weak position in a sector of average prospects.

Disinvest. Products falling within this zone are likely to be losing money already. Even if they generate some positive cash when business is good, they will lose money when business is bad. It is best to dispose of the assets as rapidly as possible and redeploy more profitably the resources of cash, feedstock and skilled manpower so released.

In general, unless the prospects for the sector have been completely transformed as the result of some rapid technological or environmental change, it will be rare for a well managed company to find that any of its business sectors lie within the disinvest area; it will be more usual for a company to be able to foresee the decline in sector prospects in the phased withdrawal stage.

The Second Order Matrix

The second order matrix enables one to combine two parameters of an *investment* decision. This is distinct from examining the parameters of product strategy, the object of the first order matrix. In this instance we are relating the product strategy parameters with our priorities in non-product strategy notably location and feedstock security aspects.

Table 16.3 shows a classification of the business sectors in Figure 16.1, in order of priority for resources. It will be noted that new ventures and double or quit businesses only receive attention after those with proven

TABLE 16.3 Classification of Business Sectors in Order of Priority

Criteria	— Matrix position
	Profit record
	— Other product related criteria
	— Judgment
Category I	Hard core of good quality business consistently generating good profits.
	Example: Engineering Thermoplastic
Category II	Strong company position. Reasonable to good sector prospects. Variable profit record.
	Examples: Dyestuffs. Chlorinated Solvents
Category III	Promising product sectors new to company.
	Example: New Chemical Business
Category IV	Reasonable to modest sector prospects in which the company is a minor factor. Variable profit record.
	Example: Chemical Solvents
Category V	Businesses with unfavorable prospects in which the company has a significant stake.
	Example: Detergent Alkylate

TABLE 16.4   Nonproduct Strategic Options

CATEGORY

1	— Joint venture to make olefins with petroleum company having secure oil feedstocks.
2	— Make maximum use of land and infrastructure at existing sites.
3	— Develop new major coastal manufacturing site in the EEC
4	— Develop a foothold in the US market.
5	— Reduce dependence upon investment in Europe in order to spread risk. Develop manufacturing presence in, *inter alia*, Ruritania.

profitability or cash generation have been allocated sufficient resources to get the best advantage from existing commitments.

Table 16.4 shows a list of nonproduct strategic options. These will usually have been developed at the corporate level and the company management will have a clear idea of relative preferences.

These two desiderata can then be combined in the second order matrix shown as Figure 16.3. It will be noted that three of the businesses appear twice, as their future development can be used to satisfy alternative nonproduct priorities, whereas three of them do not appear at all.

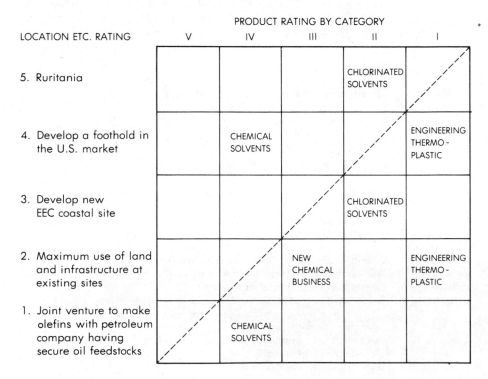

FIGURE 16.3   Second Order Matrix

This matrix gives a very convenient method of presentation of priorities and feasible alternatives, from which the most appropriate decisions can be more easily resolved.

Other Uses of the DPM

In addition to the applications described, the Directional Policy Matrix can be used in several other ways.

Analyzing the Dynamics and Financial Balance of the Portfolio

The general shape of the product matrix plot for a diversified business will give an insight into its financial position. Thus a company in which the majority of products plotted fall in the mature phase (cash generator or custodial) may be expected to generate more cash than it needs to pursue its total strategy. If so it must either seek new areas of business in the double or quit or try harder areas, or else act in effect as a banker to other businesses.

Conversely a company that has the majority of its individual product sectors in the double or quit, try harder or leadership areas will need more cash if it is to pursue the opportunities open to it.

Ideally the overall strategy should aim at keeping cash surplus and cash deficit sectors in balance, with a regular input or promising new business coming forward from research or to take up the surplus cash generated by the businesses already in or moving into the mature phase.

Building up a Picture of Competitors

The DPM can also be used to build up a qualitative picture of the product portfolios of other companies. Some insight into competitors' market positions, production capability and product R&D is in any case a prerequisite to arriving at one's own company's ranking in a particular sector. The matrix analysis will perform a useful function in codifying this information and highlighting areas where more needs to be obtained.

Once competitors' matrices have been plotted, and assuming that competitors will base their investment decisions on broadly the same logic, one can gain an insight into their likely future moves. For example, the matrix analysis will identify the points at which a competitor's production capability is weaker than his market position and hence will indicate that he is likely to lose market share unless he strengthens his position by further investment in manufacturing plant. Conversely it will also identify where production capability is stronger and a competitor is likely to seek to gain market share.

17. Strategic Marketing: Betas, Boxes, or Basics

Robin Wensley

The problem of resource allocation within the multiproduct, multimarket firm has received considerable attention in both the finance and marketing literature. Although much of the work in finance and marketing has been independent, a number of authors have recognized the potential interrelationships. Wind (1974), for instance, suggested the application of financial portfolio theory to product mix decisions, while Grant and King (1979) proposed that at a corporate level of analysis, the financial approach based on portfolio theory should be considered alongside such marketing classification schemes as the business planning matrix and the directional policy matrix. More recently, Mahajan, Wind, and Bradford (1981) have commented on the failure of many marketing schemes to reflect the distinction between risk and return that is so fundamental to the financial approaches.

This paper will develop further the comparison between the financial and marketing approaches. The current financial approach has developed from traditional capital budgeting based on discounting methods to the Capital Asset Pricing Model (CAPM) and the use of discount rates related to the systematic risk of the project, its Beta, whilst the marketing approach has relied on the classification of either products or business units into various boxes. The marketing strategy literature contains numerous individual approaches for such box classifications, but as Wind and Mahajan (1980) imply, it is possible to consider such standardized models in two broad categories: those based on univariate dimensions, best exemplified by the market share/growth matrix; and those based on composite dimensions involving the subjective weighting of a number of factors, exem-

This article first appeared in the *Journal of Marketing*, Summer 1981, pp. 173–183.

When this article was published, the author was visiting associate professor at the Graduate School of Management, UCLA, and lecturer in marketing at the London School of Business.

plified by the directional policy matrix but including others such as the A. D. Little and GE/McKinsey schemes.

In comparing resource allocation models consideration is given first to theoretical assumptions and the supporting empirical evidence and then to the relevance of each approach to crucial strategic issues at the corporate level. It is not possible to include in such a comparison the customized marketing strategy models (Wind and Saaty 1980), since as Mahajan, Wind, and Bradford (1981) recognize, such models tend to rely primarily on management's subjective judgment and, therefore, cannot be tested against either their theoretical assumptions[1] or any general empirical evidence.

A Framework for Evaluation of Corporate Level Models

In economic terms the underlying principle of corporate level models can be simply stated: They are decision rules or heuristics for detecting areas of sustainable competitive advantage whereby the firm can realize economic profits or rents. Firms have been searching for profit long before the advent of the new strategy models, but at least in principle, such techniques offer an opportunity for a more focused search. To achieve such an objective, however, any particular model must satisfy three requirements:

- an internal consistency in the implied economic processes,
- must be based on established empirical regularities,
- must focus the search along critical dimensions rather than trivial ones, even if it is claimed (Hopkins 1977) that a particular approach is to help managers think rather than give them answers.

The issue of simplicity is in itself not particularly relevant. A simple model that focuses on a particular critical dimension is likely to be more cost effective than a more complex one that concentrates on the same dimension. Indeed it has been argued that effective strategic analysis is more likely from simple add-on models that contradict the results of established analysis under certain conditions and, hence, generate a level of surprise. Provided such models are based on established empirical regularities, the simplicity of the model increases the likelihood that the surprises will be acted upon rather than the model ignored (Wensley 1979a).

Financial Models for Resource Allocation

Although the concept of discounting future cash flows has existed in economics for a long time, it was during the fifties and sixties that the Discounted Cash Flow (DCF) approach towards project selection became widely adopted in both U.S. and U.K. corporations. Considerable efforts were extended, both academically and practically, to establish the relevant Weighted Average Cost of Capital (WACC), which could then be used as the criterion for project selection or rejection (Merritt and Sykes 1963). In a number of instances it became clear that such a DCF approach was being used not only as a method of identifying attractive opportunities but also as a means of generating an exclusive ranking on the basis of each opportunity's internal rate of return.

Such developments led some strategic analysts to voice strident criticisms of such a rigidly quantified and unidimensional perspective:

> In evaluating the deployment of assets, the rigidity of quantification (DCF, for example) can distort the true picture of the various alternatives open to the firm seeking growth; those factors which do not lend themselves under conventional methods to numerical analysis tend to be left to intuition (e.g., risk analysis).
>
> The reinforcement of "minimum rates" or uniform return criteria can often result in foreclosing growth through implicitly limiting a company's strategic choices.
>
> Failure to come to grips explicitly with risk/return tradeoffs often displaces logical strategic analysis with traditional policies or "conventional wisdom" (Zakon 1971, p. 1).

The general criticism that overreliance on the now traditional means of project selection based exclusively on ranking by internal rate of return could lead to undesirable effects became widely recognized. New developments occurred in both the areas of finance and marketing partially at least in response to such problems. Such developments were, however, independent and have remained virtually unrelated; as Anderson recently commented (1979, p. 325): "A virtual revolution has occurred in financial thinking in the last two decades, but few of the new technologies and approaches from finance have filtered into marketing."

Portfolio Theory and the Capital Asset Pricing Model

The finance approach starts from the appropriate rules to construct an efficient portfolio of financial investments. The most widely developed approach is that based on the mean-variance rule suggested by Markowitz (1952). At a technical level, however, it has been recognized that the mean-variance rule is only optimally efficient under certain assumptions, in particular that the investor's utility function is quadratic and the probability distribution of returns is normal. Such issues have led to the development of rather different rules under stochastic dominance principles (Mahajan, Wind, and Bradford 1981). Whether such concerns will in the end prove significant in the area of strategic marketing is a moot point. At the moment it seems likely that the basic principles underlying the CAPM approach, which is the means to apply Markowitz' portfolio theory to re-source allocation decisions both at the level of the individual investor (Linter 1965, Mossin 1966, Sharpe 1964, and Weston 1973) and of the firm (Rubinstein 1973), will prove to be fairly robust to most of these issues.

The CAPM approach is concerned with the selection of the appropriate discount rate to apply to the cost and benefit stream for any particular project. The approach rejects the use of the same discount rate for all projects the WACC approach discussed earlier, and recommends a project specific rate related to the systematic risk of the project. The systematic risk is not the total risk but only that portion of total risk that is nondiversifiable from the point of view of the portfolio investor.

In the usual finance terminology, the level of systematic risk is characterized by its "Beta," which is strictly the covariance between the asset returns and returns from a fully diversified market portfolio. The higher the Beta of any particular project, the higher the required return for that project. A number of financial analysts have argued that there is a general relationship between increased market uncertainties and systematic risk. This would imply, for instance, that new product ventures may involve higher systematic risks than line extension projects for established products. On this basis, projects should first be sorted into different general classes:

> Various types of projects are separated into risk classes according to their perceived risk, and each risk class is assigned a discount rate . . . for example, cost reduction projects are put into Class A (low risk), scale expansion projects into Class B (average risk), new projects into Class C (high risk) (Franks and Broyles 1979, p. 118).

Then higher return targets should be set for the higher risk categories so that, for instance, the required ROI is higher for new products than for line extensions to mature products.

Limitations in the CAPM

Because the CAPM has been derived from finance theory, it has a high degree of internal consistency. There are, however, a number of problems in extending the CAPM to resource allocation decisions on projects within the firm. An analysis of the project cash flows on the basis of a discount rate related to the project's Beta gives reasonable answers. The problem is that the determinants of the correct Beta in this case are complicated and related to such factors as the link between cash flow forecast errors and the forecast errors of market return as well as asset life, the growth trend in cash flows, and the pattern of expected cash flows over time (Myers and Turnbull 1977).

On the issue of empirical evidence, despite extensive testing of the CAPM, Roll (1977) has shown that the many empirical tests purporting to show that the CAPM is descriptively valid, i.e., that the actual pricing of capital assets in the market follows the predicted behavior of the model, are, in reality, joint tests of both the CAPM and market efficiency, and that the CAPM cannot be tested directly on its own.

Finally, it has been recognized that the existence of a positive Net Present Value (NPV) against the appropriate risk adjusted discount rate cannot be taken as the automatic indicator of acceptance. A large NPV must reflect anticipated scarcity or competitive advantage. Management must, therefore, decide how much effort should be expended on the basic application of the CAPM compared with a strategic analysis of competitive advantage in any resource allocation decision.

Box Models for Resource Allocation

The Market Share/Growth Matrix

The development of the approach derived from the CAPM can be seen as one means of responding to many of the criticisms of the traditional capital budgeting methodology. Another approach to such problems has been the market share/growth box classification system, probably best described by Hedley (1977) and principally attributed to the Boston Consulting Group (BCG).

The BCG approach focuses the analysis on the two axes of market share and market growth. Market share or relative market share is seen to be important as an indicator of relative competitive position, particularly in cost terms. Such an assumption is supported by the empirical evidence of the relationship between market share and profitability (Buzzell, Gale, and Sultan 1975) as well as the somewhat more indirect evidence of the experience curve effect (Hedley 1976). Market growth is, on the other hand, seen to be important partly because of the substantial cash costs of funding activity in high growth markets; the need for substantial annual additions to both fixed and working capital often dominates any cash generated by the operation. Market growth is also seen as significant because of a hypothesized interaction effect with market share itself: It is suggested that it is easier to gain market share in high growth markets.

The BCG matrix, therefore, appears to be an appropriate means of comparing market position, in terms of share and growth, with the cash performance of any particular product. It also has the advantage that in many cases it is simple and easy to use, although problems of market definition and measurement have been recognized by other commentators (Channon 1979, Day 1977).

Limitations in the BCG Matrix

The BCG matrix has, however, been commonly extended from a simple diagnostic tool to a framework within which future strategic actions can be proposed. In such a situation we are not considering an approach derived from financial economic theory, as in the case of the CAPM, but one that is essentially ad hoc, and we need to look much more closely at two critical assumptions:

- the need for the corporation to maintain a degree of cash balance by the recycling of cash between products within the corporate port-folio,
- preferential investment in high market growth businesses.

The Need for Cash Balance

The capital market as a source of funds seems to be almost ignored in some approaches. Hedley (1977), for instance, states that most companies will have to divest themselves of certain activities solely because they will not be able to generate enough cash from other areas. The extent to which such an approach can only be effective with strict cash budgeting is left some-what unclear, but the strong implication in this direction has been devel-oped much further by other authors (Gray and Green 1976, Hall 1978).

This whole approach brings us back to the strategic mistake in seeing the corporation as an independent cash recycling entity. There are times in any corporation's history when it is difficult to raise either debt or equity, but this is very different from the assumption that in the long run the corporation cannot raise funds even if it can offer a portfolio of attractive projects to the market. This is back to defining the attractiveness of any particular investment from the market point of view. If we argue that we need an internal cash control policy to avoid investing in reasonable return projects in mature markets, then logically this must be because we are claiming that the opportunity cost of cash within the firm is above such a rate for relatively low risk projects. In this case, the corporation should probably be out in the market raising further funds.[2]

Preferential Investment in High Market Growth Businesses

In a similar approach to that of Hedley, Zakon (1971) implies that cash should be preferentially directed towards high growth markets and away from established businesses in slower growth markets. The logic behind the need for such redirection seems to rest on two further assumptions: there are more opportunities for investing in high growth areas, and the payoff for such investment is better, or at least it is easier to gain market share in high growth markets.

In a simple sense, the question of more opportunities is clearly irrele-vant because there is no need to direct cash towards a particular area when it already generates a large number of demands. The more subtle argument for such a bias rests on the assumption that it is in high growth markets that technology is changing fastest, and so the competitive advantage of investing in the latest technology is the greatest. This was an argument used very effectively by the BCG (1975) to explain the rapid demise of the U.K. motorcycle industry at the hands of the Japanese. However, while there may be some correlation between market growth and the rate of technological change, it would seem more appropriate to focus the analysis on the critical variable of technological change rather than a partial proxy such as market growth, particularly in the context of a market such as the worldwide motorcycle market.

The issue of better payoffs is potentially very relevant, but the model is not well formulated. It is, therefore, not clear to what extent the ease of gaining share in high growth markets refers to the short run cost of gaining market share or to the long run incremental benefit of increasing market share. There is very little empirical evidence, but Kijewski (1978) did undertake an analysis of the PIMS data in an attempt to estimate the cash costs of gaining market share points in different market environments. By looking at the difference between the cash flow/investment ratios for businesses that gained share as opposed to those that held share steady over one year as a means of estimating the short-term cash flow costs of gaining share, she concluded:

> Contrary to conventional wisdom, we do not find that the cash costs of gaining share vary substantially between moderate and rapid growth markets. When the cash costs are appropriately adjusted for average point change in market share in each environment, the cost of a point in share is only slightly lower in the more rapidly growing markets (and, indeed, lowest in low growth markets) (Kijewski 1978, p. 8).

On such evidence it would be difficult to make a good general case for investing in market share gains in rapid growth markets because the short-term costs were substantially lower. Indeed on such criteria there might even be a bias towards investments in low growth markets. To justify a general bias towards high growth markets there must be significant evidence that the long run incremental benefits of market share gains in such markets are greater.

If we were willing to postulate a model in which all product/markets followed the same Product Life Cycle (PLC) pattern of the same duration, then gains in market share would have greater longevity in terms of benefits if they were achieved at earlier stages in the cycle. Such a model would in fact appear to be fairly close to that implicitly assumed by those who attempt to tie budgeting procedures to the PLC (Savich and Thompson 1978). The PLC, however, has been a notable empirical failure if the analysis focuses too directly on the issue of stages (Dhalla and Yuspeh 1976, Polli and Cook 1969). Such failure led a recent reviewer to comment that "The concept of PLC stages may be hindering PLC research by diverting attention from other issues concerning product life cycles" (Rink and Swan 1979, p. 232).

It would seem that the current limited state of empirical knowledge about the costs and benefits of investing in market share shifts does not support the contention that, on average, the payoff is better from investing cash in gaining market share in rapid growth markets. The market share/growth matrix approach also fails to reflect the considerably greater degree of risk attached to major and substantial diversification moves, which has been widely recognized in more traditional work on corporate strategy since Ansoff's (1965) famous four boxes.

In conclusion, any attempt to use the market share/growth matrix for resource allocation decisions implies a preference for high market growth businesses and the need to maintain a cash balance within the firm. There is little current empirical or theoretical work to justify such a preference.

The Directional Policy Matrix

A number of other criticisms have been leveled against the market growth/share matrix. Day (1977) in the most comprehensive critique focused on the problems of assumptions, measurement, and strategic feasibility. In particular he indicated that feasibility was often dominated by other factors beyond share and market growth, which was suggestive of the nine box classification. Some other critics have chosen to concentrate solely on the oversimplistic nature of the market growth/share approach (*Marketing News* 1978). Such critics have often been much more emphatic than Day in advocating the Directional Policy Matrix or its cousins (Hussey 1978, Robinson, Hichens, and Wade 1978). In principle the Directional Policy Matrix involves expanding the dimensions of the BCG matrix so that market growth becomes a part of a composite measure of market attractiveness, and market share equally becomes a part of a composite measure of business position.

Limitations in the DPM

Applications of the DPM approach is complicated by the problem of weighting and combining different factors to generate the two dimensions, and it is in grave danger of leading the analyst to the tautological position of recommending preferential investment in those areas of highest market attractiveness and strongest business position. Hussey (1978) implicitly recognizes this with his tentative conclusion that the DPM analysis results in no surprises and, even to a limited extent, that there was a direct correlation between the discount rates shown by the projects via the normal appraisal system and those predicted by the position of the projects on the DPM. This would come as no surprise to those who see a positive net present value as a reflection of competitive advantage anyway, but Hussey does not address the question of whether he is claiming that a DPM approach would prove to be a less costly means of achieving the same result as the traditional method.

The DPM approach brings us back to the basic search for areas of sustainable competitive advantage, but there is limited evidence that it provides a useful additional form of analysis in such circumstances beyond a fairly comprehensive checklist and an idiosyncratic weighting of factors by corporate management.

Betas or Boxes: Projects or Business Units

The evaluation of the CAPM, BCG, and DPM schemes as corporate level models is given in Table 17.1.

We should have severe doubts about the theoretical and empirical support for the BCG market share/growth boxes when used to identify areas of sustainable competitive advantage. Both the CAPM and the DPM do remain focused on such an economic principle, but there remain considerable doubts as to the extent to which either can be seen as the critical determinant.

In practice the difference between financial approaches such as the CAPM and box classification systems is greater. A CAPM approach is related to individual projects, whereas box classification systems are most often applied at higher levels of aggregation, in particular Strategic Business Units. Indeed, it would be difficult to justify the cost effectiveness of box classification at the level of individual projects, since in most cases this would involve adding a more superficial approach onto the existing appraisal process within the firm.

In the context of project appraisal most evidence suggests that the sustainable competitive advantage resides in the specifics of the particular project. Hence, much of the current work on the issues of Strategic Business Units (SBUs) is likely to be based on an inappropriate grouping of product-market opportunities into a single unit. For instance, the current literature on the problems of managing units in mature markets contains the implicit assumption that few, if any, worthwhile projects will be generated by such SBU's (Hall 1978). Such an assumption challenges not only economic logic but market evidence. Goodyear, for instance, has decided quite consciously to commit its resources to increasing market share in the low growth auto tire business (*Business Week* 1978), while most of its major competitors such as Goodrich are clearly planning to reduce capacity and future capital commitments in the market. Many firms will have also experienced the fact that it is often economic for the major supplier to expand production in apparently low growth markets as have Philips N.V. in the worldwide electric light bulb market; even more will have encountered the considerable number of highly profitable cost saving investments in such areas.

It is not, of course, difficult to see why such opportunities are genuinely attractive. As the more marginal firms drop out of the business, there are real opportunities for the dominant firm(s) to pick up additional sales.

TABLE 17.1 An Evaluation of Corporate Level Models

APPROACH	EXEMPLAR	INTERNAL CONSISTENCY	EMPIRICAL EVIDENCE	CRITICAL ISSUE
Risk/Return	CAPM	OK	OK	Unlikely because numbers less important than competitive market assumptions
Unidimensional Classification	BCG	Dubious assumption about the importance of market growth	No supporting evidence for costs of gaining market share	Very unlikely because of doubts about the validity of the whole approach
Composite Dimensions	DPM	No clear theoretical or empirical statements to be assessed — seems broadly in line with competitive advantage approach but no additional empirical tests		Unlikely because it depends on management to make their own idiosyncratic assessments and adds little to current procedures

Such opportunities are reinforced when technical change requires all firms to reinvest in new facilities as the switch to radial tires has done in the U.S. market. Similar situations often occur when extra market effects such as tighter pollution regulations require significant incremental investment and, therefore, often encourage marginal firms to leave the market. The dominant firm that invests in such situations is really doing no more than building on its existing market strengths.

This all suggests that corporate management cannot avoid ensuring that each particular strategic investment proposal is assessed individually. A critical component of such an appraisal is the interrelatedness of the particular project with other current or potential activities of the firm, but such interrelatedness is not adequately represented by the generalized dimensions of box classification systems such as the DPM. Conceptually this implies that the distinction between the corporate level approach and the product/market level as proposed by Grant and King (1979) cannot yet be sustained. In principle, if we could identify classificatory systems at the corporate level that meet the classical criterion that the intraclass variability of projects was substantially less than the interclass variability, then we could maintain the distinction. We have argued that against such a criterion we really have nothing better than the traditional budgetary limits method in which projects are essentially classified purely by size or the broad categories of cost saving, line or volume extension, and new products proposed by financial analysts.

The Basic Issue: Aids to Assessing Competitive Advantage

We have argued that any analytical approach in marketing strategy must not be followed to monopolize the search for areas of sustainable competitive advantage. Wensley (1981) has argued that no economic theory can be expected to give us all the right answers, but can provide useful diagnostic questions that will indicate things to be done. Such approaches suggest, as already discussed, that any competitive advantage is much more likely to reside in the specific nature of a particular project rather than the broad characteristics of the particular business division that is sponsoring it. Economic analysis starts from the assumption that any such competitive advantage is essentially temporary but that it can be extended if the firm faces few direct competitors.

The economic analysis of barriers to direct competition starts from Bain's (1956) initial study. Bain's conception of such barriers was that new entrants into a particular market were likely to face substantial costs before being able to compete on equal terms with the established firms. The rather simplified conception of distinct but homogeneous markets inherent in this approach was, however, at variance with the market realities of customer segmentation, alternative distribution channels, and product differentiation. Caves and Porter (1977) have recently extended the barriers concept to mobility barriers reflecting the initial costs faced by any firm that wishes to change its overall position in the marketplace by opening up a new distribution channel, extending the product line, etc. The whole approach implies that because of such barriers, the level of competitive activity in any market will be less than it would otherwise be since existing firms are in some senses protected from further competition. Porter has also extended the concept to the implication that in certain declining markets the competition may also be more intense than it would otherwise be because of analogous barriers to exit (Porter 1976).

Mobility barriers distinguish between the performance of established firms in a particular market and that of new entrants. In developing markets the overall entry costs will be different for different firms; some will be better placed to develop production opportunities, while others will have better access to distribution channels and face lower entry costs in terms of this dimension. However, since there is by definition no such thing as established competition, the analysis of actual outcomes has to consider game theoretic assumptions (Shubik 1975), which creates further complications (Salop 1979).

Porter (1979) has argued that the principal empirical base of the BCG approach — the experience curve effect — can be seen as a particular form of a barrier to entry. However, the learning curve phenomena (Andress 1954, Hirschmann 1964) has been extended from direct production costs first to production overhead costs and then to all other value added items in the product. This development means that experience economies can be categorized in two ways:

- Some value added elements such as advertising should be assessed much more on the demand effect rather than actual cost
- Experience in the various value added components in the final product market can be shared with developments in other, sometimes apparently unrelated, areas.

As Day (1977) has indicated, the oversimple extension of the experience curve concept to all value added elements has created the danger that analysis is conducted in terms of building experience curve economies in the production and marketing of Product X.

More Comprehensive Analysis of Experience

In practice, in any experience analysis we should distinguish between both cost and demand effects and also specific and shared benefits. In particular, we should recognize the problems of cost based, specific analysis and the benefits of other approaches.

For instance, an obsession with reaping the benefits of experience curve cost economies can result in a strategic posture in the marketplace that is severely disadvantaged in the case of significant shifts in market

TABLE 17.2 Examples of Experience Based Strategies

	SPECIFIC	SHARED
Cost Based	Model T	Solid-state components
Demand Based	Branding	Distribution channel

response. Such a problem is clearly documented for Ford and the Model T by Abernathy and Wayne (1974), and should be uppermost in the minds of any executives if they feel they are being persuaded to take major investment decisions based on relatively naive and unchanging models of market behavior.

However, some cost based approaches require a broader sense of the related markets. For instance, the burgeoning market for solid-state devices in autos will substantially affect the scale economies for the production of such items in apparently unrelated markets (Boyd and Headen 1978) but the problem goes much further than this. The value added structure of particular products is likely to change over time, hence, the questions of relevant experience become more complex: Will the calculator market become an area where much of the value added is in distribution and marketing? If this is the case, the critical experience curve economies may well switch from production to such areas and thus change the set of corporations that are most competitively placed.

Demand based approaches may offer a way of avoiding some of these problems. For specific products the process of branding offers a way in which, if successful, a premium in the market can be maintained often over a long period. Shared opportunities come from activities in the market that provide future options for further development, such as the opening up of a new distribution channel.

We can, therefore, summarize the four broad options for experience-based strategies, and the examples in Table 17.2.

To avoid an overemphasis in our strategic analysis on specific, cost based benefits, we should recognize some of the additional advantages of the other approaches.

Additional Considerations

Demand based approaches have the advantage that, if successful, they are often difficult to imitate:

> In general there may be a high level of uncertainty as to the outcome of an advertising campaign. If advertising is successful or a new styling takes, an opponent may not be able to make a strategically successful countermove. If a price cut is successful, an opponent can counter by also cutting prices (Shubik 1959, p. 349).

In mobility barriers terms certain demand based investments can carry the additional benefit that the relevant barrier grows for those following, either because of a direct increase in costs or the need to use less effective measures because direct imitation is not feasible.

Shared experience approaches offer two potential benefits: a greater degree of flexibility in the face of market uncertainties, and the development of positions that can be exploited at a later date. Within the study of the economics of internal organizations (Alchian and Demsetz 1972, Williamson 1975), it has been recognized that firms already in a particular market have the opportunity to adapt their behavior more efficiently than potential new entrants by selective managerial intervention.

There has also been a growing body of literature on strategic analysis that has focused on this issue either directly or indirectly (Ackoff 1970, Ball and Lorrange 1979, Per Strangert 1977). However, the limited empirical evidence is rather pessimistic about the ability of particular activities to adapt to major environmental change (Cooper and Schendel 1976), and indeed suggests that such activities as more effective environmental scanning (Montgomery and Weinberg 1979) often only delay rather than avoid the threatened demise. This would suggest that corporate management should assess the flexibility in any particular project in terms of monitoring as well as future potential changes, rather than rely on statements about general management skills.

The benefit of building a position, particularly in distribution and customer terms, resides in the options that are made possible before, and often long before, these options are actually realized (Wensley 1979b). Logically, such benefits are a result of the original investment decisions, and the additional value of these optional benefits should have been considered at the time when the investments were being made to develop a positional strength.

The basic conception of positional advantages is very close to the multidimensional definition of corporate strengths proposed by Simmonds (1968), but includes the explicit recognition that today's strategy is tomorrow's history and, therefore, the strategic decisions of today are shaping the strengths and weaknesses of tomorrow. In this direction, certain strategic actions will have much greater payoffs in terms of potential benefits to future actions than others. It is important in the strategic analysis of any particular action that the nature, scale, and value of such benefits is evaluated.

Conclusion

In undertaking strategic marketing analysis of any particular investment option it is important to avoid the use of classificatory systems that deflect the analysis from the critical issue of why there is a potential sustainable competitive advantage for the corporation. The market growth/share portfolio approach advocated by BCG encourages the use of general rather than specific criteria as well as implying assumptions about mechanisms of corporate financing and market behavior that are either unnecessary or false. The DPM approach, on the other hand, appears to add little to a more specific project based form of analysis.

Both classificatory schemes would be positively harmful if used to justify some form of cash budgeting, since it is essential that any major project is assessed independent of its box classification. The financial basis of such an assessment should be an evaluation of the project's benefits against the appropriate discount rate related to the project's systematic risk or Beta. It is critical, however, that the financial analysis should not dominate a thorough evaluation of the competitive market assumptions upon which the project is based. Such a project based evaluation must focus not only on direct cost experience effects but also on the degree to which the project can be effectively imitated by others if it proves to be successful, the extent to which the project's progress will be adequately monitored and suitable changes implemented at a later date, and the particular ways in which the project will (beyond its direct substantive benefits) also enhance the firm's ability to exploit further opportunities at a later stage.

Notes

1. Customized strategy models do, of course, make implicit assumptions about the economic value of a more systematic and consistent appraisal of project characteristics. As such there are close relationships with the arguments for procedural rationality (Burton and Naylor 1980). These assumptions could also be tested against the evidence, but this is outside the scope of this paper.
2. This principle also works in the reverse situation. If the corporation is unable to find sufficient projects with adequate returns to use up all the funds available from its retained earnings, it should be returning such additional funds to its shareholders rather than investing in projects with inadequate returns.

References

Abernathy, William J. and Kenneth Wayne (1974), "Limits of the Learning Curve," *Harvard Business Review*, 52 (September–October), 109–119.

Ackoff, R. L. (1970), *A Concept of Corporate Planning*, New York: John Wiley.

Alchian, A. A. and H. Demsetz (1972), "Production, Information Costs and Economic Organization," *American Economic Review*, 62 (December), 777–795.

Anderson, Paul F. (1979), "The Marketing Management/Finance Interface," in *1979 AMA Educators Proceedings*, N. Beckwith et al., eds., Chicago: American Marketing Association, 325–329.

Andress, Frank J. (1954), "The Learning Curve as a Production Tool," *Harvard Business Review*, 32 (January–February) 87–97.

Ansoff, I. (1965), *Corporate Strategy*, New York: McGraw Hill.

Bain, J. S. (1956), *Barriers to New Competition,* Cambridge, MA: Harvard University Press.

Ball, Ben C., Jr., and Peter Lorange (1979), "Managing Your Strategic Responsiveness to the Environment," *Managerial Planning,* 28(3), (November/December), 3–9.

Boston Consulting Group (1975), *Strategic Alternatives for the British Motorcycle Industry,* London: Her Majesty's Stationers Office.

Boyd, Harper W., and Robert S. Headen (1978), "Definition and Management of the Product-Market Portfolio," *Industrial Marketing Management,* 7 (no. 5), 337–346.

Burton, Richard M. and Thomas N. Naylor (1980), "Economic Theory in Corporate Planning," *Strategic Management Journal,* 1 (no. 3), 249–263.

Business Week (1978), "Goodyear's Solo Strategy: Grow Where Nobody Else Sees It," (August 1), 67–104.

Buzzell, R. D., B. T. Gale, and R. G. M. Sultan (1975), "Market Share — A Key to Profitability," *Harvard Business Review,* 53 (January–February), 97–106.

Caves, R. E., and Porter, M. E. (1977), "From Entry Barriers to Mobility Barriers, Conjectural Decisions and Contrived Deterrence to New Competition," *Quarterly Journal of Economics,* XCI (May), 241–261.

Channon, Derek F. (1979) "Commentary on Strategy Formulation," in *Strategic Management: A New View of Business Policy and Planning,* D. E. Schendel and C. W. Hofer, eds., Boston: Little, Brown and Co.

Cooper, A. C. and D. Schendel (1976), "Strategic Responses to Technological Threats," *Business Horizons,* 19 (February), 61–69.

Day, George (1977), "Diagnosing the Product Portfolio," *Journal of Marketing,* 41 (April), 29–38.

Dhalla, Nariman K. and Sonia Yuspeh (1976), "Forget the Product Life Cycle Concept," *Harvard Business Review,* 54 (January–February), 102–109.

Franks, J. R., and J. Broyles (1979), *Modern Managerial Finance,* Chichester: Wiley.

Grant, John H. and William R. King (1979), "Strategy Formulation: Analytical and Normative Models," in *Strategic Management: A New View of Business Policy and Planning,* D. E. Schendel and C. W. Hofer, eds., Boston: Little, Brown and Co.

Gray, E. G. and H. B. Green (1976), "Cash Throw-Off: A Resource Allocation Strategy," *Business Horizons,* 19 (June), 29–33.

Hall, W. K. (1978), "SBUs: Hot, New Topic in the Management of Diversification," *Business Horizons,* 21 (February), 17–25.

Hedley, Barry (1976), "A Fundamental Approach to Strategy Development," *Long Range Planning,* 9 (December), 2–11.

——— (1977), "Strategy and the Business Portfolio," *Long Range Planning,* 10 (February), 9–15.

Hirschmann, W. D. (1964), "Profit from the Learning Curve," *Harvard Business Review,* (January–February), 125–139.

Hopkins, D. S. (1977), "New Emphasis in Product Planning and Strategy Development," *Industrial Marketing Management,* 6 (no. 6), 410–419.

Hussey, D. E. (1978), "Portfolio Analysis: Practical Experience with the Directional Policy Matrix," *Long Range Planning,* 11 (August), 2–8.

Kijewski, V. (1978), "Marketing Share Strategy: Beliefs vs. Actions," PIMS letter 9/2, Strategic Planning Institute, Cambridge, MA.

Linter, John (1965), "Security Prices, Risk, and Maximal Gains from Diversification," *Journal of Finance,* 20 (December), 587–615.

Mahajan, Vijay, Yoram Wind, and John W. Bradford (1981), "Stochastic Dominance Rules for Product Portfolio Analysis," *Management Science, 1981, Special Issue on Marketing Policy Models, Andy Zoltners, ed.*

Marketing News (1978), "Market-Share ROI Corporate Strategy Approach Can Be an 'Oversimplistic' Snare," 12 (December 15), 12.

Markowitz, H. (1952), "Portfolio Selection," *Journal of Finance,* 7 (March), 77–91.

Merritt, A. and A. Sykes (1963), *The Finance and Analysis of Capital Projects,* London: Longmans.

Montgomery, David B. and Charles B. Weinberg (1979), "Towards Strategic Intelligence Systems," *Journal of Marketing,* 43 (Fall), 41–52.

Mossin, Jan (1966), "Equilibrium in a Capital Asset Market," *Econometrics,* 34 (October), 768–783.

Myers, S. and S. M. Turnbull (1977), "Capital Budgeting and the Capital Asset Pricing Model: Good News and Bad News," *Journal of Finance,* 32 (May), 321–333.

Per Strangert (1977), "Adaptive Planning and Uncertainty Resolution," *Futures,* 9 (February), 32–42.

Polli, R. and V. Cook (1969), "The Validity of the Product Life Cycle," *Journal of Business,* 42 (October), 385–400.

Porter, Michael E. (1976), "Please Note Location of the Nearest Exit," *California Management Review,* XIX (Winter), 21–33.

———— (1979), "How Competitive Forces Shape Strategy," *Harvard Business Review,* 57 (March–April), 137–145.

Rink, David R. and John E. Swan (1979), "Product Life Cycle Research: A Literature Review," *Journal of Business Research,* 78 (September), 219–242.

Robinson, S. J. Q., R. E. Hichens, and D. P. Wade (1978), "The Directional Policy Matrix-Tool for Strategic Planning," *Long-Range Planning,* 11 (no. 3), 8–15.

Roll, Richard (1977), "A Critique of the Asset Pricing Theories Tests," *Journal of Financial Economics,* 4 (March), 129–176.

Rubinstein, M. (1973), "A Mean-Variance Synthesis of Corporate Finance Theory," *Journal of Finance,* 28 (March), 167–181.

Salop, Steven C. (1979), "Strategic Entry Deterrence," *American Economic Review,* 69 (May), 335–338.

Savich, R. S. and L. A. Thompson (1978), "Resource Allocation within the Product Life Cycle," *MSU Business Topics,* 26 (Autumn), 35–44.

Sharpe, W. F. (1964), "Capital Asset Prices: A Theory of Market Equilibrium Under Conditions of Risk," *Journal of Finance,* 19 (September), 425–442.

Shubik, M. (1959), *Strategy and Market Structure,* New York: Wiley.

———— (1975), *Games for Society, Business and War,* New York: Elsevier.

Simmonds, K. (1968), "Removing the Chains from Product Strategy," *Journal of Management Studies,* 5 (no. 1), 29–40.

Wensley, J. R. C. (1979a), "The Effective Strategic Analyst," *Journal of Management Studies,* 16 (October), 283–293.

———— (1979b), "Beyond the CAPM and the Boston Box: The Concept of Market Location," Bristol, England: Marketing Educators Group Conference.

———— (1981), "PIMS and BCG: New Horizons or False Dawn in Strategic Marketing," *Strategic Management Journal,* in press.

Weston, J. Fred (1973), "Investment Decisions Using the Capital Asset Pricing Model," *Financial Management,* 2 (Spring), 25–33.

Williamson, O. E. (1975), *Markets and Hierarchies: Analysis and Antitrust Implications*, New York: Free Press.

Wind, Yoram (1974), "Product Portfolio: A New Approach to the Product Mix Decision," *Proceedings of the 1974 AMA Conference*, 460–464.

———, and Vijay Mahajan (1980), "Design Considerations in Portfolio Analysis," working paper, Wharton School, University of Pennsylvania.

———, and T. Saaty (1980), "Marketing Applications of the Analytic Hierarchy Process," *Management Science*, 76, (July), 641–658.

Zakon, A. (1971), "Growth and Financial Strategies," working paper, Boston, MA: Boston Consulting Group.

The Development of Marketing Strategy — The Planning Process

THE ARTICLES IN THIS SECTION address the process that leads to a strategic marketing plan. The development of a strategic marketing plan involves integrating the critical inputs discussed in Section II with the concepts and planning models presented in Sections III and IV. To examine how these factors are integrated, we need to consider the relationship between the top-level managers, who are using the planning models to determine a strategic direction, and the managers at the functional-level, advertising and sales managers who must use the allocated resources to implement the strategy. Inputs from both top-level and functional-level managers are needed to develop an effective marketing strategy. The top-level managers possess a broad perspective on environmental trends and business capabilities, while the functional managers are in direct contact with the marketplace and have the best vantage point to determine what can be done. As we investigate the process of combining inputs from managers at various levels within the business, we discover that the distinction between the strategic decisions of top-level managers and the tactical decisions of functional managers becomes blurred.

Marketing Strategy Versus Marketing Tactics

In the introduction to the first section of this book, we attempted to make a clear division between a broad master strategy focusing on the selection of target product-markets and, on the other hand, tactical decisions, such as the formulation of advertising themes or of restocking policies for distributors. We suggested that the following dimensions were useful for discriminating between these two types of decisions:

317

1. Importance of decisions to business performance.
2. Level at which decisions are made.
3. Time horizon of decisions.
4. Regularity of making decisions.
5. Nature of problem in terms of definition and structure.
6. Information to make decisions.
7. Level of detail contained in decisions.
8. Ease of evaluating decisions.

In this section, we reexamine the clear distinction proposed in the introductory section. As a first step in this reexamination, we look more closely at the assumptions underlying the dimensions just listed.

Importance–Level–Time Horizon

The first three dimensions propose that strategic decisions are more important to the success of the business than tactical decisions, and thus strategic decisions are the responsibility of top-level management. As evidence of this proposition, we cited Peter Drucker's well-known aphorism that "It is more important to do the right thing than to do things right." Despite such powerful rhetoric, there is no evidence that, in terms of business unit performance, strategy dominates tactics. After an event, there may be a tendency to ascribe success to "good strategy" and failure to "poor strategy," but such an assessment is tautological.

There is a basic problem encountered in any attempt to determine whether performance is due to strategy or tactics. After the fact, many strategies can only be inferred from a set of tactical actions taken. There is little evidence that performance is improved when formal planning methods state the strategies explicitly before the tactical implementation programs are developed.[1]

In practice, both strategic and tactical decisions can have a substantial impact on business unit performance. To use a football analogy, the success for the Dallas Cowboys under Tom Landry has been attributed to the brilliance of their strategic game plans, while the success of the late Vince Lombardi's Green Bay Packers has been ascribed to effective tactics — blocking and tackling.[2]

Once we recognize that strategic and tactical decisions are so interwoven that it is difficult to determine which are more important, it becomes apparent we can no longer assume that "important" decisions are made at higher levels in the business. The blocking and tackling decisions of the Green Bay Packers are made by the linemen, in the trenches, not by the coach or general manager. And finally, consider this: just because strategic marketing plans are written formally with a ten-year horizon is not a guarantee that they will be relevant over a longer time period than the usual (tactical) marketing plan.

The General Nature of Strategic Problems

The second group of dimensions, 4 through 6, focus on the nature of strategic versus tactical problems. These distinctions between strategic and tactical problems are quite similar to those developed by Robert Anthony[3] to differentiate between the routine nature of capital budgeting and the irregular and unstructured nature of strategic response. Joseph Bower[4] subsequently found that such a distinction did not exist in large multidivisional corporations. Although the distinction between routine and non-routine problems can be made conceptual, there does not appear to be any justification for mapping this distinction onto the organizational decisions of capital budgeting and strategic reappraisal. Many strategic reappraisal decisions are imbedded in "routine" capital budgeting decisions. Thus it seems more useful to identify the strategic and routine aspects of business decisions rather than the presort decisions into routine and strategic categories on a priori criteria.

Detail and Ease of Evaluation

There is less dispute concerning the last two dimensions as a basis for discriminating between tactical and strategic decisions. Most people would agree that strategic statements are characterized by a lack of detail and thus there are problems in evaluating these decisions. Of course, one can adopt an alternative view that this difficulty in evaluating strategic decisions only goes to reinforce the preceding argument — that a distinction is not possible. If strategic decisions are difficult to evaluate, then it must be an act of faith rather than empirical evidence that leads one to regard them as important. The issues raised in this re-examination show the need for us to gain a better understanding of some of the underlying concepts about strategy itself.

Concepts of Strategy

The military perspective and an ecological viewpoint are two traditions that have influenced our thinking about the meaning of strategy in a business context. Although these analogies can provide some insight into the concept of strategy, we must recognize their limitations.

Military Analogy

Several recent articles have suggested the military model can provide the missing links in our thinking about marketing strategy.[5] Unfortunately, strategic military thinking is based on two assumptions that may not be an appropriate basis for developing marketing strategies.

The first assumption is that certain resources are available only from directly controlled supplies. Clearly, there are critical resources in a business context analogous to the military resources of men, material, and supplies. Such resources in a strategic marketing context are cash, marketing and production capabilities, and managerial know-how. In a marketing context, these resources are generally available to the business from an external source. For example, a business can raise cash from outsiders if an attractive business opportunity arises. Contracts can be made with advertising agencies to supply advertising creativity that may not be available within the firm. Independent manufacturer agents can be used to reach a new product-market.

In contrast, military strategy is based on the premise that resources may not be available at a market price when they are needed. Patton could not find an outsider to supply gasoline for his tanks.

The importance of resource control in military strategy provides an interesting focal point for marketing strategy. Perhaps, marketing strategy should focus on resources that cannot be provided efficiently by external supply markets. In the previous section, we looked at strategic planning models that focused on cash, a resource that can be provided efficiently by capital markets. However, the emphasis of military strategy suggests we should base our analysis on marketing capabilities and know-how that are not readily available from external sources.

The second assumption of military strategy is that conflict must be viewed in terms of a direct readjustment of territorial boundaries at the expense of the enemy. This view that competition is a zero-sum game contrasts directly with many marketing situations and is also at odds with the ecological model.[6]

Ecological Analogy

The ecological model is concerned with survival characteristics of various species.[7] A basic premise of the ecological model is the so-called Principle of Competitive Exclusion, which states that the environment cannot support two different species having exactly similar needs. This premise suggests a more complex model of competitive behavior and survival than the "fight to the death" view propounded by military strategists and some marketing strategic analysts.

Another interesting premise of the ecological model is the distinction between r-type species (those that survive on the basis of their rapid rate of reproduction) and k-type species (those which depend on their abilities as specialists within an ecological niche). The product life cycle model discussed in Section III suggests that the effectiveness of these two types will vary over the life cycle. In the early stages of the life cycle, r-types will be most effective because the primary concern is expanding a broadbased market. However, k-types will be more effective as the market matures because the emphasis shifts to specialization and segmentation. William

Hall has found that success in a business environment comes to companies that either achieve a low-cost position (r-type) or a highly differentiated position (k-type).[8]

The principal difference between the business and ecological perspective is that species are either one type or the other, but there is no fundamental constraint preventing an r-type business from undergoing metamorphosis to a k-type one at the appropriate stage in the market development. However, in practice, there does seem to be a very distinct problem for organizations to undertake a change. This difficulty is exemplified by the Ford Motor Company: they undertook a relentless, and very effective pursuit of efficiency in the Model T; this commitment was followed by a very costly and difficult process of readapting to different market imperatives.[9]

An ecological viewpoint suggests a limited set of alternatives. John Child, however, feels that the body of strategic choices even encompasses the selection of the environment in which the organization wishes to exist (the selection of product-markets); it also includes the organization's attempts to manipulate its environment.[10] These proactive alternatives go beyond the "ecological" alternatives related to choice of organizational form.

The ecological analogy suggests the real issue in strategy formulation is in terms of the trade-off between specialization and adaptability. Unfortunately, *before* the event, it is much easier to recognize the criteria for a good specializer than those for a good adapter. Thus it is important to have a particular strategic focus at any one time and equally important to have a means of assessing the continuing relevance of such a focus, rather than having the broad and nonoperational strategy approach of relying on adaptive potential.

Nature of the Strategic Planning Process

The strategic concept adopted by an author has a strong influence on the nature of the planning process he or she advocates. But, apart from that issue, all the articles in this section go beyond the simplistic idea that strategic planning is a one-way activity, from the top to the bottom of an organization. They share a concern for integrating top- and bottom-level perspectives, supporting the previous discussion that emphasized the intimate relationships between strategic and tactical decisions.

Multistage Iteration

One common theme for integrating top-level and bottom-level perspectives is a process of successive approximation. The first paper in this section is Article 18, "Strategy Formulation in Complex Organizations"; it was written by Richard Vancil, who, along with Peter Lorange,[11] has been one of the most important advocates of a multistage planning process. We should note, however, that the underlying assumptions of this process remain strongly hierarchical: the adjustment process accomplished lower down the organization is generally conducted within the broader guidelines set at the higher levels.

Balancing "Top-down" and "Bottom-up" Processes

Article 19, "Strategic Market Analysis and Definition: An Integrated Approach," takes the move away from a purely top-down planning process significantly further. George Day emphasizes not only that any broad definitions of strategic segments[12] or market niches must be tested rigorously against detailed product-market data for evidence of discontinuities, but also that the more specific and detailed data may often be an undervalued asset in many planning processes. Such detailed data may in fact be a valuable source of ideas for effective market strategies. The article itself is not specific about the process implications of such a rebalancing, but it assumes that the right balance can be achieved through dialogue and challenge between various managerial levels within the organization.

Adaptive Planning

The next paper in this section is "The Reality Gap in Strategic Planning," which challenges very directly the Forecasting → Plan → Monitor/Control model of the overall planning process. Rather, the emphasis is on the use of the planning process as a means to encourage adaptation[13] to changing external and indeed internal priorities; the planning also signals the existence of critical commercial risks. Again, it is assumed rather than proved that such a change in emphasis in the planning process will actually achieve the desired effects.

Strategic Incrementalism

At the opposite extreme from the dominant top-down view is the idea that the whole concept of grand strategy is fundamentally misleading. This view argues that, in reality, strategy is the outcome of the whole series of minor tactical and hence incremental moves. Article 21 is "Strategic Goals: Process and Politics," which argues this position strongly. Such a view relates strongly the development of the concept of disjointed incrementalism in public policy analysis,[14] but it should be recognized that while such a view has been accepted as having some validity in the public policy field, others have strongly suggested that more major systematic changes are also feasible in certain circumstances.[15] Similarly, while it is clearly true that in certain circumstances the grand corporate strategy has been derived after rather than before the series of tactical decisions, it is also true that such strategic decisions as the structure of the organization and its general direction and focus do exert some significant impact both on the opportunities that are perceived within the organization and the ways in which these are assessed.

Strategic Windows

The final paper in this section, Article 22, illustrates the importance of timing in making strategic decisions. This paper illustrates that there is often a narrow time period during which the unique capabilities of a business match the needs of a changing environment.

Notes

1. Robert J. Kudla, "The Effects of Strategic Planning on Common Stock Returns," *Academy of Management Journal,* 23, No. 1 (1980): 5–20.
2. While strategic parallels are often drawn between American football and business management, soccer is a more appropriate sport to use in deriving analogies. Business management like soccer is played continuously. Strategic decisions must be made while the game is being played. There are no opportunities to call time-outs in business for developing new plays. See B.S. Keirstead, "Decision Making and the Theory of Games," in *Uncertainty and Expectations in Economics: Essay in Honour of G.L.S. Shakle,* ed. C.F. Carter and J.L. Ford (Blackwell: Oxford, England, 1972), pp. 160–171.
3. Robert N. Anthony, *Planning and Control Systems: A Framework for Analysis* (Boston: Division of Research, Graduate School of Business Administration, Harvard University, 1965), in particular Appendix B: Robert H. Caplan, "Relationship between Principles of Military Strategy and Principle of Business Planning").
4. Joseph L. Bower, *Managing the Resource Allocation Process* (Boston: Division of Research, Graduate School of Business Administration, Harvard University, 1970).
5. H. Widmer, "Business Lessons from Military Strategy," *McKinsey Quarterly,* Spring 1980, pp. 59–67; and Philip Kotler and Pavi Singh, "Marketing Warfare in the 1980's," *Journal of Business Strategy,* Winter 1981, pp. 30–41.
6. Indeed even in military terms there is a distinction between the direct territorial approach of a Klauswitz and the more subtle oriental views of a writer like Suntzu.
7. Howard E. Aldridge, *Organizations and Environments* (Englewood Cliffs, N.J.: Prentice-Hall, 1979); and Michael T. Hannan and John Freeman, "The Population Ecology of Organizations," *American Journal of Sociology* 82, No. 5:929–965.
8. William K. Hall, "Survival Strategies in a Hostile Environment," *Harvard Business Review,* September–October 1980, pp. 75–85.
9. W.J. Abernathy and K. Wayne, "Limits of the Learning Curve," *Harvard Business Review,* September–October 1974, pp. 109–119 (Article 9 of this book).
10. John Child, "Organizational Structure, Environment and Performance — The Role of Strategic Choice," *Sociology* 6 (January 1972): 1–22.

11. Peter Lorange and Richard F. Vancil, *Strategic Planning Systems* (Englewood Cliffs, N.J.: Prentice-Hall, 1977).
12. Robert Garda, "A Strategic Approach to Market Segmentation," *The McKinsey Quarterly*, Autumn 1981, pp. 16–29.
13. Per Strangert, "Adaptive Planning and Uncertainty Resolution," *Futures*, February 1977, pp. 32–44.
14. C. E. Lindbloom, "The Science of 'Muddling Through,' " *Public Administration Review* 19, Spring 1959, pp. 79–88.
15. K. Archibald, "Three Views on the Expert's Role in Policymaking: Systems Analysis, Incrementalism and the Clinical Approach," *Policy Science*, 1, No. 1 (1970):73–86.

18. Strategy Formulation in Complex Organizations

Richard F. Vancil

The primary source of cohesiveness in an organization is strategy. To be effective, however, strategy must be more than just a ringing statement of purpose or objectives. It must also provide guidance that will assist subordinate managers in deciding how to proceed toward achieving the objectives. Furthermore, strategy should help to weld an organization together by developing among the members of the management team both a shared belief in the efficacy of major action programs and a shared commitment to execute those programs successfully. The purpose of this article is to discuss how strategy can be formulated in such a way that it will be more than simply a statement of purpose but will have an active role in shaping decision making in a complex organization.

Some Definitions

Before we proceed we must define three words — *strategy, objectives,* and *goals*. This is necessary because these words will be used in this article to convey a specific meaning which is not always synonymous with their common use in business.

Strategy

The strategy of an organization, *or of a subunit of a larger organization,* is a conceptualization, *expressed or implied by the organization's leader,* of (1) the long-term objectives or purposes of the organization, (2) the broad constraints and policies, *either self-imposed by the leader or accepted by him from his superiors,* that *currently* restrict the scope of the organization's activities,

This article first appeared in the *Sloan Management Review,* Winter 1976, 4–10.

When this article was published, the author was professor of management at the Harvard Business School.

and (3) the *current* set of plans and near-term goals that have been adopted in the expectation of contributing to the achievement of the organization's objectives.

This definition is intended to be read twice. Reading it first and ignoring the italicized words, the definition is not significantly different from the several that already exist in the literature.[1] The second reading, focusing on the italicized words, emphasizes three important additional aspects of this definition of strategy. First, the definition applies not only to the organization as a whole but to every major component of the organization. The "broad constraints and policies," which is what most businessmen mean by the term "strategy," may be either self-imposed or handed down from above. Strategy in a complex organization is conceived in a hierarchy and there are many levels of strategy in such an organization. Second, the strategy of an organizational component is never really "handed down"; it is conceived by an individual, the leader of the organizational unit, and this definition makes his role explicit. Third, the strategy of an organizational unit is dynamic. At any point in time, it expresses the *current* constraints, policies, and plans, but the likelihood of change in these statements is widely recognized throughout the organization. These three characteristics of strategy, as noted above, have major implications for the development of management systems in the organization.

Objectives and Goals

These two words, often used interchangeably by businessmen, can be differentiated to convey two quite different concepts, as implied in the definition of strategy above. The distinction between these two concepts is important, because a statement of strategy needs them both. The delineation of objectives and goals serves two different management purposes.

An *objective* is an aspiration to be worked toward in the future. A *goal* is an achievement to be attained at some future date. However, these short definitions fail to convey the essence of the difference between these two concepts, that is the distinction between "reach" and "grasp." For example, one of John F. Kennedy's *objectives* in 1960 was to reestablish and maintain this country's position as a leader in the fields of science and technology. One of his *goals* was to land a man on the moon and return him safely before the end of the decade.

The difference between objectives and goals may be drawn in terms of the following four dimensions.

1. *Time Frame.* An objective is timeless, enduring, and unending; a goal is temporal, time-phased, and intended to be superceded by subsequent goals. Kennedy's goal for the '60s was achieved, and it did contribute toward his objective, but new goals for the '70s are needed for the "maintenance of leadership" objective.

2. *Specificity.* Objectives are stated in broad, general terms, dealing

with matters of image, style, and self-perception; goals are much more specific, stated in terms of a particular result that will be accomplished by a specified date. It is because of their open-endedness that objectives can never be achieved while goals can. We may believe that landing the first man on the moon did reestablish our scientific leadership, but that perception may not be universally shared. To shift the analogy, we clearly won a battle, but not necessarily the war.

3. *Focus.* Objectives are usually stated in terms of some relevant environment which is external to the organization; goals are more internally focused and carry important implications about how the resources of the organization shall be utilized in the future. Objectives are frequently stated in terms of achieving leadership or recognition in a certain field. A goal implies a resource commitment, challenging the organization to use those resources in order to achieve the desired result.

4. *Measurement.* Both objectives and goals frequently can be stated in terms that are quantifiably measurable, but the character of the measurement is different. Quantified objectives are stated in relative terms. For example, the managers of one growth company have stated that their objective is "to achieve a compound rate of growth in earnings per share sufficient to place its performance in the top 10% of all (relevant) corporations." This objective may be achieved in any one year, but it is timeless and externally focused, providing a continuing challenge for the management of that company. A quantified goal is expressed in absolute terms. Several years ago, the president of a diversifying aerospace corporation stated that the company would "achieve 50% of its sales revenue from non-government customers by 1970." The achievement of that goal can be measured irrespective of environmental conditions and competitors' actions.

In order to prepare an effective statement of strategy in a complex organization, the distinction between objectives and goals must be recognized. Objectives are the first element in a statement of strategy; goals are the last. In the time that elapses between the delineation of these two statements, there must be a great deal of interplay between the managers at various levels in the organization's hierarchy. This complex process of starting with a statement of objectives and working toward the development of more specific goals will be discussed at length later in this article. First, however, we will discuss the three major elements of effective strategy.

Characteristics of Effective Strategy

The effectiveness of a particular strategy can be appraised from two different perspectives. First, of course, is the question of whether or not the strategy is right for the organization in its particular situation. Does it provide a proper match between environmental opportunities and organizational resources? Second is the more subtle question of whether or not the strategy has been constructed in such a way that it facilitates the management processes of the organization. Evaluated from this second point of view, an effective statement of strategy has three characteristics that are not commonly recognized.

Operational Guidance

The guidance that a statement of strategy provides for subordinate managers is usually cast in the form of what *not* to do rather than in the form of *what* to do. Such guidance, then, is really a set of constraints on appropriate organizational actions. These constraints are usually not stated explicitly both because it would be impractical to do so (the list would be too long) and because constraints have a negative connotation. Thus, an airline, for example, does not say that its strategy is *not* to be in the chemical business or *not* to be in the textile business, but rather that it is "to be a leader in the air transportation industry." The value of such a statement is not what it says explicitly, but the implicit message that a great many other activities which do not fall under the "air transportation industry" umbrella are to be ignored.

The guidance provided by a statement of strategy must be pervasive and operational. The statement must provide guidance to all the managers in the organization in sufficiently explicit terms to allow each manager to proceed with his tasks in the knowledge that his actions are consistent with the objectives of the organization. No single statement of strategy will suffice to provide this kind of guidance in a complex organization. Instead, many layers of strategy are needed, each layer being progressively more detailed to provide strategic guidance for the next level of subordinate managers. As the diversity and complexity of an organization increase, the degree of specificity of strategic guidance provided by corporate-level management appears to decrease. The strategy of a conglomerate corporation cannot be stated nearly as crisply as that of an airline. Nevertheless managers at lower levels of the conglomerate need guidance analogous to that provided to airline managers, and they receive it through a progressive delineation of the strategy of each major operating unit.

Personal Commitment

Another characteristic of an effective statement of strategy is that it is drafted by the manager who must carry it out. This is obviously true for a corporate president who has no superior officer to tell him what the limits should be on the scope of the corporation's activities. Surprisingly perhaps, it is equally true for several levels of subordinate managers in a well-run corporation.

A personalized strategy is feasible in a complex organization if the statement of strategy is drafted carefully. As discussed earlier, the superior manager devises his strategy and expresses it in the form of constraints on the scope of the activities of his subordinates. However, he should take care to leave them some discretion as to how they operate within those constraints. Each subordinate manager will then accept (or challenge) those constraints, devise "his" strategy within them, and in turn express his strategy to his subordinates in the form of constraints on their activities. The resulting series of progressively detailed statements of strategy are personalized, in the sense that each manager can see his imprint on his part of the series. Furthermore, they are integrated throughout the organization as a whole, because each statement is consistent with the constraints imposed by higher authority.

Two of the several advantages of personalized strategies deserve mention here. First, encouraging each manager to use his imagination to devise the best strategy he can increases the vitality and creativity of the organization. In a complex organization, no one man, not even the president, can identify all the opportunities that exist, and a framework of progressive constraints that elicits personalized strategies multiplies the sources of initiative in the corporation. Second, a personalized strategy engenders a personal commitment. As Andrews says, in discussing the relevance of personal values in the determination of strategy, "Somebody has to have his heart in it."[2]

Expectation of Change

Finally, an effective statement of strategy should recognize explicitly that it is a temporal document. Whereas the objectives of the organization, particularly if carefully drawn, may not change perceptibly over time, the scope of its activities is likely to change in an expansionist fashion and the organization's major plans are almost certain to change as it continues to adapt to its dynamic environment. The inevitability of an evolving strategy does not mean that managers should not take the trouble to make the current strategy explicit or that the task should be done in a casual manner; it does mean that any such explicit statement should be viewed as only currently useful. The implication of this is that provision must be made in the management process for a periodic review and revalidation of all levels of strategy.

Tradeoffs in Strategy Formulation

It is now necessary to look briefly at some of the problems which plague any individual manager in developing his own statement of strategy. Even if we ignore, for the moment, the complexities that arise because his organization is a part of a larger complex, his task is a difficult one. His approach to this task must be both rational and emotional, his analysis of his situation both coolly analytic and unabashedly subjective. As Professor Andrews has described so well, the strategist seeks to reconcile conflicting forces. He must deal simultaneously with four questions: What *might* we do?, What *can* we do?, What do we *want* to do?, and What *should* we do? Obviously, the strategy that results from this analysis is based on the manager's personal perception of opportunities, his personal assessment of the strengths and weaknesses of his organization, and his personal aspirations and values.

In terms of the definition given earlier, strategy consists of three elements: (1) objectives, (2) constraints and policies, and (3) plans and goals. While these three elements are not determined independently in a neat, chronological sequence, it is convenient to discuss them as though they were.

Objectives

The most personal element of an individual manager's strategy is the setting of objectives for his organization. If the task is difficult (and it need not always be), the trouble is frequently caused by a conflict between the manager's personal aspirations and values on the one hand and his professional or positional obligations on the other. Although the nature of the professional obligation varies with the level in the organization, even the highest officer must recognize that the organizational objectives he sets are not the same as his individual objectives. For the chief executive officer, the restraints imposed by his position are primarily external; his objectives for the organization must attempt to relate it to the broader society in which it exists. For a manager at a lower level, personal aspirations must be balanced off against the obligations inherent in his position as the leader of a subunit within a larger organization. For any manager, this tradeoff is essentially subjective; his aim is to frame a set of objectives for his organization which acknowledges his positional responsibilities and which is consistent with his own desires and beliefs.

Constraints and Policies

Determining the scope and balance of an organization's activities is a somewhat more analytical process and is always difficult. In simplistic terms, this task consists of finding the most appropriate match between environmental opportunities and organizational resources; the best set of activities to engage in are those which take best advantage of the organization's strengths, thus permitting the most progress toward achieving the organization's objectives. However, because the time frame involved is so long, this description of the task is insufficient. Stated more realistically, the task is to find a match between opportunities that are still unfolding and resources that are still being acquired. Substantial uncertainty exists on both counts. Opportunities may not develop in the direction or at the rate expected, and the organization may not be able to acquire new resources as effectively as the manager had hoped. Thus, determining the boundaries on an organization's sphere of activities is best conceived of as positioning the organization so that it will be able to capitalize on future opportunities. The choice that this presents for a manager is not simply the result of a neat, economic analysis. It is true that the choice needs to be wrapped in the cloak of rationality, if only to make it more communicable and to engender the commitment of subordinate managers. However, the choice is inevitably influenced, and appropriately so, by the manager's own perceptions and assessments as well as by the aspirations and obligations that he recognized in framing the organization's objectives.

Plans and Goals

The most specific element of strategy, that is the tangible plans for near-term actions and the results expected from those actions, is the most amenable to rational analysis. Here again the manager's task is to match opportunities and resources, but the choice must be based on the current situation or on what the situation will be in the very near future. The limitations on a purely rational solution occur because of the familiar tradeoff between short-term goals and long-term objectives. A manager's plan of action may be optimal, in the sense that he believes he has achieved the best balance across the time dimension, but that is still a personal belief. He may even attempt to prove the validity of his plan quantitatively, but it is almost inevitable that any such proof will ultimately rely on premises drawn from the broader elements of strategy discussed above.

A statement of strategy, then, is highly situational for two reasons. First, the strategy must reflect the organization as it now exists, its current activities, and its current set of resources. Second, and at least as important, the strategy for an organizational unit is determined by an individual; it bears the mark of his character, perceptivity, and personality. The process of permitting each manager in a complex organization to develop his own unique strategy is the topic to which we now turn.

Three Levels of Strategy

Generalizations about strategy are difficult, not simply because any statement of strategy is situational, but also because strategy in a complex organization is so detailed. Most literature on the subject stops short of exploring this detail because it is so messy. We will take the other tack here in order to provide a description that may be useful to practicing managers and more specifically to designers of long-range planning systems.

Even this first attempt at a detailed look at strategy must be simplified to some extent. In this article, we shall deal with a crude stereotype of a diversified corporation. Such a corporation, as shown in Figure 18.1, is conventionally organized into product divisions each with its own general manager which we will call the business manager. The principal subordinates of the business manager will be called activity managers.

Strategy, even in this simplest of all complex organizations, is an intricate web of personal statements by managers at each of the three levels in the hierarchy. Table 18.1 displays the elements of strategy for each of the three types of managers. In order to understand that figure, it must be read both horizontally and vertically. The horizontal reading is the most appropriate to discuss first; it will permit us to examine each statement of strategy from the point of view of the individual manager who enunciates it. Viewed from this perspective, the strategy for this illustrative organization may be conceived of as an amalgam of about three dozen individual strategies: one corporate strategy, five divisional strategies, and perhaps six activity strategies within each division. If properly prepared, these individual statements form an interrelated set. However, it is important to realize that each such statement must be capable of standing alone.

Corporate Managers

The statement of strategy expressed by the top manager of a diversified corporation can be broken into the three elements shown in Table 18.1. Corporate objectives consist of two broad types: financial and nonfinancial. Financial objectives recognize the corporation's obligation to its sharehold-

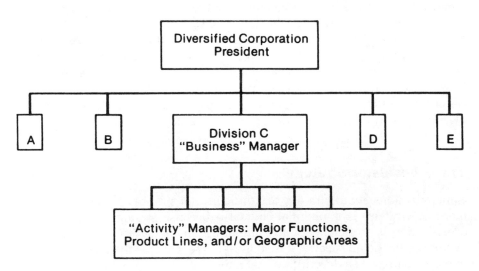

FIGURE 18.1

TABLE 18.1   Elements of Strategy in a Hierarchical Organization

Level in the Hierarchy	Objectives	Constraints and Policies	Plans and Goals
Corporate Managers	Stated in terms for: stockholders other identifiable constituencies society at large. Examples: Financial performance of the corporation Corporate citizenship and "personality" characteristics	Financial policies (debt structure, dividends, diversity of risk, etc.). Specific industries to be in, or characteristics of appropriate industries. Criteria for approving new resource commitments to businesses.	Prospective magnitude of discretionary resources to be utilized by the corporation. Prospective distribution of resources in order to affect the future mix of businesses. Performance expectations for the corporation and for each business over the next 5-10 years.
Business Managers	Stated in terms for: corporate management. Examples: Financial performance of the business Position of the business in the industry	Definition of niche in the industry; relative importance of, and interrelationships between, each activity. Priorities for changing the relative contribution from each activity.	Prospective patterns of resource allocation intended to affect the future contribution from each activity. Performance expectations for the business and for each activity over the next 3-7 years.
Activity Managers	Stated in terms for: business management. Examples: Contribution of the activity to the business Position of the activity in the industry	Delineation of limits on the scope of the entire activity. Criteria for optimizing the use of resources available to the activity.	Prospective sequence of resource utilization intended to affect the future contribution from the activity. Performance expectations for the activity and for each subactivity over the next 1-3 years.

ers and express management's aspirations for fulfilling shareholder expectations. It is increasingly rare, however, for corporate presidents to endorse the simplistic objective of "maximizing earnings over the long run." Instead, by stating the financial objectives in terms relative to what the managers of other corporations are able to achieve, the president recognizes that the performance of his company must be evaluated in the context of the economy as a whole.

In addition to setting financial objectives, many presidents today find it desirable to make explicit the social and ethical obligations of their corporation. Nonfinancial objectives may go beyond mere statements of the corporation's intention to be a good citizen; a corporate "creed" or some similar statement of the personal values shared by individuals in the organization is not uncommon. For example, such statements have been used for decades in large retailing organizations, such as J. C. Penney, Avon Products, and the Jewel Companies. The ability of these objectives to provide a set of ethical guidelines for a large number of employees dealing with an even larger group of customers would suggest that their value need not be restricted to retailing organizations.

The constraints and policies segment of corporate-level strategy consists of two types of statements. One type, statements of financial policy, may not always be critical to the success of the enterprise. Nevertheless, these statements are necessary because there are some elements of financial management, such as dividend policy, which corporate management cannot delegate to subordinates.

The other type of constraints/policies statement deals with the most crucial element of corporate strategy — the diversity of corporate activities. At a minimum, this statement identifies the industries in which the corporation is currently involved and revalidates an intention to restrict corporate activities to those industries over the long term. The top managers of corporations that are continuing to diversify have a somewhat more difficult problem. One useful way of specifying a constraint on the scope of corporate activity in such situations is to identify the major types of business opportunities which seem to capitalize on the resource capabilities of the corporation. Because the opportunities and the resources must be stated in rather general terms, the resulting statement lacks specificity. Still, this sort of statement provides a great deal more guidance for subordinates than a simple statement of the prospective financial performance that is required before a corporation will enter a new business. With the exception of only a few "pure" conglomerates, diversification actions rarely are based solely on financial criteria, and a thoughtful statement of corporate strategy can make the other criteria more explicit.

Finally, a corporate-level statement of strategy must specify the current set of major plans that are to be pursued in the years immediately ahead. In very crude terms, the feasibility of such plans must be related to corporate financial policies. The financial resources necessary to execute the plans need not be in hand, but their availability must be foreseeable. Despite the fact that the prospective distribution of funds across the range of corporate activities is highly tentative, subordinate managers must be given some idea of this distribution so that they may plan in sufficient detail. Similarly, though the prospective effects of such allocations are even more tentative, such goals must be stated in order to provide corporate management with a crude test of the feasibility of all of the elements of its strategy.

Business Managers

In terms of the hypothetical organization cited in Figure 18.1, the manager of a product division is a business manager. He has been delegated the responsibility for formulating and implementing strategy in one of the industries in which a diversified corporation is engaged. Given that set of responsibilities, the statement of strategy which the business manager enunciates contains the same three elements noted above for corporate managers, but the scope and substance of the strategy are different.

Long-term objectives for a business manager in a hierarchical corporation must acknowledge the limitations in scope that are inherent in his position. The range of his activities is usually limited to the natural boundaries of an externally definable industry. Accordingly, his objectives for the business may be stated in terms relative to the performance of other companies in the same industry. Objectives need not be limited to financial performance; statements expressing an aim to achieve (or retain) a position as the industry leader in, for example, product development or customer service are also highly desirable. Such statements serve both to express the manager's aspirations to his subordinates and to encapsulate the essence of his strategy.

The cornerstone of business strategy is the concept which Professor Andrews and his colleagues refer to as "niche." Except in the case of a total monopoly, each company in an industry seeks to find a place for itself among its competitors. A niche may be a small nook or cranny in the marketplace where the winds of competition blow with somewhat less force, or it may be the top of the mountain which is occupied by a company with a commanding market share, while the storms of competition rage below. But even staying on the mountaintop, or finding a larger and somewhat more comfortable cave higher up the slope, requires a clear understanding of the relationship between a company and its competitors who are seeking to serve the same set of customers.

The constraint/policy element of a statement of business strategy is an attempt to delineate that competitive relationship. Here the manager's task of analyzing and matching opportunities with resources can be somewhat more specific than the task of his corporate counterpart. His major competitors are unlikely to change substantially over the next decade, and the thrust of technological and market development can be foreseen, however, dimly. Some would say that delineating this crucial element of a business strategy is more challenging, and more personally rewarding, than the equivalent corporate-level task of determining the strategy of diversification.

Once a business manager has determined the broad constraints that will guide his competitive approach to the marketplace, the remaining element of his strategy is to develop implementation plans and short-term goals for achievement. Table 18.1 refers to these plans as *prospective patterns of resource allocation*. This compact phrase is intended to encompass both the expected magnitude of resources that the corporation may be able to make available to the business and the currently intended distribution of those resources among the alternative action programs which the business might pursue. Naturally, such a pattern is highly tentative. Nothing ever happens precisely as forecast, least of all such critical planning factors as the rate of market change and the nature of competitor response. Nevertheless, the performance results must also be forecast in order to permit the business manager to evaluate the cohesiveness and effectiveness of all elements of his strategy.

Activity Managers

The strategy for an activity manager, the third level in the hierarchy shown in Figure 18.1, is more difficult to generalize about because complex corporations organize their businesses in diverse ways. The principal subordinates of a business manager may be responsible for a major functional area such as manufacturing or sales, a portion of the product line, a geographical area, or some combination of the three. We will use two examples, a product line manager and a functional manager, to illustrate the elements of strategy at the activity manager level.

The first thing to be said about an activity manager of either sort is that his job is where the action is. The scope of his position is, of course, even more limited than that of the business manager to whom he reports and the statement of strategy that he drafts as a guide to his activities is accordingly more specific. However, it is the activity manager who must devise and execute the set of actions that will serve to implement the business strategy and, ultimately, the corporate strategy. The need for an activity manager to have a strategy of his own, to develop and maintain his own sense of perspective, is every bit as great as it is for his higher-ranking counterparts.

The objectives of an activity manager must be stated in terms that are appropriate to the nature of his assigned task. A product line manager's objectives might include market share, the rate of growth in sales and profitability, profit margins, and/or the image of the product in the market place. A functional manager's objectives might include costs and productivity, quality and customer service, and/or performance along these dimensions vis-à-vis competitors. For either type of activity manager, the critical characteristics of objectives defined earlier still apply; objectives are externally focused and stated in terms of the relative performance of this activity compared to similar activities performed by others.

For the activity manager the constraints/policies element of strategy is, as it was for the corporate and business managers, the most challenging aspect of strategy formulation. The product line manager's responsibility is to analyze the opportunities and to pick those that are best suited to achieve his objectives. He does this by developing a statement of constraints or priorities concerning the breadth of his product line. In it, he delineates the current and future scope and balance among the various products for which he is responsible.

Similarly, a functional manager also needs to develop a set of self-imposed constraints and policies concerning the scope of his activity. A useful concept here is that of "value added." For a functional manager, the essential question is, "What is the strategically optimal degree of vertical integration within my activity?" A manager in charge of manufacturing must worry about the strategic question of backward integration: can he capture some of the profits of his suppliers efficiently enough to increase the contribution of the manufacturing function to the business? The sales manager's analogous question concerns forward integration: to what extent could the contribution from his activity increase if he attempted to perform some of the functions now performed by others in the distribution chain between him and the ultimate consumer? Careful analysis of opportunities against resources is required to answer these questions and lead to a strategic determination of the limits on the scope of a functional activity.

Finally, the third element of every activity manager's strategy is the set of action programs that he would propose to undertake in order to implement his strategy. The necessary resources are always scarce. Therefore, priorities must be established and, in order to determine a rational sequence of actions, the performance implications of alternative sequences must be examined. Priorities will surely change as events and new opportunities unfold but, for the time at which it is made, the activity manager's strategy expresses both what he is trying to do and how he proposes to do it.

Each of the descriptions above describes the process of strategy formulation by an individual manager as though it were a neatly chronological, three-step sequence. As a practical matter, delineating a strategy is not as pedestrian as outlined, but neither is it cataclysmic in the sense of leaping full-blown from the manager's mind in one great surge of creative insight. However, the elements of a manager's strategy are related to each other, and Figure 18.2 is an attempt to illustrate that schematically.

As noted above, the most critical element in strategy formulation is that of constraints/policies. Objectives are rarely specified without recognizing their implications on the scope of a manager's activities. Similarly,

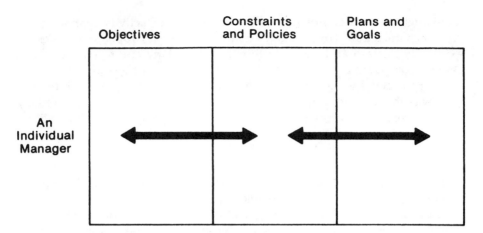

FIGURE 18.2   Strategy for an Individual Manager

the availability of an attractive action plan may lead to a modification of strategic constraints in order to legitimatize pursuing that action. Thus, we can see that constructing a cohesive statement embracing all three elements of strategy is a creative, evolutionary process. Plans and goals are expected to change over time; major policies, constraints on scope, and even objectives for the activity will also change, although the rate of evolution should be somewhat slower.

The discussion thus far has emphasized the fact that strategy must be a personalized statement enunciated by an individual manager. The fact that there may be hundreds of such managers in a complex organization does not diminish the need for personal analysis and strategic choice within the confines of each manager's positional responsibility. At the same time one would hope that the strategy of a large corporation is something more than a simple melange of independently derived statements by individuals. It is, in fact, the need to coordinate and integrate these individual statements that makes the task of strategy formulation in a complex organization so difficult.

Strategic Interrelationships

Referring back to Table 18.1 and reading it vertically this time, a different picture of strategy in a complex organization emerges. Each manager, working individually, should develop his own statement of strategy, but it is quickly obvious that these statements must still make sense when they are arranged hierarchically. Figure 18.3 is a schematic attempt to represent the nature of these interrelationships.

The cells depicted in Figure 18.3 have been numbered for easy refer-

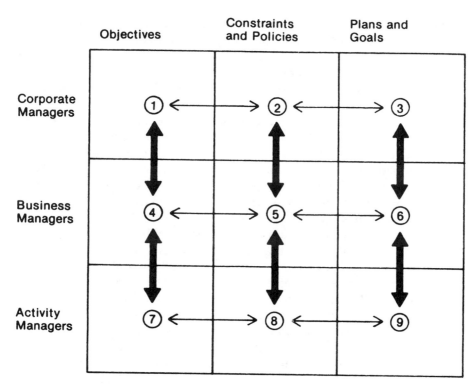

FIGURE 18.3   Hierarchical Strategic Relationships

ence in correspondence to the sequence of discussion in the preceding section. It is important to point out here that constructing such a strategic grid for a complex organization is not a chronological sequence involving nine steps. The grid is actually put together like a mosaic and, in order to see how the pieces fit together, we will examine the major elements of strategy within this context.

Objectives

The citizenship and personality objectives of a corporation in Cell 1 are the only free-standing element of strategy in the entire grid, and yet even corporate management does not have carte blanche. Articulating objectives of this sort will be effective only if they represent a codification of the values shared by most members of the organization. The value of a state-ment of strategy under these conditions is two-fold: (1) it reinforces and crystallizes the nature and extent to which values are shared in the organi-zation, and (2) it makes it somewhat easier for a prospective new member of the organization to decide whether he wishes to join it or not. Generally, as the range of diversity of a corporation's activities increases, the breadth of the values shared by all members of the corporation will decrease. Thus, a highly diverse conglomerate may not state corporate-level objectives of this sort, although such statements might be quite appropriate in some of the businesses in that corporation.

The determination of corporate financial objectives, on the other hand, is clearly not independent of other elements in the strategic grid. The relationship between Cells 1 and 2 has already been noted but, as Figure 18.3 makes clear, there is also a relationship between Cells 1 and 4. The financial performance objectives for a diversified corporation must relate to the performance objectives for each of the underlying businesses. Perhaps less obvious is the link between Cells 2 and 4, but the importance of that link becomes clear when the problem is viewed from the perspective of one of the business managers in the corporation. He cannot set performance objectives for his business without knowing something about corporate-level constraints and policies regarding diversification. How important is his business in the eyes of corporate managers? How tightly constrained should he expect to be in expanding the scope of his business? He answers these questions by defining the industry and his niche in it (Cell 5), but the delineation of his objectives is directly affected by both of the first two elements of corporate-level strategy.

Similarly, the objectives for any one of the activity managers reporting to a business manager are affected by their hierarchical relationship. The direct link between Cells 4 and 7 is only part of the story; an activity manager's objectives must recognize the constraints and policies that the business manager has specified in Cell 5. An activity manager uses his superior's constraint/policy statement for guidance in drafting an analogous statement of the limits on the scope of his own activity (Cell 8), but that same guidance is also a direct input to the activity manager's thinking as he attempts to enunciate his long-run, externally-oriented objectives.

Constraints and Policies

The difficulty of preparing an integrated set of statements of strategy is compounded when we turn to the critical task of delineating a progressive series of constraints on the scope of the organization's activities. At first glance, the integration of this element of strategy in a complex organization might appear to be as simple as following the vertical arrows in the center column of Figure 18.3. As a practical matter, tying these elements of strategy together is much more involved than that.

The focal point in preparing an integrated strategy is the statement in which each business manager defines his industry and his niche in it. This is the center cell in the strategic grid in Figure 18.3. It affects, and is affected by, many other elements of strategy. The corporate-level statement of the types of industries that the corporation will participate in (Cell 2) cannot be prepared in a vacuum; corporate managers must understand what opportunities exist in their current businesses before they can decide how to affect the future mix of businesses. Those decisions, set forth tentatively as corporate plans and goals (Cell 3), have an important, and not unintended, side effect. A business manager, trying to delineate his current and future niche in an industry, must have some idea of the magnitude of corporate resources that can be made available to his business over time. Thus, there is a direct link between Cell 5 and Cell 3, which affects the business manager's thinking about the potential scope of his business. The determination of his own plans and goals (Cell 6) also helps him to determine a reasonable set of constraints on his business.

In a similar fashion, the constraints and policies adopted by an activity manager are affected not only by the scope of the business as a whole but also by his superior's tentative plans for the utilization of resources available to the business (Cell 6). Thus, there is a direct relationship between Cell 8 and Cell 6 with regard to the availability of resources for the activity, as well as a relationship between Cells 8 and 9 which concerns how those resources might be used.

Plans and Goals

Finally, the last and most tangible element of strategy, the plans and goals at each level in the hierarchy, must also be integrated. Compared to the complex interrelationships described above, the task of integrating plans is relatively straightforward. The vertical arrows in the last column of Figure 18.3 point in both directions; the tentative allocation of corporate resources cannot be made without knowing how those resources would be used in each of the businesses, and a business manager cannot plan the use of his resources without knowing what his activity managers expect to accomplish. An activity manager's planning horizon is shorter than that of his superiors. His plans are more action-oriented and definitive, and his performance goals are frequently treated as personal commitments that can and will be achieved. At the business and corporate levels, plans and goals beyond the next year or two are more fluid; tentative plans are needed to express the other elements of strategy in a more tangible form and thus to provide guidance to subordinates. Still, all the managers involved must know that the plans will change over time.

The Strategy Formulation Process

Figure 18.4 is a graphic representation of the interrelationships discussed above. The heavy, lateral arrows in that chart are intended to emphasize the complex way that the various elements of each manager's strategy are tied together. Even so, the chart understates the extent of the interrelationships. There are several business managers and perhaps several dozen

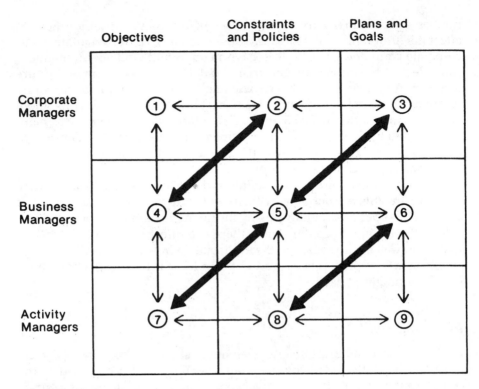

FIGURE 18.4   The Strategy Formulation Process

activity managers in a complex organization. Thus, a three-dimensional chart would really be required to express all the interrelationships.

Formulating, revising, or revalidating strategy is more than a task of individual economic analysis and personal soul-searching. In a complex organization, it is also an interactive, iterative process. Dozens, literally hundreds, of two-person agreements must be negotiated, many of them almost simultaneously. The process is never completed because the agreements continue to change and evolve. Each manager, from time to time, may attempt to express his strategy in a written statement, but it is a rare, and very temporary, event for all the managers in a complex organization to develop such statements at the same point in time. On the other hand, organizing the efforts of all the managers in the organization to attempt such an undertaking can be extremely valuable, and this is really the primary purpose of formal planning systems.

Summary

Strategy is the conceptual glue that binds the diverse activities of a complex organization together. To be effective, strategy must personally affect each manager, constraining the scope of his activities to some extent yet providing him with enough elbow room to devise his own strategy within the broader context. In such organizations it is not very useful to think about *the* strategy. Rather, one should think of the strategy as a collection of strategies, one for each manager, linked together by a progressive series of agreements on objectives, constraints and policies, and plans and goals. Each manager must have *a* strategy in which he believes and which is compatible with the strategies of his superiors, his peers, and his subordinates.

This complex web of strategies is rarely enunciated as explicitly and comprehensively as has been described here. Most of the two-party hierarchical agreements that are required take the form of an implicit understanding between a manager and one of his subordinates. The value of explicit strategies goes beyond the simple fact that a conscious choice among strategic alternatives is likely to be better than an intuitive choice. The process of formulating explicit strategies affects both the quality of the resulting choice and the likelihood that the chosen strategy will be implemented successfully. A good formal planning system is designed to provide orderly processes that permit complex organizations to achieve all three of these benefits.

Notes

1. See Andrews, K. R. *The Concept of Corporate Strategy.* Homewood, Ill.: Dow Jones-Irwin, Inc., 1971, p. 28.
2. See Andrews, K. R. *The Concept of Corporate Strategy.* Homewood, Ill.: Dow Jones-Irwin, Inc., 1971, p. 117.

19. Strategic Market Analysis and Definition: An Integrated Approach

George S. Day

Effective strategy analysis hinges on the proper definition of the market. Yet, depending on the analyst's choice of served customer segments and the treatment of such issues as substitute technologies, geographic boundaries, and levels of production or distribution, the defined market may be very broad or comparatively narrow. At the same time, there may be no defensible basis for the choice of one definition over another, although the implications of a particular choice for strategy may be profound.

To further complicate the problem, the choice of market definition may also depend on the analysis approach that is employed. Two distinct approaches have evolved from different directions, each reflecting a different set of strategic concerns.

The first objective of this paper is to compare and contrast the two approaches. Generally we will find that *top-down* approaches reflect the need of corporate and business level management to understand the capacity of a business unit to compete and apply resources to secure a sustainable competitive advantage. *Bottom-up* approaches are usually employed by marketing planners and program managers within the framework of a chosen product-market. The emphasis is on issues of product changes, advertising themes, promotional efforts, and price strategies, which imply a narrower tactical perspective.

With the increasing integration of corporate strategic planning and marketing planning (Hopkins, 1977) comes a need to reconcile the differences between market analysis approaches that might materially influence

This article first appeared in the *Strategic Management Journal*, July–September 1981, pp. 281–300.

When this article was published, the author was professor of management at the University of Toronto.

strategic choices. Our second objective is to suggest a basis for better integration of top-down and bottom-up approaches. The issue is not which of the two perspectives is more valid, but how to harness them to achieve a balanced understanding. This can be achieved through the acceptance of multiple market definitions — each more or less appropriate depending on the strategic question — and the use of a mix of market analysis methods that can accommodate a variety of strategic questions. In particular, bottom-up methods have an untapped potential to broaden management's view of their market.

A prerequisite for effective integration of differing approaches to market analysis is a common model of the principal dimensions of a market. An emerging conceptual view of the multidimensional nature of markets promises to satisfy this requirement.

Multidimensional Market Definitions

A recent review of policy research has questioned the desirability of anchoring strategy in product-market space (Hatten, 1979), because of the restrictions imposed on thought by the common meanings of these words and concepts. Similarly, Abell (1980) has argued that it is dangerous for market definitions to be perceived as simply a choice of products, or business definitions as a choice of markets. Instead, he suggests the product be considered as a physical manifestation of the application of a particular *technology* to the provision of a particular *function* for a particular *customer group*.[1] A market is defined by the choices along these three dimensions. Also, Buzzell (1979a) has suggested that *level of distribution/production* be treated as a fourth dimension. These elaborations expand the conceptual power of the basic definition of a product-market as the set of substitutes which are perceived to satisfy the needs of a strategically distinct customer segment.

Customer Functions

Products or services can be thought of in terms of the functions they perform or the ways they are used. Thus, adjustable speed drives provide a speed control function, and pasta and macaroni may be used as non-vegetable meat supplements. It is the usage situation or application contemplated by the customer that dictates the benefits being sought. Then the manufacturer provides a package of functions, which may include auxiliary services and other enhancements, to deliver these benefits (Levitt, 1980).

It is useful to think of different levels of functions in a hierarchy beginning with a generic function. Thus, the speed control function can be subdivided by size of input power source, harshness of operating environment, sensitivity of control, and so forth. As the subfunctions become more narrowly defined, they will increasingly correspond to the specific benefits sought by the customer.

Technologies

The technologies are the alternative ways a particular function can be performed. Several different technologies may provide the same function or satisfy the same needs. For example, the generic medical diagnosis function can be served by X-ray, computerized tomography, and ultrasound technologies. Whether these technologies belong in the same market is a question that is usually resolved at the subfunction level. Often two technologies compete for some of the same functions, but in some specialized subfunctions only one can feasibly perform. This situation is often encountered with industrial materials such as engineered plastics.

Customer Segments

A segment is a group of customers with similar needs, sharing characteristics that are strategically relevant.

The choice of segments to include in the market definition is dictated by the significance of the differences between segments for the decisions to be made. For this reason, it is useful to think of hierarchies of segments, with diminishing differences between segments in the lower branches. At the top are "strategic" customer segments, which must be served by totally different marketing mixes; where virtually no element of the marketing program for one segment is transferable to another strategic segment. This is the reason that tire manufacturers approach OEM markets and replacement markets as entirely separate businesses, appliance manufacturers have different marketing strategies for retail buyers and contract buyers such as home builders, and food companies often have separate divisions for institutional markets. The need for different strategies leads to totally different cost and price structures.

Within each "strategic" customer segment, there will be further levels of groupings which are meaningful for strategy development — and hence lead to opportunities for differentiation from competitors. Much of the art and science of segmentation research (Frank, Massy, and Wind, 1972) has been directed at this type of segmentation. Geographic boundaries can define segments at virtually any level, depending on the extent to which travel time or transportation costs are a large element of total costs, or the market customs and competitive practices are significantly different.

Levels of Production–Distribution

In many markets, competitors have the choice of operating at only one level in the production–distribution process (either raw materials, intermediates, components, finished products, or distribution) or integrating forward or backward in the process (Rothschild, 1976). If different competitors operate on a number of different levels, then there is a question of whether the levels should be treated separately or combined.

Total and Served Market Definitions

The definition of the total market does not proceed one dimension at a time, but instead requires simultaneous consideration of customers, technologies, and functions. There are a myriad of possibilities, as the following illustrate:

> The Snap-on Tool Company defines its market as hand tools for the professional mechanic. This customer segment is reached solely with direct sales methods. No doubt Sears, Roebuck defines the market for the hand tools it sells to encompass many customer segments, beyond professional mechanics.

> A manufacturer of automated production equipment sells integrated systems that provide many distinct functions to one customer segment, the semiconductor industry. In contrast, a scientific instrumentation company defines its market as instruments for a single testing function sold to a distinct class of laboratories.

> At one time the market for liquid oxygen and other gases was supplied with bottled gas produced in central plants and trucked to customers. This market was redefined when small liquefaction plants could be built directly on customers' premises. The functions remained the same but the new technology created a distinct market of large customers with captive plants.

Each of these market definitions represents a choice of how far to proceed along each of the multiple dimensions of the market. Markets can be as narrowly defined as a single *market cell*, where each cell is described by a discrete category along each dimension, or be defined as a number of adjacent cells.[2] For planning purposes these combinations of cells are termed product-market units, or PMUs.

Within the total market, there is a further question of whether to serve the entire market or limit coverage to specific subsegments within market cells, such as retailers with central buying offices or utilities of a certain size. The choice of *served market* will be dictated by a variety of factors, including:

- perceptions of which product function and technology groupings can best be protected and dominated,
- internal resource limitations which force a narrow focus,
- cumulative trial-and-error experience in reacting to threats and opportunities, and

- unusual competencies stemming from access to scarce resources or protected markets.

In practice, the task of grouping market cells to define a market is complicated. First, there is usually no one defensible criterion for grouping cells. There may be many ways to achieve the same function. Thus, boxed chocolates compete to some degree with flowers, records, and books as semicasual gifts (Cadbury, 1975). Do all of these products belong in the total market? To confound this problem, the available statistical and accounting data are often aggregated to a level where important distinctions between cells are completely obscured. Second, there are many products which evolve by adding new combinations of functions and technologies. Thus, radios are multifunctional products which include clocks, alarms, and appearance options. To what extent do these variants dictate new market cells? Third, different competitors may choose different combinations of market cells to serve or to include in their total market definitions. In these situations there will be few direct competitors — instead, businesses will encounter each other in different but overlapping markets, and, as a result, may employ different strategies.

Contrasting Top-down and Bottom-up Perspectives

There are pervasive differences between corporate-level planners and managers and business-level programme managers which stem from the breadth of the issues within their area of responsibility. In this and the following section we see how these differences may influence managers' views of the nature of markets and their preferences as to methods for defining markets.

The Top-down Perspective

A corporate-level planner or manager seeking to understand the strategic posture of a strategic business unit (SBU) or strategy center[3] made up of one or more PMUs will want to know the following:

What is the *scope* of the business definition? A narrow definition will circumscribe the competitive arena. For example, the Letraset company could limit its scope to supplying dry transfer graphic designs to the commercial art market. A broader definition would recognize the Letraset is in the business of meeting the needs of commercial artists for convenient methods of creating graphic designs.

What is the basis for the choice of the currently *served* market? In particular, does the choice reflect the presence of significant discontinuities between the costs to serve different segments of the market?

What is the current and forecast *performance* within the served market? What are the likely threats from present competitors finding better ways to satisfy market needs or achieve cost advantages, or from potential competitors entering from other geographic areas or offering substitute technologies?

What is the broad *strategic thrust* of the SBU, and what does it imply for resource requirements or contributions? This question will be assessed in the context of one or more portfolio representations which rely on forecasts of market share and growth, and stage of product life cycle analysis (Day, 1977; Hussey, 1978).

What are the *opportunities* for growth into new products or new markets that can best utilize the SBU experience base (Hanan, 1974)? That is, what is the most attractive growth sector for the SBU?

Underlying these questions is a view of markets as arenas of profitable competition where the corporate resources can be used to achieve a differential advantage. These resources are usually *supply factors*: such as raw materials, production processes, and technologies, plus the base of experience gained in serving the present market.

The Bottom-up Perspective

Within the SBU — and especially at the level of the product manager or market manager with responsibility for a PMU — there is a significant shift in orientation toward market analysis issues. The type and mix of markets are taken as given and the emphasis shifts to "how to be successful in the business." The salient questions thus relate in one way or another to short-run programs for enhancing performance. They include such specific concerns as:

What is our present and forecast *performance* within our served market? Elements of this question deal with specific areas of vulnerability to competition, and ability to satisfy the evolving needs of customers within the served market.

How can we improve the *efficiency* of our programs through better targeting of advertising promotions and purchase incentives, improving distribution coverage, and so forth?

What opportunities exist for improving *profitability* within the served market by price changes, repositioning, product enhancements, and additions or deletions of items in the product line?

In terms of the multidimensional market definition, these questions deal with the fine-grained structure of the product alternatives and cus-

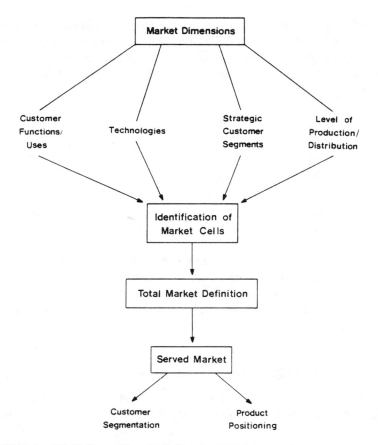

FIGURE 19.1   Multidimensional Market Analysis

tomer segments within the *market cells* (see Figure 19.1). A business may elect to serve a number of related market cells or parts of a few cells, but for each one it must tailor a marketing strategy. This is the locus of the short-run marketing plan.

The bottom-up market analysis issues can be grouped into two categories: *positioning* the company's offering and choosing *target customer segments* whose distinct patterns of needs dictate separate marketing programs. The objectives of both segmentation and positioning are the same: to seek competitive advantage through doing a better job of satisfying customer requirements.

Product positioning refers to the customer's perceptions of the place a product or brand occupies in a given market. In some markets a position is achieved by associating the benefits of the brand with the needs or life style of a customer group (as Brim decaffeinated coffee appeals to the concerned coffee drinker segment with the theme "you can drink as much as you used to"). More often, positioning involves the differentiation of the company's offering from the competition by making or implying a comparison in terms of specific attributes such as price or performance features. Thus, QYX line of computerized typewriters was introduced with a price range of $1400 to $7750, which corresponded to a gap in the IBM product line.

Customer segmentation is the process of subdividing the market into groups of customers whose members behave in the same way or have similar requirements. Actionable segments should be identifiable and accessible, represent enough volume potential to justify separate treatment (Kotler, 1977), and differ from other segments on dimensions that are meaningful for the design of strategy. This last condition means that distinctions between segments should relate to dimensions which influence the selection of one competitor over another.

The most widely used segmentation model (Wind, 1978) begins with the identification of a *basis for segmentation* — a product-specific factor which reflects differences in customer requirements and responsiveness to marketing variables. Possibilities include customers' product purchase patterns, product usage, benefits sought, price and technical service sensitivity, intentions-to-buy, and brand preference and loyalty. The choice will be largely dictated by the decision to be made.

Then, *segment descriptors* are chosen based on their ability to identify segments, account for variance in the segmentation basis, and invoke competitive strategy implications. These must be carefully tailored to the context. For example, a manufacturer of mining equipment has found that the value-in-use of his equipment (a function of initial and operating cost and productivity) relative to the competition depends less on the commodity being mined than on the specific physical profile of the mine (Johnson, 1978). Similarly, the geographic location of the mine affects its fixed cost structure and thus the comparative operating costs and productivity per unit of output for different types of equipment.

Implications of Differences in Perspective

Pervading the bottom-up perspective — and directing the search for protected market positions and target segments — is the customer's perspective. The product or market manager focuses on anticipating and reacting to shifts in the fine-grain structure of the market as a result of changes both in customers' requirements, needs, and capabilities and in the ability of competitors to satisfy these changes. This view of strategy as evolving from marketplace circumstances is very different from the top-down view which begins with supply factors. These differences are summarized and highlighted in Table 19.1. What should also be emphasized is that both perspectives are striving for the same end, which is the implementation of strategies which will yield a profitable competitive advantage.

TABLE 19.1   The View from the Top-down Versus the Bottom-up

Issue	Top-down view	Bottom-up view
1. Definition of market	Markets are arenas of competition where corporate resources can be profitably employed	Markets are shifting patterns of customer requirements and needs which can be served in many ways
2. Orientation to market environment	Strengths and weaknesses relative to competition • cost position • ability to transfer experience • market coverage	Customer perceptions of competitive alternatives • match of product features and customer needs • positioning
3. Identification of market segments	Looks for cost discontinuities	Emphasizes similarity of buyer responses to market efforts
4. Identification of market niches to serve	Exploits new technologies, cost advantages, and competitor's weaknesses	Finds unsatisfied needs, unresolved problems, or changes in customer requirements and capabilities
5. Time frame	2 to 5 years	1 to 3 years

Alternative Methods of Market Analysis and Definition

The characteristic differences between the top-down and bottom-up perspectives are reflected in their respective approaches to identifying competitive market cells.

Top-down Approaches to Market Analysis

The breadth of this perspective dictates consideration of a wide variety of present and prospective markets for resource allocation purposes. To implement this analysis, two requirements are paramount: (a) large amounts of data on market sizes, trends, plant capacities, and so forth must be in easily accessible form, and (b) the emphasis on resource allocation and competitive position puts a premium on the assessment of one's relative cost standing and the transferability of the experience base beyond presently served markets. These requirements dictate data of certain forms and types.

Supply-Oriented Approaches

The first implementation requirement means a reliance on published data, which are almost invariably organized by industry group. The industry groups are defined according to supply criteria such as similarity of manufacturing processes, raw materials, physical appearance, technology, or method of operation. The virtue of such industry groups, which are the backbone, for example, of the Standard Industrial Classification system used in the United States, is their wide acceptance due to availability of data, ease of implementation, and seeming stability.

The problems are most apparent with the function and customer dimensions of markets. Two competitive products which may serve the same function but with different technologies are almost invariably in different SIC categories. For example "polyvinyl" rain gutters and "sheet metal" gutters are in different 3-digit categories. These two technologies may not always compete directly, but when they do, they belong in the same market. This cannot be ascertained from data based on similarity of supply factors. Similarly, customer market segments defined by industries may be inappropriate either because they are too broad (and thus obscure important differences in needs and buying patterns) or too narrow (if the differences between segments are inconsequential for strategic purposes). In short, supply criteria seldom serve as a meaningful basis for grouping customers.

Identification of Cost/Investment Discontinuities

With this approach the analyst evaluates the market to see whether a significant discontinuity in the pattern of costs, capital requirements, and margins exists along one or more dimensions of the market. The resulting category boundaries represent barriers that insulate prices and profits from the activities of competitors outside the segment as well as discourage easy entry directly into the market by potential competitors. Thus, within the boundaries the relative profitability of competitors can be meaningfully compared.

The most important factors contributing to these discontinuities are:

- economies of scale,
- transferability of experience, and
- capital requirements.[4]

A boundary is encountered when participation in an adjacent category — whether a different technology, customer group, or function — is impeded by the need to enter with a large-scale operation to avoid a cost disadvantage, the need to invest substantial financial resources for fixed facilities, additional working capital, and start-up costs, or the need to employ a very different marketing mix. Conversely, barriers may not be severe if important elements of the company's experience base can be transferred. For example, a significant proportion of Texas Instrument's experience with semiconductor manufacturing is applicable to such related products as random-access memories and hand-held calculators. On the other hand, a producer of refractories for steel furnaces may find that most of its experience is limited to that specific setting.

Of course, experience is not restricted to production and technology factors but may reflect the accumulated output of all activities contributing to the value added of the product (Hedley, 1976). For example, the costs of marketing, distribution, and service often depend on experience and present a combination of scale and knowledge factors. Whether the company's experience and related resources can be employed more broadly depends on the similarity of requirements across customer segments, technologies, and functions. The identification of these similarities is analogous to the specification of the "common thread" (Ansoff, 1965).

Market boundaries identified in terms of cost discontinuities reveal opportunities for market niches which the firm can protect from competitive inroads and dominate for long-run profit.[5] Ideally there should be a minimum of direct competition within this market so the company can dominate the experience base necessary to serve that market. However, if the cost discontinuity is created by a cost element whose relative importance is declining, or the experience base is shared with outside suppliers of component parts or production technology who will sell to all prospective competitors, then the narrow market definition lacks enduring value.

When the market is defined very broadly in order to ensure competitive levels of experience and scale economies for a major cost element, it encompasses many related products whose principal common link is the shared experience base. For example, the cost position of many consumer packaged goods products is dictated by experience in sales and distribution through grocery outlets and advertising/promotion to mass markets, activities which are a significant proportion of total cost (Buzzell, 1979b). This broad perspective on market definition is very useful in the consideration of new ventures. It may be inappropriate for other purposes, such as evaluating performance in a served market, since it usually embraces a number of different competitive arenas. Similarly, a manufacturer of central air conditioners must adopt very different strategies for the modernization and new residential markets, yet product cost is dictated largely by the combined volume of sales in the two segments.

Bottom-up Approaches to Market Analysis

There is no lack of marketing research techniques that can be used for product positioning or identifying customer segments (Wind, 1978). Such methods as focus groups, problem detection studies, market mapping, conjoint analysis, trade-off analysis, and gain–loss brand switching analysis have proven their value in many applications. However, such studies are almost always undertaken from a bottom-up perspective. That is, the strategic market definition is taken as given and the focus is on the details of brand competition and customer differences within a market cell.

Yet, there is nothing inherent in many of these bottom-up techniques which mandates such a restricted role; it is a consequence of how and when they have been used. Consequently, their potential for clarifying strategic issues is largely untapped. The following discussion of one technique illustrates what can be done.

Substitution-in-Use Analysis

This category of techniques is based on the idea of strategically meaningful distinctions between functions and between technologies which represent the ways in which combinations of functions can be provided. But instead of starting with the function provided, situation-in-use analysis proceeds from the customer's perspective (Day, Shocker, and Srivastava, 1979).

Three premises underlie the concept of substitution-in-use:

1. People seek the benefits that products provide rather than the products *per se.*
2. The needs to be satisfied and the benefits which are sought are dictated by the usage situations or applications being contemplated.
3. Products/technologies are considered part of the set of substitutes if they are perceived to provide functions which satisfy the needs determined by intended usage.

Changing the perspective from function provided to benefits and needs which are contingent on the situation gives us another way of defining a market as the set of products viewed as substitutes within those usage situations in which similar patterns of benefits are sought. Customer segments are those groups for whom the usage situation is relevant.

This definition has several advantages over the technology/function approach, because the notions of benefits, usage situations, and consideration set are meaningful to customers and measurable. The introduction of intended usage into the definition also clarifies and enriches the complex nature of product "function."

Implications for Defining Markets for Strategic Planning Purposes

What is clearly needed is a dual approach to strategic market analysis, one which balances the production and cost-oriented top-down perspective with the customer's viewpoint. Otherwise, shifts in customer requirements and needs that may create new segments will be overlooked, and competitive threats from different technologies which can serve the same functions or satisfy similar needs will not be appreciated. By the same token, the customer perspective should not overwhelm the economic realities which dictate the ability to compete profitably.

This section explores various steps which can be taken to ensure that market definitions reflect a proper balance of cost and market factors and, thereby, yield meaningful strategic insights into the company's markets. The starting point is a recognition that different market definitions will be needed to satisfy different purposes, ranging from short-run performance evaluation to long-run analysis of threats and opportunities. This goal can be facilitated by ensuring that the strategic planning framework — which links business units or strategy centers and PMUs — is compatible with these different purposes. To test alternative planning frameworks for strategic relevance, explicit criteria are needed to analyze the interrelationships among PMUs. A key question is the relative importance of cost, demand, and other criteria for comparing PMUs. This question can be addressed by using the bottom-up market analysis techniques to understand the complexity of the market.

Multiple Market Definitions

There are many possible market definitions from which to choose. These alternatives are neither true nor false — only more or less useful for the purpose at hand.

Performance Evaluation and Short-Run Marketing Planning. For these purposes emphasis should be on the presently served market, since this is the arena within which the organization is trying to satisfy customer needs. A single market share measure, however, does not provide much insight. Instead, shares should be determined for all relevant customer segments.

For short-run planning, the priority is to find subgroups of customers with distinctive patterns of needs and responsiveness to marketing variables in order to use these as a basis to gain and maintain a differential advantage within the served market. Such customer characteristics as industry type, volume requirements, reliance on technical service, and so forth provide useful bases for this kind of analysis. Competitors can build defensible positions based on vendor preferences and distribution/service coverage by tailoring their overall marketing strategy to the needs of these customer segments.

To evaluate the marketing plan, one should measure efficiency of performance within these defined target segments. This can provide diagnostic insights as a basis for continuing improvements. For the latter purpose, it is important to use all feasible units of measurements, such as share of revenue, unit volume, and number of transactions such as prescriptions (Majaro, 1977).

Strategic Planning. For strategic planning, involving decisions about resource allocations within the business and product portfolio, and evaluation of financial and market performance objectives, broader market definitions may be required. The identification of strategically relevant boundaries will be guided by: (1) the extent to which relative scale economies and experience in key "cost sectors" are shared along the technology, function, and customer dimensions (Buzzell, 1979a), and (2) differentials in industry maturity or stage of life cycle as measured by current and prospective category growth, which in turn depends on untapped market potential and the presence of substitutes. Other indicators of appropriate boundaries include customer and technological stability, rate of competitive entry and exit, and the consequent distribution and stability of market shares. Patel and Younger (1978) note:

> Such an examination may reveal considerable differences in industry maturity between car radios with built-in cassette players and traditional car radios. Differences in industry maturity and/or competitive position may also exist with regard to regional markets, consumer groups and distribution channels. For example, the market for cheap car radios sold by cash-and-carry discount houses to end-users doing their own installation may be growing much faster in some countries than the market served by specialty retail stores providing installation services.

This type of analysis requires the iterative use of top-down and bottom-up analysis, where the market definitions from one perspective are tested for strategic relevance and refined from other perspectives. Neither is adequate alone. We will return to this point in the discussion of the relationship of SBUs and PMUs.

Analysis of Threats and Opportunities. Analysis of threats (competitive surveillance) and opportunities (new ventures) require the broadest definitions. As Simmonds (1968) noted, "the existence of an opportunity to make use of strengths is implicit in the definition of a strength — it implies a potentially profitable market given competitor's products, resources, and likely reactions." However, an adjacent market that represents a potential direction for future growth is also a possible source of new competition. Therefore, it is important to look at the market from the competitors' perspectives.

Various competitors may use quite different definitions for the same strategic purpose, and thus will arrive at different decisions. The concept of strategic groups (Porter, 1976) can be used to classify competitors according to the similarity or difference in their strategies, including degree of integration, extent of advertising and branding, use of captive or exclusive distributors, whether they are full-line or specialist sellers, and so forth. Each group reflects a choice which depends on its definition of the market and the resources it has available to compete.

The Strategic Planning Framework: Linking Business Units and Product-Market Units

For most multiple product firms, the SBU or strategy center form of organization is regarded as a prerequisite to effective strategic management. A business unit is an independent component of the firm for which a discrete strategy can be developed. Ideally, it should have control over most of the factors that affect business-level strategy (Hall, 1978). This ideal is seldom achieved in practice, for most SBU definitions involve compromise and trade-offs. On the one hand, it is desirable that an SBU include as few product-market units (PMUs) as possible to encourage the development of focused product-market strategies (Hofer and Schendel, 1978). On the other hand, product-market units often cannot be treated as independent strategic entities either because they share resources with other PMUs, or there would be disjointed and ineffective strategies because of excessive fragmentation (Lorange, 1980).

A PMU is both the lowest level in the organization at which strategic planning takes place, and a building block which helps to make up an SBU. The choice of PMUs to group together within an SBU will depend on their similarity on strategically relevant factors. In effect, a clustering procedure is used in which each PMU is compared with every other PMU to determine their interrelationship along a variety of top-down (cost and technology-related) and bottom-up (market) criteria. This approach was used by a manufacturer of air conditioning equipment ranging from residential air conditioners to large commercial packages (self-contained units mounted in roof-tops or slabs) to custom engineered units for large-scale industrial cooling applications. The criteria used to compare the PMUs are similar to those suggested earlier in the discussion of strategically relevant boundaries. A simplified version of this manufacturer's work sheet is shown in Table 19.2 to illustrate how the criteria were employed. One major simplification is that the geographic dimension of the PMUs is not shown.[6] Also, for confidentiality reasons, the details of the technology criteria are not revealed.

Relative Importance of Cost and Demand Factors.   A quick scan of Table 19.2 reveals a common problem; there are no evident groupings for which there is not some overlap of PMUs. In part this problem is a consequence of assigning equal importance to each criterion, which will usually be inappropriate. However, the concepts developed earlier can be employed to identify circumstances where one set of factors should dominate the other, or facilitate subjective assessments of the relative importance of each criterion. Specifically, the relative importance of cost or market factors will systematically vary with the degree of complexity of the market, as portrayed by the following dimensions:

- the number of distinctly different uses or applications for the products in the market;
- the number of usage situations encountered by each customer; and,
- the size of the consideration set (the number of product types, product variants, brands and price/feature combinations which the customer would consider during the choice process).

TABLE 19.2   Criteria for Comparing PMUs

Criteria	Room air conditioners	Central air conditioners	Furnaces	Heat pumps	Commercial roof-top units	Custom engineered units (E.M.)
Market factors						
1. Shared competitors?		×		×	×	
2. Relative market share position?		×		×	×	
3. Industry maturity?	Mature	Growth (replacement cycle)	Mature	Embryonic	Growth	Mature
4. Shared customers?						
end users		×	×	×		?
contractor or dealer		×	×	×	×	
5. Substitutability in use?	×	×		×		?
Cost factors						
1. Joint manufacturing cost?	×	×	×	×	×	?
2. Shared distribution?						
warehousing		×	×	×	×	?
transportation		×	×	×	×	
sales force	×	×	×	×	×	
Technology	×	×		×	×	×

× = PMUs are similar on this criterion.

When there is only a single use or very few uses, the product provides a single function, illustrated by farm equipment, such as bean pickers, or limited-function housewares, such as crock-pots or hamburger cookers. These may be straightforward markets to understand, depending on the number of technologies and products considered feasible for providing the basic function, e.g. slow cooking at controlled temperature.

More complex environments are created when there are many possible ways to use the product but each user only considers it for one or two distinct uses. Most industrial materials and components fall into this category. For example, engineered plastics can be used for structural or decorative parts, containers, and so forth, and in each application there are many competitive materials, including metals and a whole spectrum of plastics entailing different cost-performance trade-offs.

The most complex markets are those where each customer has many uses for the product or service and many alternatives to consider.[7] Retail

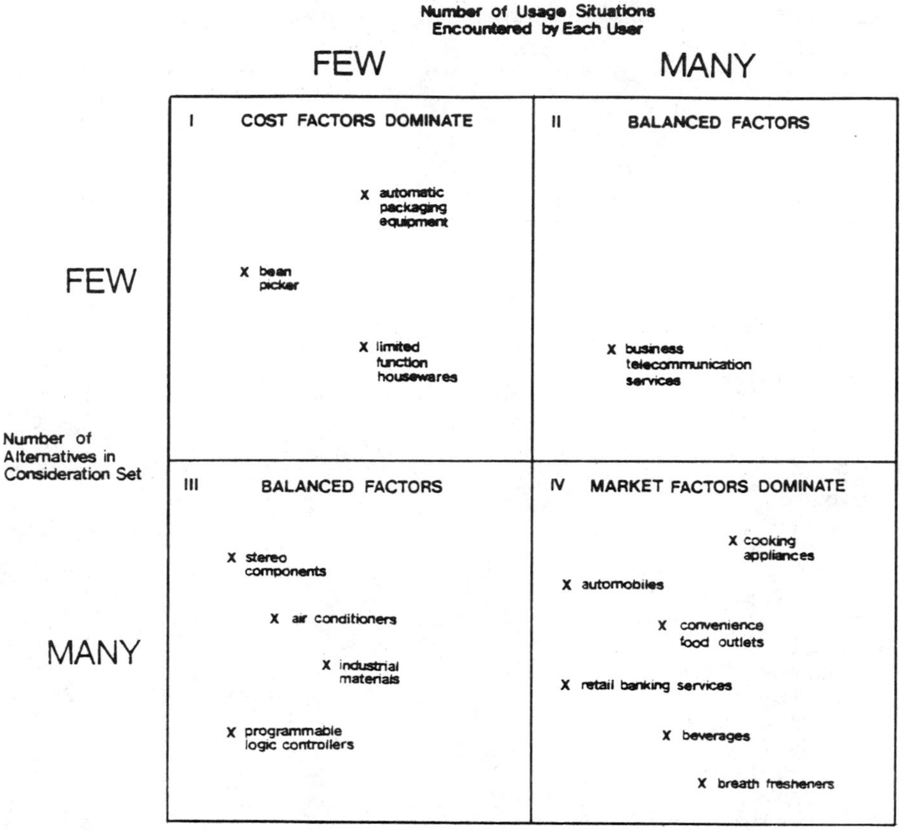

FIGURE 19.2   Product Usage Matrix

banking services are evolving toward this type of market as new competitors gain the franchise to collect deposits and give credits that was once restricted to commercial banks. Varying degrees of market complexity can be portrayed within the Product Usage Matrix of Figure 19.2.

More importantly, the matrix helps clarify the central issue in this paper — the relative balance of production and cost factors versus demand influences on the definition of the market. In general, with simpler environments the emphasis should be on cost and experience, but when there are complex usage patterns, and many alternative products/technologies which can satisfy customer needs, then the balance should shift toward a market perspective in the definition of both PMUs and SBUs. It was for this reason that General Foods redefined their product-oriented SBUs into menu categories, with SBUs like breakfast food, beverage, main meal, dessert, and pet food targeted toward specific usage situations, even though they often shared manufacturing and distribution resources (Hall, 1978).

Testing the Planning Framework.   The build-up approach to forming business units or strategy centers proceeds by grouping PMUs according to
their similarity on appropriate cost, demand and technology factors. Alternatively, one can start with a corporation or a division and follow a *divide-
up* approach, using those criteria for subdivision which yield the maximum
strategic discrimination (as illustrated in the earlier example from Patel and
Younger, 1978). Since only one or two criteria can be used at a time, the
inevitable trade-offs which have to be made between cost and demand
factors are not so evident.

Whether a build up or divide up approach is superior in any given
situation can only be answered by testing the resulting planning
framework for both strategic relevance and administrative feasibility.

(a)   *Strategic relevance tests.* The designation of a strategy center or SBU
is often a chicken-and-egg problem, in the guise of the continuing
question of which comes first, strategy or structure? Different
strategic thrusts may dictate the inclusion of different PMUs to
form the business, yet strategic planning is conducted within the
established structure of business units. Some useful questions to
guide the necessary judgments are:
(i)   is the proposed planning structure capable of stimulating
ideas for strategies which yield a future competitive advantage?
(ii)   is share of market an indication of relative cost or market
power?
(iii)   can performance be measured in terms of profit or loss?
(b)   *Administrative feasibility tests.* One set of administrative issues
deals with size and span of control trade-offs. On one hand, large
business units are likely to encompass shared resource units such
as pooled sales forces or joint production facilities, and they can
help keep the span of control manageable. However, if too many
dissimilar PMUs are lumped together, program managers may
be unable to perceive their contribution and important growth
opportunities may be submerged within the bulk of the established business. But if the business units are narrowly focused on
specific product-market opportunities the planning framework is
likely to become fragmented into many small units. This places an
unacceptable burden on the ability of corporate management to
coordinate and control the individual units. This means, for example, that opportunities for collaboration between business
units, such as adopting joint marketing programs to reach international markets, may be overlooked since no single SBU has
responsibility. Finally, if a business unit is too small it will not
have the visibility or resources to warrant the development of
separate strategic programs.

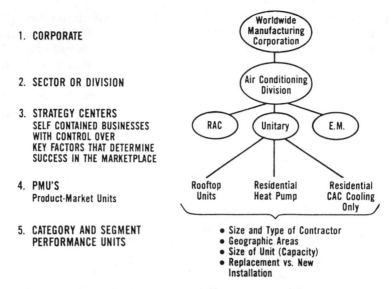

FIGURE 19.3   Strategic Planning Framework

The second administrative issue is the extent to which the planning framework of SBUs and PMUs should be forced into compatibility with the existing organization structure. If strategic realities dictate significant differences between the two structures, then, forcing them to be compatible for reasons of expediency may lead to excessive emphasis on short-run performance rather than a commitment to implementing a strategy to properly position the business in the long-run.

In the case of the air conditioner manufacturer described earlier, the strategic relevance test had primacy. The strategic planning framework which finally emerged in Figure 19.3 was adopted with the understanding that the existing organization would have to be quickly modified to ensure the desired strategic thrusts could be developed and executed.

Conclusion

Markets are complex, multidimensional arenas of competition composed of a myriad of niches and categories. The strategist seeking to understand a particular market is dealing with a moving target, for there is continuous change along each of the key market dimensions of function, technology, customer segmentation, and degree of integration. Barriers to competitive movement along these dimensions are constantly shifting, creating both threats and opportunities for protected market positions.

Both top-down and bottom-up analyses of strategic markets are necessary to avoid myopic market definitions, for there are inherent deficiencies to each approach which need to be balanced by the contrasting perspective. A top-down emphasis on markets specified in terms of company capabilities and resources can blind one to threats from competitors who are outside the presently served market, or can mean delayed response to shifts in customer requirements or usage patterns. Conversely, markets defined solely from the customer's perspective may ignore crucial economic factors which dictate relative cost position and may distort perceptions of opportunities where the competencies and experience base of the company can be effectively employed.

An integrated analysis of strategic markets begins with the acceptance of a need for multiple market definitions, each more or less suitable for particular strategic or tactical issues. Generally, broad definitions are necessary for the analysis of new ventures, or for competitive surveillance purposes, while narrower definitions are used for performance evaluation.

When the results of market analyses from the company and customer perspective are compared, it becomes evident that in many markets — especially those with complex patterns of product usage or product/service application — there is an untapped potential in methods which carefully distinguish between technologies and functions or uses. Finally, the planning process itself should have the capacity to seek out, understand, and exploit the differences in market definitions between top-down and bottom-up approaches. The pay-off will be clearer strategic thinking and faster response to emerging threats and opportunities.

Notes

1. This section relies heavily on Abell's (1980) conceptual development. See also Abell and Hammond (1979) for application of this concept.
2. This notion is developed further in Buzzell (1979a).
3. The terms business unit, strategic business unit (SBU) or strategy center will be used interchangeably to refer to self-contained businesses with control over the key factors that determine their success in the market.
4. Porter (1979) discusses several other sources of discontinuities, including product differentiation (which limits the extent to which brand names can be utilized in adjacent markets) and lack of access to distribution channels.
5. It may or may not be possible for a company to participate in the markets on both sides of a cost discontinuity. Sometimes this barrier is created by different customer segments, different patterns of needs, and responsiveness to marketing variables. For example, as some markets evolve toward maturity, the limited volume, high price, high cost-to-serve customer segment separates from the high volume, low cost-to-serve customer segment for the same function and technologies. Companies encounter serious problems in attempting to straddle two such disparate markets.
6. A good illustration of the definition of SBUs which balances global business considerations against local geographic market requirements can be found in the

Corning Glass Works: International (B) case study (Intercollegiate Case Clearing House No. 9-379-052, 1978).

7. Within this market category are two subtypes which reflect differences in the *choice resolution process*. There is a variety switching or multiple product purchase subtype, in which the customer avoids compromises among benefits sought by choosing different convenience food outlets for different occasions or stocking many types of beverages to meet the needs of different circumstances. However, in the compromise subtype, the customer's product or service choice has to meet the needs of many conflicting situations. This is true of most big-ticket purchases, such as cooking appliances and automobiles (and perhaps vacations). For example, a family car may be used for family camping trips, shopping, daily commuting, and so forth. The ultimate choice is seldom best for each specific usage situation, but may be best for the expected combination of situations.

References

Abell, Derek F. *Defining the Business: The Starting Point of Strategic Planning,* Prentice-Hall, Englewood Cliffs, N.J., 1980.

Abell, Derek F., and John S. Hammond. *Strategic Market Planning: Problems and Analytical Approaches,* Prentice-Hall, Englewood Cliffs, N.J., 1979.

Ansoff, H. Igor. *Corporate Strategy,* McGraw-Hill, New York, 1965.

Buzzell, Robert D. *Note on Market Definition and Segmentation,* Harvard Business School, Cambridge, Mass., 1979a.

Buzzell, Robert D. "The dispute about high-share businesses," *PIMS/letter 19,* Strategic Planning Institute, 1979b.

Cadbury, N. D. "When, where and how to test market," *Harvard Business Review,* May–June 1975, pp. 96–105.

Day, George S. "Diagnosing the product portfolio," *Journal of Marketing,* **41,** April 1977, pp. 29–38.

Day, George S., Allan D. Shocker, and Rajendra K. Srivastava. "Customer-oriented approaches to identifying product-markets," *Journal of Marketing,* **43,** Fall 1979, pp. 8–19.

Frank, Ronald, William F. Massy, and Yoram Wind. *Market Segmentation,* Prentice-Hall, Englewood Cliffs, N.J., 1972.

Gluck, Frederick, Stephen P. Kaufman, and A. Steven Walleck. "The evolution of strategic management," McKinsey Staff Paper, October 1978.

Hall, William K., "SBUs: hot, new topic in the management of diversification," *Business Horizons,* February 1978, pp. 17–25.

Hanan, Mack. "Reorganize your company around its market," *Harvard Business Review,* November–December 1974, pp. 63–74.

Hatten, Kenneth J. "Quantitative research methods in strategic management," in Dan Schendel and Charles W. Hofer (eds) *Strategic Management,* Little, Brown, Boston, 1979.

Hedley, Barry. "A fundamental approach to strategy development," *Long Range Planning,* December 1976, pp. 2–11.

Hofer, Charles W., and Dan Schendel. *Strategy Formulation: Analytical Concepts,* West Publishing, St. Paul, 1978.

Hopkins, David S. "New emphases in product planning and strategy development," *Industrial Marketing Management,* **6,** 1977, pp. 410–419.

Hunt, Michael. "Competition in the major home appliance industry: 1960–1970," *unpublished doctoral dissertation*, Harvard University, 1972.

Hussey, David E. "Portfolio analysis: practical experience with the directional policy matrix," *Long Range Planning*, **11**, August 1978, pp. 2–8.

Johnson, William E. "Trade-offs in pricing strategy," in *Pricing Practices and Strategies*, Conference Board, New York, 1978.

Kotler, Philip. *Marketing Management: Analysis, Planning, and Control*, Prentice-Hall, Englewood Cliffs, N.J., 1977.

Levitt, Theodore. "Marketing success through differentiation — of anything," *Harvard Business Review*, **58**, January–February 1980, pp. 83–91.

Lorange, Peter. *Corporate Planning: An Executive Viewpoint*, Prentice-Hall, Englewood Cliffs, N.J., 1980.

Majaro, Simon. "Market share: deception or diagnosis?," *Marketing*, March 1977, pp. 43–47.

Patel, Peter, and Michael Younger. "A frame of reference for strategy development," *Long Range Planning*, April 1978, pp. 6–12.

Porter, Michael E. *Interbrand Choice, Strategy and Bilateral Market Power*, Harvard University Press, Cambridge, Mass., 1976.

Porter, Michael. "How competitive forces shape strategy," *Harvard Business Review*, March–April 1979, pp. 137–145.

Rothschild, William. *Getting It All Together*, AMACOM, New York, 1976.

Simmonds, Kenneth. "Removing the chains from product strategy," *Journal of Management Studies*, February 1968, pp. 29–40.

Tilles, Seymour. "Segmentation and strategy," Perspectives Number 156, The Boston Consulting Group, Boston, Mass., 1974.

Wind, Yoram. "Issues and advances in segmentation research," *Journal of Marketing Research*, **15**, August 1978, pp. 317–337.

20. The Reality Gap in Strategic Planning

Ronald N. Paul
Neil B. Donavan
James W. Taylor

In 1976, Louis Gerstner wrote, "One of the most intriguing management phenomena of the late 1960s and 1970s has been the rapid spread of the corporate or strategic planning concept. Except for the so-called computer revolution, few management techniques have swept through corporate and governmental enterprise more rapidly or completely."[1]

Two major reasons help explain why companies have adopted the concept so rapidly. The first is that it apparently promised managements that they could now control the destinies of their organizations and achieve corporate stability no matter what happened in the external environment. It would be difficult to overstate the importance of continuity to the managements of major corporations.

The second major reason for the rapid adoption of strategic planning is that businessmen and academicians alike showed considerable agreement on what the concept was and how it should be implemented. The beautiful simplicity of the concept undoubtedly contributed to this agreement.

In 1975, Richard F. Vancil and Peter Lorange wrote, "The widely accepted theory of corporate strategic planning is simple: using a time horizon of several years, top management reassesses its current strategy by looking for opportunities and threats in the environment and by analyzing the company's resources to identify its strengths and weaknesses."[2]

When the simplicity and intuitive appeal of strategic planning are com-

This article first appeared in the *Harvard Business Review* 56, No. 3 (May–June 1978): 124–130.

When this article was published, the authors were, respectively, president and co-founder of Technomics Research Associates, Inc.; president of Gilbert H. Brockmeyer Ice Cream Company; and associate professor of marketing at California State University, Fullerton.

bined with its promise to solve the problem of uncertainty facing professional managers, the rapid adoption of the concept is quite understandable. Nevertheless, after a decade or more of experience, it is reasonable to ask whether strategic planning has lived up to its promises and, if not, in what ways has it failed. This article is an attempt to explore those questions.

Unfulfilled Promises

Although the details of execution vary from company to company, strategic planning requires each company to decide first "what it wants to be." This decision is determined by some combination of quantitative measures — dollar sales, growth in profits, return on investment — and qualitative measures — environmental concern, industry leadership, innovations.

Since only the quantitative measures can be communicated without ambiguity to all managers involved in the planning function, quantitative measures have become in practice the focal point of the typical business plan. Thus management's conception of the future of the company is thought of in terms of financial needs. These financial needs are then compared with the results of forecasts of sales and profits from the organization's existing products.

Since these estimates usually are somewhat pessimistic, this comparison almost always discloses a disparity between the bullish financial goals of top management and middle management's best expectations about the future of current products and operations. This disparity is often called the "strategic gap" and represents what strategic planning is supposed to contribute to attaining the company's goals.

Next, the future is analyzed in terms of alternative actions that the company can take to close the gap. A grid similar to the one shown in Table 20.1 is used to organize these alternatives.[3] As the table makes clear, the odds are heavily in favor of diversification as a method for closing the gap. Diversification can be accomplished in either, or both, of two ways; innovation through internal development and acquisitions.

The literature on the specific "how to" details of innovation and on

Table 20.1 Strategic Analysis Grid

	Present markets	New markets
Present products	Expansion	Diversification
New products	Diversification	Diversification

acquisition tactics is extensive, but this literature lies outside our main interests here. The central question is whether the general outline of strategic planning presented here is an accurate description of the process underlying the actual practices of strategic planning in most major U.S. corporations. We believe the outline is accurate, and we base that judgment on our experiences with dozens of major corporations over the past decade.

Unfortunate Outcomes

From a purely scientific point of view, it is not possible to say whether strategic planning has helped the corporations that have adopted it because it is not possible to know what kinds of decisions would have been made without strategic planning. However, as one examines the growing list of companies that have become entangled in financial misfortunes because of decisions apparently made in accordance with the principles of strategic planning, it seems that strategic planning may not always produce the expected results. Here are some well-publicized examples:

General Foods attempted to diversify through acquisition (Burger Chef). The 1972 annual report indicates a write-off of $39 million.

Rohr Industries attempted to diversify through internal development (urban mass transit). The 1976 annual report indicates a write-off of $52 million.

Mattel attempted to diversify through acquisition (Ringling Bros.). The 1975 annual report indicates write-offs of $25.5 million.

Outboard Marine attempted to diversify through internal development (snowmobiles). The 1975 annual report indicates write-offs of $42 million.

Singer attempted to diversify through internal development (business machines). The 1976 annual report notes a $325 million provision for discontinuance of that division.

Archer-Daniels-Midland attempted to diversify through internal development (high fructose corn syrup). The 1977 annual report will probably tell an interesting story.

The reader may have favorite candidates to add to this list, but two things should be kept in mind.

First, we have not included technical failures — as opposed to planning failures — because technical failures provide no evidence, one way or the other, about how well strategic planning actually works. For example, both DuPont (Corfam) and General Mills (Bontrae) attempted to diversify through internal development and ended with major write-offs. These products, however, were technical failures; they simply did not deliver the hoped-for benefits and results.

Second, it is usually impossible for observers outside a company to prove whether a planning failure or a performance failure occurred. A poorly *executed* plan can produce undesirable results just as easily as can a poorly *conceived* plan. However, when the management is handling its existing business in a highly competent manner, there is a reasonable basis for suspecting that planning rather than performance is at fault.

In spite of the caveats just mentioned, we believe there are two fundamental problems with the current practice of strategic planning that severely limit the likelihood of good decisions coming out of the process. One of these problems affects all organizations and the other, we suspect, affects most of them.

Unresolved Problems

The first problem is that strategic planning requires reasonably accurate long-term forecasts but that such forecasts are almost always impossible to produce. The second problem is that most strategic plans are in practice not much more than financial hopes filled with "nice" numbers. These hopes quickly turn into inexorable demands that operating management feels compelled to attain at any cost.

Forecasting the Future

The litany of strategic planning maintains that corporate weaknesses will be identified, usually defined in terms of the future, and that they should be replaced with corporate opportunities, invariably defined in terms of the future. Thus the bottom-line financial contribution of strategic planning can, at the minimum, be interpreted as the value of filling the strategic gap, but achieving this "return" assumes accurate forecasts.

In the past five years, a period no longer than most strategic planners deal with, several major changes have affected almost all U.S. corporations, including the most severe recession in modern times, severe shortages in raw materials in many basic industries, sharply rising costs for energy, a doubling of interest rates, depressed and inflated stock prices without any apparent relation to EPS, record levels of inflation and high unemployment (an impossible condition in most economic theory), and abrupt shifts in consumer income attitudes and purchasing behavior.

In hindsight, the onset of each of these changes appears to be somewhat obvious from events that preceded it. Yet there seems to be very little evidence that any one of them was forecast in anyone's strategic plan. Our point is not that the strategic planner must be a perfect seer, but rather that the future must be described with *sufficient* accuracy if management is to avoid making unalterable commitments that turn out to be in irreconcilable conflict with the future as it unfolds. Unfortunately, this modest level of accuracy appears to be beyond attainment when capital commitments are required even as little as two years in advance.

With strategic planning's dependence on accurate forecasts, it probably was not accidental that such planning gained wide acceptance during the 1960s, which were relatively stable and hence enabled forecasters to demonstrate sufficient accuracy — or at least enabled them to err on the conservative side. If one believes, as we do, that the relative stability of the 1960s is unlikely to return, then one must conclude that it is equally unlikely that the accuracy of long-term forecasts will improve materially.

Putting the Plan into Action

Strategic planning theorists repeatedly point out that the value of planning lies in the process of creating plans, not in the plan itself. While this maxim is correct, all too often this is not how things actually work. The sales and profits specified in the plan become the board of director's commitment to the stockholders and the financial community. They also become the president's commitment to the chairman and the board. Once given, these commitments become the financial establishment's gauge of the competence of the management.

In order to honor his commitment, the president must hold his vice presidents responsible for meeting their portions of the plan. Vice presidents, in turn, pass the responsibility on to division managers. In this way, plans take on a life of their own that is quite different from the original intention. Perhaps David Mahoney, chief executive officer of Norton Simon Inc., best summed it up when he said, "The way I make my number is for you guys to make your numbers."[4]

In and of itself, this development would not necessarily be bad. It could represent the way in which all the key individuals in the organization demonstrate their commitment to the corporation's future. In real life, the problem is that financial performance is invariably tied to time. Annual reports, semiannual reports, quarterly reports, and monthly reports all are made and individual performance evaluated against the goals set in the plan.

However, the key elements underlying the plan cannot be controlled on a rigid time frame. Innovation simply does not occur on an orderly month-by-month, quarter-by-quarter basis. The timing of acquisitions is equally resistant to neat, orderly calendarization.

Therein lies the second major problem of strategic planning. The same management that creates the plan ends up with the responsibility for accomplishing the financial goals of the plan without control over the events on which the plan is based. This is the management "dilemma" of planning, and it is not one to be taken lightly. We have seen managements take short-term actions to meet commitments to the plan that can only have extremely counterproductive long-term effects.

In spite of the seriousness of the problems with strategic planning, there can be no realistic argument for abandoning it, and we make none. The problems, however, are specific, and while they cannot be completely eliminated, they can be minimized. Maintaining the best elements of strategic planning within the constraints of real operating problems is the basic concept underlying what we call "adaptive forward planning."

Adapting Planning to Reality

There are ten specific actions in adaptive forward planning that will minimize the seriousness of the problems we have just discussed. None of them is revolutionary. Some of them are harder to accomplish than others. All of them presuppose a deep commitment by management to achieve the best possible results from strategic planning.

1. *Emphasize the process of planning, not the financial aspects of the plan.*

To avoid making the plan an end in itself — an inflexible, demanding mistress of performance — top management must demonstrate a real involvement in the planning *process* itself rather than assume a passive role, demanding to know "how much" and "by when." In order to select the optimum course of action, top management should concentrate its major attention on the assumptions and trends underlying the plan, not on promises of fulfillment.

William H. Spoor, chairman of the board at the Pillsbury Company, provides his division managers with alternative scenarios for 1985 and requires them to document how they would deal with the specifics of those conditions. Together, they immerse themselves deeply in examining the assumptions about possible future operating environments. More than one logical strategy has turned out to contain unexpected implications.

2. *Differentiate between risks to the balance sheet and risks to the profit and loss statement.*

On the strategic planning "Richter Scale of Management Survival," an overly bold and unrecoverable balance sheet risk is the true risk. A balance sheet risk involves a substantial commitment of corporate resources which, if unsuccessful, can seriously erode shareholder equity. The effect of a poor profit and loss risk, however, can often be managed within the time frame of the current fiscal year.

If a balance sheet risk becomes unavoidable, and top management is completely familiar with the uncertainties involved, the risk should be taken as democratically as possible. The board of directors and shareholders should be made aware of the long-term implications of the decision. A balance sheet mistake is almost always corrected by a clean sweep of existing management. A profit and loss mistake can usually be handled with a promise of better results in the future. Successful execution of strategic plans requires management continuity, and this step is designed to help achieve that continuity.

3.   *Measure the total market and competitive market shares as accurately as possible.*

It is a central premise of U.S. marketing that a successful company satisfies customer needs in a competitive environment. If a company is to understand its own position and, more important, to predict its future position in that environment, the management must have a firm grip on three factors: the company's own historical sales trends, the trend of the total market for its products, and the relative position of its competitors.

The fact that these data may not be readily available is not an acceptable excuse for not acquiring them. In fact, collecting these data is probably the most critical aspect of the entire strategic planning activity. The data not only must be accurate; they must also be the right pieces. Too many companies still measure the number of quarter-inch drill bits sold when they should be measuring the number of quarter-inch holes that customers need and want.

4.   *Gear the plan to events.*

Virtually all strategic plans are "time dependent," and expenditures, which the company can control, tend to be treated in the same way that sales dollars, which cannot be controlled, are treated. This is another example of how the numbers get a life of their own. Since the plan calls for spending a certain amount next year, another amount the following year, and so on, the momentum of this planned commitment of resources acts to sweep middle management people past warning yellow and red signal lights.

To put it another way, the person in the middle is like a gambler who has so much in the pot that he thinks he cannot afford to fold a marginally acceptable hand. If expenditures depend on events — "X" dollars will be spent for plant construction only when "Y"% of target consumers prefer the new product over competition in in-home use tests — automatic restraints are built into the process. The key words are *if* and *when*. Plans geared to events minimize the likelihood of an inadvertent balance sheet mistake.

5.   *Plan to expend money step-by-step.*

The engineering department will always argue that the most efficient and most profitable plant size is the biggest one that can be built, and the financial department can be counted on to argue that now is the cheapest possible time to build it. They are both probably right, but both miss the real point. Capital expenditures almost always represent balance sheet risks, and such risks must be minimized because of the difficulty in accurately forecasting the future. Therefore, smaller scale plans that can be steadily expanded are the most prudent choice for the long term even though they may appear less profitable on paper today.

6. *Build a second plan based on time.*

In addition to the basic strategic plan that specifies financial goals, such as "X number of dollars of sales and profits by a particular date," prepare a plan that indicates what planned performance will be considered acceptable if the goals are reached between "Time X" and "Time Y." This second plan is an extremely useful tool in reviewing the basic strategic plan. It also helps avoid giving the numbers a life of their own because it provides a second perspective for evaluating progress.

7. *Decide in advance the criteria for abandoning a project.*

Most plans say nothing about "folding a bad hand," but they should because it is inevitable that bad hands will turn up in any extended period of time. The opposite side of adapting a plan to events is including a specification, agreed on in advance, for abandoning every strategic project undertaken.

Each project should have a time *and* dollar bail-out signal attached to it: "If sales are not X by the end of Fiscal 19 —— , the project will be abandoned," or "If a shelf life of 24 months cannot be achieved after 6 months of R&D effort, the project will be abandoned."

These specifications should, of course, be built around the key elements of the project's anticipated success. The similarities between selecting abandonment criteria and gearing a plan to events (Step 4) should not be allowed to obscure the fact that there are also significant differences between the two.

Events control the rate at which resources are devoted to a project; abandonment criteria determine whether further resources will be devoted at all.

8. *Set up a monitoring system.*

The fundamental idea of adaptive forward planning is one of regular review and refinement of strategic plans. If this activity is going to achieve the maximum value, the review process must be based on accurate and timely information. A substantial portion of this information is likely to be different from the kinds of information that the company normally has available in managing its day-to-day operations.

Therefore, a separate information system is necessary to monitor the company's progress toward its future business. All the reasons that well-run companies need information to manage their existing business are even more important when it comes to managing their future business with all the inherently greater risks and uncertainties.

For example, perhaps McDonald's and the Colonel missed the rapid growth in pizza and Mexican fast-food opportunities because they focused only on hamburgers and chicken, instead of on the causes leading to the growth in fast-food sales in general. These causes were: increased disposable income, more working wives, greater mobility of the average consumer, and the consequent decline in the number of family meals at home. The management apparently assumed that hamburgers and chicken were the only ways to satisfy this rapidly changing market.

9. *Make a new five-year plan every year.*

Any business plan that is over 12 months old in today's rapidly changing state of economic and social affairs is an extraordinarily dangerous document. At the very least, management should review *all* the basic assumptions and trends underlying the overall strategic plan annually. Then it should conduct a careful review of the interim progress that has been made and clearly identify the reasons for underperformance or overperformance.

This step is absolutely mandatory on an annual basis and is desirable on a more frequent basis. The reason is that what management has least expected to happen has often actually come to pass since the plan was first completed. Therefore, the plan must be changed on a regular basis and that can only happen when it is scheduled.

10. *Avoid excessive publicity about long-term financial goals.*

All too often, there is an unfortunate tendency to announce, and publicize, goals as if forecasted earnings were "chickens already hatched in the fifth year out." The presence of a strategic plan is used to create an image of professionalism about the management and to create an image of precision about management's forecasts.

If the strategic plan is well done, and top management has had a deep involvement, management is acutely aware of just how much real error exists in the forecasted numbers. This step will go a long way toward avoiding giving the numbers a life of their own.

In Summary

Strategic planning has experienced widespread and rapid adoption by U.S. business because it promised a high degree of control over the future of the company. Fulfilling that promise has brought to light two major problem areas. One is the inability of strategic planners to forecast the long-term external environment with sufficient accuracy and the other is the unintended use of plan forecasts as day-to-day management control procedures. The effects of these problems can be substantially reduced by incorporating flexibility into existing planning practices.

Adaptive forward planning is not a theoretical construct; it is a response to real problems that have been experienced in using the strategic planning process in business organizations. The ten steps we have out-lined can minimize the consequences of forecasting errors by requiring a frequent and detailed review process. They can also minimize the use of strategic forecasts for inappropriate purposes by involving top management in the planning process and providing it with a set of tools for evaluating planned progress.

Notes

1. Louis V. Gerstner, Jr., "Can Strategic Planning Pay Off?" *Marketing Management — Perspectives and Applications* (Homewood, Ill.: Richard D. Irwin, 1976), p. 174.
2. See Richard F. Vancil and Peter Lorange, "Strategic Planning in Diversified Companies," HBR January–February 1975, p. 81.
3. See H. Igor Ansoff, *Corporate Strategy* (New York: McGraw-Hill, 1965); George A. Steiner, *Top Management Planning* (London: Macmillan, 1969).
4. "What Makes David Mahoney Run?" *Forbes*, February 15, 1972, p. 26.

21. Strategic Goals: Process and Politics

James B. Quinn

Executives are constantly under pressure to: (1) define specific goals and objectives for their organizations; (2) state these goals clearly, explicitly and, preferably, quantitatively; (3) assign the goals to individuals or organizational units; and (4) control the organization toward established measurable goals.

These have become almost biblical mandates for most managers. Yet at the strategic level in large companies one often finds that successful executives announce only a few goals. These are frequently broad and general. Only rarely are they quantitative or measurably precise. Further, managements tend to arrive at their strategic goals through highly incremental "muddling" processes rather than through the kinds of structured analytical processes so often prescribed in the literature and "required" according to management dogma.

This article documents why top managers act as they do. It also asserts that their practices are purposeful, politically astute and effective. They do not represent breakdowns in management technique, sloppiness, or lack of top management sophistication — as critics of these practices so often suggest. Managers at all levels can be more effective if they understand the logic and process behind such "broad goal setting" and "incremental" techniques.

The conclusions in this article come from systematic observation of some 10 organizations over a period of several years. Examples are selected from these observations, from secondary sources and from a current project on "Strategy Formulation in Major Organizations," in which the author

This article first appeared in the *Sloan Management Review*, Fall 1977.

When this article was published, the author was the William and Josephine Buchanan Professor of Management at the Amos Tuck School of Business Administration, Dartmouth College.

has interviewed some 100 top managers in large US and European companies.

Keeping Goals Vague

Why don't top executives simply arrive at goals and announce them in the precise, integrated packages advocated by theoretical strategists and expected by their organizational constituents? In fact, they may establish a few broad goals by decree. But more often — and for good reason — they avoid such pronouncements. Why?

Undesired Centralization

Effective top managers understand that goal "announcements" centralize the organization. Such statements tell subordinates that certain issues are closed and that their thoughts about alternatives are irrelevant. Successful top executives know they cannot have as much detailed information about products, technologies and customer needs as their line colleagues do. In formulating goals, they want both to benefit from this knowledge and to obtain the genuine participation and commitment of those who have it. For example:

> Mr. James McFarland said that, shortly after he became chief executive officer: "I asked myself what was expected of me as CEO. I decided that my role was really to build General Mills from a good into a great company. But I realized this was not just up to me. I wanted a collective viewpoint as to what makes a company great. Consequently, we took some 35 top people away for three days to decide what it took to move the company from 'goodness' to 'greatness'. Working in groups of six to eight we defined the characteristics of a great company from various points of view, what our shortcomings were and how we might overcome these." Over time these broad goals were translated into charters for specific divisions or groups. They became the initial guidelines that stimulated the company's very successful development over the next decade.

> The president of another large consumer products company was trying to develop a posture to deal with ever-increasing government regulation in his field. He said: "I have started conversations with anyone inside or outside the company who can help me. I don't know yet what we should do. And I don't want to take a stand we can't all live with. Before we make any irrevocable decisions, I'll want a lot of advice from those people in the company who understand the specific problems better than I do. And I'll want everyone pulling together when we do set our course."

Far from stimulating desired participation, goal announcements can centralize the organization, rigidify positions too soon, eliminate creative options and even cause active resistance to the goals themselves.

Focus for Opposition

Further, explicitly stated goals — especially on complex issues — can provide focal points against which an otherwise fragmented opposition will organize. Anyone with political sensibilities will understand this phenomenon. For example, President Carter's stated energy plan immediately drew the adverse comments of many parochial interests who only opposed a specific part of the plan. But soon these highly fragmented forces appeared unified in their opposition to the total plan and each fragment gained added credibility from this apparent unity. In a like manner, a "land use plan" or a "zoning ordinance" quickly becomes a coalescing element for many disparate interests in a town. In industry, department or division heads who compete fiercely on most issues can become a formidable power bloc against some announced thrust which would affect each of them only marginally. For example:

> In a textile fibers company strong marketing, production and R&D managers — who fought each other constantly — formed a potent coalition to resist a "product management" scheme to coordinate the very things that caused their friction. And in decentralized companies, powerful product division heads have forced new chief executives to give up, get out, or revert to acquisitions — rather than accept new interdivisional goals pushed from the top.

Because of such potential opposition, experienced executives are reluctant to put forward complete "goal packages" which could contain significant points of controversy. Instead they progress by building consensus around one — or a few — important new goal(s) at a time. This in part explains the "incrementalism" so often observed in organizations.

Cause of Rigidity

Once a top executive publicly announces a goal, it can become very difficult to change. Both the executive's ego and those of people in supporting programs become identified with the goal. Changing the goal broadcasts that the executive was in error and that all those pursuing the goal were on the wrong track. As a consequence, people tend to doggedly prolong seriously outmoded — but publicly committed — goals, rather than swallow their losses and move on.

> The government constantly continues obsolete military, energy and social programs for just such reasons. Corporate bankruptcy lists

are rampant with conglomerates, banks, transportation companies and real estate ventures under duress because their officers tried frantically to fulfill announced — but unrealistic — growth goals.

By contrast, the vice chairman of a multibillion dollar consumer products company said: "We don't announce growth goals in new areas precisely because we don't want to be trapped into doing something stupid. We might be tempted to acquire a company when we shouldn't. Or we might hang on to an operation we really should sell off. Public statements can sometimes generate powerful expectations — internally and externally — that can pressure you to do the wrong thing."

Top managers generally like to keep their options open as long as possible, consistent with the information they have. One way to accomplish this is to define only broad directions, then respond to specific, well documented proposals. There is an additional advantage to this approach. The proposers are more likely to identify with their proposition and see it through. Again, this is part of the logic behind incrementalism. As one vice president in charge of diversification said:

> Our management doesn't state a specific diversification goal requiring so many millions in profits and sales within five years. Instead we say "we want to be a competitive factor in (a designated) industry in five years." This keeps us free to approach each field flexibly as opportunities develop. And we don't get committed until we have concrete numbers and proposals to look at.

Threat to Security

There are still other good reasons why effective top managers do not announce goals explicitly or widely. In any healthy organization good people constantly bubble out to head other enterprises. Thus top executives are justifiably reluctant to provide potential competitors with specific information about their future moves.

When talking to the investment community or his vice presidents, Tex Thornton was never very specific about the sequence and timing of "his plan" during Litton's rapid growth phase. Advance knowledge of Litton's interest could have inflated an acquisition's stock price, activated other potential acquirers, or caused third parties to intervene. With large numbers of Litton executives being sought by other companies, it would have been folly to disclose acquisition goals in detail. In addition, more general goals allowed Litton needed flexibilities to consider new opportunities as they became available.

Further, as one chief executive said, "the future can make fools of us all." There are many examples of former high executives ousted because unforeseen events made it impossible to fulfill ambitious announced goals.

In the late 1960s the president of a large consumer products company announced to all his goal of 10 percent profit growth per year. But many in the company regarded this as "his goal" — not theirs. Despite some impressive successes, the president was hung for a failure to meet his goal in two successive years while he was trying to develop some entirely new ventures within the company. When these were slow in materializing, his vice presidents gleefully saw to it that the original goal was well remembered at board level. The embarrassed board, which had earlier approved the goal, terminated the president's career.

There are many other situations — like divestitures, consolidations, or plant closures — where managers may not announce goals at all until after they are accomplished facts. These are just some of the reasons why top managers do not follow the conventional wisdom about announcing goals. The few goals top managers do announce tend to: (1) reflect or help build a developing consensus; (2) be broad enough in concept to allow opportunism; and (3) be sufficiently distant in time that a number of possible options could ensure their achievement.

The Case for General Goals

Conventional wisdom also requires that effective goals be specific, measurable and, preferably, quantitative. Many managers actually express embarrassment or frustration when they cannot reach this "ideal." But more sophisticated executives find such highly precise goals useful only in selected circumstances. As an executive vice president of a major automobile company said:

> The decisions where we can set specific numerical goals are the easy ones. Establishing the image of your car line, deciding what posture to take vis-à-vis developing legislation, determining what features the public will want in a car three years from now, setting goals for dealing with worker representation or host country demands abroad . . . those are the tough questions. And they don't have numerical answers.

One can attempt to be verbally precise in such areas. Yet very often a broad goal statement is more effective than its narrower, more measurable counterpart might be. Why?

Cohesion

A certain generality in goals actually promotes cohesion. Many can support "continued growth," "greater freedom," "equal opportunity," "full disclosure," or "quality products" as organizational goals. But oddly enough, adding more specific dimensions to these broad concepts may quickly complicate communications, lose some individuals' support and even create contention.

If a community tries to agree on its precise goals in building a new school, it may never reach a sufficient consensus for action. People can differ irreconcilably on whether a traditional, experimental, pre-college, classical, or vocational approach should predominate. Yet they might easily agree on a goal "to build a new school." Once the broad program is approved, they can resolve some very fundamental value differences by compromising on the much less emotionally charged architectural details.

Similarly, top managers can often avoid serious rifts by focusing agreement on very broad objectives where substantial agreement exists, then treating more specific goal issues as decisions about concrete proposals or program details. Again, incrementalism is logical. For example:

> The new principal stockholder in a mechanical equipment company wanted the company to grow relatively rapidly by selective acquisitions. One of the stockholder's board representatives prepared a detailed outline containing proposed areas for growth and diversification. Some other board members — based on limited experience — immediately took a rigid stance against one specific proposal, i.e., acquisitions in "service areas" supporting the company's line. Little progress could be made until the principal stockholder's representatives went back and sold the board on an idea they could all agree to, i.e., growth through acquisition. As the board becomes more comfortable with this broad concept, the principal stockholder's representatives still hope to bring in some "service company" candidates and allay their fellow directors' fears in terms of a specific example.

Identity and Elan

Broad goals can create identity and elan. Effective organizational goals satisfy a basic human need. They enable people to develop an identity larger than themselves, to participate in greater challenges, to have influence or seek rewards they could not achieve alone. Interestingly enough, many employees can better identify with broad goals like being "the best" or "the first" in an area than they can with more specific numerical goals. As the chief executive of a major consumer products company said:

> We have slowly discovered that our most effective goal is *to be best* at certain things. We now try to get our people to help us work out what these should be, how to define *best* objectively, and how to *become best* in our selected spheres. You would be surprised how motivating that can be.

Most companies devote great attention to measurable output goals — like size, productivity, profits, costs, or returns — that lack charisma and provide no special identity for their people. Yet they often fail to achieve these goals precisely because their people do not identify sufficiently with the company. To forge a common bond among individuals with widely diverse personal values, expectations and capacities, such numerical goals must be teamed with goals that satisfy people's more basic psychological needs: to produce something worthwhile, to help others, to obtain recognition, to be free or innovative, to achieve security, to beat an opponent, or to earn community respect. While such organizational goals must be general enough to achieve widespread support, they must also clearly delineate what distinguishes "us" (the identity group) from "them" (all others).

To improve their competitive postures, executives often consciously define the "uniqueness" or "niche" of their company's products, processes, technologies, services, or markets. More thoughtful top managers also carefully analyze whether one strategic goal or another will better attract the skilled people and personal commitments they want. These people's talent and dedication then become the central strengths upon which the organization's success is built. An IBM salesman, a Bell Labs researcher, a *New York Times* stringer, or a Steuben glassblower all enjoy a special elan — as do millions of others whose organizations achieve a unique identity. This elan provides a special psychic compensation for the people involved, and symbiotically it becomes their organization's most priceless asset. More often than not such elan develops around broad conceptual goals, rather than precise mathematical targets.

The Case for Specific Goals

Contrary to conventional wisdom, relatively few strategic goals need to be mathematically precise. Properly derived, those few can provide essential focal points and stimuli for an organization. However, they should be generated with care and used with balance.

Precipitating Action

By making selected goals explicit at the proper moment, managers can create a challenge, precipitate desired discussions or analyses, or crystallize defined thrusts. For example:

> The president of a major packaging company wanted to move his organization in new directions. He first unleashed a series of management, staff and consulting studies to help define the company's weaknesses and major opportunities for improvement. These were circulated as "white papers" for discussion by his top management team. After a while consensus began to emerge on critical issues and options. The president began to reinforce one: "The need to work existing assets much harder." In further discussions his organization crystallized this concept into a specific target return on net assets — vastly higher

than the current return — as a principal goal for 1981. This goal triggered the shutdown of excess facilities, a new focus on profitability rather than volume, and a profit-centered decentralization of the whole organization.

Under these circumstances, after building consensus around a broad goal, the top executive may merely approve its specific manifestation. Although the goal is a challenge, his own organization has recommended it. The executive knows that it is feasible, and key people understand and support the goal. The time horizon is sufficiently distant to allow for alternative approaches which will ensure its achievement.

Major Transitions

Specific new goals can also help signal a major change from the past. Properly developed, they can challenge lower levels to propose specific solutions, yet not unduly constrain their approaches. To be effective they must build on some accepted values in the organization and leave time enough for proposed new programs to reach fruition. For example:

> After much discussion, an aerospace company's top management established the goal of moving 50 percent into nongovernment business within a decade. This started a furor of creative proposals. Research put forward new technical concepts. Each division proposed how it could best realign its own business. Corporate staff units investigated industries and specific companies for acquisitions. The administrative vice president recommended a new control system to handle diversification. Revised banking relations were proposed. And so on. From all these thrusts top management slowly chose its desired pattern of internal vs. external growth, market sectors, organizational form and financial structure. Throughout, lower levels felt their ideas were appreciated, and they identified with changes made.

After a prolonged disaster or a major trauma, an organization often needs distinct and clear new goals. Typically, these must combine a broad definition of longer-term success and some specific, achievable, short-term goals to build confidence. Without visible intermediate goals, people can become frustrated and give up on the ultimate challenge.

Limited Number

At any given moment, an executive can push only a few specific new goals, giving them the attention and force they need to take hold. Fortunately, a top executive rarely needs to press more than a few significant changes simultaneously. In fact, the essence of strategy is to identify this small number of truly essential thrusts or concepts and to consciously marshal the organization's resources and capabilities toward them. Then — to capture the organization's attention — the executive must consistently reinforce these strategic goals through his statements, his decision patterns and his personnel assignments. He must be willing to put his credibility on the line and use the power and sanctions of his office to achieve them. Still, the typical organization's ongoing momentum and resource commitments will allow it to absorb only a few major changes at once.

Two examples illustrate the complex interactions that lead to success or failure when setting specific goals at the top level.

> In 1969, RCA's chairman, Robert Sarnoff, initiated several major new thrusts simultaneously. While repositioning RCA in its traditional electronics–communications markets, he actively diversified the company through acquisitions. At the same time he also strove to: (1) build RCA's computer activities into an effective direct competitor of IBM; (2) move the company's technological efforts from research toward applications; and (3) strengthen the company's lagging marketing capabilities. He implemented much of this through an enlarged central corporate staff. It was difficult for the organization to absorb so much top-level-initiated change at once. Various aspects of the program met intense resistance from existing divisions. The computer venture failed and Mr. Sarnoff's credibility with the organization became strained to the breaking point.

> By contrast, shortly after Philip Hofmann became chairman of Johnson & Johnson, he announced a specific new goal of $1 billion in sales (with a 15 percent after-tax return on investment) before his retirement some seven years later. Annual sales were then approximately $350 million. Though the challenge was startling in scale, it built upon an established growth ethic in the company, and it did not constrain potential solutions. Instead it stimulated each division to define how it could best respond, thus maintaining the company's intended decentralization. It also allowed sufficient time for managers to propose, initiate and carry out their new programs. Performance ultimately surpassed the goal by a comfortable margin.

At some point, of course, planning processes must refine goals into specific operational targets. As the examples of successful goal setting illustrate, this is best achieved through incremental, iterative processes which intimately involve those who have to implement the proposed strategic thrusts.

The Need for Effective Goals

All of the concepts above help insure that strategic goals are set (1) at the right time; (2) with maximum input from those who have the most specific knowledge; and (3) with the genuine commitment of those who must achieve results. Why should managers take such care in developing and expressing organizational goals?

Effective strategic goals do more than provide a basis for direction setting and performance measurement. They are essential to establishing and maintaining freedom, morale and timely problem sensing in an enterprise. The benefits of effective goal setting are greatest when people throughout the organization genuinely internalize the goals and make them their own.

Freedom with Control

If people share common purposes, they can self-direct their actions with minimum coordination from executive or staff groups. This is especially critical for those groups whose activities involve creative work, such as research and development, advertising, or strategic planning. Without such goal congruence, control of these activities is impossible. No amount of ex-post-facto performance measurement can insure that creative people imaginatively identify proper problems, generate imaginative alternatives, or invent new or responsive solutions. Such actions must be stimulated before the fact by ensuring that well-selected people understand and internalize goals.

Maintaining Morale

Morale is a goal-oriented phenomenon. In a "high-morale" organization people intensely share common performance goals. They ignore internal irritations and adapt rapidly to external stimuli which help or hinder goal accomplishment. Entrepreneurial organizations, project teams on urgent tasks, dedicated medical groups, or even whole societies (like Israel or Japan) exhibit these characteristics. A specific industrial example suggests how powerful the symbiotic effect of a stimulating goal and talented people can be:

> From 1970 to 1976 tiny KMS Industries supported the world's most advanced laser fusion program for commercial energy production. As one executive said: "I don't know any of us who didn't agree that this was the most important task in the world. We thought we could lick the fight. If successful, we would have a new basis for creating energy, hydrogen and hydrocarbons. It would make the United States and other nations independent of world energy markets. People on the fusion program had extremely high morale. They would work all night. They were thoroughly committed." On May 1, 1974 — despite much larger AEC and Russian expenditures in the field — a KMS team achieved the world's first "unambiguous" release of neutrons from laser fusion.

A contrasting example makes the opposite point:

> The dominantly shared goal of many a government (or staff) department is the preservation of its members' positions and budgets. Lacking shared — or often even understood — performance goals, such organizations become "hotbeds of inertia." They focus extraordinary energies on minor internal irritants. When disturbed by external stimuli they operate with awesome tenacity to re-establish accepted interpersonal and political equilibria — even to the point of negating their own output and jeopardizing their continuation.

Often managers spend enormous amounts of time trying to ease or resolve the interpersonal tensions in such organizations, but they accomplish little until they can get people to accept a new sense of common purpose.

Problem Sensing

Finally, goals help define problems. Organizations without a strong sense of broad purpose can precipitate their own demise by ignoring major problems or overlooking alternatives. Some companies define their services, concepts and goals with such limited vision that they screen out major opportunities. Others have elaborately worked-out goal statements covering broad issues, but their control and reward systems reinforce — and cause people to internalize — only a few. And when people are not encouraged to internalize an adequate range of goals, the consequences can be extremely costly.

> In the late 1960s many conglomerates proudly concentrated on "managing the business as a financial enterprise." Their control and reward systems focused so much attention on continuously improving short-term financial performance that their managers often screened out other important issues as "nonproblems." This led them to undercut research and technology, product and personnel development, plant investments, international relations, and perhaps even ethics to an extent that sometimes jeopardized their companies' very viability.

> Recently, the chairman of a multibillion dollar diversified company publicly decried the $35 million his divisions would expend on depollution measures. It was clear that he perceived "environmentalism" only as a threat. Yet one division of his company (auto exhaust systems) was likely to sell an additional $600 million-plus of its product annually — with corresponding profits — because of the same environmental standards he resisted as "a total loss to the company."

Using Conventional Processes

If goals are to stimulate freedom with control, high morale and creative problem solving, people throughout the organization must understand and actively identify with them. Usually this requires the genuine participation of many individuals in setting and modifying the goals. Yet the manager must not lose control over this vital process. He must carefully blend consultation, participation, delegation and guidance to achieve his purposes. How can he manage this complex art?

Bottom Up

The philosophers' ideal is to arrive at goal consensus through democratic discussion or through "bottom-up" proposals. These views often prevail within small-company, Japanese, or "Theory Y" managements, and they clearly have merit for some organizations.

However, such approaches are very time-consuming and can prove to be frustrating, wasteful, or even divisive. Opaque committee discussions can go on endlessly and still leave individuals with different views of what goals were agreed on. People may expend extraordinary time and energy on proposals that management later rejects as "irrelevant." They feel angry or manipulated when "their" carefully prepared proposals or goals are overruled for other organizational purposes only fully appreciated from on high.

Unwitting Bureaucracy

Managers of larger enterprises rarely feel they can afford a purist approach to democratic goal setting. At the same time, they sense the shortcomings of goals announced from above. Consequently, a pragmatic compromise emerges. Top managers often provide a framework of broad goals for their subordinate units. They then encourage lower-level managers to make proposals which respond to these goals through planning, budgetary and ad hoc processes. Before the proposals reach final approval stages, a series of staff interventions, personal discussions and intermediate reviews tune them toward what various people think top management wants and will accept.

This process brings a kind of collective wisdom to bear. There is some personal involvement at all levels. But often a bland, committee-like consensus emerges. This process works moderately well for routine modifications of existing thrusts, but it discourages significant changes in organizational goals. Thus, unwittingly, most large enterprises become conservatively bureaucratized. They continue existing momenta and overlook major external changes or new opportunities.

Evolving Effective Strategic Goals

Dramatic new strategic goal-sets rarely emerge full blown from individual "bottom-up proposals" or from comprehensive "corporate strategic planning." Instead a series of individual, logical, perhaps somewhat disruptive decisions interact to create a new structure and cohesion for the company. Top managers create a new consensus through a continuous, evolving, incremental and often highly political process that has no precise beginning or end. A well documented example — one with which many readers will be familiar — illustrates important dimensions of this "logical incremental" approach to strategic goal setting.

IBM's strategic goal of "introducing its 360 computers simultaneously as a single line with compatibility, standard interface, business and scientific capability, hybrid circuitry and the capacity to open new markets" probably started in 1959 when T. Vincent Learson became head of the Data Systems and General Products divisions. The divisions' product lines had begun to overlap and proliferate, causing software, cost and organizational problems. Top managers sensed this, but no clear solutions were at hand.

In 1960–61 various specific decisions began to eliminate alternatives and define key elements of the new goal. Proposals for two new computers, "Scamp" and the 8000 series, were killed to avoid further proliferation. In mid-1961 Learson and a subordinate, Bob O. Evans, arrived at a broad concept "to blanket the market with a single product line," and they initiated exploratory studies on a new product line called simply "NPL." During 1961 a special Logic Committee recommended that IBM use "hybrid circuitry" — rather than integrated circuits — in any major new line. In late 1961 NPL was foundering. Learson and chairman Watson started a "series of dialogues on strategy" with division heads, but no clear concept emerged. Consequently, they formed the SPREAD committee of key executives to hammer out basic concepts for a new line. In January 1962, the committee reported and top management approved its recommended concepts for a new integrative product line, now worked out in some detail. Broad top management support and a genuine organization momentum were building behind the new concept.

In 1962 development began in earnest, and IBM's board approved a $100-million manufacturing facility for hybrid circuits. Still, technical difficulties and differences in viewpoint persisted. In late 1962 a special programming meeting was held at Stowe to discuss software development, but major programming problems remained unresolved. In 1963 various groups openly resisted the new line. The opposition was broken up or removed. In December 1963, Honeywell precipitated action by announcing a strong competitor for IBM's successful 1401 computer. Shortly thereafter, in January 1964, Learson conducted a performance "shoot out" between the 360/30 and the 1401. The 360/30 was judged good enough to go ahead. Final pricing, marketing and production studies were now made. In March 1964, top management approved the line in a "final risk assessment session" at Yorktown. And on April 7, 1964, Watson announced the 360 line. The decision now appeared irrevocable.

But in 1965 and later, new time-sharing features, smaller and larger computers, and peripheral equipment units were announced or "decommitted." IBM raised $361 million of new equity in 1965 to support the line — ultimately investing some $4.5 billion in the 360. Further changes occurred in the line and its supporting hardware and software. Finally, well into the 1970s, the 360 series provided IBM's essential strategic strength, its massive installed computer base. The decision and its impact extended over some 15 years.

The pattern is common. At first there are simply too many unknowns to specify a cohesive set of new directions for the enterprise. More information is needed. Technical problems must be solved to determine feasibilities. Investments must be made in programs with long lead-times. Trends in the marketplace must crystallize into sufficiently concrete demands or competitive responses to justify risk taking. Various resource bases must be acquired or developed. Different groups' psychological commitments must be diverted from ongoing thrusts toward a new consensus. Lead-times for all these events are different. Yet logic dictates that final resource commitments be made as late as possible consistent with the information available — hence the emergence of incrementalism.

To reshape an organization's accepted culture significantly, an executive must often overcome some potent psychological and political forces. His success will depend on the very group whose perceptions he may want to change. If he moves too precipitously, he can undermine essential strengths of his organization. All too easily he can alienate his people, lose personal credibility and destroy the power base his future depends on. Unless a crisis intervenes, he cannot change the organization's ethos abruptly. Instead he usually must build commitment — and his own political support — incrementally around specific issues or proposals. The real art is to thoughtfully blend these thrusts together, as opportunities permit, into patterns which slowly create a new logical cohesion.

Managing the Incremental Process

Changing strategic goals typically involves managing a complex chain of interacting events and forces over a period of years. How do successful managers approach this challenge?

For the reasons cited above, a kind of "logical incrementalism" usually dominates strategic goal setting. This process is purposeful, politically astute and effective. It starts with needs that may only be vaguely sensed at first and incrementally builds the organization's awareness, support and eventual commitment around new goals. The stages in this process — though not always the same — commonly recur. These are set forth below. The management techniques used at each stage — also outlined below — are not quite the textbook variety. But seeing these in the context of the total process helps explain their wide use and notable effectiveness. It also explains some of the seeming anomalies and real frustrations of management in large organizations. Managers at all levels should understand how this process operates and how they can best fit into and manage their roles in it.

Sensing Needs

Top executives very often sense needs for strategic change in quite vague or undefined terms, like IBM's "organizational overlap" or "too much proliferation." Early signals may come from almost anywhere, and they may initially be quite indistinct. Long lead-times are often needed to make significant changes. Consequently, effective executives — like Mr. Learson — consciously seek multiple contact points with managers, workers, customers, suppliers, technologists, outside professional and government groups, and so on. They purposely short-circuit all the careful screens an organization builds to "tell the top only what it wants to hear" and thus delay important strategic signals. They constantly move around, show up at unexpected spots, probe and listen.

Building Awareness

The next step is very often to commission study groups, staff, or consultants to illuminate problems, options, contingencies, or opportunities posed by a sensed need. These studies sometimes lead to specific incremental decisions. More often they merely generate broadened or intensified perceptions of future potentials. At this stage managers may need to offset the frustration of study groups, who frequently feel they have failed because their studies do not precipitate direct action. But the organization is not yet ready for a decision. Key players are not yet comfortable enough with issues, variables and options to take a risk. Building awareness, concern and a "comfort factor" of knowledge about a situation is a vital early link in the practical politics of change.

Broadening Support

This stage usually involves much unstructured discussion and probing of positions. Earlier studies may provide data or the excuse for these discussions — as in the case of the "strategic dialogues" at IBM. At this stage top executives may actively avoid decisions, other than agreeing to explore options. Instead, they may encourage other key players to see opportunities in a new light, define areas of indifference or concern and identify potential opponents and points of contention. Whenever possible, the guiding executive lets others suggest new thrusts and maintains the originator's identity with the idea. He encourages concepts he favors, lets undesired or weakly supported options die, and establishes hurdles or tests for strongly supported ideas he may not agree with, but does not want to oppose openly. His main purpose is to begin constructive movement without threatening major power centers. Typically, goals remain broad and unrefined.

Creating Pockets of Commitment

Exploratory projects — like NPL — may be needed to create necessary skills or technologies, test options, or build commitment deep within the organization. Initially, projects may be small and ad hoc, rarely forming a comprehensive program. The guiding executive may shun identity with specific projects to avoid escalating attention to one too quickly or losing credibility if it fails. To keep a low profile he may encourage, discourage, or kill thrusts through subordinates, rather than directly. He must now keep his options open, control premature momentum and select the right moment to meld several successful thrusts into a broader program or concept. His timing is often highly opportunistic. A crisis, a rash of reassignments, a reorganization, or a key appointment may allow him to focus attention on particular goals, add momentum to some, or perhaps quietly phase out others.

Crystallizing a Developing Focus

Ad hoc committees — like the SPREAD committee — are a favorite tool for this. By selecting the committee's membership, charter and timing, the guiding executive can influence its direction. A committee can be balanced to educate, evaluate, or neutralize opponents. It can genuinely develop new options, or it can be focused narrowly to build momentum. Attention to the committee's dynamics is essential. It can broaden support and increase commitment significantly for new goals. Or it can generate organized opposition — and a real trauma — should top management later overrule its strong recommendations.

At crucial junctures the guiding executive may crystallize an emerging consensus by hammering out a few broad goals with his immediate colleagues and stating some as trial concepts for a wider group to discuss. He may even negotiate specific aspects with individual executives. Finally, when sufficient congruence exists or the timing is right, the goal begins to appear in his public statements, guidelines for divisions and other appropriate places.

Obtaining Real Commitment

If possible, the executive tries to make some individual(s) explicitly accountable for the goal. But he often wants more than mere accountability — he wants real commitment. A major thrust, concept, product, or problem solution frequently needs the nurturing hand of someone who genuinely identifies with it and whose future depends on its success. In such cases, the executive may wait for a "champion" to appear before he commits resources, but he may assign less dramatic goals as specific missions for ongoing groups. Budgets, programs, proposals, controls and reward systems must now reflect the new goal, whether or not it is quantitatively measurable. The guiding executive sees to it that recruiting and staffing plans align with the new goal and, when the situation permits, reassigns its supporters and persistent opponents to appropriate spots.

Continuing Dynamics

All of the above may take years to effect — as it did in IBM's case. Over this time horizon, the process is rarely completely orderly, rational, or consistent. Instead the executive responds opportunistically to new threats, crises and proposals. The decision process constantly molds and modifies his own concerns and concepts. Old crusades become the new conventional wisdom; and over time, totally new issues emerge.

Once the organization arrives at its new consensus, the executive must move to ensure that this does not become inflexible. In trying to build commitment to a new concept, an executive often surrounds himself with people who see the world the same way. Such people can rapidly become systematic screens against other views. Hence, the effective executive now purposely continues the change process with new faces and stimuli at the top. He consciously begins to erode the very strategic goals he has just created — psychologically a very difficult task.

Conclusion

Establishing strategic goals for complex organizations is a delicate art, requiring a subtle balance of vision, entrepreneurship and politics. At the center of the art one finds consciously managed processes of "broad goal setting" and "logical incrementalism." Management styles vary, but effective top executives in larger enterprises typically state a few broad goals themselves, encourage their organizations to propose others, and allow still others to emerge from informal processes. They eschew the gimmickry of simplistic "formal planning" or "MBO" approaches for setting their major goals. Instead they tend to develop such goals through very complicated, largely political, consensus-building processes that are outside the structure of most formal management systems and frequently have no precise beginning or end.

Those who understand these processes can contribute more effectively, whatever their position in the organization. Those who wish to make major changes in organizations should certainly comprehend these processes, their rationale and their implications. Those who ignore them may find the costs very high.

22. Strategic Windows

Derek F. Abell

Strategic Market Planning involves the management of any business unit in the dual tasks of *anticipating* and *responding* to changes which affect the marketplace for their products. This article discusses both of these tasks. Anticipation of change and its impact can be substantially improved if an organizing framework can be used to identify sources and directions of change in a systematic fashion. Appropriate responses to change require a clear understanding of the alternative strategic options available to management as a market evolves and change takes place.

Dynamic Analysis

When changes in the market are only incremental, firms may successfully adapt themselves to the new situation by modifying current marketing or other functional programs. Frequently, however, market changes are so far reaching that the competence of the firm to continue to compete effectively is called into question. And it is in such situations that the concept of "strategic windows" is applicable.

The term "strategic window" is used here to focus attention on the fact that there are only limited periods during which the "fit" between the key requirements of a market and the particular competencies of a firm competing in that market is at an optimum. Investment in a product line or market area should be timed to coincide with periods in which such a strategic window is open. Conversely, disinvestment should be contemplated if what was once a good fit has been eroded — i.e., if changes in market requirements outstrip the firm's capability to adapt itself to them.

Reprinted from *Journal of Marketing*, July 1978, pp. 21–26, published by the American Marketing Association.

When this article was published, Derek F. Abell was an associate professor of business administration at the Graduate School of Business Administration, Harvard University.

Among the most frequent questions which management has to deal with in this respect are:

Should funds be committed to a proposed new market entry? Now? Later? Or not at all? If a commitment is to be made, how large should it be?

Should expenditure of funds of plant and equipment or marketing to support existing product lines be expanded, continued at historical levels, or diminished?

When should a decision be made to quit and throw in the towel for an unprofitable product line or business area?

Resource allocation decisions of this nature all require a careful assessment of the future evolution of the market involved and an accurate appraisal of the firm's capability to successfully meet key market requirements. The strategic window concept encourages the analysis of these questions in a dynamic rather than a static framework, and forces marketing planners to be as specific as they can about these future patterns of market evolution and the firm's capability to adapt to them.

It is unfortunate that the heightened interest in product portfolio analysis evident in the last decade has failed to adequately encompass these issues. Many managers routinely classify their various activities as "cows," "dogs," "stars," or "question marks" based on a *static* analysis of the *current* position of the firm and its market environment.

Of key interest, however, is the question not only of where the firm is today, but of how well equipped it is to deal with *tomorrow*. Such a *dynamic* analysis may foretell non-incremental changes in the market which work to disqualify market leaders, provide opportunities for currently low share competitors, and sometimes even usher in a completely new cast of competitors into the marketplace. Familiar contemporary examples of this latter phenomenon include such products as digital watches, women's pantyhose, calculators, charter air travel, office copiers, and scientific instrumentation.

In all these cases existing competitors have been displaced by new contenders as these markets have evolved. In each case changing market requirements have resulted in a *closing* strategic window for incumbent competitors and an *opening* window for new entrants.

Market Evolution

The evolution of a market usually embodies more far reaching changes than the relatively systematic changes in customer behavior and marketing mix due to individual product life cycles. Four major categories of change stand out:

1. The development of new primary demand opportunities whose marketing requirements differ radically from those of existing market segments.
2. The advent of new competing technologies which cannibalize the existing ones.
3. Market redefinition caused by changes in the definition of the product itself and/or changes in the product market strategies of competing firms.
4. Channel changes.

There may be other categories of change or variants in particular industries. That doesn't matter; understanding of how such changes may qualify or disqualify different types of competitors can still be derived from a closer look at examples within each of the four categories above.

New Primary Demand

In a primary demand growth phase, decisions have to be reached by existing competitors about whether to spend the majority of the resources fighting to protect and fortify market positions that have already been established, or whether to seek new development opportunities.

In some cases, it is an original entrant who ploughs new territory — adjusting his approach to the emergent needs of the marketplace; in other cases it is a new entrant who, maybe basing his entry on expertise developed elsewhere, sees a "strategic window" and leapfrogs over the original market leader to take advantage of the new growth opportunity. Paradoxically, pioneering competitors who narrowly focus their activities in the early stages of growth may have the most difficulty in making the transition to new primary demand growth opportunities later. Emery Air Freight provides an example of a company that did face up to a challenge in such a situation.

Emery Air Freight.   This pioneer in the air freight forwarding business developed many of the early applications of air freight in the United States. In particular, Emery's efforts were focused on servicing the "emergency" segment of the market, which initially accounted for a substantial portion of all air freight business. Emery served this market via an extensive organization of regional and district offices. Among Emery's major assets in this market was a unique nationwide, and later worldwide, communications network; and the special competence of personnel located in the district offices in using scheduled carriers in the most efficient possible way to expedite deliveries.

As the market evolved, however, many new applications for air freight emerged. These included regular planned shipments of high value-low weight merchandise, shipments of perishables, "off-line" service to hard-to-reach locations, and what became known as the TCC (Total Cost Concept) market. Each of these new applications required a somewhat different approach than that demanded by the original emergency business.

TCC applications, for example, required detailed logistics planning to assess the savings and benefits to be obtained via lower inventories, quicker deliveries and fewer lost sales through the use of air freight. Customer decisions about whether or not to use air freight required substantially more analysis than had been the case for "emergency" use; furthermore, decisions which had originally been made by traffic managers now involved marketing personnel and often top management.

A decision to seek this kind of business thus implied a radical change in Emery's organization — the addition of capability to analyze complex logistics systems and to deal with upper echelons of management.

New Competing Technologies

When a fundamental change takes place in the basic technology of an industry, it again raises questions of the adaptability to new circumstances of existing firms using obsolete technology.

In many cases established competitors in an industry are challenged, not by another member of the same industry, but by a company which bases its approach on a technology developed outside that industry. Sometimes this results from forward integration of a firm that is eager to develop applications for a new component or raw material. Texas Instruments' entry into a wide variety of consumer electronic products from a base of semi-conductor manufacture is a case in point. Sometimes it results from the application by firms of a technology developed in one market to opportunities in another. Or sometimes a breakthrough in either product or process technology may remove traditional barriers to entry in an industry and attract a completely new set of competitors. Consider the following examples:

> Watchmakers have recently found that a new class of competitor is challenging their industry leadership — namely electronic firms who are seeking end market applications for their semi-conductors, as well as a new breed of assemblers manufacturing digital watches.

> Manufacturers of mechanical adjustable speed drive equipment found their markets eroded by electrical speed drives in the early 1900's. Electrical drives were based on rotating motor-generator sets and electronic controls. In the late 1950's, the advent of solid state electronics, in turn, virtually obsoleted rotating equipment. New independent competitors, basing their approach on the assembly of electronic components, joined the large electrical equipment manufacturers in the speed drive market. Today, yet another change is taking

place, namely the advent of large computer controlled drive systems. This is ushering yet another class of competitors into the market — namely, companies whose basic competence is in computers.

In each of these cases, recurrent waves of new technology fundamentally changed the nature of the market and usually ushered in an entirely new class of competitors. Many firms in most markets have a limited capability to master all the technologies which might ultimately cannibalize their business. The nature of technological innovation and diffusion is such that most *major* innovations will originate outside a particular industry and not within it.

In many cases, the upheaval is not only technological; indeed the nature of competition may also change dramatically as technology changes. The advent of solid state electronics in the speed drive industry, for example, ushered in a number of small, low overhead, independent assemblers who based their approach primarily on low price. Prior to that, the market had been dominated by the large electrical equipment manufacturers basing their approach largely on applications engineering coupled with high prices and high margins.

The "strategic window" concept does not preclude adaption when it appears feasible, but rather suggests that certain firms may be better suited to compete in certain technological waves than in others. Often the cost and the difficulty of acquiring the new technology, as well as the sunk-cost commitment to the old, argue against adaption.

Market Redefinition

Frequently, as markets evolve, the fundamental definition of the market changes in ways which increasingly disqualify some competitors while providing opportunities for others. The trend towards marketing "systems" of products as opposed to individual pieces of equipment provides many examples of this phenomenon. The situation of Docutel illustrates this point.

Docutel. This manufacturer of automatic teller machines (ATM's) supplied virtually all the ATM's in use up to late 1974. In early 1975, Docutel found itself losing market share to large computer companies such as Burroughs, Honeywell, and IBM as these manufacturers began to look at the banks' total EFTS (Electronic Funds Transfer System) needs. They offered the bank a package of equipment representing a complete system of which the ATM was only one component. In essence their success may be attributed to the fact that they redefined the market in a way which increasingly appeared to disqualify Docutel as a potential supplier.

Market redefinition is not limited to the banking industry; similar trends are underway in scientific instrumentation, process control equipment, the machine tool industry, office equipment, and electric control gear, to name but a few. In each case, manufacturers basing their approach on the marketing of individual hardware items are seeing their "strategic window" closing as computer systems producers move in to take advantage of emerging opportunities.

Channel Changes

Changes in the channels of distribution for both consumer and industrial goods can have far reaching consequences for existing competitors and would-be entrants.

Changes take place in part because of product life cycle phenomena — the shift as the market matures to more intensive distribution, increasing convenience, and often lower levels of channel service. Changes also frequently take place as a result of new institutional development in the channels themselves. Few sectors of American industry have changed as fast as retail and wholesale distribution, with the result that completely new types of outlets may be employed by suppliers seeking to develop competitive advantage.

Whatever the origin of the change, the effect may be to provide an opportunity for a new entrant and to raise questions about the viability of existing competitors. Gillette's contemplated entry into the blank cassette tape market is a case in point.

Gillette.   As the market for cassettes evolved due to increased penetration and new uses of equipment for automotive, study, business, letter writing, and home entertainment, so did distribution channels broaden into an increasing number of drug chains, variety stores, and large discount stores.

Presumably it was recognition of a possible "strategic window" for Gillette that encouraged executives in the Safety Razor Division to look carefully at ways in which Gillette might exploit the cassette market at this particular stage in its evolution. The question was whether Gillette's skill in marketing low-priced, frequently purchased package goods, along with its distribution channel resources, could be applied to marketing blank cassettes. Was there a place for a competitor in this market to offer a quality, branded product, broadly distributed and supported by heavy media advertising in much the same way that Gillette marketed razor blades?

Actually, Gillette decided against entry, apparently not because a "strategic window" did not exist, but because profit prospects were not favorable. They did, however, enter the cigarette lighter business based on similar analysis and reportedly have had considerable success with their *Cricket* brand.

Problems and Opportunities

What do all these examples indicate? *First*, they suggest that the "resource requirements" for success in a business — whether these be financial requirements, marketing requirements, engineering requirements, or whatever — may change radically with market evolution. *Second*, they appear to suggest that, by contrast, the firm's resources and key competencies often cannot be so easily adjusted. The result is a *predictable* change in the fit of the firm to its market — leading to defined periods during which a "strategic window" exists and can be exploited.

The "strategic window" concept can be useful to incumbent competitors as well as to would-be entrants into a market. For the former, it provides a way of relating future strategic moves to market evolution and of assessing how resources should be allocated to existing activities. For the latter, it provides a framework for diversification and growth.

Existing Businesses

Confronted with changes in the marketplace which potentially disqualify the firm from continued successful participation, several strategic options are available:

1. An attempt can be made to assemble the resources needed to close the gap between the new critical marketing requirements and the firm's competences.
2. The firm may shift its efforts to selected segments, where the "fit" between requirements and resources is still acceptable.
3. The firm may shift to a "low profile" approach — cutting back severely on all further allocation of capital and deliberately "milking" the business for short-run profit.
4. A decision may be taken to exit from that particular market either through liquidation or through sale.

All too frequently, however, because the "strategic window" phenomenon is not clearly recognized, these strategic choices are not clearly articulated. Instead, "old" approaches are continued long after the market has changed with the result that market position is lost and financial losses pile up. Or, often only half-hearted attempts are made to assemble the new resources required to compete effectively; or management is simply deluded into believing that it can adapt itself to the new situation even where this is actually out of the question.

The four basic strategic choices outlined above may be viewed hierarchically in terms of *resource commitment*, with No. 1 representing the highest level of commitment. Only the company itself can decide which position on the hierarchy it should adopt in particular situations, but the following guideline questions may be helpful:

To what extent do the changes call for skills and resources completely outside the traditional competence of the firm? A careful analysis has to be made of the gap which may emerge between the evolving requirements of the market and the firm's profile.

To what extent can changes be anticipated? Often it is easier to adapt through a series of minor adjustments — a stepping stone approach to change — than it is to be confronted with a major and unexpected discontinuity in approach.

How rapid are the changes which are taking place? Is there enough time to adjust without forfeiting a major share of the market which later may be difficult to regain?

How long will realignment of the functional activities of the firm take? Is the need limited to only some functions, or are all the basic resources of the firm affected — e.g., technology, engineering, manufacturing, marketing, sales, and organization policies?

What existing commitments — e.g., technical skills, distribution channels, manufacturing approaches, etc. — constrain adaption?

Can the new resources and new approaches be developed internally or must they be acquired?

Will the changes completely obsolete existing ways of doing business or will there be a chance for coexistence? In the case of new technologies intruding from outside industry, the decision often has to be made to "join-em rather than fight-em." Not to do so is to risk complete obsolescence. In other cases, coexistence may be possible.

Are there segments of the market where the firm's existing re sources can be effectively concentrated?

How large is the firm's stake in the business? To the extent that the business represents a major source of revenues and profit, a greater commitment will probably need to be made to adapt to the changing circumstances.

Will corporate management, in the event that this is a business unit within a multi-business corporation, be willing to accept different goals for the business in the future than it has in the past? A decision not to adapt to changes may result in high short-run returns from that particular business. Looking at the problem from the position of corporate planners interested in the welfare of the total corporation, a periodic market-by-market analysis in the terms described above would appear to be imperative prior to setting goals, agreeing on strategies, and allocating resources.

New Entrants

The "strategic window" concept has been used implicitly by many new entrants to judge the direction, timing, and scale of new entry activities. Gillette's entry into cigarette lighters, major computer manufacturers' entry into ATM's, and Procter & Gamble's entry into many consumer markets *after* pioneers have laid the groundwork for a large scale, mass market approach to the specific product areas, all are familiar examples.

Such approaches to strategic market planning require two distinctly different types of analysis:

1. Careful assessment has to be made of the firm's strengths and weaknesses. This should include audits of all the key resources of the company as well as its various existing programs of activity.
2. Attention should be directed away from the narrow focus of familiar products and markets to a search for opportunities to put unique competencies to work. This requires a broader appreciation of overall environmental, technical and market forces and knowledge of many more markets, than is encountered in many firms today. It puts a particular burden on marketing managers, general managers, and business planners used to thinking in terms of existing activities.

Analysis of patterns of market evolution and diagnosis of critical market requirements in the future can also be of use to incumbent competitors as a forewarning of a potential new entry. In such cases, adjustments in strategy can sometimes be made in advance, which will ultimately deter would-be new competitors. Even where this is not the case, resource commitments may be adjusted to reflect the future changes in structure of industrial supply.

Conclusion

The "strategic window" concept suggests that fundamental changes are needed in marketing management practice, and in particular in strategic market planning activities. At the heart of these changes is the need to base marketing planning around predictions of future patterns of market evolution and to make assessments of the firm's capabilities to deal with change. Such analyses require considerably greater strategic orientation than the sales forecasting activities which underpin much marketing planning today. Users of product portfolio chart analysis, in particular, should consider the dynamic as opposed to the static implications in designating a particular business.

Entry and exit from markets is likely to occur with greater rapidity than is often the case today, as firms search for opportunities where their resources can be deployed with maximum effectiveness. Short of entry and exit, the allocation of funds to markets should be timed to coincide with the period when the fit between the firm and the market is at its optimum. Entering a market in its early stages and evolving with it until maturity may, on closer analysis, turn out to be a serious management error.

It has been said that while the life of the product is limited, a market has greater longevity and as such can provide a business with a steady and growing stream of revenue and profit if management can avoid being myopic about change. This article suggests that as far as any one firm is concerned, a market also is a temporary vehicle for growth, a vehicle which should be used and abandoned as circumstances dictate — the reason being that the firm is often slower to evolve and change than is the market in which it competes.

Section VI

Implementation and Control of Marketing Strategy

FROM ANY POINT OF VIEW, it is clear that a strategy becomes effective only when it influences action. However, as we have suggested repeatedly in the book, this noncontroversial assertion masks a very intractable dilemma in the application of strategic analysis.

Implementation is the process of translating strategic imperatives into various operating forms — tactical actions, for example, organizational designs or the control and reward system. No implementation decision excludes all others nor is it totally consistent within itself. At one end of the spectrum of decision types is an overemphasis on the definition of detailed tactical actions at a high level in the organization; it seems suspiciously like the classic foolishness of "buying a dog and then barking oneself." At the other end, a reliance on the full feedback loop of monitoring, control, and adjustment can require such overall delays that, to use another old aphorism, "the stable is locked after the horse has bolted." In this last section, we examine readings that cover in more detail all these various options. Of course, each article is characterized by an emphasis on the benefits of the particular form of implementation it is considering.

Translating Strategy into Tactical Actions

The first two readings in this section consider some of the tactical issues in the following specific contexts: the specific issues in low market share businesses, and the problems of weak products. The process of market planning demonstrates the need for both senior management involvement and the guidance and encouragement of product managers. In the end, however, detailed planning must be done at the product market level. The necessity of developing detailed plans at lower levels in the organization reinforces the view that broad objectives, such as gaining a given percentage in market share, may fail to reflect crucial information and concerns for a specific product or business unit.

As Richard Rumelt has observed, the portfolio models and decision rules (described in Section IV) should not be criticized for their simplicity.[1] They should be examined in terms of whether the simplification focuses on critical or trivial dimensions for the particular organization! Since many of the developments in marketing strategy analysis have been based on the central concept of market share, it is not surprising that a number of authors have concentrated on those situations in which a market-share-based form of analysis might prove to be dangerously misleading. In the case of high market share companies, two specific circumstances have been identified. First, the extent to which the resource demands of high market share strategies are fully recognized at the outset[2] and second, the extent to which such strategies must be modified in the light of antitrust regulation.[3]

In the case of low market share companies, the first reading (Article 23), "Strategies for Low Market Share Business," expresses the concern that the value of differentiation and segmentation may be underemphasized in strategic analysis. Then, as Article 24, "Harvesting Strategies for Weak Products," indicates, we must recognize that not all products in the corporate portfolio are set for growth and expansion. Hence the ways in which weaker products are actually managed can have very significant impacts on overall corporate performance.

Organization and Control

Strategy can also be implemented through choices in terms of organization and control. Both the actual form of the organization and the criteria for selecting and controlling those who manage are important aspects of implementation. Article 25, "SBUs: Hot, New Topic in the Management of Diversification," focuses on the most popular current choice in organizational form to implement strategies in diversified firms. In fact, the choices available, as well as the marketing strategy implications, suggest that other options need to be considered — including both functional and matrix forms. The appropriate choice may be significantly affected by the nature of the firm's environment.[4]

Article 26, "Wanted: A Manager to Fit Each Strategy," considers another area of crucial organizational choice — the selection of the individual management. The issue of the degree to which individual managers can be effective when operating one sort of marketing strategy is obviously contentious, but it is certainly likely that some persons are more comfortable with one approach rather than with another.

Article 27 is "A Strategic Framework for Marketing Control"; it looks at how the control system can be used to reinforce the chosen strategic direction for the firm. It is apparent, of course, that if we introduce an organizational form, employ managerial types, and use a control system in a manner consistent with our chosen strategy, then the initial choice had better be right: the self-reinforcing system takes a long time to respond effectively to any evidence of its own inappropriateness. An awareness of the overall strategic impact of the monitoring, control, and reward system is important even when no such explicit choices have been made. Even apparently unrelated decisions on the nature of the reporting of accounts are likely to have a very significant impact on the evaluation of the performance of marketing units. This is particularly true in situations of a greater emphasis on effective use of the replacement value of capital within the activity rather than pure sales volume or even gross margin.[5]

Some Cautions

Having started with articles that considered how a chosen strategy might be implemented, we also need to consider a few cautions. For instance, Robert Hayes and William Abernathy[6] have expressed concern that an overreliance on short-term performance measures (such as market share and profitability) can lead to a longer run decline in competitive position. Such undesirable effects are, of course, increased when senior executives set hurdle rates for the returns on new investments, rates that exceed those derived from the financial markets, as discussed in Section III. Further problems are created when the crucial importance of timing is not recognized, and too much emphasis is placed on certainty. If we wait too long to be certain that a marketing opportunity exists, then it will have passed us by because a competitor has responded more quickly.[7]

Article 28, "Strategic Responses to Technological Threats," provides an important, if restricted, test of the frequent underlying assumption that recognition of technological change in its markets provides the means for the dominant firm to react effectively by adapting. The actual evidence is distinctly pessimistic. Technological change often changes the nature of the market itself so much that previous competitive strengths count for little or, even worse, prove to be real handicaps. Next, "The Malaise of Strategic Planning" (Article 29), raises the concern that too much of strategic planning seems, in practice, to be directed to broad and often trivial generalized strategies[8] — such as cost leadership or market niches — rather than to understanding the specifics and the opportunities of the product-market in question.

A Partial Synthesis

As we suggested in Section I, our introduction to strategic marketing — and as many of the subsequent readings testify — the relationship between marketing strategy and action (implementation) poses a number of unresolved questions. Hence the final conclusion in the current state of knowledge must be a personal one. Such a situation does not absolve us as authors from making our own position clear; but it does require us to emphasize both that it is very much our position and also that readers must make up their own minds on the basis of the conflicting arguments.

We would choose to emphasize three particular aspects of strategic marketing. First, we believe that the process of thinking and indeed acting strategically is a critical part of effective operations within the organization. Second, it is most useful to consider marketing strategy at the corporate level, in broad terms of structure and organizational design, and to encourage more detailed market-based analysis at the operating level. Third, to the extent that marketing strategy analysis embodies the evidence of empirical regularities in the competitive marketplace, a good understanding of the rules is a good basis upon which to judge particular opportunities to beat the competition.

In summary, any student or practitioner of marketing strategy would be well advised to spend some time considering the following comment by Kiechel:

> Strategic concepts may be a bit like the rules of the Assassins. That curious medieval sect of Muslim fanatics, we are told, had several orders or ranks, each with its own place in an ascending hierarchy. Upon being promoted into the next highest order, initiates would be given a new, and presumably loftier, set of rules to live by. After years during which these structures became second nature to them, the devout might even find a place in the ninth, or highest order. These few would wait with hushed reverence as the sect's leader welcomed them individually into the elect, whispering into the ear of each the final, ultimate wisdom. The message: "There are no rules."[9]

Notes

1. Richard P. Rumelt, "Evaluation of Strategy: Theory and Models," in *Strategic Management: A New View of Business Policy and Planning*, ed. D. E. Schendel and C. W. Hofer (Boston: Little, Brown, 1979).
2. William E. Fruhan, "Pyrrhic Victories in the Fight for Market Share," *Harvard Business Review*, September–October 1972, pp. 100–107.
3. Paul N. Bloom and Philip Kotler, "Strategies for High Market Share Companies," *Harvard Business Review*, November–December 1978, pp. 95–102.
4. For a much more extensive discussion, see Barton Weitz and Erin Anderson, "Organizing the Marketing Function," in *Annual Review of Marketing 1981*, ed. B. Enis and K. Roering (Chicago: American Marketing Association).
5. Fredrick E. Webster, Jr., James A. Largay III, and Clyde P. Stickney, "The Impact of Inflation Accounting on Marketing Decisions," *Journal of Marketing*, 44, Spring 1981, pp. 9–17.
6. Robert M. Hayes and William J. Abernathy, "Managing Our Way to Economic Decline," *Harvard Business Review*, July–August 1980, pp. 67–77.

7. This and related issues in the application of economic analysis to the identification of competitive opportunities are discussed in greater detail in Robin Wensley, "PIMS and BCG: New Horizon or False Dawn," *Strategic Management Journal,* April–June 1982, pp. 149–158.

8. Michael Porter, in his book *Competitive Strategy: Techniques of Analyzing Business, Industry, and Competitors* (Englewood Cliffs, N.J: Prentice-Hall, 1981), uses the term generic rather than generalized to describe such strategies. Generic, however, implies that each is distinctly independent and the classification is not susceptible to further simplification. In fact, his three "generic" strategies (of cost-leadership, differentiation and focused) are all subsets of the basic strategy of maintaining competitiveness in a defensible market sector.

9. Walter Kiechel III, "Playing the Rules of the Corporate Strategy Game," *Fortune,* 24 September 1979, pp. 110–115.

23. Strategies for Low Market Share Businesses

R. G. Hamermesh
M. J. Anderson, Jr.
J. E. Harris

During the past several years, a great deal of research on profitability and market share has uncovered a positive correlation between the two. One study shows that "on the average, a difference of ten percentage points in market share is accompanied by a difference of about five points in pretax ROI."[1] Although in general market share and return on investment do go hand in hand, many of the inferences that both managers and consultants have been drawing from this finding are erroneous and misleading.

One of the most dangerous inferences drawn from this generality is that a low market share business faces only two strategic options: fight to increase its share or withdraw from the industry. These prescriptions completely overlook the fact that, in many industries, companies having a low market share consistently outperform their larger rivals and show very little inclination to either expand their share or withdraw from the fight. Perhaps the best example of this situation is the steel industry, where producers such as Armco Steel, Inland Steel, and Kaiser Steel have consistently earned a higher return on equity than their much larger competitors, United States Steel and Bethlehem Steel.

Often, planning systems that are based on this generality also have serious flaws. Most of these systems place a business in one of four categories, according to its market share and the industry's growth rate.[2] Depending on the category a business falls in, a strategy is automatically prescribed. Low market share businesses in low-growth industries should be

This article first appeared in the *Harvard Business Review*, May–June 1978, pp. 95–102.

When this article was published, the authors were, respectively, assistant professor of business administration at the Harvard Business School, marketing manager at IBM, and consultant for Agricultural Corporation in Atlanta.

divested; high market share businesses in low-growth industries should be "milked" or "harvested" for cash; high market share businesses in high-growth industries should maintain their growth; and low market share businesses in high-growth industries should increase their market share.

Although each classification system has its own nuances, all such systems share the same shortcoming: they define strategy at such a high level of abstraction that it becomes meaningless. A successful business strategy must be specific, precise, and far-ranging. It should state the markets in which a business will compete, the products that will be sold, their performance and price characteristics, the way in which they will be produced and distributed, and the method of financing. By taking the attention of corporation executives away from these essential details and instead focusing their attention on abstractions, many planning systems do a great disservice.

Finally, such sweeping generalities offer little consolation to those businesses that, for one reason or another, find themselves in a poor market position. Since only one competitor enjoys the highest share of any given market, most businesses must face the disadvantage of not having the highest market share. They must devise a specific strategy that will lead to the best possible performance, regardless of their position.

During the past several months, we have been studying businesses that have outperformed other much larger companies in their industries. We have identified four important characteristics that most of these successful businesses share. In this article, we shall discuss these characteristics.

Indications of Performance

Although there are numerous ways to define successful performance and low market share, we have chosen two straightforward definitions. Low market share is less than half the industry leader's share, and successful companies are those whose five-year average return on equity surpasses the industry median. Applying these criteria to the over 900 businesses in 30 major industries listed in *Forbes Annual Report on American Industry* revealed numerous successful low share businesses. From a list of these companies, we chose three — Burroughs Corporation, Crown Cork & Seal Co., Inc., and Union Camp Corporation — for close study. These three companies have surpassed not only their industries' average return on equity but have actually led their industries in several important performance categories.

Consider Burroughs. During the mid-1960s, many analysts predicted that the corporation, with its narrow line of computers, aging accounting machines, and market share of less than 3%, would soon withdraw from

TABLE 23.1   Comparative Performance of Major Mainframe Computer
Manufacturers Through 1976

Company	Total sales (in millions of dollars)	Net profit margin	Return on equity (five-year average)	Annual sales growth (five-year average)	Earnings per share growth (five-year average)
IBM	$16,304	14.7%	20.5%	12.8%	14.1%
Burroughs	1,871	9.9	14.3	14.5	17.1
Sperry Rand	3,203	4.8	13.1	11.1	12.9
NCR	2,312	5.0	11.8	9.6	46.0
Honeywell	2,495	4.5	9.7	8.5	5.1
Control Data	1,331	2.5	4.7	12.4	−0.1

SOURCE: Annual reports of the above companies and *Forbes*, January 9, 1978.

the mainframe computer market. Today, Burroughs competes more effectively with IBM than does any other computer company. Its market share
is still dwarfed by that of IBM, but during the past five years, its sales and
earnings per share have grown faster than IBM's. And although Burroughs's net profit margin and return on equity trail IBM's, they exceed
those of NCR, Sperry Rand, Honeywell, and Control Data by a substantial
margin.

It is significant that results by line of business, which are reported in
10-K statements and which distinguish businesses such as Control Data's
finance and insurance lines and Honeywell's controls line, also indicate
that on a return-on-sales basis, Burroughs's computer line greatly outdis-
tances that of all its rivals except IBM. (See Table 23.1 for detailed comparisons of the financial positions of mainframe computer manufacturers.)

Crown Cork & Seal is another successful low share company. In fact,
as Table 23.2 shows, its financial performance over the past decade has
consistently been the highest of the major metal can manufacturers. Yet
Crown Cork & Seal has not always enjoyed such success. In early 1957, the
company was near bankruptcy, and with sales of $115 million in 1956, it
had to compete with American Can (1956 sales of $772 million) and Conti-
nental Can (1956 sales of $1 billion).

Today, Crown Cork & Seal is still much smaller than its two giant

TABLE 23.2   Comparative Performance of Major Metal Can Manufacturers
Through 1976

Company	Net sales (in millions of dollars)	Net profit margin	Return on equity (five-year average)	Annual sales growth (five-year average)	Earnings per share growth (five-year average)
Crown Cork & Seal	$ 910	5.1%	16.2%	14.7%	14.5%
Continental	3,458	3.8	14.1	10.5	14.3
National Can	917	2.5	12.2	16.5	5.9
American Can	3,143	3.3	12.0	9.2	16.9

SOURCE: Annual reports of the above companies and *Forbes*, January 9, 1978.

TABLE 23.3   Comparative Performance of Major Forest Products Companies Through 1976

Company	Sales (in millions of dollars)	Net profit margin	Return on equity (five-year average)	Annual sales growth (five-year average)	Earnings per share growth (five-year average)
Union Camp	$1,003	11.1%	21.7%	13.6%	24.9%
Weyerhaeuser	2,868	10.2	19.5	15.4	18.1
Mead	1,599	5.6	17.4	7.5	31.7
International Paper	3,540	6.0	16.2	11.0	21.5
Boise Cascade	1,932	5.2	12.0	1.2	Not applicable

SOURCE: Annual reports of the above companies and *Forbes*, January 9, 1978.

rivals, but with profits of $46 million (15.8% return on equity), the prospect of bankruptcy has long since passed. Although Crown Cork & Seal's competitors have all diversified, an analysis of 10-K statements for 1976 shows that the pretax returns on sales of their metal packaging businesses were all below 6%; Crown Cork & Seal's pretax return on sales was nearly 10%.[3]

Our third company, Union Camp, competes in the extremely competitive, highly fragmented forest products industry. Over 3,000 companies have major product lines in this industry, and it has been highly volatile and plagued with overcapacity, depressed prices, pollution control problems, and high construction costs.

Despite these problems, Union Camp's earnings per share have increased by almost 27% annually over the past five years, and average return on equity has been over 20%. As the ninth largest company in its industry, Union Camp competes with such giants as International Paper and Weyerhaeuser, which are three and a half and two and a half times larger than Union Camp. As shown in Table 23.3, Union Camp's weak market position has not prevented the company from outperforming its larger competitors. Comparisons of the pretax return on 1976 sales of the paper and paperboard portions of these companies shows that Union Camp leads the pack with a 28% return. The next highest rate was posted by Boise Cascade's paper operations.

Elements of Strategy

Except for their low market share positions and exceptional performances, Burroughs, Crown Cork & Seal, and Union Camp seem to have little in common. Certainly their competitive environments are extremely different. Computer mainframes constitute a highly technological, rapidly growing industry that is dominated by one company. The metal container industry is extremely mature and, with only four major competitors, is a classic oligopoly. The forest products industry is also mature, but it is very fragmented.

Given these rather substantial differences in industry settings, are there any common strategies that these three successful low share companies have implemented to yield profits? Our research suggests four characteristics that these companies share: they carefully segment their markets, they use research and development funds efficiently, they think small, and their chief executives' influence is pervasive.

Segment, Segment, Segment

First, to be successful, most businesses must compete in a limited number of segments within their industry, and they must choose these segments carefully. Thinking in broader terms than only the range of products offered and the types of customers served, most successful companies define market segments in unique and creative ways. For example, besides products and customers, a market can also be segmented by level of customer service, stage of production, price performance characteristics, credit arrangements with customers, location of plants, characteristics of manufacturing equipment, channels of distribution, and financial policies.

The point is an important one. To be successful, a low share company must compete in the segments where its own strengths will be most highly valued and where its large competitors will be most unlikely to compete. Whether that strength is in the type and range of products offered, the method by which the product is produced, the cost and speed of distribution, or the credit and service arrangements is irrelevant. The important thing is that management spend its time identifying and exploiting unique segments rather than making broad assaults on entire industries.

Aerosol and Beverage Cans. Although the metal container industry sells to numerous industries and faces competition from glass, aluminum, fiberfoil, and plastic containers, Crown Cork & Seal has elected to concentrate on two product segments: (1) metal cans for hard-to-hold products such as beer and soft drinks and (2) aerosol cans. In an industry where transportation costs represent a large proportion of total costs, Crown Cork & Seal has built small single-product plants close to its customers instead of large and possibly more efficient multiproduct plants located at some distance from its customers.

The two market segments Crown Cork & Seal serves have both grown more rapidly than the total industry, but they also require expert skills in container design and manufacturing. The company has a particular advantage over competitors in the soft drink and brewing industries because it is the largest supplier of filling equipment to these companies. Thus Crown Cork & Seal has segmented its market by products, customers, customer service, and plant location. It is significant that the company sells to growth segments in which it has special expertise.

Four Large Paper Mills.   In the forest products industry, Union Camp has had to overcome the disadvantages of having a relatively small timberland holding — only 1.6 million acres — in contrast to International Paper's 23.7 million acres and Weyerhaeuser's 16.7 million acres. Although this difference makes Union Camp's raw material prices higher, the company has achieved consistently lower operating costs than its large rivals. Since the location of plants is important, Union Camp, like Crown Cork & Seal, operates only four very large mills, strategically situated in deep water ports close to both Union Camp's southern timberlands and its eastern customers.

For example, at its Franklin, Virginia plant, Union Camp operates the largest fine-paper machine in the world. As a low-cost producer of paper products, this corporation produces large volumes of only a limited number of paper products, and in bleached paper, Union Camp is not fully integrated. Instead, it sells most of its output to end-product converting companies. By selling to a rather small number of paper converters, the corporation has established a superior service record.

Thus Union Camp has segmented its market by stage of production, manufacturing policies, prices, products, customers, and services.

Three Distinct Computer Lines.   Unlike Union Camp and Crown Cork & Seal, which do not offer complete lines in their industries, Burroughs offers a full line of computers. But in developing its full product line, the corporation has taken advantage of historical ties to the financial community, where it has been a major supplier of accounting machines for decades. Today, Burroughs possesses an 18% share of the banking segment, almost three times its overall market share.

In designing its large computers, the B5000 series, Burroughs has emphasized ease and flexibility of programming at the expense of efficient use of main memory. This form of segmentation has been justified by the tenfold decrease in memory costs since 1964, while talented programmers have become both scarce and expensive.

In medium-size computers, Burroughs has chosen to imitate IBM's design and to compete on price. The company has reportedly underbid IBM by considerable amounts on some large government contracts. In the small computer market, Burroughs has continued to upgrade its electronic accounting machines and has given them the capability to serve as either terminals to a larger computer or as free-standing accounting machines.

Thus, although Burroughs offers a full line of mainframe computers, within each line it has segmented the market to capitalize on its particular skills and resources.

That Crown Cork & Seal, Union Camp, and Burroughs have had to compete in unique market segments in order to attain their success should not be surprising. But what these three companies reveal is that the opportunities to segment an industry are enormous and extend to every facet of a business. When a business segments its markets in unique and creative ways, it can far surpass the performance of its larger competitors. The marketing vice president of one high market share business once commented:

> For years, we have been unable to understand why our profits have been mediocre despite our strong market position. The expert planners at corporate staff have been of little help. About a year ago, we decided to do a detailed study of our industry. We found that, although we had the highest market share, in all of the important and more profitable market segments, we were taking a beating. We were leading the pack, however, in the unappealing segments of the markets.

Use R&D Efficiently

Although low market share companies can improve their performance by pursuing narrow market segments, their larger rivals still seem to have a tremendous advantage, because of their size, in research and development. Our research suggests that smaller companies seldom win R&D battles but that they can channel their R&D spending into areas that are the most likely ones to produce the greatest benefits for them.

Lower Process Costs. At both Crown Cork & Seal and Union Camp, for example, R&D is focused on process improvements aimed at lowering costs. A Crown Cork & Seal executive has noted:

> We are not truly pioneers. Our philosophy is not to spend a great deal of money for basic research. However, we do have tremendous skills in die forming and metal fabrication, and we can move to adapt to the customer's needs faster than anyone else in the industry.[4]

Alexander Calder, Jr., Union Camp's chairman, has adopted a similar R&D strategy:

> We are known to be very strong in process and in the manufacturing of industrial products. . . . We do little basic research like Du Pont. But we are good at improving processes, developing improved and some new products, and helping to build new manufacturing capabilities.[5]

Another R&D strategy Union Camp and Crown Cork & Seal have developed is to work closely or jointly with their largest customers on major developments. For example, Crown Cork worked closely with large breweries in the development of the drawn-and-ironed cans for the beverage industry. As a result, the company beat all three of its major competitors in equipment conversion for the introduction of this new product.

Concentrate on Innovations. For Burroughs, the problem of developing an R&D strategy is much more difficult and crucial than for the other two companies because of the rapid changes and high technology in the computer industry. Although Burroughs spends 6% of its sales on R&D compared with IBM's 7.5%, in dollar terms the difference is staggering — $112 million versus $1.2 billion. To compensate, Burroughs runs an extremely efficient R&D operation and concentrates on truly innovative products. And because of its low share position, these products are able to attract enough new customers to more than offset the trading up by Burroughs's existing customers.

IBM, on the other hand, has paced its innovations because, whenever it introduces a new system, a significant amount of its leased equipment is exchanged for the new system. As a result, Burroughs is recognized as one of the technological leaders in the computer industry.

Burroughs also runs an extremely efficient R&D operation. Its chairman, Ray Macdonald, spends a great deal of time at his R&D center and exerts tremendous pressure on his engineers.

Think Small

Another characteristic of successful low market share companies is that they are content to remain small.[6] Most of them emphasize profits rather than sales growth or market share, and specialization rather than diversification.

Limit Growth. Macdonald limits Burroughs's growth in the rapidly growing computer industry to 15% per year because he maintains that fast growth does not allow for the proper training of people and the development of a management structure. And in an industry where giants such as General Electric and RCA have faltered because they have found the pursuit of market share to be too costly, Burroughs has been consistently profitable despite only slow and modest gains in market share. Macdonald notes:

> There are two theories of growth in this industry. One is ours, where you plan to grow at a sustainable and affordable rate and put market share low on the list of objectives. Then there are others who thought that this rate was inadequate and took risky measures to increase their growth and market share. They were moths around a candle on that one.[7]

Union Camp and Crown Cork & Seal have also emphasized profits rather than size. At Crown Cork & Seal, management decided not to continue to compete in the oil can market even though the company had a 50% share of this segment. Despite the loss of sales, management decided that it had other more profitable opportunities and that new materials such as fiberfoil provided too great a threat in the motor oil can business.

During the 1973–1975 recession, Union Camp's management resisted customer pressure to produce a broad line of white papers. To Union Camp, the extra sales could not be justified by the added production costs.

Diversify Cautiously. Unlike many of their larger competitors, most successful low market share companies are not diversified. For example, both Continental Can and American Can have diversified widely, while Crown Cork & Seal has continued to concentrate on making metal cans. When successful low market share companies do diversify, they tend to enter closely related areas. For example, Union Camp has diversified into wood-based chemicals and retail distribution of building materials. Union Camp's vice chairman, Samuel Kinney, Jr., explained another element of Union Camp's diversification strategy:

> You must have someone in the parent organization who really understands the [new] business before it gets heavy. Other paper companies have had troubles along these lines. They had these MBAs who, I am sure, were intelligent. But once they failed, there wasn't a damn thing anyone could do back at headquarters. They didn't know the business, and they were completely out on a limb.[8]

Ubiquitous Chief Executive

The final characteristic of these companies we found striking is the pervasive influence of the chief executive. John Connelly of Crown Cork & Seal, Alexander Calder of Union Camp, and Ray Macdonald of Burroughs have all been described as extremely strong-willed individuals who are involved in almost all aspects of company operations.

To a large extent, it is understandable that leaders of low market share companies are dynamic, tough people who see obstacles as challenges and enjoy competing in unorthodox ways. It may simply take a strong-willed leader to convince and inspire an organization to "beat the odds."

This is not to imply that the chief executives of large share companies are not also strong-willed, dynamic, and tough. But most often these executives work with teams of other senior managers and limit their responsibilities to a few key areas. In successful low share companies, the influence of the chief executive often extends beyond formulating and communicating an ingenious strategy to actually having a deep involvement in the daily activities of the business.

At Union Camp, for example, Calder still retains responsibility for sales and marketing. Macdonald of Burroughs is deeply involved in both the development and the marketing of new products.

Of course, the pervasive influence of the chief executive in low market share business makes the problem of management succession an extremely difficult one. Connelly, now 72, has yet to retire or to pick a successor. While Macdonald retired in December 1977, he has retained the position of executive committee chairman, and analysts are already questioning Burroughs's prospects without him. Though reports differ about what the actual situations are, only Union Camp's Calder seems to have been able to delegate significant responsibilities and to practice a more participatory style of leadership than the others have.

Alternative to Growth

Although this article has an optimistic tone, we must acknowledge that there are some serious obstacles a low market share business must overcome. These usually include small research budgets, few economies of scale in manufacturing, little opportunity to distribute products directly, little public and customer recognition, and difficulties in attracting capital and ambitious employees. Moreover, previous research indicates that, on the average, the return on investment of low share businesses is significantly less than that of businesses with high market shares.

We have made no attempt to refute these research findings or to deny the obstacles facing low share businesses. But we have sought to demonstrate that many of the inferences being drawn from these findings are simplistic and misleading. Simply put, not all low share businesses are "dogs."

Rather, we have found that a small market share is not necessarily a handicap; it can be a significant advantage that enables a company to compete in ways that are unavailable to its larger rivals. We believe that these findings are significant.

For the independent low share company, these findings represent an alternative to bankruptcy and the high costs and risk associated with efforts to increase market share.

To the large diversified company, the findings suggest that formal planning systems must go beyond simply placing each division in one of several categories. Categorization schemes can provide a useful conceptual handle for top executives, but the best planning systems are those which encourage and enable a division to seek the best fit between the opportunities in the competitive environment and the particular skills, strengths, and resources each division possesses.

In sum, our findings indicate that, in a division or in an independent company, management's first objective should be to earn the maximum return on invested capital rather than to achieve the highest possible market share.

Notes

1. Robert D. Buzzell, Bradley T. Gale, and Ralph G. M. Sultan, "Market Share — A Key to Profitability," *Harvard Business Review,* January–February 1975, p. 97.
2. See *Perspectives on Experience* (Boston: Boston Consulting Group, Inc., 1968 and 1970) for a description of a typical classification system.
3. For a more comprehensive description of Crown Cork & Seal, see E. Raymond Corey, "Key Options in Market Selection and Product Planning," *Harvard Business Review,* September–October 1975, p. 119.
4. "Crown Cork & Seal and the Metal Container Industry," Harvard Business School case study, ICCH No. 6-373-077 (Boston: Intercollegiate Case Clearinghouse, 1973), p. 30.

5. "Union Camp Corporation," Harvard Business School case study, ICCH No. 9-372-198 (Boston: Intercollegiate Case Clearinghouse, 1972), p. 6.

6. For an excellent discussion of the risks of attempting to build market share, see William E. Fruhan, Jr., "Pyrrhic Victories in Fights for Market Share," HBR September–October 1972, p. 100.

7. "How Ray Macdonald's Growth Theory Created IBM's Toughest Competition," *Fortune*, January 1977, p. 98.

8. "New Growth at Union Camp," *Dun's Review*, March 1975, p. 43.

24. Harvesting Strategies for Weak Products

Philip Kotler

A division manager in the XYZ Company broke the news to Jim Smith that the company had decided to "harvest" his business unit. Smith had been running his business in the "maintenance mode" for years. Now he was told that his budget for the next year would be cut 20 percent, yet he should not let sales revenue slip by more than 10 percent.

Smith was shaken by the company's decision, especially since he saw some new opportunities on the horizon. He outlined them to the division manager, but in the end the "harvest" decision stuck. Top management was set on reallocating resources from his business to other businesses with a brighter future in the company. Smith's mandate was to maximize the short-term cash flow from his business. Smith thought over his options: raising prices, cutting promotional expenses, reducing product quality, or reducing technical service. He decided in favor of a personal option: He quit.

The decision to harvest a business entity — whether a division, product line, specific product, or brand — is clearly a controversial step. After all, management has three other options for handling a weak business entity. It can pour money into this unit to make it stronger (building strategy), it can budget enough money to maintain sales and profits at the present level (maintenance strategy), or it can abandon the business (divestment strategy). Harvesting the business is a fourth choice by which the company decides to reduce its investment in a business while hoping to "harvest" reasonable earnings or cash flow.

Although much has been written about building, maintaining, and divesting strategies, little has been written on the theory and practice of

This article first appeared in *Business Horizons*, August 1978, pp. 15–22.

Philip Kotler is currently at the Graduate School of Management, Northwestern University.

harvesting. This neglect is surprising in view of the growing application of this strategy and the many subtle issues that it raises. General Electric was one of the first companies to assign harvesting missions on a planned basis to its weaker business entities.[1] The Boston Consulting Group popularized harvesting in application to what it called "weak cash cows."[2] H. J. Heinz Company uses the term "milkers" for those businesses that it wants to manage for cash flow. General Foods uses "harvest business" as one of its category management concepts. One business executive told me:

> Many businesses are attempting to make deliberate decisions using these four strategies, but this is all rather new and I'm not sure how well it has been thought out. Of the four, harvesting is most difficult because of the delicate balance required and also because it implies ultimate decline and liquidation. The decision to liquidate is much easier — get out of a bad situation and go on to something better.

Companies applying harvesting strategies have not always been happy with the results. Some business entities should not, in retrospect, have been harvested because total demand later turned around. Other businesses that were put into a harvesting pattern promptly nose-dived into oblivion and destroyed the cash flow expectation. Harvesting is not a strategy to be undertaken lightly. Let us consider the following questions:

- How does harvesting differ from maintaining a business on the one hand and abandoning a business on the other?
- What kinds of products and businesses should be harvested?
- What strategies are effective for harvesting a business?
- What is the best way to implement and control a harvesting program?

The Nature of Harvesting

Harvesting is not a newly discovered business strategy. The vice president of marketing for a major food company told me that his company has been harvesting products for years without ever calling it that. Unfortunately, the company seemed to have a knack for assigning entrepreneurial managers to manage harvested businesses and maintenance managers to manage growth businesses.

One of the first things to recognize about harvesting is that it is a fuzzy term. "Harvesting" conjures up the image of gathering up the crops after a long season of growth — which suggests, in the business context, that the product has matured and the company is now going to extract the remaining value from the business. Thus harvesting implies the sunset or twilight stage of a product or business in its life cycle. Milking — a term used interchangeably with harvesting — suggests drawing the "milk," or value, from an asset — the opposite of investing or feeding the asset. These two terms are semantically colorful but functionally fuzzy for business decision purposes.

For our purposes, I will define harvesting as *a strategic management decision to reduce the investment in a business entity in the hope of cutting costs and/or improving cash flow.* The company anticipates sales volume and/or market share declines but hopes that the lost revenue will be more than offset by the lowered costs. Management sees sales falling eventually to a core level of demand. The business entity will be divested if money cannot be made at this core level of demand or if the company's resources can produce a higher yield by being shifted elsewhere.

Harvesting steers a middle course between a maintenance and an abandonment objective. Maintenance of a business entity requires an adequate level of reinvestment to keep up product quality, plant size and efficiency, and customer services. A maintenance objective is appropriate for business units enjoying a stable market, a good market share, and an important position in the company's lineup. "Strong cash cows" are not harvested — they are maintained.

Harvesting differs from abandonment in that the latter decision calls for finding a buyer or arranging for asset liquidation. The company will normally prefer abandonment to harvesting for business units that are losing money. If the company cannot find a buyer, it may sometimes harvest the business temporarily.

The main reason for harvesting a business entity is to pull out cash that can be put to better uses in the company. Too many of yesterday's breadwinners absorb company resources at the expense of keeping the organization from focusing on high opportunity areas. As Peter Drucker has suggested, "When an organization focuses on opportunity, also-rans have to make do with what they have or with less." Harvesting amounts to placing a tax on products that are going nowhere to support the creation of tomorrow's breadwinners.

It should be noted that harvesting can be implemented at different rates. Slow harvesting means very gradually reducing the budget support for the business unit so that it almost appears to be a maintenance strategy. Fast harvesting means substantially reducing the budget support for the business unit so that it almost appears to be an abandonment strategy. This distinction is reflected in Union Carbide's description of its Category 4 and 5 products.[3]

> *Category 4:* Strategic planning units (SPUs) are assigned to this category when the primary objective, and the criterion on which performance is evaluated, is maximization of cash flow. These SPUs will receive limited resource support.
> *Category 5:* SPUs in this category are candidates for withdrawal either because of competitive weaknesses, incongruence with corporate objectives, or projections of unsatisfactory financial performance. These SPUs will receive limited resource support for a defined period of time.

Thus one of the major decisions in a harvesting strategy is the rate at which investment in the business entity should be reduced.

Identifying What's Harvestable

Management gets interested in harvesting a business under three different circumstances. In the first instance, the business may be one that is losing money in spite of a heavy budget and which has little prospect for a turnaround. Harvesting seems to be a way to lower the costs and cut losses. However, it can be argued that termination may make more sense in this case than harvesting. In one executive's words, "It is hard to milk a dog. The best thing is to get rid of the dog."

In the second instance, the business may be making money but not going anywhere, and the company may see better opportunities elsewhere. So instead of maintaining the cash cow indefinitely, the management decides to milk the cow for needed funds to invest in more promising areas.

In the third instance, the business entity may be a product that is about to become obsolete. Management will soon have a replacement product ready and therefore decides to harvest the existing product. A divisional manager at General Electric told me:

> If a dominant product of ours is facing sharp price cutting by competitors, we won't necessarily lower our price to save our market share. If we have a new and better product in the works, we will lose market share knowing this is only temporary. We will harvest the old product until the new one comes along.

Thus, a harvesting strategy may be resorted to in quite different business situations. There is no single indicator that reliably points to candidates for harvesting. Any identification scheme must rest on a multiple set of indicators. The following seven indicators are the most important:

1. The business entity is in a stable or declining market.
2. The business entity has a small market share, and building it up would be too costly; or it has a respectable market share that is becoming increasingly costly to defend or maintain.
3. The business entity is not producing especially good profits or may even be producing losses.
4. Sales would not decline too rapidly as a result of reduced investment.
5. The company has better uses for the freed-up resources.
6. The business entity is not a major component of the company's business portfolio.
7. The business entity does not contribute other desired features to the business portfolio such as sales stability or prestige.

If all seven conditions are present, the business entity appears ideal for harvesting. If fewer conditions are met, the harvesting decision becomes more debatable.

Indicator three warrants a comment. The actual impact of a harvesting decision on profits should be evaluated on both an incremental and fully-allocated basis. If, by reducing sales volume, allocated corporate expense carried by that business is reduced and the noncancellable portion is spread to other growing parts of the corporation, there could be an attractive paper profit improvement but not a penny more in the bank.

Indicator four is perhaps the hardest to evaluate. What will happen to sales volume and revenue if the harvesting decision is implemented? Much depends on the specific harvesting strategy chosen and on the speed and vigor of competitive reaction. Ideally, sales should not fall far below their current level, at least in the short run. If they are expected to fall precipitously, the company should consider instead a "maintain or abandon" decision.

One clue as to where sales will settle can be found by looking at the number of entering and exiting customers from period to period. Suppose 15 percent of the customers in a typical period are new. When the budget is cut, the percentage of new customers will fall since the company will probably reduce its spending to attract new customers. Suppose, also, that old customers fall away at the rate of 5 percent each period. This customer loss rate will continue after harvesting is introduced, and may accelerate if price is pushed up or product quality and service are noticeably reduced. By estimating the likely impact of the particular harvesting strategy on the customer attraction and holding rates, respectively, management can develop a "guestimate" of the expected sales decline.

Some harvested products have displayed a remarkable staying power long after their marketing support levels have been reduced or removed. Consider the following:

> Bristol-Myers sold the venerable Ipana toothpaste brand rights to two entrepreneurs who continued to produce it and to stock distributors while stopping all advertising. The brand's sales continued for years at a "hard core" level, making good profits for the two entrepreneurs.[4]

> General Foods produced La France (a bluing agent) and Satina (a starch) long after they were superseded by more effective aerosol products, and they continued to sell — at somewhat reduced levels — with virtually no marketing support.

> Lifebuoy, a successful soap in the 1940s, fell into disfavor later because of its strong medicinal smell. Yet Lever Brothers continues to distribute Lifebuoy with virtually no advertising or promotional support. Because the product is priced higher on a per-ounce basis than

many leading soaps, it produces enough profit for the company to justify its continuation.

General Electric decided several years ago to harvest its artillery manufacturing division located in Vermont. Although the division was profitable, GE did not want to risk bad public relations by getting deeper into the arms business. In spite of reducing its investment over a number of years, letting the plant run down, doing little research and development, and raising prices, GE found the demand for these products persisting at a high level. Ironically, the decision to harvest produced a substantial increase in profits.

Thus, the sales of a product can decline to a level of "petrified demand," the term suggested by one marketing investigator as a contingent stage in the product life cycle following a sales decline.[5]

Preparing a Harvesting Plan

The marketing plan for harvesting a product should contain the same elements that are found in any marketing plan. The manager decides, or is told, to sell a certain volume or produce a certain revenue with a stated budget. If objectives are set for both volume and revenue, the setting of a certain price in the harvesting strategy is implied. If only a revenue goal is set, the harvesting manager is free to set the price-volume objectives on the basis of his or her understanding of the demand curve.

The harvesting manager faces a number of options in formulating a plan to achieve the given sales and profit objectives. Every line item in the budget is potentially reducible. One useful way of classifying the available actions is by their degree of competitive visibility. Ideally, the harvested business does not want to alert competitors to its intention. Reducing the plant and equipment expenditures and reducing research and development expenditures are two actions that have minimal competitive visibility. These actions are normally not detectable by the competition. A more visible action would be to reduce certain marketing expenses such as sales force effort or advertising effort. If these expenses are reduced in select cities where there is lower profitability to begin with, they would not necessarily alert competitors to a harvesting intention. Still another action is to raise the product's price. The most visible indications of a harvesting intention are actions taken to trim the quality of the product, reduce the number of items in the line, or cut certain services. If, furthermore, price is raised along with service and marketing cuts, this could clearly indicate a harvesting strategy.

Although a harvesting decision calls for reduced levels of marketing support, the marketing tools at the given resource levels must be handled creatively in order to keep sales as high as possible. It is a good idea, for example, for management to occasionally "splash" some advertising. Sporadic spurts of advertising will recapture consumer and dealer attention and indicate an intention to continue the product in the line. In the same vein, the company should extend occasional deals to the trade to maintain its interest in stocking the product. It is even conceivable that packaging might be freshened or the advertising message altered in order to maintain as much interest in the brand as possible.

If the harvest manager decides on a fast harvest, the best move is to cut all plant, equipment, and research and development expenditures; reduce the marketing budget; reduce product quality and service; and raise prices sharply. This will produce a large cash flow increase, albeit for only a short time. If the harvest manager decides on a slow harvest, the first stage calls for expenditure reductions in plant, equipment, and research and development. Later, marketing expenditures can be reduced and prices slightly raised. Still later, product quality and service can be trimmed. This approach produces a smaller increased cash flow but one lasting over a longer period.

Formulating the optimal harvesting plan is not easy. Considerations will differ according to whether the business entity is a division, product line, product, or item. If the business entity is a single product, the management may be able to test alternative harvesting strategies by trying them out in different cities to gauge their impact on sales and profits. If the business entity is a division, the decision has more finality, involves more cost and more people, and must include a larger set of considerations than does the decision to harvest a single product.

Implementing the Harvesting Plan

Company management can proceed to implement a harvesting decision in one of three ways. The first way is for management to gradually reduce the budget of the business entity's manager without claiming to harvest the business. As George C. Michael has written, "It is the policy of several corporate managements not to disclose to operating-level management a formal decision to harvest or withdraw support from a product line in order to avoid friction or loss of morale at that level." It can use all kinds of excuses, such as tight money, the need to finance other parts of the company, or the amount of current uncertainty surrounding the business. The manager will be upset about the budget crunch, but not as demoralized as he would be if informed of the harvesting decision. The cost of doing things this way, however, is to cause erratic planning from year to year and a loss of the unit manager's confidence in corporate management.

The second way to implement a harvesting decision is to appoint a new manager to head the business unit, one who is an experienced harvester.

Just as some executives are good at producing growth and others at maintaining sales, still others are good harvesters. The problem with this solution is that these harvesting managers become well known inside and outside of the company and signal the company's decision to harvest the business. The harvesting executive's appearance, like that of the Grim Reaper, has serious repercussions for morale and productivity. It might be better to use him as a backdoor consultant than to give him operating responsibilities.

The third way calls for top management to inform the business unit manager of the harvesting decision. Top management will present the reasoning in the light of all the indicators of a harvesting situation. The unit manager will normally ask for a chance to argue against this decision and should be given this opportunity. If the unit manager can convince company management that the business has more potential than they recognize, they may be willing to change their mind and provide adequate funds on a trial basis.

When the unit manager and company management agree on a harvest decision, the decision should be implemented as inconspicuously as possible. The unit manager may share the decision with one or two close associates, but it is not advisable to spread the word broadly. Employee morale is likely to deteriorate in a business unit that is programmed for harvesting. More able employees may leave for other jobs, while others may slacken their productivity.

However, if the company is large and can reassign employees to other jobs, the demoralization impact will be lessened. The unit manager will be judged on the ability to meet the revenue and cash flow objectives set for the harvested business. The manager's reward is based on success in accomplishing the planned objectives. At General Electric, the harvest manager receives a bonus based on meeting the harvesting objectives, with 72 percent of the weight based on current financial results, 16 percent on future benefit performance, and 12 percent on other factors.[6] If the business is harvested successfully, the manager's career opportunities will be as good as those facing other managers in the company.

Competitors must be prevented, as long as possible, from learning of the harvesting decision. Competitors will normally increase their attack on a business that has been put into a harvesting mode. They will increase their marketing expenditures and lower their prices, forcing the harvested unit to "put up or shut down." The harvest manager will need reinforcements to fight back or will have to consider product abandonment. Therefore, competitors must be kept guessing about management's real intention.

Is it possible to hide the harvesting decision from the competitors for very long? This varies in different industries. A consumer packaged goods executive said that his company always made an effort to minimize the visibility of the harvest decision but went on to say:

I also believe that the decision to harvest or not to harvest must assume that competition will learn of the decision instantaneously. If the success of our harvesting strategy depends on competition not learning of our decision for some period of time, divestiture is a more appropriate course of action.

The company will also want to keep customers in the dark about the harvesting as long as possible. Customers will lose their confidence in a company that has decided to let its plant run down, stop its search for product improvements, reduce its sales force and service, and in general, take steps that reduce the value of the offer. To the extent that customers learn of the harvesting decision, their rate of switching to competitors will accelerate and bring about a faster sales deterioration than anticipated.

Monitoring the Decision

A harvesting decision must not be undertaken lightly. It should be based on convincing indicators that the business should be harvested. Once decided, the company should stick to this decision unless there is overwhelming new evidence that the decision should be reviewed. A company that vacillates between a harvesting and a maintenance decision — and even a growth decision — is responding too much to current events. It finds itself building up market share at a great cost after giving it up so easily.

At the same time, the company has to be alert to signs that the harvesting decision may have been a mistake and that profits can be made by reversing the decision. This can happen under two different circumstances. First, management may discover that its decision was based on erroneous information about the current situation. The present sales potential may have been underestimated, or the costs of doing business may have been overestimated. Or management may have thought that a competitor was coming into the market or that a new technology was going to make the business obsolete.

Second, management may have made the correct decision at the time, but new factors caused the marketing environment to change drastically. The sudden onset of inflation and recession in the early 1970s led a lot of consumers to rediscover less expensive products whose sales had been slipping in the affluent 1960s, products like oatmeal, Kool-Aid, and home permanents. Price-conscious consumers migrated to products and brands which in many cases had been put into a harvesting mode. Increased publicity about public health problems was another factor leading consumers to shift to neglected products such as filter-tipped cigarettes and decaffeinated coffee. One frequent argument for harvesting instead of terminating a product is that sudden macroenvironmental changes may bring the product back into favor. At the same time, this argument is used too often by management as an excuse for not vigorously pursuing new opportunities.

Harvesting is not so much a new strategy as a fuzzy strategy. Companies have been using it for years without having a systematic grasp of its principles and procedures. The Boston Consulting Group, General Electric, and other companies have recently called attention to this strategy. However, very little is known about what, when, and how to harvest.

Most companies today manage a line of products in different stages of their life cycle. They deserve differential resource support depending on their profit outlook and their importance in the company's product portfolio. Between the decision to maintain a product and to phase out a product is the decision to phase it down. Reducing the support given to a product, if the reduction is going to kill the product overnight, does not make sense. However, reducing the support makes sense if the cost can be brought down without sales falling by as much. This is the harvesting solution. It calls for the effective identification of those products that warrant harvesting, the development of an optimal harvesting plan, and the implementation of a harvesting action program that does not alert competitors or alarm employees or customers. As companies gain more experience with harvesting, they will place more of their products in this decision mode and presumably enjoy comparable increases in economic efficiency.

Notes

1. See "Strategic Planning: Three New Slants," *General Electric Monogram,* November–December 1973: 2–6.
2. The Boston Consulting Group, *The Product Portfolio,* No. 66, 1970.
3. David S. Hopkins, *Business Strategies for Problem Products* (New York: The Conference Board, 1977): 8.
4. "Abandoned Trademark Turns a Tidy Profit for Two Minnesotans," *Wall Street Journal,* October 27, 1969: 1.
5. George C. Michael, "Product Petrification: A New Stage in the Life Cycle Theory," *California Management Review,* Fall 1971: 88–91.
6. Michael G. Allen, "Diagramming G.E.'s Planning for What's Watt," *Planning Review,* September 1977: 8.

25. SBUs: Hot, New Topic in the Management of Diversification

William K. Hall

It started in 1971 in the executive offices at General Electric, the world's most diversified company. Corporate management at GE had been plagued during the 1960s with massive sales growth, but little profit growth. Using 1962 as an index of 100, dollar sales drew to 180 by 1970; however, earnings per share fluctuated without growth between 80 and 140, while return on assets fell from 100 to 60. Thus, in 1971, GE executives were determined to supplement GE's vaunted system of management decentralization with a new, comprehensive system for corporate planning.

The resulting system was based upon the new concept of strategic business units — SBUs, as they are now commonly called. Not only did this new system change the direction of planning at GE; it subsequently affected the corporate strategies and the planning processes in hundreds of other diversified firms around the world as well.

The SBU concept of planning is an intuitively obvious one, based on the following principles:

The diversified firm should be managed as a "portfolio" of businesses, with each business unit serving a clearly defined product-market segment with a clearly defined strategy.

Each business unit in the portfolio should develop a strategy tailored to its capabilities and competitive needs, but consistent with the overall corporate capabilities and needs.

The total portfolio of business should be managed by allocating capital and managerial resources to serve the interests of the firm as a

This article first appeared in *Business Horizons*, February 1978, pp. 17–25.

When this article was published, William K. Hall was professor of management at Michigan State University.

whole — to achieve balanced growth in sales, earnings, and asset mix at an acceptable and controlled level of risk. In essence, the portfolio should be designed and managed to achieve an overall corporate strategy.

As might be expected, the successful implementation of this intuitive approach provides a number of complex management choices and challenges. As a result, a heightened understanding of the benefits and costs of the SBU approach to the management of diversification is essential to the practice of general management. The objective of this article is to add to this understanding by summarizing the principles behind the SBU approach, and by examining the alternatives, benefits, and problems encountered to date in its successful implementation.

A Look at Traditional Planning

In order to put the SBU concept of planning into a proper context, it is necessary to review briefly the traditional planning and resource allocation processes in large, diversified firms. These traditional processes grew out of the massive movement toward divisionalization and decentralization during the period 1920–1965. This movement began as a response to growth, diversity, and overall complexity in the large, diversified firm. In essence, the movement was essential, as one general manager put it, "to tailor responsibilities down to the size where a general manager could get his arms around them."

As the decentralized, divisionalized structure matured in the 1960s, formal planning became a way of life in the well-managed, diversified firm. Typically, the approach was initiated with the delineation of overall corporate mission, objectives, targets, and environmental assumptions. These were disseminated annually to the various divisions, where plans, projections, and sub-unit targets were developed as a response to these guidelines. Then a delicate, iterative process of "bottom up — top down" negotiation and consensus-seeking eventually resulted in an "approved plan" for the upcoming planning period.

This approach to formal planning had a number of advantages:

It forced divisional managers to be explicit in their target-setting and goal-seeking, often on a profit center or investment center basis.

It allowed the corporate entity to add up the divisional pieces in advance, adjusting resource allocations and pushing divisions toward different targets when discrepancies against corporate objectives arose.

It allowed the development of sophisticated control systems to project, measure, and interpret deviations from the planned divisional results.

At the same time, however, this approach to planning and control was not without deficiencies. Divisional plans were frequently either overly optimistic or overly pessimistic. Depending upon the corporate "culture," they typically were based on one of three scenarios: extrapolated results, a philosophy that "next year things will get better," or a philosophy that "it's better to plan things a little conservatively so that we come out looking good at the end." Often, management commitment to plans was incomplete — either at the corporate or divisional level. Variances were frequently explained by unforeseen external factors, inadequate divisional resources, or deficiencies in the target-setting process itself. The total corporate plan, formed by adding up the divisional plans, often left corporate management without a clear grasp of either divisional or corporate strategy. Moreover, division plans were frequently approved (or rejected) without an explicit understanding of the strategy behind the plans or the risks and opportunities associated with this strategy. As one divisional general manager commented, "Planning without an understanding of corporate strategy was a lot like throwing darts in a darkened room."

In short, the traditional corporate plan almost always contained notebooks full of facts, figures, and forecasts, but it frequently failed to digest these in a way that provided key insights into strategies and business success factors at both the divisional and the corporate levels. The result, for many firms, was a decade of "profitless growth."

The SBU Alternative

In an attempt to deal with inadequacies in its traditional planning process, General Electric, guided by a task force of senior general managers and assisted by a team of management consultants, developed the SBU alternative to corporate planning. This process, now applied under a variety of names and in a variety of ways in other diversified firms, is almost always based on four steps:

- identification of strategic business elements, or units,
- strategic analysis of these units to ascertain their competitive position and long-term product-market attractiveness,
- strategic management of these units, given their overall positioning, and
- strategic follow-up and reappraisal of SBU and corporate performance.

Identifying SBUs

The fundamental concept in the identification of SBUs is to identify the discrete, independent product-market segments served by the firm. In essence, the idea is to decentralize on the basis of strategic elements, not on the basis of size or span of control. This can be accomplished, as one general manager observed, by "identifying natural business units which correspond to the degrees of freedom a manager has available to compete."

Thus, within GE, nine groups and forty-eight divisions were reorganized into forty-three strategic business units, many of which crossed traditional group, divisional, and profit center lines. For example, in three separate divisions, food preparation appliances were merged as a single SBU serving the "housewares" market. A very small part of the Industrial Components Division was broken out as a separate SBU, serving a distinct industrial product-market niche in the machine tool industry. Within Union Carbide, another firm adopting the SBU approach, fifteen groups and divisions were decomposed into 150 "strategic planning units," and these were then recombined into nine new "aggregate planning units."

Ideally, an SBU should have primary responsibility and authority for managing its basic business functions: engineering, manufacturing, marketing, and distribution. In practice, however, traditions, shared facilities and distribution channels, manpower constraints, and business judgments have resulted in significant deviations from this concept of autonomy. In General Foods, for instance, strategic business units were originally defined on a product line basis, even though several products served overlapping markets and were produced in shared facilities. Later, these product-oriented SBUs were redefined into menu segments, with SBUs like breakfast food, beverage, main meal, dessert, and pet foods targeted toward specific markets, even though these, too, shared common manufacturing and distribution resources.

The General Foods example, and examples from many other firms adopting the SBU concept, point out that identification and definition are ultimately managerial decisions reflecting philosophical and pragmatic resolutions of the question: "What are our businesses and what do we want them to be?" As one general manager succinctly put it, "In our company an SBU ultimately becomes whatever subdivision corporate management wants it to be."

Strategic Positioning

The subsequent process of positioning an SBU is typically driven by two criteria: long-term attractiveness of the product-market segment served by the SBU, and the SBU's competitive position (business strength) within that product-market segment. A conceptual 2 × 2 matrix illustrating this positioning is shown in the following figure:

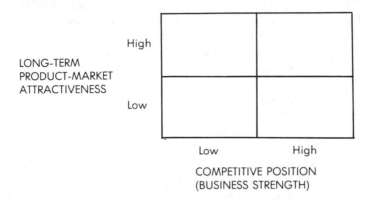

LONG-TERM
PRODUCT-MARKET
ATTRACTIVENESS

High

Low

Low   High

COMPETITIVE POSITION
(BUSINESS STRENGTH)

Here again, the scales of measurement and the precision of measurement along both scales vary significantly in practice. Since the choice of a measurement scale is more important then the degree of detail in measurement along the chosen scale, it will be discussed in some detail.[1]

Long-Term Product-Market Attractiveness.   Two distinctive philosophies have evolved in ranking SBUs on this dimension. The first uses a single measure, almost always defined as the long-term projected real growth rate of the product-market segment.[2] (The split between high and low growth rates is sometimes arbitrarily set at 10 percent; other times it is set at the level of growth of the economy as a whole or at the level of growth of some sector of the economy.) Support for the growth rate definition of product-market attractiveness is clearly based upon a life cycle theory. With such a theory, attractive product-market segments are those in the development or "take-off" stage, and less attractive segments are in maturity or decline. Ideally, the long-term growth rate measures life cycle position and, hence, long-term product-market attractiveness.

The second methodology for assessing product-market attractiveness uses a set of measures, some qualitative and others quantitative. There, the choice of measures and the actual assessment of SBU position against these measures can be made at the SBU level, the corporate level, or jointly. In corporate practice, I have seen all of these possibilities being utilized. At General Electric, for example, SBU product-market attractiveness is determined by examining and projecting ten criteria: segment size, segment growth rate (units and real dollars), competitive diversity, competitive structure, segment profitability, and technological, social, environmental, legal, and human impacts.

Competitive Position (Business Strength).   As in the case of assessing long-term attractiveness, two alternative philosophies have evolved for ranking competitive position. Here again, the first is based on a single measure, generally defined as segment share or as segment share relative to competition.[3] Support for this single factor concept comes from the theory of experience curves, an approach to strategy formulation developed by the Boston Consulting Group.[4]

This theory suggests that the unit costs of production, marketing, and distribution drop proportionately (in real terms) each time total output (experience) doubles. This decrease in unit costs presumably comes from learning effects, scale effects, substitution of lower cost factor inputs, redesign, and technology. Thus, if one believes that costs in an SBU are on an experience curve, it follows that there should be strong relationships between high market share (experience), lower costs, and higher profitability.[5] In essence, high market share (or relative market share) becomes a surrogate measure of business strength relative to competition within the product-market segment.

In many firms, however, the market-share–experience-curve approach to assessing competitive position is viewed as overly simplistic or even erroneous. In this regard, a number of arguments have emerged:

> The competition with the most experience may be the "oldest" competitor. If this older firm has dedicated plant and equipment, it may not be able to exploit new, cost-reducing technology as rapidly as an emerging competitor.

> Shared experience obtained from other related product-market segments may be as important as accumulated output in lowering costs. (That is, experience cannot be measured independently for each product-market segment).

> External factors, technology breakthroughs, and other events may be as important as accumulated output in lowering (or in raising) costs.

In those firms that have either partially or totally rejected the experience-curve rationale, multiple measures of business strength have emerged. These measures are generally a mixture of qualitative and quantitative factors, and, depending upon the company, they can be defined and assessed either at the corporate or at the SBU level. At General Electric, for example, competitive position is evaluated on the following dimensions: segment size and SBU growth rate, share, profitability, margins, technology position, skill or weaknesses, image, environmental impact, and management.

Strategic Handling. The strategic plan for an SBU is ultimately derived from its position with respect to long-term attractiveness (potential) and competitive position. Four combinations are possible.

Low Potential/Low Position. An SBU in this category is clearly an unattractive member of the firm's portfolio for both the short run and long run.

Furthermore, an infusion of resources to improve position will still leave the SBU in a low-potential segment. In essence, the SBU in this category is unworthy of major future commitments.

In the evolving jargon of the field, this "low/low" SBU is typically given the title of "cash trap," "mortgage," or "dog." Regardless of the title, the recommended strategic handling is always the same — manage the SBU to maximize short-term cash flow. In some cases this strategy can be accomplished through closing the SBU down or through rapid divestiture. In other cases, it can be handled by "harvesting" cash from the operation through ruthless cost cutting, short-term pricing policies, and sometimes through giving up market share and growth opportunities that absorb short-term cash.

Low Potential/High Position.   Here an SBU is serving an unattractive product-market segment from a position of strength. Typically called a "bond" or "cash cow" in SBU parlance, the recommended strategic handling is to "milk" the entity for cash, although without the aggressiveness with which one would handle a "dog." The idea of selective cash "milking" is to preserve market position while generating dollars in an efficient fashion to support other growth-targeted elements of the portfolio. Carefully targeted growth segments, stabilized pricing, differentiated products, selective cost reduction, less creative marketing, and selective capital investment are all means of achieving this goal.

High Potential/Low Position.   SBU elements in this category are typically termed "question marks," "problem children," or "sweepstakes" competitors. These elements are in an awkward position, for if they do not strengthen their competitive position, someone will almost certainly attack their product-market segment aggressively. Yet, the costs of strengthening their competitive position may not warrant the effort.

Thus, these elements are in a "get up or get out" strategic handling situation. Rigorous planning alternatives must be generated, evaluated, and costed. And then, the SBUs in this category must be moved, either upward or out of the firm's portfolio through divestiture or consolidation.

High Potential/High Position.   SBUs in this category would seem to have the best classification. As "stars" or "savings accounts," these represent the businesses that must be groomed for the long run. As such, they should be given the resources and corporate support to grow faster than the market segment in sales, profits, and cash flow.

The recommended strategic handling of portfolio SBU elements can be summarized as follows:

> Dogs and cash cows are managed for short-term cash flow. Over the long run, dogs are divested or eliminated, while cash cows ultimately become dogs as their competitive position declines.

Question marks must either get into the star category or get out of the portfolio. In the first case, they should make the move with carefully developed strategic plans so that major risk elements are identified and contained.

Stars are short-run cash consumers and are managed for long-term position. Over the long run, as their segment attractiveness ultimately declines, they will become cash cows, generating cash to support the next round of stars.

Strategic Follow-up and Reappraisal

In most explanations of the SBU process, the typical discussion stops after an explanation of SBU identification, classification, and handling. Unfortunately, failure by corporations to exploit the last element — follow-up and reappraisal — has probably resulted in most of the frustrations and failures encountered with the SBU process to date. To be successful, the SBU process must be iterative and ongoing, incorporating strategic planning and reappraisal, as well as managerial control.

Strategic Planning.   Simply saying that a business is a star or cash cow will not make anything happen. Once a decision on strategic handling has been reached in this regard, detailed strategic goals and action plans must be evaluated and implemented. Such planning clearly offers alternatives; as one manager put it, "Some companies forget that there's more than one kind of cow." Detailed analysis and conceptual thinking are both required here, focusing on key success factors and major risk elements apt to be encountered along the way.

Strategic Reappraisal.   A one-time evaluation and strategic positioning are also insufficient. In most companies in which SBUs are successful, strategic reappraisal is routinely conducted on an annual or biannual basis. In one large company, for instance, each SBU manager must completely reassess his competitive position and strategy in an annual presentation before corporate management. Simultaneously, a staff review group will present and evaluate alternatives to this positioning on a total portfolio basis.

In other organizations, such as GE, reappraisal is initiated when a strategic "trigger point" — an external factor projected to have a significant impact on SBU performance — occurs. One GE manager described this system as follows: "For each business unit we require that management identify the sensitivity to these key external factors. These sensitivities must be identified in advance, and specific contingency plans must be ready in advance. Thus, we at least face the future with our eyes open!"

Managerial Control.   Senior managers in many large firms also argue that the SBU approach to the management of diversification requires major changes in systems for budgeting, capital appropriation, measurement, reward, and managerial development. One general manager described the problem in his firm as follows: "To me it makes little sense to go through a sophisticated SBU analysis and then continue to allocate capital simply on discounted rate of return. Moreover, it makes even less sense to continue to measure and reward SBU management on annual performance against a profit budget."

Very little information is available on the modifications in managerial control that accompany the SBU concept.[6] However, General Electric has provided some interesting information on their systems in public sources.

SBU control systems with GE are based on key success indicators (called business screens). For each SBU, performance measurements are monitored on five broad criteria: market position, competitive position, profitability/cash flow, technological position, and external trigger points. Standards for each criteria are set and weighted differently, depending upon how the SBU is categorized. In addition, a "quality of performance" ranking is maintained as a measure of how well individual SBU managers have attained their standards of performance. As one GE manager put it, "the maturity of our SBU planning process could be measured when we began to bridge the gap between budgeting and the strategic plan."

The measurement and reward of managerial performance was perhaps the biggest shift in the revised GE system. Under the previous system of reward, GE had compensated key managers on the basis of residual earnings — controllable profits during the planning period less a charge for corporate services and capital. Under the SBU system, however, SBU managers in different sectors of the matrix are measured and compensated differentially according to a bonus schedule, as shown in the table.

SBU Classification	Current Performance (Residual Income)	Future Performance (Strategy)	Other Factors
Invest/Grow	40%	48%	12%
Selectivity	60	28	12
Harvest/Divest	72	16	12

Clearly, SBU elements with an invest-and-grow classification are being rewarded on the basis of long-term (strategic) contributions. While GE has recognized the difficulty of such a long-term appraisal, key managers in the company agree that an invest-and-grow manager can be evaluated and rewarded on the quality of his long-run strategy through a careful appraisal of his manpower plans, facilities plans, action programs, and competitive evaluation. As one GE manager described the system, "Of course, it has measurement problems, but so do most good compensation systems.

In the end, I'm convinced that our revised executive incentive compensation system is the key that will make the SBU process work."

Management development in GE has also shifted to reflect differential needs in differential business elements. Invest-and-grow business managers are developed to foster entrepreneurial characteristics. Cash cow (selectivity) business managers are developed to take sophisticated and hard looks at their businesses, and harvest and divest managers are developed with a heavy orientation toward experience, operations, and cost-cutting.

The philosophy behind the GE management system is a classical one: Effective strategy implementation decisions will be made only if managerial selection, appraisal, and incentives are consistent with the strategy and with the planned results. As one manager in a large, diversified company recently observed, "Most firms have gone only half way with the SBU concept — they position their product-market segments and then go right on rewarding and promoting managers on traditional criteria. In the end the companies which make the SBU concept work will be those which change all management systems; developing and rewarding SBU managers differentially depending upon their SBU position and the strategic handling which is appropriate for their element of the portfolio."

Pitfalls in SBU Analysis

Failure to Go All the Way

As discussed above, the failure to tie all management systems to the SBU approach is frequently a key pitfall in SBU analysis. In addition, there is the ever-present danger that short-term perturbations in the economy may drive invest-and-grow managers away from the long-term orientation required by the SBU approach. One senior manager commented on this problem as follows: "The 1974–1975 recession came when many companies were moving onto the SBU system. Unfortunately, indiscriminate cost cutting and cash conservation caused many of these firms to cover their heads with a blanket, going back to the 'good old ways' of doing business. In the end, the good companies of the 1980s will be those that stayed with their strategies during the recession — repositioning themselves in the short run to strengthen themselves for the long run."

Doctrinaire Approaches

There is a wide variety of alternatives for identifying product-market segments, for evaluating these segments, and for developing an SBU strategy vis-à-vis competition. The application of a single methodology in a doc-trinaire fashion is likely to create dissension, confusion, and misleading results. SBU-based planning, even more than traditional corporate planning, must be conducted to generate "multibusiness insights" — that is, to learn more about one's businesses than the competitor knows about his. As one manager succinctly observed, "The real payback from SBU planning is an intangible one — it comes slowly as you develop a strategic understanding of your businesses and your portfolio."

Transition Costs

Both the measurable and the hard-to-measure costs of moving from the traditional corporate planning process to the portfolio planning process must also be considered. Managers who have risen through the ranks of a firm to positions of leadership in groups and divisions are not apt to "jump for joy" when they are reorganized and retitled "dogs," "cows," or "question marks." Moreover, their subordinates are apt to be even more unsure as they assess their future employment, career development, and promotion prospects. One middle manager in a business redefined as a cash cow commented on this problem:

> I spent two years in an MBA program learning how to run a business as a profit/investment center. Now, suddenly I'm told to manage my department as a cash center.
>
> Then the corporation turns down a major expansion proposal from our division, reallocating investment funds to another set of businesses. I don't understand it, I don't like it, and I really wonder what my future looks like with the XYZ company.

In addition to these costs of managerial adjustment, there is some question as to whether traditionally trained managers can manage cows or dogs at all. A related question is whether or not a firm can develop and keep the diversified managerial talent necessary for managing diversified portfolio elements. And finally, "going all the way" with SBU implementation involves the high costs of adding new managerial systems or organization, planning, and control.

Transition costs can (and are) being handled in part by executive development programs within companies and within management education institutions. While these programs are useful — perhaps even essential — to a company shifting to the SBU philosophy, management transition takes time and involves some painful reallocations. It remains to be seen how much time and pain will be incurred as organizations shift and how many of these organizations will be able to endure these transition costs. The key issue, as one middle manager put it, will be "to convince managers that there are other ways to heaven than a star."

New Ventures and R&D

A fourth unresolved problem with the SBU approach to date involves corporate strategies toward new ventures and research and development — that is, toward the businesses of the future.

In theory, it would appear that R&D in a cash cow should be eliminated or restricted to short-term projects generating cost reductions. It is possible that a major R&D effort in a cow could result in major new markets or products that could ultimately turn the cow into a star (or lengthen the life during which the cow continues to generate cash). However, failure to maintain a competitive advantage in R&D within a cow could give competitors market leadership, accelerating, in effect, the cow's movement toward the dog category.

SBU theory would also seem to indicate that new ventures, R&D, and acquisition-merger policies should be directed at potential stars. The question is, how does one identify future stars in business segments where the firm has little or no experience, and should one develop these business segments internally or through acquisition-merger?

Determining the role of new technology and searching for stars of the future that are outside of the firm's existing portfolio are difficult — in theory and in practice. In essence, while the SBU philosophy has provided new insights into the management of existing businesses, new concepts are needed for managing additions to the portfolio effectively.

SBUs in Nondiversified Firms

It is obvious that SBU analysis has evolved as a powerful concept in the management of diversification. Still, while diversification has been a major trend throughout world corporations for the past quarter-century, many large, nondiversified businesses — even entire corporations — remain, in effect, single SBUs.

The question must be asked: Are there any concepts that would aid in strategy formulation within a nondiversified firm? Clearly there are some:

- consideration of resegmenting the existing single product-market segment into new segments to gain improved competitive position and segment attractiveness, and
- consideration of using cash flow from the existing single product-market segment to develop new stars — either through acquisition or through internal development (that is, manage the base business as a cow to feed the stars of the future).

While these ideas have conceptual merit, they are not without problems. Resegmentation takes time, money, and managerial skill. Diversification does also, and diversification raises the additional question of direction. Unfortunately, it is uncommon for the nondiversified firm to possess simultaneously all three elements — time, money, and skill in shifting strategies. Even when these three factors are present to some degree, reinvestment decisions in the base business tend to claim priorities on these scarce resources.

This strategic dilemma of the maturing, nondiversified firm is a major challenge to management and to society. While SBU analysis aids in understanding the dilemma, it has not as yet provided the conceptual framework to aid in the resolution.

There is little question that formal SBU analysis — identification, positioning, handling, and follow-up — provides new insights into the management of diversification. While the total number of diversified firms adopting some variant of this approach is unknown, one estimate is that 20 percent of the "Fortune 500" manufacturing firms are utilizing the concept. And while after only five years of experience it is too early to assess its impact, some testimonials provide a feel for preliminary management reaction:

> *General Electric:* "GE is growing rapidly as a result of its strong financial controls and marketing strategies. . . . Two basic failures — an absence of strategic planning and a dearth of financial controls have brought [their major domestic competition] to an [unfortunate] pass."[7]

> *Mead Paper:* "Our track record for earnings won't validate it, but we will make this thing (SBU analysis) work. You can't help but improve a company if you get rid of the losers and step up the winners. Our program is the common thread running through the company."[8]

> *Union Carbide:* "Business strategies that reflect the category assigned to the business have been developed for each strategic planning unit. . . . At present, about 60 percent of Union Carbide's total sales is concentrated in businesses in growth categories. For the period 1975 to 1979, about 80 percent of forecasted (capital) expenditures has been allocated to these businesses."[9]

> *Armco Steel:* "We [now] know the businesses we should pursue aggressively, those to maintain at the current level, and those to deemphasize or phase out. We can set goals that are reasonable . . . as they are attractive. And, importantly, we can have confidence in achieving our goals."[10]

However, the concept of portfolio management, like any other concept, must continue to evolve and mature as a philosophy for the effective management of diversification. And this evolution must come to grips with a number of issues that still are not fully resolved: tailoring and restructuring planning and control systems, avoiding doctrinaire approaches, and effectively managing transition costs. In addition, the handling of research and development and new ventures, as well as the application of the SBU concept to the nondiversified firm, provide major challenges to both business and business research.

There is little question, however, that the SBU approach to the management of diversification will leave a major mark — just as the movement to divisionalization and decentralization did twenty-five years ago. As one senior executive put it, "SBU analysis makes planning discontinuous. . . . It forces general managers to develop competitive and multibusiness insights at a strategic level. . . . And in the uncertain, rapidly changing world of the 1980s, this kind of strategic planning will become a way of life."

Notes

1. I have seen primarily 2×2 matrices, although 3×3 and 4×4 matrices are used in some organizations.
2. In a few cases, I have also seen projected long-term return on assets used as a measure of segment attractiveness.
3. Relative share is defined as the ratio of the SBU's dollar sales in the product-market segment to the dollar sales of the SBU's major competitor (or in some cases, competitors).
4. See, for example, the article by Hedley, "A Fundamental Approach to Strategy Development," *Long Range Planning* (December 1976), pp. 2–11.
5. See Buzzell, "Market Share: Key to Profitability," *Harvard Business Review* (January–February 1975), for an empirical study lending some support to this hypothesis.
6. Recently, Richard Bettis and I initiated a research project at the University of Michigan on these issues.
7. "The Opposites: GE Grows While Westinghouse Shrinks," *Business Week* (January 31, 1977), pp. 60–66.
8. J. W. McSwiney, Chairman, in "Mead's Technique to Sort Out the Losers," *Business Week* (March 11, 1972), pp. 124–127.
9. *1975 Annual Report*, Union Carbide Corporation, p. 6.
10. C. W. Verity, Chairman, in "Why a Portfolio of Businesses?" *Planning for Corporate Growth*, Planning Executives Institute (December 1974), pp. 54–60.

26. Wanted: A Manager to Fit Each Strategy

Business Week

Manpower planning and strategic planning have become two of the most popular catchphrases in management parlance. Of chief executives responding to a recent survey, 85% listed manpower planning as one of the most critical management undertakings for the 1980s. The popularity of strategic planning — and particularly the phase known as product portfolio analysis — is pointed up by the growing practice of diversified companies to identify products by market share and growth potential, and to base long-range capital allocations and operational goals on individual product life cycles. Under this concept, products with a high market share but a low growth potential, for example, are used as cash cows to fund star performers that may not yet be self-sufficient in cash flow.

A Joint Concept

All too often, however, chief executives speak of manpower and strategic planning as though they were separate functions. Management experts warn that corporations failing to link the two concepts may be sounding a death knell for both. The problem, as these experts perceive it, is that corporate manpower officers still tend to weigh specialized, product-line knowledge more heavily than general management skills in making executive assignments. They ignore the fact that the entrepreneurial type of manager who brought a product line from only, say, a 2% share of market to 20% in three years may not be the right person to continue managing that line with equal effectiveness once it becomes a mature product with little growth potential. Very likely the entrepreneurial type's forte is risk-

This article appeared in *Business Week*, February 25, 1980, pp. 166–173.

taking and innovating, while cost-cutting and pushing productivity — the essence of operating a mature, cash-generating business — may well be an anathema to him.

"Too often it's like trying to put your best guard into the quarterback's slot — it just can't work," says consulting psychologist Harry Levinson, of Belmont, Mass. Adds Richard J. Hermon-Taylor, vice-president of Boston Consulting Group: "I just don't think companies give a lot of explicit attention to the personality attributes of management when they are considering significant changes in strategy."

But some companies do recognize the link between manpower and strategic planning and are striving to match a manager's personal orientation or style with operating strategy.

Chase Manhattan Bank

When the trust manager retired, corporate management decided that the department, whose operations had been essentially stable, should focus on a more aggressive growth strategy. Instead of seeking a veteran banker, Chase hired a man whose main experience had been with International Business Machines Corp. "We felt he had that strong IBM customer marketing orientation," explains Alan F. Lafley, Chase's executive vice-president for human resources. Similarly, when Chase reoriented its retail banking business from a low-margin operation, in which the stress was on keeping down costs, to a more expansionary enterprise offering broader consumer financial services, it hired — because of his entrepreneurial skills — an executive who had been a division chief for a small industrial firm overseas. The former head of retail banking, who was viewed as a strong cost-cutter, is now successfully whipping some of Chase's European operations into better financial shape.

Heublein's United Vintners Inc.

The subsidiary split its wine operations in two in 1977, forming a premium wine division to stress quality over volume and a standard division to emphasize aggressive pricing and efficient volume production. The company chose a wine professional, Robert M. Furek, its previous marketing vice-president for all wines, to run the premium wine business. But it tapped Harold G. Spielberg, formerly personal products manager for Gillette Co., to be general manager of United's new Standard Wines Div. The sales staff was drastically reshuffled along similar quality-vs.-volume lines. "People in our premium wine company tend to have more wine background, while those in our standard wine company come out of consumer products and food companies," an official concedes.

Corning Glass Co.

It had projected fast growth for its fledgling optical fibers business over the next decade, and it shifted the head of the company's television tube business to direct the new venture. The growth of the tube business had leveled, and its manager had shown himself to have entrepreneurial flair, says Richard A. Shafer, Corning's director of management and professional personnel. "Optical fibers is clearly an entrepreneurial thing," Shafer explains. "We don't know what the i's and t's are, so we can't get someone who dots i's and crosses t's." A manager from Corning's more mature electronics business replaced the television tube head.

In December, ironically, Corning reshaped its electronics strategy, deciding that the market was starting to expand again, and that it needed a growth-oriented manager. It placed a manufacturing specialist who had "shown a great deal of flair in working with customers" in the top marketing slot for electronics, and, says Shafer, "it looks like he's turning it around."

Although such moves sound simple to arrange, many companies are reluctant to choose managers primarily on the basis of managerial orientation or personality traits. Appointing outsiders as managers can be demoralizing for executives who assumed they were next in line. Finding a challenging spot for a competent manager whose only fault is that his department's strategy has changed can also be a problem, particularly for companies that do not have the luxury of numerous divisions and products. Moreover, appraising an individual's managerial orientation or style and determining the type needed for a specific job are imprecise tasks at best. "Too few people are keeping adequate records of their employees' behavior patterns, and too few companies are writing job descriptions focusing on needed behaviors," Levinson says.

The TI Story

It can be a hit-or-miss proposition. For example, Texas Instruments Inc. has adopted a manpower planning policy that sounds as if it comes out of a behavioral science textbook. "As a product moves through different phases of its life cycle, different kinds of management skills become dominant," says Charles H. Phipps, manager of strategic planning. "It may be in the nature of an entrepreneurial manager to continue to take risks, but if the business gets too large, then top management can no longer tolerate wide swings in performance."

But although TI takes great pains to assess its managers in terms of personal orientation, it failed to capitalize on its early lead in integrated circuits largely because it misjudged the style needed to manage the product line. The story goes back two decades. Jack Kilby, one of TI's foremost researchers and a pioneer in integrated circuit technology, had been pegged as a brilliant scientist but not a strong manager. In 1959, when TI formally launched its IC development program, it placed an executive skilled in administrative chores in charge, with Kilby subordinate to him. The company ignored Kilby's "strong desire to lead his brainchild into the marketplace," Phipps recalls.

To placate Kilby, TI moved the new manager elsewhere in 1961 and let Kilby manage the fledgling IC department. Not surprisingly, Kilby stressed innovation and research at the expense of financial controls, and a few years later he was gently eased out of the department and back to research. Top management brought in managers from TI's technically mature germanium transistor department to provide tighter cost controls.

The tighter controls were introduced, but TI failed to recognize that Kilby's research orientation was really what the IC department needed at that stage. The new management team did not provide the technical push needed to get the IC operation, still in the development phase, off to a fast commercial start. When J. Fred Bucy became head of TI's semiconductor operations in 1967, he swept out most of the IC management and again put in technically oriented people. The result: TI went on to pioneer brilliantly in bipolar integrated circuits and became a competent follower, though not a leader, in the newer metal oxide semiconductor technology.

A chastened TI has since redoubled its efforts to match management orientation with job needs. Bucy, now president, personally reviews the records of the top 20% of TI's managers. But Phipps admits that the company still has no all-encompassing answer as to how to fit the manager to the strategy.

Several companies are trying hard to formalize programs that will at least keep them heading in the direction of making perfect managerial meshes. Chase's Lafley, a 27-year veteran of General Electric Co. who was recruited in 1975 to set up a strategic manpower planning program, says his group has "started at the top of the bank and addressed every one of the positions, checked the strategy of the division, and checked whether the people leading the divisions had the proper [behavioral] criteria." It has not been painless. Lafley says that 200 to 300 people have left the bank, "at least half of whom were encouraged to leave because their skills didn't fit our strategies."

"Growers" Versus "Undertakers"

At GE, an adherent of product portfolio analysis, strategic objectives for the company's wide-ranging products are defined as "grow," "defend," and "harvest," depending on the product life cycle. Now its general managers are being classified by personal style or orientation as "growers," "caretakers," and — tongue-in-cheek — as "undertakers" to match managerial type with the product's status. Notes one consultant and GE-watcher: "I hear they have a shortage of growers, but they are making great efforts to remove the undertaker types who are heading up growth businesses."

A look at the game of musical chairs recently played in GE's Lighting Business Group in Cleveland tends to support that observation. "The lighting business is mainly mature, but we just designated international operations as a growth area in our five-year forecast," explains Harry T. Rein, the group's manager for strategic planning. John D. Hamilton, the manager responsible for its manpower planning, says he and the executive manpower staff at corporate headquarters "looked at the whole pool of corporate talent." They decided to move in a manager from GE's motor division who had an industrial rather than lighting background, but who seemed to show an entrepreneurial flair.

Corning's Match-ups

Perhaps the most formal integration of personal managerial styles and strategic objectives is being done by Corning Glass. A personnel director has been assigned specifically to assess the company's top 100 managers for such qualities as entrepreneurial flair. Each of 11 other personnel development managers is responsible for gathering skills data for about 300 lower-echelon managers. "We're asking incumbents and their bosses what you need to have on the job, because we want to know what goes into success," Richard Shafer says.

The process is easier for small companies, which can assess the types of managers employed by larger competitors and emulate their approach to staffing. In 1974, Prime Computer Inc., a Wellesley Hills (Mass.) minicomputer maker, had sales of only $6.5 million and was operating in the red. The next year, Kenneth G. Fisher left Honeywell Inc. after 20 years to become Prime's president, and he immediately started to hire new managers from companies like his former employer.

"We wanted people from big companies that had already been through what we were going through," Fisher explains. "We assumed that we were going to succeed extraordinarily, and we needed men who had been through all the plateaus before." Fisher has since increased the managerial staff from 15 to 260 people. Last year, Prime's sales were up to $153 million and net income to $17 million, but Fisher is still looking for managers from much larger companies. "We're building a management substructure that can manage a $500 million company," he says.

Doubts about It All

Fisher notes that recruitment of executives with the sophistication gained at giant companies induced Prime to automate its process for laying out printed circuit boards much earlier than competitors of its own size. Similarly, Prime computerized factory scheduling, material control, and other functions long before sales volume justified such an investment. This has let the company operate with an administrative staff at least one-third smaller than would otherwise have been required. Fisher boasts that Prime gets revenues of about $70,000 per employee, compared with an average in the minicomputer industry of about $35,000.

Despite such successful results from strategic manpower planning, many companies remain uninterested in the concept. Says Chairman James L. Ketelsen of Tenneco Inc., who prefers versatile, jack-of-all-trades managers: "It doesn't make that much difference to us whether it's a growth business or a stable business per se. Most good managers can run any kind of business." Many behavioral scientists shudder at such views, but they hope that 10 years from now fewer chief executives will hold them.

27. A Strategic Framework for Marketing Control

James M. Hulbert
Norman E. Toy

The decade of the 1960s led many companies down the primrose path of uncontrolled growth. The turbulence of the 1970s has drawn renewed attention to the need to pursue growth selectively, and many companies have been forced to divest themselves of businesses which looked glamorous in the 1960s, but faded in the 1970s. Simultaneously with this reappraisal has come a much more serious focus on problems of control — a concern with careful monitoring and appraisal to receive early warning on businesses or ventures that are suspect.

Yet, despite the extent to which control is stressed by authors,[1] there does not exist a generally agreed upon strategic framework for marketing control, and there has been little successful integration of concepts in marketing strategy and planning with those of managerial accounting. In particular, the work of the Boston Consulting Group,[2] the results of the PIMS study,[3] and a variety of other sources[4] have stressed the importance of market share objectives in marketing strategy, coincidentally emphasizing the need to know market size and growth rate and thus the importance of good forecasts. Typically, however, procedures for marketing control have not been related to these key parameters. (Incredibly, market size is sometimes even omitted from marketing plans, according to one knowledgeable author.)[5]

In this article we seek to remedy that state of affairs by outlining a strategic framework for marketing control. Using the key strategic concepts discussed above, we first present a framework for evaluating marketing

This article first appeared in *Journal of Marketing*, April 1977, pp. 12–20.

When this article was published, the authors were associate professor at the Graduate School of Business and dean of the School of Public Health at Columbia University, respectively.

performance versus plan, thus providing a means for more formally incorporating the marketing plan in the managerial control process.

The plan, however, may well provide inappropriate criteria for performance evaluation, especially if there have been a number of unanticipated events during the planning period. A second stage of this article, therefore, is to provide a means of taking these kinds of planning variances into account, so as to provide a more appropriate set of criteria for performance evaluation. Two conceptual developments are shown as Part I and Part II of the Appendix.

Performance Versus Plan

In Table 27.1 we show the results of operations for a sample product, *Product Alpha*, during the preceding period. In the analysis which follows, we shall focus on analysis of variances in profit contribution. As we discussed elsewhere,[6] an analysis of revenue performance is sometimes required; the procedure here is analogous. Organizationally, one of the results we would like to achieve is to be able to assign responsibility, and give credit, where due.

A variety of organizational units were involved in the planning and execution summarized in Table 27.1, and an important component of control activity is to evaluate their performance according to the standards or goals provided by the marketing plan. We should also note, however, that

TABLE 27.1   Operating Results for Product Alpha

Item	Planned	Actual	Variance
Revenues			
Sales (lbs.)	20,000,000	22,000,000	2,000,000
Price per lb ($)	0.50	.4773	0.227
Revenues	10,000,000	10,500,000	500,000
Total Market (lbs.)	40,000,000	50,000,000	10,000,000
Share of Market	50%	44%	(6%)
Costs			
Variable cost per lb ($)	.30	.30	—
Contribution			
Per lb ($)	.20	.1773	.0227
Total ($)	4,000,000	3,900,000	(100,000)

the type of analysis we shall discuss has limited potential for *diagnosing* the causes of problems. Rather, its major benefit is in the *identification* of areas where problems may exist. Determining the factors which have actually caused favorable or unfavorable variances requires the skill and expertise of the manager.

The unfavorable variance in contribution of $100,000 for *Product Alpha* could arise from two main sources:[7]

1. Differences between planned and actual quantities (volumes).
2. Differences between planned and actual contribution per unit.

Differences between planned and actual quantities, however, may arise from differences between actual and planned total market size and actual and planned market share (penetration) of that total market. The potential sources of variation between planned and actual contribution, then, are:

1. Total market size.
2. Market share (penetration).
3. Price/cost per unit.

This format for variance decomposition permits assignment into categories which correspond to key strategy variables in market planning.[8] The analysis proceeds as follows.

Price-Quantity Decomposition

In order to measure volume variance with the standard yardstick of planned contribution per unit, actual quantity is used to calculate the price/cost variance. (This procedure is standard accounting practice.) To be more concise, we utilize the following symbols:

- S — share of total market
- M — total market in units
- Q — quantity sold in units
- C — contribution margin per unit

We use the subscript "a" to denote *actual* values, and "p" to denote *planned* values. The subscript "v" denotes *variance*. Thus the price/cost variance is given by

$$(C_a - C_p) \times Q_a = (.1773 - .20) \times 22,000,000$$

$$= -\$500,000;$$

and the volume variance is given by

$$(Q_a - Q_p) \times C_p = (22,000,000 - 20,000,000) \times .20$$

$$= \$400,000.[9]$$

The sum of these contribution variances therefore yields the overall unfavorable contribution variance of $-\$100,000$ shown in Table 27.1.

Penetration — Market Size Decomposition

The second stage of the analysis is the further decomposition of the volume variance in contribution into the components due to penetration and total market size. Figure 27.1 is helpful in the exposition of the analysis.

As a first step, we should like to explain differences in quantities sold $(Q_a - Q_p)$, where actual and planned quantities are the product of the market size times share $(Q_a = S_a \times M_a$, and $Q_p = S_p \times M_p)$. From Figure 27.1, rectangles I and II are clearly assignable to share and market size, respectively. Rectangle III, however, is conceptually more complex.

We argue that discrepancies in forecasting market size should be evaluated using the standard yardstick of planned share, just as the dollar value of the quantity variance is measured using the standard of planned contribution. Thus, actual market size is used to calculate share variance, while both share and forecast components (which together comprise the quantity variance) are measured using planned contribution. This procedure is also consistent with recommended accounting practice.[10]

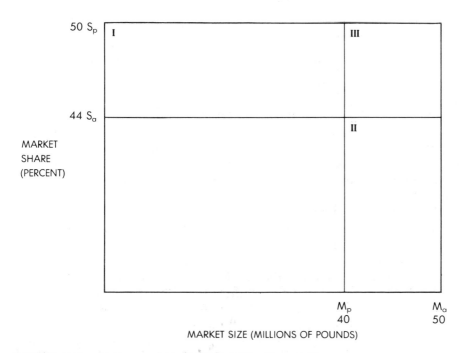

FIGURE 27.1 Variance of Total Market Size Versus Share

Then the variance in contribution due to share is given by

$$(S_a - S_p) \times M_a \times C_p$$
$$= (.44 - .50) \times 50{,}000{,}000 \times .2$$
$$= -\$600{,}000;$$

and the market size variance is given by

$$(M_a - M_p) \times S_p \times C_p$$
$$= (50{,}000{,}000 - 40{,}000{,}000) \times .5 \times .2$$
$$= \$1{,}000{,}000.$$

The sum of the market size and share variances yields the overall favorable volume variance in contribution of $400,000 derived in the previous section.

We may now summarize the variances which in total constitute the overall variance as follows:

Planned profit contribution		$4,000,000
Volume variance		
Share variance	(600,000)	
Market size variance	1,000,000	
		400,000
Price/cost variance		(500,000)
Actual profit contribution		$3,900,000

Interpretation

Conceptually, variances may occur because of problems in forecasting, execution, or both. In using the results of the analysis for performance evaluation, however, responsibility will have to be assigned. Generally, variances in total market size, for example, will be viewed as the responsibility of the market forecasting group.

Share or penetration variances present a more difficult case. They may arise due to incorrect forecasts of what "expected performance" should be, or due to poor performance itself. Apportioning responsibility in this case clearly necessitates managerial judgment. However, where marketing and sales personnel participate in the development of market share objectives, or where share declines relative to previous performance, the burden of proof is more likely to fall on the operating unit rather than on a separate planning or forecasting group.

Responsibility for price variances may also be difficult to assign. For example, prices may be seriously affected by changes in market or general economic conditions beyond the control of the operating group but which should have been foreseen by forecasters or planners. On the other hand, prices are an integral part of the marketing mix, and variances may well indicate problems in marketing or selling tactics.

With these considerations in mind, we may now review the results of the variance analysis:

First, *the favorable volume variance of $400,000 was in fact caused by two larger variances cancelling each other out. And while one of these variances was positive, the other negative, both are undesirable! By not achieving planned share of market, we lost $600,000 in profit contribution.*

The loss of market share may be due to poor planning, poor execution, or both . . . and managerial judgment is the key factor in diagnosing the causes of this discrepancy.

This unfavorable share variance was more than compensated for — or so it appears — by the $1,000,000 positive contribution variance due to the fact that the market turned out to be much larger than was forecast. This variance is unequivocally the responsibility of the forecasting group, though whether or not they should have been able to foresee the expansion is an issue which the manager must decide.

However, this nominally favorable variance is, in fact, a danger signal. *We seriously underestimated the size of the market, which was 25% greater, at 50 million pounds, than the forecast (40 million pounds).* As the dominant competitor, we have lost market share in what is apparently a fast-growing market, the kind of error which can soon lead to loss of competitive position.[11]

In this instance, then, the share/size decomposition of the volume variance serves to emphasize the importance of good planning — and good information for planning — in terms directly related to two crucial variables in strategy design. This form of decomposition, we submit, generates considerably more useful insight into issues of marketing control *than isolation of only the volume variance, which is much less clearly interpretable.*

The final variance component is the unfavorable price variance of $500,000. Again, interpretation is the job of the manager. However, we should note that the accounting procedures used here (and generally) treat price and volume variances as if they were separable. *Yet, for the vast majority of products and services, demand is price-elastic to some degree so that variances in total revenue are the combined result of the interaction, via the demand function, of unit prices and quantities.*

In this example, for instance, the lower levels of prices may well have been an important factor in expanding industry and company demand. Nonetheless, the fact remains that failure to attain planned price levels led to a $500,000 decrease in actual versus planned profit contribution. The reasons for this variance may lie with performance (e.g., poor tactics) or planning (e.g., inaccurate forecasts).

Diagnosis and responsibility assignment procedures will be explored in more detail in the following section.

Monday Morning Quarterbacking

A crucial issue, which we have thus far skirted, is the appropriate criterion for performance evaluation. This is a basic yet nagging problem underlying the whole area of strategic control. In the foregoing analysis, for example, we assumed that the marketing plan provides an appropriate set of criteria. The objectives therein are usually derived after considerable participation, discussion, and negotiation between interested parties,[12] and may well represent the most appropriate set of criteria that are available, at least at the beginning of the planning period.

In many companies, however, performance during the previous planning period serves as an additional set of evaluation criteria. In fact, the search for more "objective" criteria for performance evaluation led to the origins, at General Electric, of the PIMS project and the subsequent "par" criterion.[13]

The facts are, of course, that the marketing plan — which we used as our criterion — is generally based upon the best information which is available on an *ex ante* basis. The conditions which are manifest during the planning period, however, may be vastly different from those envisaged at the time of plan development. In some company planning systems, some of these changes may be encompassed by contingency planning, while in others the plan is updated when major environmental changes occur.[14] In many other instances the plan is not updated — at least in any formal way.[15]

Nonetheless, irrespective of the comprehensiveness of systems to provide flexibility in plans, when the time arrives to review performance, most marketing managers use some *ex post* information. In other words, the criteria of evaluation — implicitly or explicitly — are generally "what performance should have been" under the circumstances which actually transpired. Nor is this "Monday morning quarterbacking" undesirable, for it is eminently more sensible than blind adherence to a plan which is clearly outdated by violation of planning assumptions.[16]

For example, supply may be affected unexpectedly; a major competitor may drop out of the market — or an aggressive new competitor may enter; or demand may have an unexpected change — e.g., because of weather. Either of these would likely change the appropriate par market share for the company. The purpose of this second stage of the analysis, therefore, is to provide a variance decomposition which permits comparison of performance versus the criterion of "what should have happened under the circumstances."

Naturally, there are inherent dangers in such a process. Re-opening the issue of what constitutes an appropriate criterion for performance evaluation may mean opening a Pandora's Box. Equally clearly, however, there are frequently occasions when unforeseen events can significantly affect what target performance should be. In such instances, it is surely preferable that any adjustment process be systematic and orderly, explicit and visible.

Using "Expert" Information

Continuing with our previous operating results, then, let us construct the scenario which occurred during the planning period, using the *ex post* information which would be available to the marketing manager at the time of performance review:

1. A new competitor — Consolidated Company — entered the market early in the year. The competitor was a large, well-financed conglomerate, which used an aggressive promotional campaign and a lower price to induce trial purchase.
2. A fire in the plant of a European manufacturer led to totally unforeseeable foreign demand for one million pounds of *Product Alpha*.

With a small amount of additional work by the manager, we may now develop an appropriate *ex post* performance analysis. For example, the fact that the new competitor was quite prepared to subsidize his entry into our market out of his other operations was an important cause of the price deterioration, and also guaranteed that he would "buy" a share of market sufficient for him to run his new plant at close to standard capacity. At the same time, this aggressive entry and the price competition which ensued was an important factor in further expanding total industry demand.

In quantitative terms Consolidated's effective mean selling price for the year was $0.465 per lb. We had forecast an industry mean of $0.495 and a price for our own product of $0.475, and we realized $0.4773 per lb. Competitive intelligence informed us that Consolidated's new plant had a capacity of only 1.33 million pounds so that its inability to supply more set a lower limit for market prices, above that of Consolidated's introductory price.

We now reconstruct the discrepancy between conditions forcast at the time of planning and the conditions which subsequently prevailed.

Market Share

As noted, our intelligence estimates indicated that Consolidated's capacity would be 1.33 million pounds. Our historical market share had hovered around 50% for some time, so that *everything being equal*, we might expect that 50% of Consolidated's sales would be at our expense. However, knowing that we were (a) the dominant competitor and (b) the premium-price competitor, we also know that we were the most vulnerable to a price-oriented competitive entry. Consequently, we used as a planning assumption the supposition that 60% of Consolidated's sales would be at our expense. That is, we assumed that .6 × 1.33 million pounds, or 800 thousand pounds of sales volume which we would otherwise have obtained, would be lost to Consolidated. Thus, we had the following two conditions:

If no entry: Forecast market share equal to 20.8 ÷ 40 = 52%

With entry: Forecast market share equal to 20 ÷ 40 = 50%

Since we were certain that Consolidated would enter early in the year, we used the latter assumption. However, while our intelligence estimates on the size of Consolidated's plant were excellent, we did not glean the information that they would use 3-shift operation rather than two shifts which have been standard practice for the industry. As a result Consolidated's effective standard capacity was raised from 1.33 to 2.0 million pounds. Under these conditions, then, assuming the 60% loss rate holds, we should have expected to lose .6 × 2.0 or 1.2 million pounds to Consolidated, rather than 800,000 lbs. Thus, with perfect foresight we *should have* forecasted a market share of 19.6 ÷ 40, or 49%.

Price

We had forecast an industry mean price of $0.495 per pound, and planned for a net price to us of $0.50 per pound. This $.005 per pound premium had been traditional for us because of our leadership position in the industry, with a slightly higher quality product and excellent levels of distribution and service.

The actual industry mean price was $0.475 per pound, and our net mean price was $0.4773, so that we only received a premium of $0.0023 per pound.[17] Here, then, we have some basis for separating the planning variance from the performance variance.

Although the basis for this distinction again involves managerial judgment, for present purposes we assume that the planning group should have foreseen that Consolidated's entry would be based on a low price strategy which would lead to an overall deterioration in market prices. On the other hand, our selling and marketing tactics were responsible for the deterioration in our price premium.

Market Size

Finally, there was no possibility that our planning group could have foreseen the European fire, and it would be demonstrably unfair to hold them responsible for this component of the variance.

On the other hand, the remainder of the market expansion should have been foreseen, and the responsibility should be assigned to them. Their failure in this regard was no doubt related to the oversight in the pricing area, for it seems entirely plausible that demand was more price elastic than we had realized, and the price decrease brought a whole new set of potential customers into the market.

Variance Decomposition

The full *ex post* decomposition using this information is displayed in Figure 27.1.[18] To simplify the exposition, we employ a third subscript, "r," which indicates the standard which "should have been" — in other words, the plan as *revised* by *ex post* information. A number of useful insights are generated by the tableau.

The first issue is the nature of planning variances, which is somewhat counter-intuitive. Consider, for example, the planning variance in market share — a negative $98,000. What this is really telling us is that, considering only this factor in isolation, our planned market share was set unrealistically high, and that adjusting for this factor alone would have implied planning for a total contribution of $4,000,000 less the $98,000, or $3,902,000. Conversely, however, positive (or favorable) planning variances are in fact undesirable and represent, potentially, opportunity losses.

For example, the $900,000 favorable planning variance in market size, which is responsible for the fact that overall variance is favorable, represents lost profit contribution due to the fact that we had not correctly anticipated the market growth rate (given, of course, that there were no short-run capacity constraints). The $88,200 performance variance in market size is viewed as unassignable in this instance. We have decided that the planners could not have foreseen the foreign demand, and that we don't feel it should be assigned to sales.

Similar issues arise with the price variance. The planning group's failure to correctly predict market prices is responsible for the bulk of the price variance. However, there is no way that this component might have been recovered; it simply indicated the fact that our plan was subsequently shown by events to be unrealistic in its price expectations. In contrast, the failure of the marketing department to maintain our traditional price premium is reflected in the unfavorable performance variance in price of $60,000.

Again, however, we should point out that the most important element of the analysis is the market size/market growth rate issue. Picture the poor salesmen as they operate during the planning period. They know they are feeling some price pressure, to which, as we have seen, marketing responded. However, they also know that their quantity of sales is up — 22 million pounds of product versus a planned amount of 20 million pounds.

Thus, it is entirely feasible that our salesmen were not pushing that hard, since they appeared to be having a banner year, handsomely exceeding their monthly volume quotas and prior periods' performance. In fact, during this period we were frittering away our market position through our ignorance of the rate at which the market had expanded.

However, accurate and timely industry sales statistics, in combination with a flexible planning system which could readily incorporate these data in a revised plan and set of sales quotas, would preempt a problem which, by the time we recognized it, had developed into a fair-sized disaster. While market information is always important, it truly takes on new meaning for the company competing in a high-growth market.

Finally, we should note that the aggregate variances for quantity (including share and market size) and price/cost shown in Table 27.2 do not agree with those developed in the first part of the article. The reason is, of course, that there are now two possible criteria or yardsticks against which to compare actual results: the original plan (subscripted "p") and the revised plan (subscripted "r").

Following the conceptual development of Part II of the Appendix,

TABLE 27.2 Expost Performance Evaluation: Analysis of Contribution

Item	Composition	Type of Variance: Planning Variance	Type of Variance: Performance Variance	Variance Totals	Reconciliation
PLANNED CONTRIBUTION					$4,000,000
QUANTITY VARIANCE					
SHARE					
Planning Variance	$(S_r-S_p)\cdot M_r\cdot C_p = (.49-.50) \times 49{,}000{,}000 \times .20$	(98,000)			
Performance Variance	$(S_a-S_r)\cdot M_a\cdot C_r = (.44-.49) \times 50{,}000{,}000 \times .18$		(450,000)		
Total				(548,000)	
MARKET SIZE					
Planning Variance	$(M_r-M_p)\cdot S_p\cdot C_p = (49{,}000{,}000-40{,}000{,}000) \times .5 \times .20$	900,000			
Performance Variance	$(M_a-M_r)\cdot S_r\cdot C_r = (50{,}000{,}000-49{,}000{,}000) \times .49 \times .18$		88,200		
Total				988,200	
TOTAL QUANTITY VARIANCE					440,200
PRICE VARIANCE					
Planning Variance	$(C_r-C_p)\cdot Q_r = (.18-.2) \times 24{,}010{,}000$	(480,200)			
Performance Variance	$(C_a-C_r)\cdot Q_a = (.1773-.18) \times 22{,}000{,}000$		(60,000)		
Total				(540,200)	
TOTAL PRICE VARIANCE					(540,200)
TOTAL PLANNING VARIANCE		321,800			
TOTAL PERFORMANCE VARIANCE			(421,800)		
TOTAL VARIANCE				(100,000)	
ACTUAL CONTRIBUTION					$3,900,000

therefore, we have used what we believe to be the soundest analysis. Alternative decompositions, which permit the retention of identical aggregate variances to the preliminary "versus plan" comparison are possible, but their conceptual framework is less defensible.

Summary

To be useful to the marketing manager, a framework for control should be related to strategic objectives and variables and, whenever possible, should permit assignment of responsibility for differences between planned and actual performance. The procedures described in this article utilize the key strategic variables of price, market share, and market size as a framework for marketing control.

The framework was first used to analyze marketing performance vs. plan, decomposing quantity variance into components due to under- or over-achievement of planned market share and over- or under-forecasting of market size. Then, recognizing that the plan may well not constitute an adequate criterion for evaluation, we extended the example to illustrate how *ex post* information might be utilized to develop more appropriate evaluative criteria, which permitted isolation of the planning and performance components of the variance.

While there is evidently a considerable amount of managerial judgment involved in the decomposition procedure, marketing planning and control has never been exactly bereft of managerial judgment. There is nothing radical about the procedure, which simply recognizes that it is not always possible to update and modify plans to reflect changing conditions, but that such changes may nonetheless be taken into account in appraisal and evaluation via *ex post* revision of the plan.

The example we worked with also indicates the dangers of not continuously monitoring markets and revising plans and objectives, particularly when market conditions are fluid. In such markets, good tracking procedures[19] and responsive tactics are essential for any company seeking to maintain or increase its market position. The importance of marketing control — so long a stepchild — will surely increase in the years ahead. The markets of the late 1970's will differ considerably from those of the 1960's, and pressures of costs and competition will force companies to be more effective in performance appraisal and evaluation.

Notes

1. See, for example, V.H. Kirpalani and Stanley S. Shapiro, "Financial Dimensions of Marketing Management," *Journal of Marketing*, Vol. 37 No. 3 (July 1973), pp. 40–47; David J. Luck and Arthur E. Prell, *Marketing Strategy* (En-

glewood Cliffs, N.J.: Prentice-Hall Inc., 1968); Philip Kotler, *Marketing Management: Analysis, Planning and Control* (Englewood Cliffs, N.J.: Prentice-Hall Inc., 1972).

2. Boston Consulting Group, *Perspectives on Experience* (Boston: Boston Consulting Group, 1968); see also, Patrick Conley, "Experience Curves as a Planning Tool," in S.H. Britt and H.W. Boyd, eds., *Marketing Management and Administrative Action* (New York: McGraw-Hill, 1974), pp. 257–68; William E. Cox, "Product Portfolio Strategy: A Review of the Boston Consulting Group Approach to Marketing Strategy," in *Proceedings*, 1974 Marketing Educators' Conference (Chicago: American Marketing Association), pp. 465–470.

3. Sidney Schoeffler, Robert D. Buzzell and Donald F. Heany, "Impact of Strategic Planning on Profit Performance," *Harvard Business Review*, Vol. 52 (March–April 1974), pp. 137–145; Robert D. Buzzell, Bradley T. Gale and Ralph G.M. Sultan, "Market Share — A Key to Profitability," *Harvard Business Review*, Vol. 53 (January–February 1975), pp. 97–106.

4. See Bernard Catry and Michel Chevalier, "Market Share Strategy and the Product Life Cycle," *Journal of Marketing*, Vol. 38 No. 4 (October 1974), pp. 29–34; C. Davis Fogg, "Planning Gains in Market Share," *Journal of Marketing*, Vol. 38 No. 3 (July 1974), pp. 30–38.

5. F. Beaven Ennis, *Effective Marketing Management* (New York: Association of National Advertisers, 1973), p. 11.

6. James M. Hulbert and Norman E. Toy, "Control and the Marketing Plan," paper presented to the 1975 Marketing Educators' Conference of the American Marketing Association.

7. To simplify this example, no variances in either variable costs or marketing program costs are included.

8. (For algebraic exposition, see Appendix, Part I.)

9. Algebraically, we have:
$$(C_a - C_p)Q_a + (Q_a - Q_p)C_p$$
$$= C_aQ_a - C_pQ_a + C_pQ_a - C_pQ_p$$
$$= C_aQ_a - C_pQ_p$$

10. "Report of the Committee on Cost and Profitability Analyses for Marketing," *Accounting Review*, Supplement to Vol. XLVII (1972), pp. 575–615.

11. Boston Consulting Group, *Perspectives on Experience*, same as reference 2 above.

12. John A. Howard, James M. Hulbert and John U. Farley, "Organizational Analysis and Information System Design: A Decision Process Perspective," *Journal of Business Research*, Vol. 3.

13. Schoeffler, Buzzell and Heany, same as reference 3 above.

14. Ennis, same as reference 5 above, p. 57.

15. Noel Capon and James M. Hulbert, "Decision Systems Analysis in Industrial Marketing," *Industrial Marketing Management*, Vol. 4, 1975, pp. 143–160.

16. Joel S. Demski, "An Accounting System Structured on a Linear Programming Model," *The Accounting Review*, Vol. 42 (October 1967), pp. 701–712.

17. Some judgment is evidently involved here. Percentage differentials might well be used instead of absolute differentials.

18. For algebraic exposition, see Appendix, Part I.

19. John U. Farley and Melvin J. Hinich, "Tracking Marketing Parameters in Random Noise," in *Proceedings*, 1966 Marketing Educators' Conference.

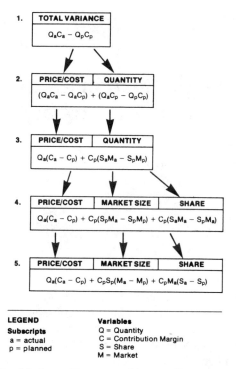

LEGEND

Subscripts	**Variables**
a = actual	Q = Quantity
p = planned	C = Contribution Margin
	S = Share
	M = Market

APPENDIX, PART I   Variance Decomposition — Comparison with Plan

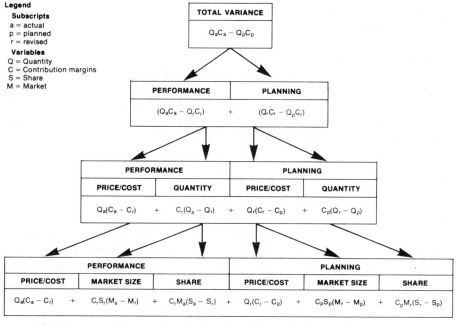

APPENDIX, PART II   Variance Decomposition — Use of *Ex Post* Information

28. Strategic Responses to Technological Threats

Arnold C. Cooper
Dan Schendel

Technological innovation can create new industries and transform or destroy existing ones. At any time, many businesses are confronted with a host of external technological threats. Managements of threatened firms realize that many threats may not materialize, at least in the short run. However, one or more of those potential threats may develop in ways that will have devastating impact. Providers of kerosene lamps, buggy whips, railroad passenger service, steam radiators, hardwood flooring, passenger liner service and motion pictures all have had to contend with such threats. Few environmental changes can have such important strategic implications.

A typical sequence of events involving the traditional firm's responses to a technological threat begins with the origination of a technological innovation outside the industry, often pioneered by a new firm. Initially crude and expensive, it expands through successive submarkets, with overall growth following an S-shaped curve. Sales of the old technology may continue to expand for a few years, but then usually decline, the new technology passing the old in sales within five to fourteen years of its introduction.

The traditional firms fight back in two ways. The old technology is improved and major commitments are made to develop products utilizing the new technology. Although competitive positions are usually maintained in the old technology, the new field proves to be difficult. In addition to the major traditional competitors (who are also fighting for market share in the new field), a host of new competitors must be confronted.

This article first appeared in *Business Horizons*, February 1976, pp. 61–69.

When this article was published, both authors were faculty members at the Kannert Graduate School of Business Administration, Purdue University.

Despite substantial commitments, the traditional firm is usually not successful in building a long-run competitive position in the new technology. Unless other divisions or successful diversifications take up the slack, the firm may never again enjoy its former success.

Most previous research on technological innovation has been concerned with the practices and problems of innovators. This research is concerned with major technological innovations from the viewpoint of firms in established industries threatened by innovation.

Threatened Industries

The industries and technologies selected for study were the following:

- steam locomotives versus diesel-electric,
- vacuum tubes versus the transistor,
- fountain pens versus ball-point pens,
- boilers for fossil fuel power plants versus nuclear power plants,
- safety razors versus electric razors,
- aircraft propellers versus jet engines, and
- leather versus polyvinyl chloride and poromeric plastics.

Within these traditional industries, twenty-two separate firms were studied, using data available in the secondary literature where over 200 separate sources were examined. Table 28.1 lists these firms. Two broad questions are of concern to the study:

> What was the nature of the substitution of the new technology for the old?

> What response strategies were used to counter the technological threats?

The findings must be regarded as tentative. The data are incomplete in some areas, as should be expected from secondary data. For example, data on the performance and strategies of smaller firms in the threatened industries are not readily available. The relatively small number of industries studied and the complexity of the processes prevent definitive conclusions. However, the experiences of these industries and firms suggest a number of conclusions with implications for managers of threatened firms.

The first section which follows deals with substitution patterns of new technology for the old. The second deals with response strategies by the threatened firms, a subject which has received very little previous attention in the literature. Finally, a section is devoted to implications and conclusions.

TABLE 28.1   Traditional Industries Studied

	LOCOMOTIVES	VACUUM (RECEIVING) TUBES	FOUNTAIN PENS	SAFETY RAZORS	FOSSIL FUEL BOILERS	PROPELLERS	LEATHER INDUSTRY
Sales decline immediately after new technology introduced?	No	No	*	No	No	No	Yes[1]
Sales eventually begin long-term decline?	Yes	Yes	Yes	No	No	Yes	Yes
Time from introduction of new technology until sales of new technology exceeded old.	Fourteen years[2]	Eleven years	Nine years	Twenty-five years[3]	Not during the twenty years since first sale	Five years[4]	†
New markets created by new technology?	No	Yes	Yes	No	No	No	Yes
New technology limited in application or crude at first?	Yes	Yes	Yes	Yes	Yes	Yes	Yes
New technology applied sequentially to submarkets?	Yes	Yes	Yes[5]	No	No	Yes	Yes
First commercial introduction by a firm in traditional industry?	‡	Yes	No	No	§	Yes[6]	No
First commercial introduction by a new firm?	No	No	Yes	Yes	No	No[6]	Yes
Old firms participate in new technology?	Yes	Yes	Yes (4 of 5)	Yes (briefly)	Yes	Yes (2 of 3)	No (1 of 4)[7]
Acquisitions a means of participating in new technology?	No	Yes Raytheon	Yes Parker	Yes Gillette[8]	No	No	Yes Allied Kid

	Locomotives	Vacuum tubes	Fountain pens	Safety razors	Propellers	Fossil fuel boilers	Leather
Old technology improved after new technology was introduced?	Yes	Yes	Yes	Yes	Yes	Yes	Yes
Traditional firms involved in improving old technology and in entering new technology?	Yes	Yes	Yes (4 of 5)	Yes (participation in electric razors short-lived)	Yes	Yes	Yes
Attempt to establish barriers to new technology?	No	No	No	No	No	No	No

Firms Studied

Locomotives: American Locomotive Co., Baldwin Locomotive Works. *Vacuum (receiving) tubes:* Columbia Broadcasting System (CBS), Radio Corp. of America (RCA), Raytheon Mfg. Co., Sylvania Electric Products, Inc. *Fountain pens:* Esterbrook Pen Co., Eversharp, Inc., Parker Pen Co., Sheaffer Pen Co., Waterman Pen Co. *Safety razors:* American Safety Razor Corp., Gillette Safety Razor Co. *Fossil fuel boilers:* Babcock & Wilcox Co., Combustion Engineering Inc. *Propellers:* Koppers Corp., Curtiss-Wright Corp., United Aircraft Corp. *Leather industry:* A. C. Lawrence Leather Co., Armour Leather Co., Allied Kid Co. (Cudahy), Seton Leather Co.

1. Production of three of the four types of leather declined in the year after vinyl was first used as a leather substitute.
2. Available sales data relate to units sold rather than sales dollars, but it appears that diesel-electric sales exceeded steam locomotive sales by 1938, fourteen years after the first diesel-electric switcher was introduced. Subsequently, steam locomotive unit sales exceeded diesel-electric unit sales during World War II, but steam locomotive sales then dropped sharply after the War.
3. During 1956-1958, electric razor sales exceeded sales of razor blades. Subsequently, however, razor blades regained a sales lead and have maintained it to the time of the study.
4. Unit production of jet engines exceeded unit production of piston engines during a three-year period in the early 1950s. It appears that the dollar value of jet engines produced exceeded the value of the smaller, less powerful piston engines within about five years of their introduction in the United States.
5. The pen market is segmented by price. Initially, the ball-point pen was relatively expensive.
6. Power Jets, a new British firm, developed the first jet engine. General Electric developed and introduced the first American jet engine, relying upon Power Jets' designs.
7. Allied Kid bought Corfam from DuPont in 1965. Also, all the firms began coating hides with synthetic materials to improve their qualities.
8. Gillette acquired Braun, A. G., and thereby entered the overseas market for electric razors. Gillette has not reentered the U.S. market since 1938, when its internally developed electric razor was introduced and subsequently withdrawn.

* Data were not found to indicate whether sales of fountain pens declined the year the ball-point pen was introduced.

† Results are mixed by type of application. By 1950, synthetics had captured 50% of the shoe sole market.

‡ The first mainline diesel-electric was introduced by General Motors, a firm which never made steam locomotives. However, American Locomotive had earlier introduced an experimental diesel-electric switcher.

§ The first nuclear power plant was developed by Westinghouse, a firm with a strong position in turbines. However, for the producers of boilers, it was not a traditional competitor which introduced the new technology.

Patterns of Substitution

The nature of the substitution of one technology for another is not well known. The product life cycle concept suggests that products move through a classical S-shaped curve: this implies that the sales of a new product grow, slowly at first and then rapidly, and finally mature to a plateau from which they decline. Presumably, this would apply to the sales of a new technology, with the sales of the old technology declining accordingly.

Empirical studies of ethical drug products and of nondurable goods found that new products did not always follow the S-shaped sales curve.[1] J. C. Fisher and R. H. Pry postulated that the substitution of one technology for another follows a hyperbolic tangent or S-shaped curve.[2] On a semilog scale, the market share of the new technology divided by the market share of the old technology plots as a straight line. They reported on some seventeen substitutions, most of which closely followed this pattern. Kenneth Hatten and Mary Louise Piccoli tested the Fisher-Pry model on over forty substitutions and reported that the model was useful, so long as care was exercised in the selection of units and in the application of the results.[3] Generally, then, an S-shaped curve of growth for the new technology and a similar S-shaped curve of decline for the old technology would be expected.

The data required to plot the product life cycles for the new and old technologies are not always available in the form desired. For instance, the unit sales of piston engines and of jet engines over time do not accurately reflect the much greater horsepower of jet engines. Comparison of leather and vinyl is made difficult by the wide range of uses of both materials, often in applications where they do not compete with each other. Nevertheless, a number of questions of managerial interest can be considered with the data available.

An examination of the sales over time for both the new and old technologies showed variable patterns which do not always duplicate the classical S-shaped pattern. Analysis of this sales data, coupled with extensive examination of other information, leads to a number of conclusions concerning the substitution pattern of new for old technologies.

> After the introduction of the new technology, the sales of the old technology did not always decline immediately; in four out of seven cases, sales of the old technology continued to expand.

> In two cases, sales of the old technology continued to expand for the entire period studied, despite growth in sales of the new technology.

> When sales of the old technology did decline, the time period from first commercial introduction to the time when dollar sales of the new

technology exceeded dollar sales of the old ranged from about five to fourteen years.

The first commercial introduction of the new technology was, in four out of seven cases, made by a firm outside the traditional industry. It might have been expected that the traditional competitors would have been the logical sources of industry innovation because of their strong customer relationships, well-developed channels of distribution and organizations oriented toward serving those industries.

In three of the four industries in which capital requirements were not excessive, new firms were the first to introduce the new technology.

The new technology often created new markets which were not available to the old technology. Although the initial ball-point pens were expensive, low-priced pens were later developed which opened up a new market — the "throw-away" pen. It was also estimated that 50% of the applications for the transistor were in equipment made possible by the invention of the transistor. Vinyls were used in floor coverings and building materials, applications not open to leather.

The new technology was expensive and relatively crude at first. Often, its initial shortcomings led observers to believe it would find only limited applications. Although the first ball-point pens wrote under water, they blotted, skipped and stopped writing on paper and even leaked into pockets; after an initial fad phase, public disenchantment set in and sales dropped dramatically. The first transistors were expensive and had sharply limited frequencies, power capabilities and temperature tolerance; some observers thought they would never find more than limited application. The jet-powered airplane was initially thought to be suitable only for the military market.

The new technology often invaded the traditional industry by capturing sequentially a series of submarkets. Although the new technology was crude it often had performance advantages for certain applications. Some submarkets were insulated from competition for extended periods. General Motors' diesel-electric locomotive first invaded the submarket for passenger locomotives, subsequently the submarket for switcher locomotives, and then freight locomotives — the major submarket — accounting for about 75% of industry sales. The transistor found early application in hearing aids and pocket radios, but not in radar systems and television.

The new technology did not necessarily follow the standard S-shaped growth curve. Erratic patterns were caused by abnormal economic and social conditions (World War II in the case of the electric razor, propellers and steam locomotives), by faddish phases of sales (ball-point pens), and by a newer technology replacing the original new technology (transistors and integrated circuits).

Some Pitfalls of Appraisals

Many factors affect the rate of penetration of a new technology: it does not capture markets overnight. Substantial sales opportunities may exist in the old technology for extended periods. It may be difficult for management in the traditional firms to judge the eventual impact of a developing threat, but at least there is usually time to develop a new strategy.

However, response presumes the ability to recognize and assess the threatening innovation. Intelligence activities focusing only upon traditional competitors are not enough, inasmuch as nontraditional competitors and new firms may be the originators of the threatening technology. It may be necessary to monitor a variety of innovations, many of which may never have significant impact.

Surviving past technological threats does not confer future immunity. In 1934, when General Motors introduced the first mainline diesel-electric locomotive, the producers of steam locomotives could look back upon two earlier threats which they had survived: the electric locomotive, and, in the 1920s, passenger cars with individual gasoline-powered engines. Both of these prior threats captured only small segments of the American locomotive market. There was no indication that the next threat, the diesel-electric, would destroy the traditional industry within fifteen years.

It would be a mistake to wait until decline in sales of the old technology triggered the need for appraisal of the threat. By then, much of the lead time would have passed. However, this means that the new technology must be appraised when it is still relatively crude. In an earlier article, James C. Utterback and James W. Brown emphasized that hypotheses about directions for change aid in selection of parameters which can be observed and evaluated.[4] For instance, early diesel engines had such a high weight-to-horsepower ratio that a diesel-electric locomotive would have been impossibly large. Managements of steam locomotive firms might have hypothesized that any changes leading to improvements in this weight-to-power ratio were of critical importance and deserved continuous monitoring.

It is not enough to judge that someday a new technology will replace an old one. Rates of penetration must be determined. When the Baldwin Locomotive Works was founded in 1831, it would have been of little value to tell founders that someday their principal product would be obsolete. However, when Sylvania introduced a new line of vacuum tubes for computers in 1957, the rate of improvement of transistors then taking place was extremely relevant.

The forecaster needs to understand differences in needs of market segments and relate these to probable improvements in the new technology. Some market segments in a traditional industry are threatened earlier and to a greater extent than others. Firms should consider strategies involving emphasis on the less threatened segments.

Response Strategies

Once the threat has been recognized, what kind of response is made by the traditional firm? If it decides not to participate in the new technology, management might elect one or a combination of the following specific actions.

Do nothing.

Monitor new developments in the competing technology through vigorous environmental scanning and forecasting activity.

Seek to hold back the new threat by fighting it through public relations and legal action.

Increase flexibility so as to be able to respond to subsequent developments in the new technology.

Avoid the threat through decreasing dependence on the most threatened submarkets.

Expand work on the improvement of the existing technology.

Attempt to maintain sales through actions not related to technology, such as promotion or price-cutting.

A firm might, however, choose to participate in the new technology. The degree of commitment could vary widely, ranging from a token involvement, such as defensive research and development, to seeking leadership in the new technology through major and immediate commitments. Important dimensions of a strategy for participation in the technology include decisions about the level of acceptable risk, the magnitude of commitments to the new technology, the timing of those commitments and the extent of reliance on internal development versus acquisition. Against this background of possible responses, the seven industries were studied to determine the response strategies actually used by the threatened firms. Their strategies are shown in the accompanying table.

Participation in the New Technology

Of the twenty-two firms studied, all but five made at least some effort to participate in the new technology. Fifteen of the firms made major efforts to establish positions in the new technology. Firms with small market shares in the old technology were not the focus of this study. However, it does appear that they either did not attempt to establish positions in the new technology, or they achieved no visible success. For instance, the hundreds of small razor blade firms never had successful electric razors, and the five smallest locomotive producers never made the transition to diesel-electrics.

Nature of Participation

The timing of traditional firms' entries in the new technology varied widely. Raytheon and RCA vacuum tube producers were among the first to enter the transistor market. By contrast, Parker Pen brought out its first ball-point pen nine years after its first commercial introduction. Of the nine firms which had traditionally emphasized research and development in their various divisions, six were early entrants in the new technology. By contrast, only two of the firms with a low research and development emphasis were early entrants.

Acquisition was not a widely used means of entry into the new technology. Only four of twenty-two traditional firms used acquisition, and two of these used acquisitions to supplement their internal development. Parker acquired the Writing Division of Eversharp as a means of successfully entering the low-priced ball-point pen market after having first developed a high-priced ball-point pen. Raytheon, having previously made major commitments to germanium transistors, acquired Rheem Semiconductor as a means of entering the silicon transistor field.

Emphasis on Old Technology

In every industry studied, the old technology continued to be improved and reached its highest stage of technical development *after* the new technology was introduced. For instance, the smallest and most reliable vacuum tubes ever produced were developed after the introduction of the transistor. No threatened firm adopted a strategy of early withdrawal from the old technology in order to concentrate on the new. Moreover, all but one of the twenty-two companies continued to make heavy commitments to the improvement of the old technology.

Most of the firms followed a strategy of dividing their resources, so as to participate in a major way in both the old and new technologies. Baldwin Locomotive developed both advanced turbine-powered electric locomotives and diesel-electric locomotives. CBS and Raytheon developed new lines of vacuum tubes and also made major investments in research and development and production facilities for transistors. This dual strategy was not usually successful, particularly in relation to building a strong competitive position in the new technology. There were no apparent actions taken by the traditional firms to create or strengthen the barriers to adoption and diffusion of the innovations.

Firms that pioneered the new technology generally did not enter the old technology. The only exception was BIC, a successful French producer of low-priced ball-point pens, which acquired Waterman, an American fountain pen manufacturer. The acquisition was apparently for Waterman's U.S. distribution system rather than its product line, inasmuch as the fountain pen line was discontinued four years later.

Overall Performance

The new technical innovations did not always lead to immediate financial returns and, in fact, sometimes presented all participants with severe competitive challenges. The nuclear power field involved very heavy investments for many years by all participants before the first profits were earned. The precipitous sales decline, which occurred after the first cycle of ball-point pen sales, drove more than 200 new firms, as well as several established firms, from the market. DuPont's poromeric leather substitute, Corfam, reportedly resulted in losses of $100 million: Goodrich and Armstrong were also entrants who later withdrew from the leather substitute field.

The new technology often evolved rapidly. Transistors, nuclear power plants and jet engines all confronted participants with a succession of decisions about commitments to evolving technologies. Early leaders, such as Raytheon in transistors and Curtiss-Wright in jet engines, lost their competitive positions as the technology changed.

Where the old technology continued to grow, traditional firms were able to maintain their competitive positions and enjoy financial success. But many of the most successful firms in the new technology had never participated in the old technology. In industries in which capital barriers were not great, new firms were among the most successful. Examples of successful new firms were Papermate in ball-point pens, Fairchild Semiconductor in transistors and Schick in electric razors.

Over the long run most of the traditional firms that tried to participate in the new technology were not successful. Of the fifteen firms making major commitments, only two, Parker in ball-point pens and United Aircraft in jet engines, enjoyed long-term success as independent firms participating in the new technology.

Patterns of Commitment

Managers of threatened firms must decide how to allocate resources in choosing between improving the old technology and attempting to establish a competitive position in the new. If sales of the old continue to grow, as in safety razors or fossil fuel power plants, then the strengthening of the firm's position in the business it knows so well can be rewarding. However, if sales of the old technology are declining, heavy, across-the-board commitments seem questionable. Management should carefully segment its markets and identify those which appear protected from the threat. Strategies based upon maintaining strong competitive positions in these segments seem justified.

It is interesting that the traditional firms studied here continued to make substantial commitments to the old technologies, even when their sales had already begun to decline because of the competitive pressures of the new technologies. Perhaps this demonstrates the difficulty of changing the patterns of resource allocation in an established organization. Decisions about allocating resources to old and new technologies within the organization are loaded with implications for the decision makers; not only are old product lines threatened, but also old skills and positions of influence.

It was common for spokesmen for the traditional firms to emphasize the shortcomings of the new technology with comments such as "It is no wonder if the public feels that the steam locomotive is about to lay down and play dead," and "It is certain that substantially all airplanes which operate at speeds of 550 mph or less will use propeller propulsion." The executives who make these statements, conditioned by life-long involvements with the old technology, may have been slower than others to recognize the declining opportunities for their traditional products.

Commitment to the new technology, with its expanding opportunities and lack of entrenched competitors, may seem attractive. Certainly most of the firms studied here made such strategic investments. Yet such decisions are fraught with risk, as evidenced by the traditional firms being relatively unsuccessful in the new fields.

For these companies, the patterns of commitment seem to be related to the firm's characteristics. One group of firms was relatively undiversified and did not have strong research and development orientations. The producers of locomotives, fountain pens, safety razors and two of the leather producers might be so classified. Except for several of the pen companies, these firms usually were *not* early entrants, and furthermore, never captured substantial market shares in the new technologies. It is tempting to conclude that an innovative technical and managerial organization is required to make a successful transition from the old to the new technology.

Another group of firms had relatively strong research and development traditions and were accustomed to managing multibusiness organizations. Most of this group, which included the producers of vacuum tubes, boilers and propellers, made major commitments to the new technologies and in several instances achieved substantial early success. However, these technologies continued to evolve rapidly, so that it was necessary to generate successive generations of successful new products. Here, companies such as Curtiss-Wright in jet engines and RCA and Raytheon in transistors were unable to continue their early successes.

The reasons for these firms' inability to build and maintain strong competitive positions are not obvious. Resource limitations apparently were not a major factor in the transistor industry, inasmuch as a number of new companies were relatively successful. The traditional firms not only had to develop new products based upon different technologies, but also had to adapt to changing methods of marketing, servicing and manufacturing. Their lack of long-term success may be an indication of the relative difficulty of changing organizational strategy successfully. The skills, attitudes and assumptions which undergird successful strategy in a traditional technology may require modification in ways both major and subtle to bring about equivalent success in the new technology. Apparently, many organizations found this difficult to do.

Managers of threatened firms should consider carefully commitments to the new technology. Where such commitments are made, it is desirable to recognize explicitly the different strategic requirements for success in the new field. Acquisition, although not widely used by the firms studied here, merits particular consideration. This may be a way to acquire not only technical capabilities, but also organizations attuned to competition in the new field. There are no easy paths to success when faced with major technological threats. However, the experiences of these firms illustrate some of the approaches and pitfalls which management should consider.

Notes

1. William E. Cox, "Product Life Cycles in Marketing Models," *Journal of Business* (October 1967), pp. 375–384.
   Rolando Polli and Victor Cook, "Validity of the Product Life Cycle," *Journal of Business* (October 1969), pp. 385–400.
2. J. C. Fisher and R. H. Pry, "A Simple Substitution Model of Technological Change," *Technological Forecasting and Social Change* (1971), pp. 75–88.
3. Kenneth Hatten and Mary Louise Piccoli, "An Evaluation of a Technological Forecasting Method by Computer Based Simulation" (Proceedings of the Division of Business Policy and Planning, Academy of Management, August 1973).
4. James C. Utterback and James W. Brown, "Monitoring for Technological Opportunities," *Business Horizons* (October 1972), pp. 5–15.

29. The Malaise of Strategic Planning

J. Quincy Hunsicker

More and more top managers are today questioning the value added by their increasingly time-consuming and sophisticated strategic planning processes. One such executive complained to me recently: "We spend an awful lot of time and effort on strategic planning these days, but somehow I find it hard to point to a clear case where our business is really better off or even substantially different for it. It's not the process itself I'm concerned about, because that works reasonably well. And I have to say that the strategies that result seem logical enough. But for the life of me I can't think of any really new ideas that have resulted from all this effort. To top it all off, we really got caught off balance last year when one of our foreign competitors came out of the blue with an offer to acquire one of our largest domestic distributors. After a lot of pushing and pulling in emergency meetings, we finally made a successful counter offer. But I have to say we ended up paying far too much for something we really didn't want in the first place, and the whole affair has left us somewhat shaken."

A second manager had similar misgivings: "I guess our strategic planning system was fine a few years ago. We were in a consolidation mode then, trying to improve the quality of our earnings and conserve capital — the job was to figure out which businesses we belonged in and which we didn't. But now all that's changed and we seem to be stalled. Somehow we've got to get our motor restarted and get the company back on a growth track. But it seems to me our planning processes just don't generate the kind of innovative ideas that we're in real need of. There's a pile of analysis there but damn little nourishment."

A third manager fumed: "Our planners do an absolutely first-rate job in describing and documenting our problems in Cinemascope and Technicolor, but the solutions they come up with are pathetic. They'll tell us

This article first appeared in *The Management Review*, March 1980, pp. 8–14.
When this article was published, Quincy Hunsicker was managing director of the Zurich office of McKinsey and Company.

that the market for such and such a product is mature and our position is weak compared to our competition, so we ought to divest. Nothing wrong with that logic — but if we were to withdraw from all our problem businesses, even assuming that we could get the unions and such to go along, we just wouldn't have very much left."

The three executives I have quoted are not isolated cases. Variations on the same theme have cropped up repeatedly in disucssions I have had with executives of several large companies over the past year or so. Other observers of the business scene — both professional and academic — have reported more or less the same phenomenon. This vague discontent with strategic planning seems to be more and more prevalent at the top management level, and it is perhaps most acute in companies with the most highly developed strategic planning systems. Clearly, what chief executives find most frustrating is the disproportion between the time and money expended on the strategic planning effort, on the one hand, and the substantive value of the resulting strategies, on the other. The much-maligned "gut feel" that permeated the planning efforts of the past has been replaced by research and voluminous analysis. Yet the new strategies, for all their elaborate methodological underpinnings, rarely seem to result in a great leap forward. Nor, as business headlines frequently remind us, have they helped very much to avoid the occasional disaster.

If, somewhere along the line, strategic planning systems have gone off the track, I believe we need not look too far for an explanation.

Responding to Change

Planning systems, like other institutional structures and processes, normally develop in response to needs and demands arising internally or impinging on the organization from outside. Ineffective systems eventually collapse or are replaced; effective ones tend to survive, sometimes outliving the needs they were created to fill.

During the 1960s and early 1970s, growth was the dominant fact of the economic environment, and the planning systems that developed in response were typically geared to the discovery and exploitation of entrepreneurial opportunities. Decentralized planning was the order of the day. Top management focused on reviewing major investment proposals and approving annual operating budgets. Long-range corporate plans were occasionally put together, but they were primarily extrapolations and were rarely used for strategic decision-making purposes.

All this changed abruptly in late 1973 with the sudden quadrupling of energy costs, followed by a recession and rumors of impending capital crisis. Setting long-term growth and diversification objectives was suddenly an exercise in irrelevance; "zero growth" and the capital crunch became top management's preoccupations. Soon, reflecting these new management needs and concerns, a systems orientation aimed at more centralized control over resources began to pervade corporate planning efforts. Sorting out winners and losers, setting priorities and husbanding capital became the name of the game.

Not by accident, it was in these years that sophisticated, centrally controlled strategic planning systems burgeoned in many large companies. Most of the currently popular planning concepts, including the concept of a strategic portfolio, were well suited for dealing with the resource allocation needs of the period. Product and geographic markets were depressed and capital was presumed to be short, so there was a brief hiatus in the search for new markets to conquer. The competitive structures of most industries remained relatively stable; most companies concentrated on strengthening their core businesses.

New Game Rules

But now the business picture is subtly changing again. Many, perhaps most, companies have become convinced that times are not going to get better, and that to succeed in a slower-growing economy (which implies growing at the expense of their competitors) they must actively seek new opportunities — including, once more, aggressive product and market diversification. Finding the funds, for most, is no great problem; by and large, the predicted capital shortage has failed to materialize. Today, in fact, there is something of a capital glut around the world, and most larger companies are awash with cash. It is the growth opportunities that are hard to find. As companies begin once more to invade each other's markets in search of these growth opportunities — often with fresh technical or marketing approaches — the relatively stable and compartmentalized competitive picture of the mid-1970s has blurred.

These changes in the strategic planning environment are only just beginning to affect the substance of most corporate strategic planning efforts. Some companies are already consciously reshaping their strategic planning, but most are still clinging to their accustomed approaches.

Viewed in the light of today's strategic requirements, their planning processes seem to focus far too much effort on developing "optimal" strategies, rather than on challenging the assumptions on which these strategies are based. Too much time and energy, moreover, is devoted to the evaluation, as opposed to the generation, of ideas and proposals. And too much analytical effort is concentrated on overall market trends and the company's own economics, rather than on the nature, economics and probable strategy of competitors, from whom most of its growth will have to come.

Ironically, in further refining their sophisticated planning systems, many companies have fallen victim to a kind of "paralysis of analysis" in planning. The remedy, I believe, is a shift in the basic focus of corporate planning efforts from optimizing to challenging assumptions, from a market perspective to an emphasis on competition, from the meticulous evaluation of pedestrian alternatives to the generation of innovative options. Let us look at each of these in turn.

Challenging Versus Optimizing

The recent surge of research and literature on strategic planning has encouraged reliance on various standard analyses of the market and of the company's competitive position. In some cases, this reliance has developed into an almost mechanistic processing of data: managers simply input specified variables on market size, growth rate, competitive share, and so on, and the system then proceeds to crank out an "optimum" strategy for the product — for example, invest for growth by pricing aggressively to build market share, or milk by sacrificing market share to hold prices.

The trouble is not that these standardized strategies are wrong — although occasionally they are embarrassingly off target. Their real drawbacks are that (1) they leave the company vulnerable to competitors who choose not to play by the rules, and (2) they lock management into a static (and dangerously predictable) repertory of strategic options.

Competitive Vulnerability

Some of the most useful planning tools of the past decade have themselves fostered a kind of "tunnel vision." Followers of learning-curve theory are often slow to discern that competitors don't always follow the same learning curve and that differences in technology or approach can make learning-curve theory irrelevant in many situations. Apostles of portfolio analysis often tend to derive their strategies from the positions of their products on a strategic matrix without considering whether these positions could and should be changed. Devotees of statistics on the relationships among such variables as market share, R&D investment and profitability tend to forget the less-publicized but strategically far more significant company-to-company variations that remain hidden behind the published averages.

Companies that put too much reliance on such standardized approaches have repeatedly been badly hurt by competitors who defy the conventional wisdom of the industry, or simply refuse to play by the rules. In fact, most rapid changes in market share come about when one competitor chooses a basically different technology or strategy. Consider these examples:

> For years, supermarket operators in the United States followed the maxim that "big was beautiful" and that larger stores were not only

more attractive but more efficient to operate. As a result, average store size increased steadily throughout the 1960s. Then along came the convenience-store operators with limited varieties and longer hours of operation to take over as the fastest-growing industry segment.

The Swiss watch manufacturers were well down the learning curve for mechanical watches when they were first approached with the idea of an electronic movement. Reasoning that it offered only slightly greater accuracy, required battery replacement and, most important, would cost more to produce than mechanical movements, the Swiss passed up the opportunity — and the rest is history. Their real mistake lay not in misjudging the technology, but in underestimating the importance of the vastly greater economies of scale that could be attained with electronics.

Specialized microprocessors have been in use for years in automobiles, machine tools, and so on. Until the mid-1970s, however, each microprocessor was preprogrammed for a specific task and the quantities produced for each application were limited. Then one competitor, Intel, came up with the idea of a general-purpose microprocessor that could be programmed to fit many different applications, thus permitting mass production and correspondingly lower costs. Almost immediately, the new Intel 8080 microprocessor became the standard model for the industry, and most competitive semiconductor manufacturers were forced to follow suit.

It seems obvious that any planner or manager who has lived with a business for a long time may be especially prone to "tunnel vision," the inability to see genuinely different alternatives. Yet time and again, even the most sophisticated companies have been overtaken by competitors who challenged the prevailing assumptions, looked at the business in a new way and came up with a winning strategy.

Static Assumptions

The second great drawback of standardized strategic approaches is that they tend to elevate past planning assumptions to the status of eternal truths. They foster the dangerous notions that the key factors for success in a given industry don't change, that basic environmental factors remain constant, and that there is no reason to reexamine current definitions of market segmentation and competitors. Such static preconceptions foreclose any possibility of arriving at really innovative strategies based on the perception of actual or potential changes in the "givens."

Changes in the key success factors in particular businesses have repeatedly threatened established industry leaders and handed important opportunities to their more alert competitors, or even to industry newcomers. Consider:

In the 1960s, DuPont was the undisputed leader in the US chemical industry, thanks to its success in developing new products and new applications. Then, as the market for synthetics matured and the string ran out on substitution opportunities for other materials, low-cost production replaced technological prowess as the key success factor in the industry. DuPont lost its lead to Dow Chemical, which had for some time seen the change coming and had concentrated on developing a low-cost raw material position.

When gas liquefaction processes were originally developed, scale economies dictated that liquid oxygen and other gases should be produced centrally and then trucked to customers. But over the years, the technology and the economics changed, and in the 1950s a newcomer to the field, Air Products, capitalized on these changes to carve out a major share of the market by erecting small liquefaction plants directly on customers' premises.

The concept of the gasoline service station was developed by the major oil companies in an age when automobiles needed frequent and rather elaborate servicing. Over the years, improvements in design and materials drastically reduced these service needs, but until quite recently the majors held fast to their outdated full-service approach. Meanwhile, the independents were quick to respond to the new conditions and move to lower-cost self-service or limited-service stations.

Similarly, gradual or sudden changes in the business environment often have important, though not always obvious, strategic implications. For example:

The steady increase in labor costs for certain trades, such as carpenters, electricians and plumbers, led some companies to reexamine prevailing assumptions about how much work people were willing to do themselves. Result: a boom in "do-it-yourself" items and retail outlets.

The potential opportunities that fair trade legislation could offer for strengthening their position vis-à-vis the trade have led several EEC food manufacturers to consider actively campaigning for government regulation, an intervention which they once regarded as anathema.

Changes in the assumptions that have traditionally been made about market segmentation can likewise have an important strategic impact. For example:

The structure of the residential air conditioning business has been profoundly altered by the rise of the replacement market, with its unique requirements. Some companies that once regarded service as an economically unattractive necessity and confined their service to their own units have begun aggressively servicing competitive units in order to build a stronger position in the replacement segment.

Today, almost the entire airline industry is busily segmenting and resegmenting the travel market in an effort to discover whether the customers who are willing to sign up and pay for tickets in advance are the same as those who are willing to stand by for last-minute seats, and whether or not charter passengers are a separate breed.

Changes in key success factors, environmental conditions or market segments often create the most important strategic threats and opportunities of all, but they can seldom be identified or successfully addressed by the use of standardized approaches. Such bold strategic moves as General Electric's recent acquisition of Utah International are not arrived at by formula. Rather, they require the wit to perceive and the ingenuity to exploit and shape significant change in the "givens" underlying a business.

Competitive Versus Market Focus

Ten years ago, a well-known printing ink company developed a revolutionary printing process, involving completely new equipment. Unable to sell its process and its inks to existing printers, the company decided to enter the market directly. For the first eight years it was spectacularly successful, but suddenly everything seemed to go wrong. Once the market leader, the company lost share rapidly and its profits plummeted. With the benefit of hindsight, the explanation was clear. Once the market for its new process had developed, attracting other producers, the company found itself competing head-to-head with others who — using the same process — had profiled themselves against certain distinct segments of the market. While the source of its potential volume had shifted decisively from process substitution to gaining competitive share, the company's strategy was still oriented toward penetration of the overall market.

The example, once more, is not an isolated one. A significant consequence of the transition to a slow-growth economy has been a basic shift in the potential source of additional volume available to growth-minded companies. Growth potential is no longer provided by the expansion of the overall market. Rather, the growth of one company has to come out of the hide of another. This means that it has become more important than ever to know who your competitors are and to understand their economics in depth.

The president of one of the world's largest banks stated not too long ago: "Our biggest problem these days is to figure out just who our competitors are. Until fairly recently, we commercial banks had a franchise on collecting deposits and giving credits. But now it seems that almost everybody can do this in one way or another. So before we can do a really good job of developing our own strategy, we have to find out who it is we are fighting against."

Most well-managed companies keep a fairly sharp eye on their traditional competitors, but many have been surprised by competition from an unexpected corner. Consider:

> A large glass products manufacturer had what he felt was a well-thought-out strategy for dealing with his major competitor when one of his largest customers unexpectedly announced plans to integrate backward. Overnight, virtually all his carefully worked-out strategic plans had to be completely rethought.

> In the packaging industry, traditional lines between suppliers and customers have become increasingly blurred. On the one hand, suppliers of paper, aluminum and glass have moved forward into container production; on the other, several large packaging customers have integrated backward. Each of these participants brings to the business a different background and a different economic perspective; each views the market in a slightly different way. Analyzing competitive economics in the industry and predicting competitive behavior has therefore become a complex and tricky task.

> Large machinery suppliers to the chemical and construction industry find themselves increasingly in competition with the same engineering firms that are among their biggest partners and customers. Here, the competition is not for market share but rather for share of contract value added, and for control over the responsibility for specification.

Such problems are becoming more and more frequent as companies cast about for growth opportunities in one another's backyards.

Not too long ago, a leading US machinery manufacturer found itself under intense pressure from a Japanese firm whose products sold for almost 40 percent less. To find out how this was possible, the American company bought one of its competitor's machines, "reverse-engineered" it, and costed it out with the help of available Japanese data on parts costs, labor costs and so on. At the end of the day it found it could account for no more than half of the apparent cost differential.

It was only later that the company discovered that in Japan the entire cost structure of this industry is different from that in the United States. American manufacturers normally value-engineer each model to determine the optimum part specifications and tolerances to produce that machine at the lowest cost; then they turn these specifications over to subcontractors. Japanese manufacturers, in contrast, design their machines as far as possible from standard parts available more or less off the shelf from their suppliers. Consequently, their assembly costs are somewhat higher, but their suppliers' costs are much lower, because far fewer parts in total are required to supply the industry. Since the total manufacturing cost of this type of machinery is roughly 60 to 70 percent parts and 30 to 40 percent assembly, the Japanese system optimizes the higher value-added sector, yielding a lower overall cost.

Sometimes, as this example shows, competition from an unfamiliar source may demand a very fundamental examination of the basic economics and other policy underpinnings of a competitor's activities.

Innovation Versus Evaluation

After a long strategic planning session in which the strategy of a troubled division was reviewed by managers and their staffs, one executive remarked to me: "It was an exhausting day. We spent hours going around and around in circles trying to decide what to do about our Japanese operation. It's pretty clear that more of the same isn't going to get us anywhere and simply pulling out just won't make anybody happy. But nobody seems to have any other ideas."

It is a familiar complaint. In many companies, the process of proposing a new idea, justifying it and defending it against "challenges" by corporate staff and senior management is so intimidating that all but the most confident entrepreneurs are inclined to stick to less imaginative approaches that are easier to quantify and defend. Indeed, the more quantitatively oriented and sophisticated a planning process becomes, the harder it is for most managers to come up with fresh approaches. By its very nature, the system tends to suppress new ideas — ideas that may only be questions, vague feelings, or hunches at the start.

In many companies, the planning process itself is largely to blame for the pedestrian quality of the strategies that result. Typically, strategic plans in most companies begin with a detailed analysis of statistics and trend figures for market size, market share, economics and profitability, and go on from there. Few attempt the more difficult task of identifying, analyzing and thinking about the key factors for success in the business, how they are changing and, even more important, how they might be deliberately shaped.

This is not to disparage sound analysis. It is needed in any strategic plan. My assertion is simply that conventional strategic planning approaches tend almost to substitute quantitative analysis for judgment and intuition. In practice, I find that quantitative analyses are often most useful for providing an information base and for confirming hypotheses that have been conceived with a liberal dose of hunch, intuition, judgment and experience. Even Einstein developed his general theory of relativity before there was much empirical evidence to support it.

True creativity is probably largely inborn, and it is a very scarce commodity to be sure. Almost certainly fewer than 5 percent of the world's scientists, for example, account for more than 95 percent of the really important scientific developments. Given the scarcity of creative talent, few companies can afford to stifle it. Yet fewer still, it seems, try very hard to dispel the creativity-inhibiting factors with which their organizations' atmosphere is often saturated: rigid hierarchical authority structures; internal competition for leadership or credit; the requirement that all proposals be supported by "completed staff work;" compartmentalized planning or research responsibilities; and/or a nonsupportive or harshly critical review or evaluation process.

Concluding Note

The task of improving a company's strategic decisions is rarely a simple one, nor are there any rules that can guarantee good results. The main lessons of experience are that planning processes ought to change with the planning needs of the company; that analytical tools can supplement, but not supplant, good thinking, and that a successful strategy cannot be developed without creative ideas at the beginning and management commitment at the end.

30. The Anatomy of Strategic Thinking

J. Roger Morrison
James G. Lee

As corporate systems develop over the years, they tend to become ever more cumbersome, bureaucratic and inward-looking. Proliferating paperwork diverts management's attention from the substance of strategy to the mechanics of the planning process. Strategic planning becomes a time-consuming annual chore. Frequently, future strategy focuses on maintaining the existing product or market position of the business rather than on attempting to change it. Scant attention is paid to the competitive situation. In such a climate, imaginative and creative strategic thinking is nipped in the bud.

Yet it is superior strategic thinking, not sophisticated planning systems, that underlies successful competitive strategies. Effective strategic thinking focuses on achieving competitive advantage — on gaining and holding the initiative.

Competitive advantage, of course, may be gained in various ways. Sometimes a company may be able to exploit a unit-cost advantage through scale of manufacturing, low-cost sources of raw materials, or wider distribution. Another company may position its products competitively by creating new market segments, or by basing marketing strategies on distinctive strengths such as product "life cost," premium quality, value for money, reliability, status and the like. Still another may exploit some flexibility in the range and synergy of products, forward or backward integration, or new technologies that others lack. Or competitive advantage may be gained through speed of response and through sheer agility, always keeping one or two steps ahead of the next competitor.

This article first appeared in *The McKinsey Quarterly,* Autumn 1979, pp. 2–9.

When this article was published, Roger Morrison was managing director and James Lee was a principal in the London office of McKinsey and Company.

Whatever their strategy, companies that are adept at strategic thinking seem to be distinguished from their less successful competitors by a common pattern of management practices. First, they identify and emphasize more effectively than their competitors the key success factors inherent in the economics of each business. Second, they segment their markets so as to gain decisive competitive advantage. Third, they base their strategies on the measurement and analysis of competitive advantage. Fourth, they anticipate their competitors' responses. Fifth, they exploit more, or different, degrees of freedom than do their competitors. Finally, they give investment priority to businesses that promise a competitive advantage. Let us look at each of these six points in turn.

Key Success Factors

The key success factors in any business will depend on the economics of the industry. In the airline industry, with its high fixed costs and relatively inflexible route allocations, a high load factor is critical to success. In the automobile industry, a strong dealer network is a key success factor, since the manufacturer's sales crucially depend on the dealer's ability to finance a wide range of model choices and offer competitive prices to the customer.

The successful strategic thinker, then, is guided by a clear business concept based on a thorough understanding of the economics of his business and of the success factors in his industry. The manager who talks of "growing at 10 percent" or "achieving 20 percent return on capital" when asked to explain his business concept is no strategic thinker. The strategic thinker's reply will run along quite different lines: "We are a high-fixed-cost business. Utilization is the name of the game. Our product line and pricing policies are designed to sustain high levels of utilization." Or, "We have the lowest-cost sources of raw materials. Our sources are being threatened. We are investing heavily to protect them." Or, "Reliable spares service is the key because our products have no competitive advantage, but the cost to our customers of a shut-down far exceeds the price of our products. So we are constantly improving our service and distribution system to keep one step ahead of our main competitor, who has a weaker system but is improving fast."

A company that has a clear business concept will use a wide range of market and economic analyses to identify the key success factors in its business and will make these factors the basis of its strategy for beating the competition. Take the case of a certain package tour operator. This man knows that he has a high-fixed-cost business and that load factor is all-important to his success. His business concept is based on achieving a high load factor by limiting his product line (many travel operators do the exact opposite), choosing high-density routes, consolidating undersubscribed tours, and using special pricing deals to fill marginal capacity. As a result, he achieves a load factor of 97 percent in an industry where the average is 91 percent. Not surprisingly, his business is profitable.

Segmenting Markets

The traditional approach to market segmentation — a concept used by consumer marketers for decades, but discovered only recently by industrial companies — is to segment markets according to certain market characteristics, most commonly customer needs. The strategic thinker typically bases his market segmentation on competitor analysis. Thus, he may separate segments according to the strengths and weaknesses of different competitors. This enables him to concentrate on segments where he can both maximize his own competitive advantage and avoid head-on competition with stronger competitors.

Again, the case of the package tour market provides a good illustration of the technique. This market has three distinct segments: the bona fide affinity group, the convenience affinity group, and the individual purchaser of travel packages. Different competitors with different competitive advantages operate in each of the segments. The purchasing decisions of the potential customers in each segment differ both in timing and in nature.

This particular operator, knowing that his greatest strength is his superior distribution to the bona fide affinity group, concentrates first on that segment. Almost nine months before the beginning of the holiday season, he starts his mail-order campaign to bona fide travel groups. In the first three months he fills perhaps 75 percent of capacity. In the next four months or so he shifts his marketing strategy to the second segment, the so-called convenience groups — again using mail order, but with a different approach. At the same time he consolidates origins and dates. When he has thus increased load to between 85 and 90 percent, he turns his attention to the third market segment, individual travellers, again using a different strategy. First, he markets at full price; later, he discounts heavily through selected retail travel agents, to reach 95 to 98 percent loading. Thus, capitalizing on the key factor for success in his business, he builds on his relative competitive strength in each segment.

Few travel operators have articulated their business concepts as clearly as this firm, and few are so successful. Occasionally a more complex business may need a correspondingly complex business concept. But it is interesting to note that the best business concepts are often surprisingly simple.

Analyzing Competitive Advantage

Successful strategies not only capitalize more effectively on the key success factors in the industry; they build on advantages over competition, or seek to minimize disadvantages. Essential to this type of strategic thinking is a sound basis for assessing a company's advantages relative to its competitors. Using market share as the sole measure of competitive position is not enough. Market share is almost always the result of a number of performance variables that may be crucial to the company's success in a given business — for example, product performance, distribution effectiveness, pricing and credit terms, after-sales support, and manufacturing economics.

The methods used by companies in assessing each of these elements vary from simple subjective judgment to highly sophisticated analysis. But the method may be less important than the thinking it stimulates: how can the company best exploit a competitive advantage or minimize a competitive disadvantage once it has been identified?

A certain manufacturer of electronic medical equipment competes in two distinct market segments: custom-designed systems and modular standard systems. This company once had the advantage in the custom-designed segment; in fact, it built the leading share. But in the course of a few years the decisive edge it had held in product features and technology was lost to competitors, and as its market lead eroded its cost advantage began to slip away as well. Competitor analysis revealed, however, a very different picture with respect to the company's second main product line, modular standard systems. Here it stood second in market share — but it still possessed a commanding lead over the competition in product features, technology and unit cost. Accordingly, management took the decision to shift the company's strategic thrust from custom-designed to modular standard systems. Of late its sales in that segment have been growing at a record pace, confirming the wisdom of the strategy.

Here, once again, an effective competitive strategy resulted from strategic thinking.

Anticipating Competitive Response

Good strategic thinking also implies an understanding of how situations will change over time. Business strategy, like military strategy, is a matter of maneuvering for superior position and anticipating how competitors will respond, and with what measure of success. Successful strategists aim to keep always one step ahead of the main competitor. They plan their moves well in advance and have contingency plans for the most likely outcomes.

A consumer electronics company was preparing to launch a line of high-fidelity components aimed at the middle-price market. Aware that its competitors were likely to retaliate, it developed a strategic "roadmap," shown schematically in Figure 30.1, plotting the steps it would take to respond to the anticipated competitive counterattack, and prepared its manufacturing economics and design and development to follow this strategy. Once the competitors had reacted to the initial launch of middle-price

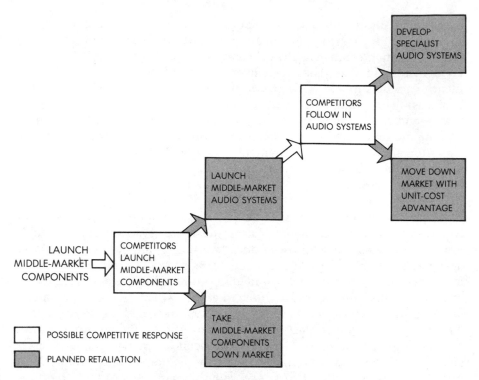

FIGURE 30.1   A Strategic Roadmap for Meeting Competitive Threats

components, it would follow up by introducing a new line of integrated hi-fi systems for the middle market, taking the original range of middle-market components down market at the same time. Management even went a further step in their strategic thinking, anticipating the competitors' reactions to these moves. In the event, the company was able to retain the strategic initiative.

Exploiting Degrees of Freedom

The market leader will not only try to achieve and retain competitive advantage over time; he will also try to control the initiative by striving to dominate the *nature* of the competition — that is, to choose the ground on which the competitive battle will be fought out. The advantages are obvious: if the leader's position is threatened he can deflect the threat by changing tack in a direction that he hopes his competitor will find hard to follow.

The strategic thinker is therefore always searching for new ways to compete — that is, for more and different strategic degrees of freedom.

The more degrees of freedom he has relative to his competitors, the likelier he is to win.

British food manufacturers, for example, have seen their marketing strength decline in inverse relation to the growing power of the grocery chains. A strategic response to this threat might take one of three forms. The food manufacturers could intensify their product marketing efforts by introducing better products or more competing brands, extending their product lines, creating new segments for specialty customer groups, or battling on retail price. Or they could respond by competing in trade marketing — strengthening the key account management function, offering better trade discounts and deals, or agreeing to provide more and more in-store services at their own expense. Or they could compete on cost advantage — a very different strategy indeed, implying much greater concentration on operations management and less on marketing. For example, they could strengthen the distribution system and achieve economies of scale in manufacturing; rationalize the product line and concentrate on high-volume commodity products; apply food technology to reduce waste; and maybe even integrate backward to capture cost-efficient sources of supply. Figure 30.2 illustrates these three degrees of freedom available to UK food manufacturers.

Most UK food companies seem to be concentrating their strengths on the first two approaches. Were they to think strategically and examine their relative competitive advantage along all three degrees of freedom, some of them might well decide to change direction, or at least begin to prepare contingency plans.

Investing Strategically

Continuity of growth, particularly in a diversified company, requires constant reallocation of resources. Capital must be shifted from products that have matured to those that show potential for the future. Without deliberate and sometimes ruthless intervention, maturing products tend to go on absorbing the biggest share of capital. Strategic thinkers are rarely in doubt as to which of their businesses should be absorbing funds and which should be managed to provide funds.

Since competitive advantage is the theme of strategic thinking, the resource allocation process must be geared to the measurement of competitive advantage. One European company measures its potential competitive advantage (not just its existing strengths) in terms of market share, customer base, product performance, unit cost advantage, distribution power and customer service, and any other competitive factors that it has determined to be specifically relevant to the industry. It allocates funds only to those businesses it considers attractive from both an industry and a competitive point of view — and it regards as unattractive any industry in

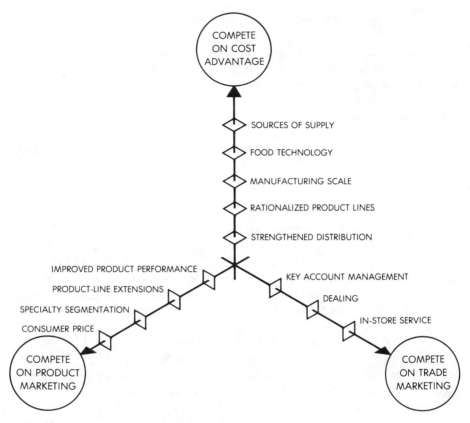

FIGURE 30.2   Degrees of Freedom in UK Food Manufacturing

which no single competitor can easily gain a significant advantage. Obviously, no such classification can long remain static: investment priorities will change over the years with changes in either industry attractiveness or the potential for competitive advantage.

Concluding Note

If a company's strategies fail to reflect the six elements considered in this article the chances are that strategic thinking is being crowded out by the mechanics of its strategic planning processes, or that both are inadequate. But the likelihood is that management's planning energies need to be redirected from forms and systems back to the substance of effective strategy: beating the competition.

(continued from page iv)

served. *Article 7:* "An Application of the Capital Asset Pricing Model to Divisional Required Returns" by James C. Van Horne. Reprinted from *Financial Management*, Spring 1980, pp. 14–19. Used by permission of the Financial Management Association and the author. *Article 8:* Reprinted with permission from *Long Range Planning*, Vol. 9, No. 6, Barry Hedley, "A Fundamental Approach to Strategy Development." Copyright 1976, Pergamon Press, Ltd. *Article 9:* Copyright © 1974 by the President and Fellows of Harvard College; all rights reserved. Reprinted by permission of the *Harvard Business Review*. "Limits of the Learning Curve" by William J. Abernathy and Kenneth Wayne, September–October 1974, pp. 109–119. *Article 10:* "The Product Life Cycle: A Key to Strategic Marketing Planning" by John E. Smallwood. Reprinted from *MSU Business Topics*, Winter 1973, pp. 29–35. Used by permission from Michigan State University. *Article 11:* Copyright © 1976 by the President and Fellows of Harvard College; all rights reserved. Reprinted by permission of the *Harvard Business Review*. "Forget the Product Life Cycle Concept!" by Nariman K. Dhalla and Sonia Yuseph, January–February 1976, pp. 102–112. *Article 12:* "Planning for Profit" by Bradley T. Gale. Reprinted from *Planning Review*, January 1978. Published by the North American Society for Corporate Planning, 1406 Third National Building, Dayton, OH 45402. *Article 13:* "PIMS: A Reexamination" by Carl R. Anderson and Frank T. Paine. Reprinted from the *Academy of Management Review*, July 1978, pp. 602–612. Used by permission of the *Academy of Management Review*. *Article 14:* Reprinted with permission from *Long Range Planning*, Vol. 10, No. 1, Barry Hedley, "Strategy and the 'Business Portfolio.' " Copyright 1977, Pergamon Press, Ltd. *Article 15:* "Diagnosing the Product Portfolio" by George S. Day. Reprinted from the *Journal of Marketing*, published by the American Marketing Association, April 1977, Vol. 2, pp. 29–38. *Article 16:* Reprinted with permission from *Long Range Planning*, Vol. 11, S. I. Q. Robinson, R. E. Hichens, and D. P. Wade, "The Directional Policy Matrix — Tool for Strategic Planning." Copyright 1978, Pergamon Press, Ltd. *Article 17:* "Strategic Marketing: Betas, Boxes, or Basics," by Robin Wensley. Reprinted from the *Journal of Marketing*, published by the American Marketing Association, Summer 1981, pp. 173–183. *Article 18:* "Strategy Formulation in Complex Organizations" by Richard F. Vancil. Reprinted from *Sloan Management Review*, Vol. 17, No. 2, pp. 1–18, by permission of the publisher. Copyright © 1976 by the Sloan Management Review Association. All rights reserved. *Article 19:* "Strategic Market Analysis and Definition: An Integrated Approach" by George S. Day. Reprinted from *Strategic Management Journal*, Vol. 2, No. 2, pp. 281–299. Used by permission. *Article 20:* Copyright © 1978 by the President and Fellows of Harvard College; all rights reserved. Reprinted by permission of the *Harvard Business Review*. "The Reality Gap in Strategic Planning" by Ronald N. Paul, Neil B. Donovan, and James W. Taylor, May–June 1978, pp. 124–130. *Article 21:* "Strategic Goals: Process and Politics" by James B. Quinn. Reprinted from *Sloan Management Review*, Vol. 19, No. 1, pp. 21–37, by permission of the publisher. Copyright © 1977 by the Sloan Management Review Association. All rights reserved. *Article 22:* "Strategic Windows" by Derek F. Abell. Reprinted from the *Journal of Marketing*, published by the American Marketing Association, July 1978, pp. 21–25. *Article 23:* Copyright © 1978 by the President and Fellows of Harvard College; all rights reserved. Reprinted by permission of the *Harvard Business Review*. "Strategies for Low Market Share Business" by R. G. Hamermesh, M. J. Anderson, Jr., and J. E. Harris, May–June 1978, pp. 95–102. *Article 24:* "Harvesting Strategies for Weak Products" by Philip Kotler. Reprinted from *Business Horizons*, August 1978, pp. 15–22. Copyright 1978, by the Foundation for the School of Business at Indiana University. Reprinted by permission. *Article 25:* "SBUs: Hot, New Topic in the Management of Diversification" by William K. Hall. Reprinted from *Business Horizons*, February 1978, pp. 17–25. Copyright 1978, by the Foundation for the School of Business at Indiana University. Reprinted by permission. *Article 26:* "Wanted: A Manager to Fit Each Strategy," reprinted from the February 25, 1980 issue of *Business Week* by special permission, © 1980 by McGraw-Hill, Inc., New York, NY 10020. All rights reserved. *Article 27:* "A Strategic Framework for Marketing Control" by James M. Hulbert and Norman E. Toy. Reprinted from the *Journal of Marketing*, published by the American Marketing Association,

Index